Exacting Beauty

Exacting Beauty

Theory, Assessment, and Treatment
of Body Image Disturbance

J. Kevin Thompson
Leslie J. Heinberg
Madeline Altabe
Stacey Tantleff-Dunn

American Psychological Association

Washington, DC

RC
569.5
.B65
E93
1999

Exacting beauty

Copyright © 1999 by the American Psychological Association. All rights reserved. Except as permitted under the United States Copyright Act of 1976, no part of this publication may be reproduced or distributed in any form or by any means, or stored in a database or retrieval system, without the prior written permission of the publisher.

Published by
American Psychological Association
750 First Street, NE
Washington, DC 20002

Copies may be ordered from
APA Order Department
P.O. Box 92984
Washington, DC 20090-2984

In the U.K., Europe, Africa, and the Middle East, copies may be ordered from
American Psychological Association
3 Henrietta Street
Covent Garden, London
WC2E 8LU England

Typeset in Goudy by EPS Group Inc., Easton, MD
Printer: Data Reproductions Corp., Auburn Hills, MI
Dust jacket designer: Minker Design, Bethesda, MD
Technical/Production Editor: Amy J. Clarke

Library of Congress Cataloging-in-Publication Data
Exacting beauty : theory, assessment, and treatment of body image disturbance / by
   J. Kevin Thompson ... [et al.].—1st ed.
     p.   cm.
   Includes bibliographical references and index.
   ISBN 1-55798-5410-3 (hardcover : acid-free paper)
   1. Body image disturbance.   I. Thompson, J. Kevin.
   RC569.5.B65E93   1998
   616.85'2—dc21   98-35202
                                                                    CIP

British Library Cataloguing-in-Publication Data
A CIP record is available from the British Library.

Printed in the United States of America
First Edition

CONTENTS

LIST OF EXHIBITS AND TABLES

LIST OF APPENDIXES

PREFACE

When a 2-year-old was asked "When your hair grows out, do you want it like your mother's hair?" she replied "want hair like Barbie." This anecdote might offer reason enough to explore the field of body image; the fact that the young girl is one of our daughters underlies an even more compelling motivation for this book.

Actually, the time seems right to attempt an integration of theory, assessment, and treatment for the rapidly expanding field of body image disturbance. First, descriptive data now suggest that dissatisfaction with appearance is problematic for a wide array of individuals who vary on such characteristics as ethnicity, gender, age, body weight, avocational or athletic status, type of clinical disorder, and sexual orientation. Second, recent investigations yield great advances in theoretical explanations for the onset and development of body image disturbance. Third, recent advances in assessment methods and treatment approaches give clinicians a variety of tools to work with clients having different body image problems.

The phrase used in our book's title, *exacting beauty*, is meant to convey the negative effects on the individual that result from extreme attractiveness standards. Webster's *Ninth New Collegiate Dictionary* defines this adjective as "tryingly or unremittingly severe in making demands" (p. 431). Certainly, beauty ideals have existed for hundreds of years in many and diverse societies, and we believe that the toll of trying to meet increasingly unrealistic models of beauty has never been more exacting.

Originally, we had included the term *integrating* in the title; however, this concept still remains a central theme of the book. We view an appreciation of risk factors and theoretical perspectives as integral to the selection and application of assessment and treatment strategies. Basic research findings that form the supportive data for a specific explanation of body image disturbance indicate measures or procedures that may also be useful for clinical assessment. In turn, these assessment instruments may provide information essential for the selection of specific treatment approaches, optimizing client–treatment matching. Bridging research and practice is the hallmark of the scientist–practitioner model; bridging theory, assessment, and intervention may yield great benefits for the researcher and clinician.

As noted in the Introduction, we focus exclusively on an appearance-related notion of body image disturbance. Our coverage of evolving theoretical explanations, assessment practices, and interventions focuses on four primary areas: social and societal, interpersonal, feminist, and behavioral–cognitive. Therefore, we have somewhat narrowed down the potential literature for our review, with a goal of focusing on the major areas with empirical support. Certainly in future years, novel findings may force a reconsideration of this structure.

As a warning, you may find this book a bit different from most, if not all, such "guidebooks" devoted to theory, assessment, or treatment. We fill it with information that is designed to be easily accessible, including appendices of actual assessment measures, tables with descriptions of measures (including author contact information), figures illustrative of concepts that range from art to covariance structure models, and exhibits that provide an up-close examination of a topic. In addition, we include numerous case histories and anecdotes to introduce, inform, or summarize a clinical issue or research finding. These vignettes serve to illustrate not only the significant distress that many individuals feel about their appearance but also the powerful role of societal and interpersonal factors in shaping one's body image.

We hope you find our presentation of information useful for your research and clinical work. We endeavor to provide a guide that is useful for researchers and clinicians interested in the ever-expanding field of body image disturbance.

Several individuals made this book possible. First, great thanks go out to the staff at APA Books, especially Margaret Schlegel, Ed Meidenbauer, Mary Lynn Skutley, Amy Clarke, Olin Nettles, and Julia Frank-McNeil. Several individuals read specific chapters and offered feedback, including Ruth Striegel-Moore, Eric Stice, Myles Faith, and Rick Gardner. Tom Cash and James Rosen gave us permission to include their assessment measures and reproduce material illustrative of their many research findings and treatment methods. Thanks go to Joan Altabe who provided consultation for artwork selection. Finally, appreciation is extended to Diane Dwyer and Marianne Bell for their patience, work ethic, and good humor.

J. Kevin Thompson
Leslie J. Heinberg
Madeline Altabe
Stacey Tantleff-Dunn

Exacting Beauty

AN INTRODUCTION TO THE CONCEPT OF BODY IMAGE DISTURBANCE: HISTORY, DEFINITIONS, AND DESCRIPTIONS

Image is everything. (Andre Agassi, tennis star and advertising icon, circa early 1990s)

Agassi may be onto something; however, perhaps he was only partially correct and not sufficiently specific. We might modify his statement to read "Body image is everything." For it is not so much our actual appearance or how we seem to others but our own internal view of how we look, how we think we appear to others, and how we feel about our looks, that is, indeed, "everything." We offer a wealth of evidence in the next 11 chapters to support this somewhat hyperbolic claim; however, we need look no further than a few simple correlations from Feingold's (1992) classic meta-analysis of attractiveness research to find support for the relative distinctiveness of the subjective versus objective nature of attractiveness. He found that the correlation between the objective level of attractiveness and one's own self-rating of appearance was .24 for men and .25 for women, which means that just over 6% of one's own view of one's appearance (i.e., body image) is explained by actual attractiveness (researchers take the square of the simple correlation to compute this statistic). In addition, Feingold found that one's own self-rating of attractiveness, but not that of objective raters (i.e., actual attractiveness level), was significantly associated with global self-esteem.

Body image is the term that has come to be widely accepted as the internal representation of your own outer appearance—your own unique perception of your body. Cash (1990b) has referred to this as the "view from the inside" (p. 51), which he contrasted with an external rating of appearance, the "view from the outside" (p. 51). Your internal view is associated with feelings and thoughts and may even modify your behavior in certain situations. In some cases, the feeling that results from your evaluation of your appearance may be positive; but in other cases, it may be so negative that it leads to depression. The thoughts that accompany a positive rating of your looks may hearten your self-esteem and lead to bold, successful interpersonal or business ventures, whereas cognitions resulting from a poor view of the physical self may weaken your confidence sufficiently to eliminate any possibility of leaving the safe confines of your home.

This book is about the uniquely individual experience of body image. Although the term has been used by researchers in other areas of psychology to study phenomena ranging from phantom limb pain to conditions resulting from certain types of brain damage (Altabe & Thompson, 1994; S. Fisher, 1990; J. K. Thompson, 1990), we focus our examination on the appearance-based aspects of body image. In fact, we look at this topic from a clinical viewpoint, endeavoring to define, describe, and explain disturbances in one's view of one's looks. These disturbances may affect one emotionally, cognitively, and behaviorally—indeed, in extreme cases, they may lead to such clinical conditions as anorexia nervosa, bulimia nervosa, and body dysmorphic disorder. In addition, the disturbances may be present in individuals of widely varying avocations and conditions, from gymnasts and bodybuilders to individuals who have cancer, facial disfigurement, or visual impairment. And let us not overlook the often forgotten overweight or obese person, who is subject to constant disparagement and stigmatization from a society and its individuals who continue to discriminate against one of the few socially acceptable targets of prejudice (Rothblum, 1992).

To frame the material that is to follow, we provide in this introduction a bit of background material. First, we briefly address the early days of body image research, noting its historical roots, and trace the evolution of the field of appearance-based body image research. Second, we note the various definitional subtleties of body image, with a goal of parsing the distinctions among dissatisfaction, disturbance, schema, and multiple other ways of describing appearance-related conceptualizations. Third, we review explanations for the development and maintenance of clinically severe disturbances in body image, with a focus on the major theoretical approaches that receive in-depth coverage later in the book. Finally, we offer a road map of the material that follows.

BODY IMAGE DISTURBANCE: A BRIEF HISTORY

Although the study of body image has almost become synonymous with the study of appearance satisfaction, its roots are far more eclectic (S. Fisher, 1986, 1990; J. K. Thompson, 1992). Neurologists and neuropsychologists have been intrigued for many years by the often bizarre modifications in self-image produced by certain types of brain damage. For instance, *anosognosia* is a condition whereby an individual may not be aware of the existence of a large portion of his or her body; *autotopagnosia* refers to an inability to distinguish the right from the left side of the body (S. Fisher, 1990). *Phantom limb pain*—the residual feeling of pain in an arm or leg lost to injury or amputation—also has a rich research tradition (Shontz, 1974). Investigations of the neurological basis of body image in the early years of the 20th century by such researchers as Bonnier (1905), Pick (1922), and Head (1926) were instrumental in forming an initial interest in this concept. In particular, Head's coining of the term *body schema* in 1926 and his description of an integrative cognitive process presages one of the current revolutions in body image research, namely, the study of cognitive processes and the possible existence of a schema that serves as a reference point for organizing new information about one's appearance.

Schilder (1914, 1923, 1950) is generally credited with providing one of the first multidimensional conceptualizations of body image, extracting it from its narrow neurological roots. His focus was on the psychological self-awareness of body image, and he added theoretical notions related to psychoanalysis and sociology (Schilder, 1950). He believed that both conscious and unconscious processes contributed to the total image one has of one's own body and entertained such contributing factors as emotions, attitudes, wishes, and social relationships. Freeing body image from its localization within the study of brain damage led other theorists, in particular individuals with a psychodynamic background (which, after all, dominated clinical psychology from roughly 1900–1950), to postulate psychological concepts of body image. Dominant among these and based on the early writings of Sigmund Freud, Alfred Adler, and Carl Jung was the "body boundary" formulation (S. Fisher & Cleveland, 1968). S. Fisher and Cleveland's ideas emanated from early clinical work with projective techniques and observations showing boundary differences in inkblot perceptions for patients with diverse psychosomatic symptoms (S. Fisher, 1990).

The onset of a specific focus on self-perceptions of appearance seems to have begun in the 1940s and 1950s, perhaps starting with the work of Burgess and Wallen (1944), who measured self-ratings of attractiveness by 350 married couples (Feingold & Mazzella, 1996). Later, Secord and Jourard (1953; Jourard & Secord, 1955) created some of the first scales designed to assess self-rating of subjective appearance. In the 1960s and early 1970s, researchers turned their attention to clinical populations with eating- and weight-related disorders. Stunkard and colleagues, in two landmark articles, offered convincing evidence for the importance of body dissatisfaction as a factor in the distress associated with obesity, particularly, juvenile onset obesity (Stunkard & Burt, 1967; Stunkard & Mendelson, 1967). Unfortunately, there has been a dearth of follow-up work in this area until recent years (e.g., J. K. Thompson, 1996b; J. K. Thompson & Tantleff-Dunn, 1998).

However, the field of eating disorders has generated a great deal of academic and popular interest in body image, beginning with the classic work of Bruch (1962), Russell (1970), and Slade and Russell (1973). These early works include a specific focus on a particular aspect of disturbed body image as a central component of the symptomatology of anorexia nervosa. Following Bruch's suggestion that a disturbance in body image was one of the three central features of anorexia nervosa, Russell's (1970) emphasis on the fear of fatness as central to the psychopathology of the disorder, and Slade and Russell's finding that these individuals actually overestimate the size of their emaciated bodies, the *Diagnostic and Statistical Manual of Mental Disorders—Third Edition* (DSM-III; American Psychiatric Association, 1980) includes diagnostic criteria related to body image disturbance as a necessary feature for the diagnosis of anorexia nervosa. An influential review article by Garner and Garfinkel (1981) heightened interest in the connection between body image and anorexia nervosa. Additionally, research on bulimia nervosa exploded onto the scene in the early 1980s, and findings of the presence of high levels of either dissatisfaction with appearance or overestimation of body size (in a manner similar to individuals with anorexia nervosa) in persons with this eating disorder led to the addition of a body image criterion for bulimia nervosa in the revised DSM-III (DSM-III-R; American Psychiatric Association, 1987; J. K. Thompson, Berland, Linton, & Weinsier, 1986).

During this period, however, findings emerged from individuals without eating disorders, indicating that they also had disturbances in body image. J. K. Thompson and Thompson (1986) found that college women without any sign of an eating disorder overestimated their body dimensions; Cash, Winstead, and Janda (1986), in a nationwide survey, found that only 7% of women expressed little concern with their appearance. Rodin, Silberstein, and Striegel-Moore (1985) coined the now classic phrase *normative discontent* to describe the widespread dysphoria that women have regarding their appearance. It was around this time that S. Fisher (1986) published his exhaustive two-volume series devoted specifically to an assimilation of the diverse literature on body image. This treatise brings together for the first time the rich complexity of the diversity of body image; it is essential reading for any clinician or researcher who wishes to put any current work in a historical context. S. Fisher's book, as much as any seminal theory or empirical work, can be credited for propelling the field of body image into the forefront of psychology. A few years later, Cash and Pruzinsky (1990) presented an edited volume that provided information on newly emerging pockets of body image research, such as physical disability, cosmetic and reconstructive surgery, and objective bodily damage. In that same year, J. K. Thompson (1990) offered an overview of theoretical models, assessment strategies, and treatment interventions for body image disturbance that focused specifically on the appearance-related dimension of body image.

One final historical influence that has been somewhat relegated to the periphery of the field of body image until recent years is body dysmorphic disorder (J. C. Rosen, 1996a). Body dysmorphic disorder has a long descriptive and clinical history, beginning with classic case studies of individuals with extreme disparagement of an aspect of physical appearance by Morselli (1886) and Janet (1903), but a relatively short research history. The first English-language article was published by Hay in 1970, and the disorder was first included in the *DSM-III-R* in 1987. Recent advances in the description, assessment, and treatment of body dysmorphic disorder indicate that it will become one of the most active areas in the entire field of body image in the next millennium (e.g., Phillips, 1996; J. C. Rosen, 1996a; more on body dysmorphic disorder is in the next chapter).

THE CONTINUUM OF BODY IMAGE DISTURBANCE

The story of body image is not only a history of pathological disturbance but one of basic, exploratory work, designed to describe and measure "normal" or basic issues in its phenomenology. This tandem focus on the "disturbed" and "normative" facets of an appearance-based body image has generated much interest. However, clearly delineating where normal appearance concern or dissatisfaction becomes problematic disturbance, leading to distress and specific diagnosable clinical conditions, is no easy task. In addition, body image has gradually developed over time into a *sponge phrase*, absorbing many different connotations and meanings. We now discuss the continuum issue and definitional problems in greater detail.

In reality, a *continuum* model may be the best way to conceptualize body image, with levels of disturbance ranging from none to extreme and most people falling near the middle of the range, experiencing mild–moderate concern, distress, or dissatisfaction. This continuum approach fits with much of the work in this field, which finds that higher levels of body image disturbance are associated with higher levels of other measures indicative of clinical problems, such as eating disturbance and depression (e.g., J. K. Thompson, 1996b). At the highest end of the disturbance continuum, one is likely to find a body image disturbance so severe as to be associated with significant impairment in social functioning, occupational functioning, or both.

Also at this upper end of disturbance, one is likely to encounter behaviors indicative of an eating disorder, such as starvation, bingeing, and purging. In addition, if the concern with an appearance feature is extreme, suggesting that the individual's view of his or her own appearance "defect" is one of disparagement, then a clinical condition of body dysmorphic disorder should be considered. This disorder, covered in more detail in chapter 1, represents the far end of our body image continuum and is associated with great impairment in an individual's ability to function effectively (Phillips, 1996). Body dysmorphic disorder is the only category in the DSM-IV (American Psychiatric Association, 1994) that is specific to a dysfunctional body image, although J. C. Rosen (1992) has conceptualized body image as a disorder and J. K. Thompson (1992) has offered guidelines for a DSM-based body image disorder.

Note that some levels of body image disturbance, perhaps at the low–moderate range of the continuum, might conceivably be beneficial, leading to "healthy" exercise and eating behaviors. For instance, in terms of motivations for exercise, two studies show that appearance, weight control, and body fitness–tone are reasons for exercise that significantly relate to levels of body dissatisfaction (Cash, Novy, & Grant, 1994; McDonald & Thompson, 1992). (It is interesting to note that other reasons for exercise, such as health, fitness, mood, socializing, and enjoyment, were not found to be related to level of appearance dissatisfaction.) In keeping with this idea, Heinberg, Haythornthwaite, Rosofsky, McCarron, and Clarke (1996) found that obese women with low levels of body dissatisfaction were less likely to maintain weight lost for health reasons—an unhealthy body image may have possibly served as a motive for greater compliance. Cash (1996) has developed a scale (the Appearance Orientation Scale) that measures investment in appearance (i.e., appearance-related behaviors and cognitions) and has found that scores on this scale are independent of dissatisfaction level. Thus, researchers and clinicians need to consider the potential that some level of disturbance may actually have beneficial aspects. In addition, not all measures of body image, even an appearance-based notion of the construct, are solely measures of pathology (e.g., Cash's Appearance Orientation Scale). This leads us now into the often convoluted and always controversial area of defining body image disturbance.

DEFINITIONS

In this introductory chapter, we have already offered multiple terms for describing components of body image and have partially explored definitions of several of these conceptualizations. Now, it may be useful to consider more specifically how we use certain terms throughout this book that relate to the range of disturbance in body image. First, we have found it useful to consider body image disturbance as an umbrella term, which can be conceptualized as including all subcomponents or different types of body image (hence the title of this book). Other writers have used a similar strategy—one notable exception is Cash (1996; Cash & Pruzinsky, 1990), who prefers *disturbances* because it reflects the multiple components of body image. Therefore, when we use the phrase *body image disturbance*, we are simply referring to the complex construct of body image, which as noted previously we confined to a physical appearance-based definition.

A specific disturbance may take many forms, as we noted at the outset of this Introduction, including affective, cognitive, behavioral, and perceptual features. When one is upset, distressed, or anxious about one's appearance, the disturbance is in the affective vein. A *cognitive* component might consist of an unrealistic expectation for a certain appearance feature, for example, wishing to look like a fashion model. A *behavioral* aspect includes avoidance of certain situations that elicit body image scrutiny, such as swimming or working out at a fitness club. A *perceptual* component has traditionally been defined as an overestimation of one's body size. (However, the distinctiveness of this component from an affective disturbance is currently being questioned; for more on this, see chapter 10.) Someone with a severe body image disturbance may have affective, cognitive, behavioral, and perceptual facets associated with their dysfunction and may present clinically with a diagnosable disorder, such as body dysmorphic disorder. Alternatively, someone with only mild impairment in one system (e.g., distress only during the summer beach season when wearing a swimsuit) might be conceptualized as fitting at the low-disturbance end of our continuum.

Body dissatisfaction is another widely used phrase in the field of body image. Several measures (see chapter 2) actually include this definition in their name, and it usually denotes a scale designed to target the satisfaction–dissatisfaction continuum of disturbance. Most researchers, ourselves included, conceptualize this component of disturbance as perhaps the most important global measure of distress because it captures the essence of one's subjective evaluation. In addition, much of the available research in the field (see chapter 1) is based on studies defining disturbance as dissatisfaction. For our purposes, it is important to consider that dissatisfaction may be associated with certain affective, cognitive, and behavioral features; however, these facets of disturbance can be measured with scales designed specifically for the assessment of their unique domain (e.g., a scale that solely indexes body image avoidance).

Now comes the tricky part. There are many other terms used to define the different components of body image, and in some cases, researchers and clinicians use these terms interchangeably when perhaps they should not. We present some of these terms and offer some guidance to an understanding of the relatedness or distinctiveness of these concepts in Exhibit 0.1. For instance, terms such as weight concern, appearance concern, and body concern may or may not reflect the same underlying type of body

EXHIBIT 0.1
Definitions of *Body Image*

Weight satisfaction—Satisfaction with current weight, which might be assessed by measuring discrepancy between current and desired weight.

Size perception accuracy—Accuracy of estimation of the size of body sites, which is commonly referred to as body image distortion (but we hope this term fades away rapidly).

Body satisfaction—Satisfaction with an aspect of one's body; usually scales define which sites are rated (e.g., waist, hips, thighs, breast, hair, etc.).

Appearance satisfaction—Satisfaction with overall appearance; usually scales contain items that address issues such as facial features, weight-related areas, and hair; items might also address broader features, such as sex appeal.

Appearance evaluation—Rather than asking for a satisfaction rating, these scales may ask for a range of agreement (agree–disagree), with statements about broad appearance features.

Appearance orientation—A measure of cognitive–behavioral investment in one's appearance reflected by items that assess the frequency of appearance-related thoughts and behaviors.

Body esteem—Probably most similar to body satisfaction, these items reflect agreement with positive versus negative features about one's body; they may capture broader concepts (i.e., "I am proud of my body").

Body concern—(At this point, it starts to become murky.) This may reflect dissatisfaction, or it may mean a simple focus on one's body (see appearance orientation); one must examine the specific study and measure to be sure.

Body dysphoria—Also problematic, this might mean dissatisfaction, or it might mean distress, as a function of dissatisfaction; each actual study and measure must be evaluated.

Body dysmorphia—Typically refers specifically to the *Diagnostic and Statistical Manual of Mental Disorders* definition of body dysmorphia that reflects an extreme disparagement, which may be excessive or even imagined (see the definition of body dysmorphic disturbance in Exhibit 0.2).

Body schema—A construct tied closely to cognitive-processing theories and models; this generally means a hypothesized preexisting cognitive framework for interpreting appearance-related information; evidence is indirectly inferred from experiments that typically consist of a priming manipulation (see chapter 10 for more information).

Body percept—(see above).

Body distortion—Typically used to refer to size estimation accuracy; however, it has been used to describe bizarre perceptual experiences (e.g., schizophrenia).

Body image, body image disturbance, and body image disorder—These global constructs are almost useless without a specification of which particular subjective, affective, cognitive, behavioral, or perceptual processes are intended and whether the foci are specific body sites or a more global aspect of overall appearance.

Definitions are presented in relative order of precision.

image (e.g., "appearance" has a much broader body-related reference than "weight"). In addition, body schema and body percept may be unrelated to other, more specific definitions—these terms are usually used by researchers interested in cognitive-processing models of disturbance. Appearance orientation, as noted earlier, has actually been shown empirically to be distinct from appearance evaluation, body satisfaction, body anxiety, and body-image-avoidant behaviors (T. A. Brown, Cash, & Mikulka, 1990; J. K. Thompson, Altabe, Johnson, & Stormer, 1994). Finally, perhaps body image distortion has been the phrase of greatest abuse; we recommend that this phrase is retired and *size perception accuracy* is used when researchers and clinicians want to refer to a size-estimation component of body image.

Given what we have just covered regarding definitions and the continuum model of body image disturbance, it is interesting to evaluate the types of formal definitions used for diagnosing Body Dysmorphic Disorder or other *DSM* disorders for which there are body-image-related criteria (i.e., anorexia nervosa and bulimia nervosa; see Exhibit 0.2). For contrast purposes, some of the suggested criteria for a body image disorder are provided (e.g., J. K. Thompson, 1992). As noted in Exhibit 0.2, the current *DSM* definition of anorexia nervosa contains two criteria that denote an aspect of body image disturbance:

> fear of gaining weight or becoming fat . . . disturbance in the way in which one's body weight or shape is experienced, undue influence of body weight or shape on self-evaluation, or denial of the seriousness of the current low body weight. (American Psychiatric Association, 1994, pp. 544–545)

The sole body image-related criterion for bulimia nervosa focuses on the effects of disturbance on one's self concept, requiring that "self-evaluation

EXHIBIT 0.2
Diagnostic and Statistical Manual of Mental Disorders-Related Definitions of *Body Image*

Anorexia nervosa: Intense fear of gaining weight or becoming fat, even though underweight. Disturbance in the way in which one's body weight or shape is experienced, undue influence of body weight or shape on self-evaluation or denial of the seriousness of the current low body weight.[a]

Bulimia nervosa: Self-evaluation is unduly influenced by body shape or weight.[a]

Body dysmorphic disorder: Preoccupation with an imagined defect in appearance. If a slight physical anomaly is present, the person's concern is markedly excessive.[a]

Body image disorder: A persistent report of dissatisfaction, concern, and distress that is related to an aspect of physical appearance. Some degree of impairment in social relations, social activities, or occupational functioning must be present.[b, c]

---

[a]From American Psychiatric Association (1994). [b]From J. K. Thompson (1992). [c]Subcodes for rating the severity of symptoms (mild–severe), target of disturbance (weight vs. nonweight), and "objectiveness" of disturbance (valid–delusional) are provided.

is unduly influenced by body shape and weight" (American Psychiatric Association, 1994, p. 550). J. K. Thompson (1992) focused on a "persistent report of dissatisfaction, concern, and/or distress" (p. 43) that is associated with "some degree of impairment in social relations, social activities or occupational functioning" (p. 43). Clearly, the multiple views of body image disturbance have made their way into the available diagnostic systems.

This brings us to one of the more complex issues in the field of body image and one that we return to throughout this book: the problems inherent in defining, measuring, and creating theoretical models and in treating a disorder as broad and multifaceted as body image, even if we can confine it to an appearance-related definition. We hope that defining some of the terms can serve as a guidepost, and we have endeavored to specify when referring to individual studies the aspect of body image under investigation. For the remainder of this book, we try to use concrete terms and refer specifically to one or more aspects of an appearance-related disturbance that we have described in this Introduction.

EXPLANATIONS OF BODY IMAGE DISTURBANCE

Explanations, hypotheses, and, ultimately, well-constructed theories of body image disturbance are crucial to the development of the field beyond its current stage. It is interesting to note that a wealth of research documents the incidence of disturbance in diverse populations and focuses on the evaluation of intervention programs for treating body image dysfunctions (Cash, 1995b, 1996, 1997; Cash & Pruzinsky, 1990; J. C. Rosen, 1996a, 1996b, 1997; J. K. Thompson, 1990, 1996b). Only recently have researchers in systematic studies sought to examine risk factors for the onset of disturbance, and we are just beginning to understand the multitude of influences that may be potentially found as important in precipitating and contributing to the maintenance of body image problems (M. P. Levine, Smolak, & Hayden, 1994; Smolak, Levine, & Striegel-Moore, 1996).

Biological, social, and interpersonal factors have a tremendous impact on one's body image, and these influences form the backdrop for the exposition of the emerging models and schools of thought reviewed in this book. The sociocultural factor includes the pernicious pressures associated with striving to fit societal ideals and the negative impact of making social comparisons with "attractive" reference groups. We position the two chapters that review evidence for a sociocultural role in body image formation and maintenance at the outset of our discussion of theories because we believe that societal mores form and shape the more intimate social and interpersonal experiences that also affect body image. For instance, the chapter on appearance-related feedback details the negative effects of critical comments, teasing, and seemingly benign appearance commentary;

however, it is doubtful that such verbalizations would take place at such an alarming frequency (or have such a negative impact) if we did not live in a society that places such a premium on attractiveness. Additionally, the influences of such close associates as family and friends, including modeling one's parents' or peers' dieting and appearance behaviors, might not be so powerful in a society that did not emphasize adherence to idealized standards of appearance.

Certainly, society has a role in other theoretical examinations, yet several of these approaches offer their unique slant on causes and consequences of body image disturbance. Feminist interpretations consider biological sex and the multitude of unique experiences encountered by girls and women to be crucial for making sense of the extraordinary concerns, pressures, and body dysphoria felt by them. Similarly, the tragedies of sexual abuse and sexual harassment, although also associated with clinical conditions such as depression and extreme feelings of powerlessness, yield conceptualizations that offer much in terms of understanding body image. Two conceptual models used to guide many different aspects of psychological functioning—behavioral and cognitive explanations—also offer excellent frameworks for understanding the onset and perpetuation of body image disturbance. These two approaches focus on such factors as critical conditioning experiences, behavioral avoidance, cognitive biases, and cognitive schemata as concepts for grasping the onset and continuance of body image problems.

OVERVIEW OF THE BOOK

Geena was a chubby clarinet player who liked to read and play chess. She was more interested in computers than makeup and in stuffed animals than designer clothes. She walked to her first day of junior high with her pencils sharpened and her notebooks neatly labeled. She was ready to learn Spanish and algebra and to audition for the school orchestra. She came home sullen and shaken. The boy who had his locker next to hers had smashed into her with his locker door and sneered, "Move your fat ass." That night she told her mother, "I hate my looks. I need to go on a diet." (Pipher, 1994, p. 55)

As a child and teenager . . . I learned that I was grotesque, actually burlesque. I came to believe that my body was afflicted. Yet, unlike the bent limb, the marked face, or the twisted frame, this affliction was a crime. And I was the criminal. Condemned by a jury of my peers, I was indicted as weak. They said I caused my burden, and because I did, I legitimized their abuse. I had a scar I was blamed for. (an overweight boy quoted in LeBow, 1995, p. 10)

We close out this Introduction with these two quotes because they exemplify the traumatic and powerful societal and interpersonal influences that affect body image, especially for young boys and girls. In addition, they reflect one strategy that we use throughout this book, the generous allotment of anecdotes, case histories, and sound bites as exemplars to introduce theoretical and clinical material. We hope that these excerpts will not only enlighten research discussions but also capture the essence of the often tragic causes and consequences of body image disturbance. In some cases, we hope the material will illustrate the absurdities associated with any society's obsession with image.

Our goals in the first section of this book are to offer background material, illustrate the diversity of body image, and examine current assessment and treatment approaches. Chapter 1 provides an overview of the scope of body image disturbance, highlighting its connection to individuals of incredibly diverse backgrounds and clinical conditions. In chapter 2, we offer an overview of assessment and treatment strategies, including an analysis of measures designed to quantify levels of subjective dissatisfaction and related definitions of body image, and an overview of treatment strategies found successful in improving one's body image.

The next four sections contain eight chapters that form the bulk of this book. This material details the background and evidence for various explanations of the development and maintenance of body image disturbance. We generally refer to these as *explanations* rather than *theories* because well-developed and empirically tested theories have yet to emerge in some areas. However, we purposefully selected these four broad explanatory areas because the emerging evidence is quite robust in relating these influences to the onset and perpetuation of body image problems. More important, this is the first book to outline the measurement of these risk variables and relate specific treatment options that target such factors.

In the section Societal and Social Approaches, we review the role of broad and pervasive sociocultural forces, such as the media (TV, print), and examine the more specific factor of social comparison, a tendency to evaluate one's own appearance to that of proximal (i.e., friends) or distal (i.e., celebrities) others. In these two chapters, we not only examine the evidence indicting the media or one's own comparison strategies as contributing factors but also review state-of-the-art methods for measuring (quantifying) these influences and describe how treatment programs attempt to modify one's own internalization of media-driven societal values or upward social comparison tendencies (i.e., selectively choosing to compare with more attractive others).

The section Interpersonal Approaches brings the focus closer to home, so to speak, with two chapters that examine the role of interpersonal factors. In chapter 5, we review a wealth of data determining that feedback from others about one's looks, typically in the form of "teasing" comments, may have devastating effects on one's body image. Chapter 6 details other interpersonal factors, particularly from one's close relationships (family, peer, partner), which may play a role in the development and persistence of body image problems. In this chapter, issues such as parental modeling of dieting or weight concerns and how one's romantic partner evaluates one's appearance are reviewed. Multiple measures that reflect an interpersonal influence are provided, and treatment strategies, especially those that target the pernicious effect of teasing, are explored in these two chapters.

The Feminist Approaches section offers a detailed examination of one of the most rapidly emerging fields of study in body image. These two chapters deal with issues critical to understanding the particular reasons that women are at greater risk for body image problems. In particular, political and economic conceptualizations are reviewed as well as emerging theories based on feminist writings. The role of sexual abuse and harassment are also explored, along with factors that moderate and explain the negative effects of these traumatic experiences on body image. Assessment and treatment methods predicated on feminist theory and practice are also offered.

The Behavioral, Cognitive, and Integrative Approaches section provides an examination of how two of the dominant psychological theoretical orientations conceptualize the area of body image. In chapter 9, we provide a behavioral conceptualization, based on traumatic conditioning or critical experiences, for the initial formation of body image disturbance and we offer behavioral avoidance as an explanation for the maintenance of such distress. Measures for detecting and defining contextual factors and avoidance are provided, and exposure methodologies for treating disturbance are outlined. In chapter 10, cognitive-processing models for understanding a body image-related cognitive schema are reviewed, and research strategies are explained. Relating such schematic processing to clinical assessment and treatment possibilities is a relatively new enterprise; however, in this chapter, we explore the many possibilities for such a connection.

Finally, we conclude with a chapter entitled "Future Directions: Integrative Theories, Multidimensional Assessments, and Multicomponent Interventions." In this chapter, we provide an overview of recent integrative models of body image formation and maintenance. These emerging conceptualizations, based on attempts by researchers to create multidimensional models, may serve as a guide for future reformulations and extensions of the explanations of body image contained in this book. We also note the existence of multidimensional assessment batteries for both the measurement of body image disturbance and its associated risk and protective factors. Innovative developments in treatment are covered, and the need for comparative outcome studies is emphasized. We conclude with a call for carefully controlled research on the evaluation of the ever-proliferating number of strategies for modifying body image disturbance.

I

AN OVERVIEW: PREVALENCE, DIVERSITY, ASSESSMENT, AND TREATMENT

1

THE SCOPE OF BODY IMAGE
DISTURBANCE: THE BIG PICTURE

As one scans the current scientific literature dealing with the psychological experience of one's own body, the quantity and diversity of studies are impressive. Research dealing with this topic has gone off in all directions. (S. Fisher, 1990, p. 3)

In this first chapter, we attempt to provide a framework for the material to follow by offering a "big picture" overview of the multiple and diverse individuals of widely divergent backgrounds and body sizes who share a common bond—their body image has a significant influence on their day-to-day functioning. This review is not meant to be comprehensive—entire books have been written on some of the single topics to follow—instead, we intend to choose contemporary and illustrative research and clinical reports in an effort to expose the importance of body image for many individuals of both genders and a wide array of ethnic and cultural backgrounds. In this and subsequent chapters, readers will also find scattered throughout our presentation of scientific and clinical material numerous quotes and minicase vignettes designed to capture experientially the often academic discussion of a particular topic. It is our hope that these inserts will highlight contemporary and often highly personal aspects of the experience of body image disturbance.

JUST HOW DISSATISFIED ARE PEOPLE?

The Big Surveys

Several large-scale surveys from a wide variety of sources indicate that a substantial number of individuals are unhappy with how they look. A good place to begin this overview of dissatisfaction is a perusal of the three large-scale surveys conducted over the past 25 years by *Psychology Today*. Although the representativeness of the readers who responded to the *Psychology Today* questionnaire to all men and women in the general population is questionable, these data provide some intriguing information regarding change in body image over time. Table 1.1 contains the results from the surveys, conducted in 1972, 1985, and 1997, for several aspects of physical appearance. For instance, overall appearance dissatisfaction increased from 23% to 56% for women and from 15% to 43% for men. Women were especially unhappy with their mid torso, lower torso, and weight; men were quite a bit more dissatisfied with the mid torso than lower torso, almost equaling women in the waist area (63% vs. 71%). It is interesting to note that men were more unhappy with their chest area (38%) than women were with their breasts (34%). (The *Psychology Today* survey also has a wealth of information regarding influences on the development of body image, so we return to its findings periodically in other chapters.)

Some of the recent large-scale studies, conducted by researchers using randomized and stratified sampling procedures, yield perhaps more reliable data than the *Psychology Today* results, which may have been influenced by a sample bias (i.e., individuals who were most concerned with appearance may have disproportionately responded to the survey). In 1993, the Centers for Disease Control and Prevention in Atlanta reported on their Youth Risk Behavior Survey, which was a self-administered questionnaire given to a random sample of 11,467 high school students in 1990 (Serdula et al., 1993). Their primary measure of interest for our purposes was an index of "trying to lose weight," which is not, of course, synonymous with body dissatisfaction but can serve as a direct reference variable for one's

TABLE 1.1
Sources of Discontent: The Results of Three
U.S. Surveys on Body Image

Disliked physical attributes	1972 survey		1985 survey		1996 survey	
	Men	Women	Men	Women	Men	Women
Mid torso	36	50	50	57	63	71
Lower torso	12	49	21	50	29	61
Upper torso (breast–chest)	18	27	28	32	38	34
Weight	35	48	41	55	52	66
Muscle tone	25	30	32	45	45	57
Height	13	13	20	17	16	16
Face	8	11	20	20	*na*	*na*
Overall appearance	15	23	34	38	43	56

Note. All figures are in percentages. From *The Body Image Workbook: An 8-Step Program for Learning to Like Your Looks* (p. 40), by T. F. Cash, 1997, Oakland, CA: New Harbinger. Copyright 1997 by New Harbinger Publications (www.newharbinger.com). Reprinted with permission.

unhappiness with weight. Table 1.2 contains some of their findings, indicating that female students in Grades 9–12 were much more likely to be attempting weight loss (42.5–45.3%) than were male students (14.5–16.0%). Of special note here is the finding that boys were more likely to be interested in gaining weight (22.2–29.4%) than losing weight and much more likely to be invested in this goal than women (only 5.6–7.9% of women were attempting to gain weight). These data illustrate a key finding that we return to later: Men may often be dissatisfied because of a low weight or, more likely, their goal of gaining weight reflects a desire to add muscle mass.

In this same study, Serdula et al. (1993) surveyed 60,861 adults. Table 1.3 contains these results. The percentages of female participants attempting to lose weight were comparable with the high school sample, with percentages of women in four age categories from 18 to 59 years old, ranging from 40.4% to 44.6% (27.1% of those age 60 or older were trying to lose weight). The percentages for men were somewhat higher than for the high school male students, however a direct comparison is suspect given that the men did not have the option of responding that they wanted to gain weight.

Of considerable interest are the findings in both surveys regarding individuals of different ethnicities. As both tables reveal, there were relative similarities in findings for different ratings across White, Black, Hispanic, and "Other" designations of background. For instance, for the high school students, the percentages were roughly comparable, for both male and female students, with the possible exception that Black female and male students were less interested than other groups in losing weight and more interested in gaining weight (see Table 1.2). However, these numbers were more consonant across all groups for the adults—there was almost no ethnicity difference in those trying to lose weight (37.7–38.9%).

This issue of ethnicity and weight modification efforts was also examined recently by a study conducted by the Heart, Lung, and Blood Institute (Schreiber et al., 1996). Table 1.4 contains some of the findings from this study of 2,379 girls, ages 9 and 10. Overall, there was no statistical difference in either age or ethnicity of girls trying to lose weight. For 9-year-olds, 42% of Black girls and 37% of White girls were trying to lose weight; the comparable figures for 10-year-olds were 44% and 37%, respectively. Although not contained in the table, the authors reported that controlling for differences in overall level of obesity (body mass index [BMI]) even eliminated these small differences between Black and White girls. Some other interesting findings regarding BMI are contained in the table. For instance, more of the Black girls were in the higher BMI categories, and these girls were trying to lose weight or were "chronic dieters" at roughly the same levels as White girls. However, in the lower BMI levels,

TABLE 1.2
Prevalence of Weight-Control Practices From the Youth Risk Behavior Survey, 1990

Characteristic	Female students						Male students				
	n	% trying to lose weight	% trying to maintain weight	% trying to gain weight	% not doing anything	n	% trying to lose weight	% trying to maintain weight	% trying to gain weight	% not doing anything
Grade[a]											
9	1,443	42.5	25.0	7.9	24.6	1,311	15.0	16.7	22.2	46.1
10	1,487	45.3	24.9	7.0	22.8	1,459	14.5	14.7	28.6	42.2
11	1,523	43.4	27.3	5.9	23.4	1,375	16.0	14.0	29.4	40.6
12	1,425	43.7	28.7	5.6	22.1	1,429	15.3	15.1	23.3	46.2
Race											
White	3,163	47.4	27.3	3.6	21.7	3,106	16.2	14.6	23.3	46.0
Black	1,233	30.4	26.7	16.1	26.8	1,003	10.0	15.7	39.4	35.0
Hispanic	1,171	39.1	24.5	11.2	25.2	1,084	16.7	16.3	29.0	38.0
Other	315	45.6	18.7	8.1	27.6	392	13.7	17.2	22.4	46.8
Total	5,882	43.7	26.4	6.6	23.2	5,585	15.2	15.1	26.0	43.7

Note. From "Weight Control Practices of U.S. Adolescents and Adults," by M. K. Serdula, M. E. Collins, D. F. Williamson, R. F. Anda, E. Pamuk, and T. E. Byers, 1993, *Annals of Internal Medicine, 119,* p. 668. Copyright 1993 by American College of Physicians. Reprinted with permission.
[a]Excludes 15 students who were in ungraded classrooms.

TABLE 1.3
Prevalence of Weight-Control Practices From the Behavioral Risk Factor Surveillance Survey, 1989

Characteristics	Women				Men			
	n	% trying to lose weight	% trying to maintain weight	% neither	n	% trying to lose weight	% trying to maintain weight	% neither
Age (in years)								
18–29	7,200	40.4	29.3	30.3	6,326	18.7	27.0	54.3
30–39	7,949	42.9	28.6	28.5	6,797	25.5	29.4	45.2
40–49	5,384	44.6	28.2	27.2	4,616	29.9	28.9	41.2
50–59	4,041	41.7	28.3	30.0	3,132	28.9	27.5	43.6
Older than 60	9,873	27.1	27.5	45.4	5,543	21.8	26.9	51.3
Race								
White	28,654	38.4	28.8	32.9	22,223	24.2	27.9	47.9
Black	3,274	38.6	24.0	37.4	2,020	21.7	25.1	53.2
Hispanic	1,486	37.7	29.6	32.7	1,231	29.6	27.3	43.1
Other	1,033	38.9	29.1	31.9	940	24.8	33.9	41.3
Total	34,447	38.3	28.4	33.3	26,414	24.3	27.9	47.8

Note. From "Weight Control Practices of U.S. Adolescents and Adults," by M. K. Serdula, M. E. Collins, D. F. Williamson, R. F. Anda, E. Pamuk, and T. E. Byers, 1993, *Annals of Internal Medicine, 119,* p. 670. Copyright 1993 by American College of Physicians. Reprinted with permission.

TABLE 1.4

Girls in the National Heart, Lung, and Blood Institute Growth and Health Study: Baseline Data, 1987–1988

Age and Body Mass Index quartile[a]	N		% trying to lose weight		% chronic dieters[b]		% trying to gain weight	
	Black	White	Black	White	Black	White	Black	White
9-year-olds								
1st	119	178	13	12	2	2	50***	16
2nd	132	150	27	29	6	2	22***	5
3rd	124	160	43	41	12*	4	7	3
4th	160	125	74	77	25	18	3	2
Total	535	613	42	37	12***	6	19***	7
10-year-olds								
1st	137	168	7*	16	2	2	43***	12
2nd	168	132	28	24	8*	3	19***	2
3rd	158	141	43	48	8	7	9**	1
4th	201	100	82	74	24	32	2	1
Total	664	541	44	37	12	9	16[b]	5

Note. From "Weight Modification Efforts Reported by Black and White Preadolescent Girls: National Heart, Lung, and Blood Institute Growth and Health Study," by G. B. Schreiber, M. Robins, R. Striegel-Moore, E. Obarzanek, J. A. Morrison, and D. J. Wright, 1996, Pediatrics, 98, p. 66. Copyright 1996 by American Academy of Pediatrics. Reprinted with permission.
[a]Quartile cut points were calculated separately for 9- and 10-year-old girls.   [b]Chronic dieters reported that they were usually or always trying to lose weight.
*p < .05. **p < .01. ***p < .001 in a two-sided test.

the percentage of individuals trying to gain weight was much greater for Black versus White girls.

Certainly, dieting may be a behavior driven by concerns other than those related to a poor body image. Perhaps health reasons, among other motivations, explain the decision to lose weight, and conceivably, there may be ethnic differences in these motivations for dieting. Striegel-Moore, Wilfley, Caldwell, Needham, and Brownell (1996) evaluated a large number of attitudes and behaviors of 324 dieting Black and White women (drawn from a pool of over 20,000 subscribers to *Consumer Reports*). They assessed nine different reasons for undertaking a weight-loss program, including desires to improve appearance, concerns about health pressures from others, and feeling physically uncomfortable. None of the comparisons between Blacks and Whites for any of the nine measures were significantly different. However, a comparison of the strength of the ratings across different items reveals that desires to improve appearance and "wanted to feel better about self" were the highest rated in terms of importance (see Table 1.5).

In a recent large-scale study, D. E. Smith, Thompson, Raczynski, and Hilner (in press) evaluated body satisfaction and investment in appearance (i.e., the importance of physical appearance to the individual) in a large sample of Black and White men (1,838) and women (1,898). It is interesting to note that Black men and women were more invested in appearance than White men and women but were also more satisfied with their appearance. This finding indicates that cognitions and behaviors associated with appearance issues—which is what the items on the appearance in-

TABLE 1.5
Importance of Reasons for Undertaking One's
Most Recent Weight-Loss Program

Reason	Black women		White women		F
	M	SD	M	SD	
Concerns about health	3.81	1.26	3.82	1.13	0.81
Wanted to improve appearance	4.47	0.79	4.41	0.74	0.44
Pressure from others	1.89	1.19	1.92	1.15	0.65
Wanted to feel better about self	4.33	0.93	4.25	0.93	0.53
An upcoming event	1.59	1.07	1.79	1.34	2.09
Wanted to have more energy	3.73	1.26	3.76	1.20	0.67
Wanted to improve social life	2.22	1.41	2.26	1.41	0.08
Wanted to do better at work	1.81	1.20	2.04	1.20	4.01
Felt uncomfortable physically	3.89	1.17	3.81	1.19	0.00

Note. *n* was 162 for both groups. Questions were rated on a scale ranging from 1 (*not at all important*) to 5 (*extremely important*). Using Bonferroni correction, the *p* level for this set of variables is $p = .05/9 = .006$. None of the univariate comparisons were statistically significant. From "Weight-Related Attitudes and Behaviors of Women Who Diet to Lose Weight: A Comparison of Black Dieters and White Dieters," by R. H. Striegel-Moore, D. E. Wilfley, M. B. Caldwell, M. L. Needham, and K. D. Brownell, 1996, *Obesity Research, 4,* p. 113. Copyright 1996 by *Obesity Research*. Reprinted with permission.

vestment measure assess—do not necessarily translate into dissatisfaction with one's looks. Indeed, Rucker and Cash (1992) had similar findings, and Cash and colleagues have repeatedly found that investment and satisfaction are independent constructs (see the Introduction and T. A. Brown, Cash, & Mikulka, 1990). One possible explanation for these ethnic differences in findings for the two aspects of body image was offered by one of our graduate students. Her observation was that Black women's body image may not be as dependent on weight or size as that of White women. Overweight Black women, she noted, focus on a variety of appearance features (e.g., dress, hair, make-up), whereas White women are so focused on weight that this component of appearance dominates internal feelings about their looks. Of course, this is only one hypothesis, and research to test it and other possible explanations is needed.

Finally, in one of the most thorough surveys, Cash and Henry (1995) evaluated 803 women, ranging in age from 18–70 years old, from five regions of the United States (Northeast, Southeast, West Coast, Southwest, and Midwest). The sampling was conducted to represent the U.S. population in terms of race, age, income, education, and geographical region. Table 1.6 reveals that levels of disturbance on measures of dissatisfaction, appearance evaluation, and overweight preoccupation were remarkably consistent across ages. On only one dimension, appearance evaluation, was there any difference across the 18–70 age range, with 18- to 24-year-olds rating their bodies more positively than did all other ages. The findings on ethnicity were clear-cut on all measures: Blacks were more satisfied than

TABLE 1.6
Body Image Comparisons as a Function of Age and Race–Ethnicity

Demographic variables and group	Multidimensional Body Self-Relations Questionnaire subscales					
	Appearance Evaluation		Body Areas Satisfaction		Overweight Preoccupation	
	M	SD	M	SD	M	SD
Age in years (n)						
18–24 (128)	3.07_a	.48	3.37	.69	2.95	.97
25–34 (198)	2.94_b	.48	3.22	.74	2.87	.89
35–44 (168)	2.92_b	.48	3.18	.74	2.83	.91
45–54 (150)	2.88_b	.48	3.18	.71	2.86	.92
55–70 (159)	2.86_b	.48	3.22	.80	2.77	.88
Race–ethnicity						
Black (n = 76)	3.20_a	.48	3.65_a	.80	2.57_a	.85
Hispanic (n = 50)	2.95_b	.48	3.29_b	.86	2.83_a	.95
White (n = 672)	2.90_b	.48	3.18_b	.71	2.89_a	.91

Note. For each demographic variable, groups (columns) with different subscripts are significantly different ($p < .05$). From "Women's Body Images: The Results of a National Survey in the U.S.A.," by T. F. Cash and P. E. Henry, 1995, Sex Roles, 33, p. 24. Copyright 1995 by Plenum Publishing Corporation. Reprinted with permission.

Hispanics and Whites on all measures, and there was no difference in the satisfaction of Hispanic and White samples.

There is more to one's body image than simply overall weight or size, although the great majority of the research has been "weighted" in this dimension. We now turn to a few examples that may help broaden our appearance horizon.

Breast–Chest Size

> One out of five respondents said that at least once in her life, a man has said he wished her breasts were a different size. (Plus, a startling 58 percent have been taunted or teased because of their breasts.) (P. Grant, 1996, p. 189)

> Cosmetic surgery to enlarge the breasts (which does not include reconstruction after mastectomy) is gaining popularity after falling out of favor in 1992. That year, the Food and Drug Administration banned silicone-gel-filled implants amid worries about potential health problems from silicone leaking out of the pouches. The number of operations plunged to 32,607, from a high of an estimated 120,000 to 150,000 in 1990. But the count has been climbing back up and exceeded 122,000 last year ... the states with the most operations are Florida, Texas and California, and plastic surgeons report that women in Texas request bigger implants than those in any other state. (Grady, 1998, p. B13)

Literally millions of women have sought augmentation cosmetic surgery to enlarge breast size, and increasingly, men are opting for pectoral implants to expand their chests (discussed later in this chapter in the "Costs" of Body Image Disturbance). These decisions to engage in expensive, and possibly, risky surgery suggests a level of dissatisfaction with this body site that has also been documented by researchers. As Table 1.1 notes, 38% men and 34% women disliked this aspect of their appearance.

J. K. Thompson and Tantleff (1992) developed the breast–chest rating scale, which consists of five sizes ranging from small to large, and asked men and women to rate their current size and their ideal size. Both men and women preferred to have larger chest and breasts than they currently possessed. In addition, there were some interesting findings related to stereotypical beliefs about the ideal size ratings of other individuals. In general, men and women overestimated the ideal size they thought others would choose, indicating that people are not actually as enamored of large breasts and chests as the raters thought. Jacobi and Cash (1994) had similar findings for the breast size: Women's own size rating was smaller than their ideal, and they overestimated the ideal breast size picked by men. Recently, Tantleff-Dunn, Thompson, Sellin-Wolters, and Ashby (1997) completed a longitudinal study of size preferences covering 6 years, from 1990–1996, and found that women and men have been very consistent in their dissatisfaction with breast–chest size: Ratings of actual size were smaller than ideals for each of the four measurement periods during the 6 years.

Recently, Koff and Benavage (1998) evaluated breast size satisfaction, along with several other measures of body image, in samples of Caucasian and Asian American college women. They used a modification of the J. K. Thompson and Tantleff (1992) measure: The figures were truncated at the hip–thigh junction to focus attention more directly on the upper body, and the figures were modified to appear more ethnically neutral. Caucasian women rated themselves as having larger breast sizes and had larger ideal breast size ratings than did the Asian American women; it is interesting to note that the groups did not differ on measures of overall appearance satisfaction.

Self magazine conducted a survey in 1996 of over 4,000 women and found that over half would change their breasts if they could (P. Grant, 1996): Forty-three percent thought that their breast size made a "difference to their partner's enjoyment" (p. 210), and 62% of that group stated that they had this opinion because of specific comments from their partners. (In chapters 5 and 6, we explore in more detail issues related to one's partner's judgments of appearance attributes.)

Facial Features

> My hatred of my appearance began when I was 12 . . . I became obsessed with my nose; I thought it was too big and shiny. It started when I heard a boy in my class make a comment about Jimmy Durante. I can't even remember what he said, but he was snickering, and I was sure it was a mean comment. I thought he might be making fun of me—of my nose. I couldn't be sure, but I kept worrying that maybe there *was* something wrong with my nose, even though I'd never worried about it before. After that, I started lifting up my lips to raise my nose so it wouldn't look so big. (a woman in her mid-30s, as quoted in Phillips, 1996, p. 38)[1]

Many aspects of the face are foci of dissatisfaction among individuals of different backgrounds. For instance, Hall (1995) noted that eyelid surgery to modify the *epicanthic fold* (the fold of the skin of the upper eyelid over the inner angle or both angles of the eye) and nose reconstruction are common among Asian women. Rhinoplasty (nose surgery), rhytidectomy (face lift), and blepharoplasty (eyelid lift) are among the most common cosmetic surgeries performed each year (American Society of Plastic and Reconstructive Surgeons, 1996). Ear surgery, jaw surgery, chin aug-

---

[1]From *The Broken Mirror: Understanding and Treating Body Dysmorphic Disorder*, by Katherine A. Phillips, New York: Oxford University Press. Copyright © 1996 by Katherine A. Phillips, MD. Used by permission of Oxford University Press.

mentation or reduction, brow or forehead lift, and cheek surgery are also popular facial sites for intervention. (See Tables 2.2, 2.3, and 2.4 in the next chapter for more information about the broad range of cosmetic procedures available for the facial area.)

Male Pattern Hair Loss

> Before my hair problem began, I didn't have much trouble talking to people when I went out. I was never the life of the party, but I'd go out. I liked to see people, and I never avoided social events that I wanted to go to. But it's really hard for me now because of how I look. When I do go out, it's hard for me to talk with people—I can't concentrate on the conversation. All I can think about is whether my hair looks okay and whether they're noticing how thin it is. I constantly check out their hair and compare it to mine. Then I usually feel worse because I think their hair looks better. (a young man, as quoted in Phillips, 1996, p. 16)[2]

Androgenetic alopecia, or male pattern baldness (MPB), affects the majority of men over the age of 50 (Cash, 1990a, 1990b), and this change in appearance may have dramatic effects for the emotional well-being of the individual. Cash (1990a, 1992) found that 60% of men with extensive MPB described negative social or emotional effects from the hair loss. In fact, hair transplant or restoration surgeries are by far the most popular cosmetic surgery for men (American Society of Plastic and Reconstructive Surgeons, 1996; see also chapter 2). Cash, Price, and Savin (1993) directly compared female and male participants with MPB and found that the consequences were significantly more deleterious for women. Women reported more adverse psychosocial events, reported a reduction in positive life events, and were more dissatisfied on a measure of overall appearance evaluation than were men.

Muscularity

As noted in Table 1.1, dissatisfaction with muscle tone for both men and women has increased over the past 25 years, now reaching 45% for men and 57% for women. In their study of satisfaction of multiple body areas, Jacobi and Cash (1994) also found that both male and female participants preferred a more muscular physique than they currently possessed. Furnham, Titman, and Sleeman (1994) found that physical activity status moderated women's positive perception of muscularity: Women who were involved in active sports, such as bodybuilding and rowing, had higher

---

[2]From *The Broken Mirror: Understanding and Treating Body Dysmorphic Disorder*, by Katherine A. Phillips, New York: Oxford University Press. Copyright © 1996 by Katherine A. Phillips, MD. Used by permission of Oxford University Press.

acceptance ratings of muscular female body shapes than did sedentary controls. Tantleff-Dunn and Thompson (1997) found that men's dissatisfaction with chest size (i.e., wanting to be larger than they were) was associated with greater overall appearance dissatisfaction. Extreme concerns with muscularity may also be an indication of the existence of body dysmorphic disorder (as discussed shortly), the use of steroids (Blouin & Goldfield, 1995), or both.

Individual Difference Variables

> I was at my ob/gyn and I had gained 26 pounds in 26 weeks of pregnancy. He told me that if I didn't watch out I would gain another 40 pounds! He's sending me to the dietician. I've been so upset I've been crying all day—really stressed. I don't know what to do. (a 35-year-old woman pregnant with her first child)

Gender

Because of their biological sex, women encounter body image-related experiences that men do not—a fact that becomes apparent as you read this book, especially chapters 3 and 8 on sociocultural pressures and sexual abuse–harassment. McGrath, Keita, Strickland, and Russo (1990) mined similar territory with regard to gender and depression, considering the psychological reaction to changes associated with being female, such as menstruation, pregnancy, and menopause. Certainly if the experience of being female is important to the gender difference in depression where the sex ratio is 2:1, consider its possible relevance for eating disorders where the sex ratio is 9:1 and the main symptom is feeling unhappy with one's body.

Perhaps the transition through the pubertal years has received more evaluation than any other biological aspect of being female (J. K. Thompson, 1990). Most of this research focuses on the timing of menarche or of physical maturation in conjunction with that of one's peers. In both cases, early maturation (usually defined by menarche prior to age 11 or a self-rating of physical maturation before one's peers) has been associated with greater body dissatisfaction (Brooks-Gunn & Warren, 1985; J. K. Thompson, 1990); however, there has also been conflicting data (e.g., Heinberg, 1996). In recent years, a synchronous model, based on the timing of puberty and life events as opposed to the singular timing of puberty, has achieved more consistent support. Smolak, Levine, and Gralen (1993) found that the confluence of early maturation and dating produced the highest levels of body dissatisfaction and eating disturbance. M. P. Levine, Smolak, Moodey, Shuman, and Hessen (1994) found that the addition of academic stress to the above equation resulted in an even greater scenario of risk for disturbed eating.

Puberty certainly presents unique body-related challenges for girls, which boys do not encounter. Girls' bodies change physically in a manner that is not reinforced by prevailing cultural standards, that is, the preference for a thin, noncurvaceous shape. Boys, however, live in a society that values a large and muscular physique in its men; therefore, the natural physical changes that occur during this epoch for boys are supported by current mores. It is thought that these factors, at least partially, may account for the more negative view of puberty by girls and the decrease in self-esteem that occurs for them at this time (Smolak & Levine, 1996). Related to this idea is the finding that adolescent dancers have a more negative attitude toward puberty than swimmers (Brooks-Gunn, Attie, Burrow, Rosso, & Warren, 1989). The different aspects of puberty change may also be associated with different body image effects, for instance, breast development may be connected with an enhancement of self-esteem and body satisfaction (Slap, Khalid, Paikoff, Brooks-Gunn, & Warren, 1994). Recent evidence indicating that girls are developing pubertal characteristics at younger ages suggests that body image issues should be examined in this context for girls, even as young as 8–10 years of age (Herman-Giddens et al., 1997).

The menstrual cycle is a second part of the female experience that is associated with a number of physical changes, such as fluid retention, neurotransmitter modifications, and blood sugar perturbations, that may affect self-image. Although the research in this area is minimal, Altabe and Thompson (1990) found that appearance dissatisfaction was exacerbated both immediately prior to and during menstruation, findings that were replicated by Carr-Nangle, Johnson, Bergeron, and Nangle (1994).

Given the vast physiognomical changes that accompany pregnancy, it is almost astounding that such minimal attention has been devoted to this factor and body image. In one of the few studies in this area, Slade (1977) tested size estimation accuracy at 4 and 8 months, finding that women were more accurate at the latter time. Davies and Wardle (1994) found that pregnant women were more satisfied than nonpregnant controls about their body size and had less weight concern. However, the pregnant women's rating of ideal size did not change as a function of pregnancy, and they expressed concerns about postpartum weight changes. Sternberg and Blinn (1993) found that the diaries of pregnant teenagers had a predominance of negative entries about the body.

These body image issues related to pregnancy should be of concern for health practitioners. Fears of weight gain are especially intense among dieters and individuals with eating disturbance (Fahy & O'Donoghue, 1991). Low weight gain and eating-disorder symptoms are associated with increased pregnancy complications for mother and baby (Franko & Walton, 1993). In addition, the postpartum period may be associated with weight concerns and disordered eating and may actually lead to the onset of eating disorders (A. Stein & Fairburn, 1996). Psychoeducational programs to deal with this critical time may be warranted (A. Stein & Fairburn, 1996).

Thus, there is evidence that female physical changes, puberty, menstruation, pregnancy, and the postpartum period are associated with vulnerability to body image problems. The degree to which these factors help understand the gender difference in body image disturbance is open to question—certainly other issues that may differentially have an impact on women versus men (e.g., sexual abuse and harassment; see chapters 7 and 8) may also contribute to this discrepancy. However, the unique physical and biological factors that affect only women deserve further study. In particular, extending the research timeline to include an analysis of how older women react to physical changes is needed.

In fact, research shows that the gender differences in body image distress are actually increasing. Feingold and Mazzella (1996) recently conducted a meta-analysis of 222 studies from the past 50 years, evaluating gender and age-related trends for three measures of body image: self-rating of attractiveness, body satisfaction, and a mixed category, which they noted contained measures that assessed a combination of satisfaction and self-evaluation. Their findings revealed that women were more disturbed than men, the difference was widening rather than narrowing, and the gender discrepancies were most pronounced in the adolescent years. These findings, especially with adolescents, are quite disconcerting and fit with new evidence indicating that girls are engaging in risky behaviors related to body image concerns. Yesalis, Barsukiewicz, Kopstein, and Bahrke (1997) reviewed national and state surveys for anabolic–androgenic steroid use among boys and girls. Their estimates were that 375,000 boys and 175,000 girls use steroids; more important, the results also suggest that rates were declining or stable for boys but were increasing for girls. Finally, recent evidence suggests that diabetic girls may skip insulin injections as a method of losing weight, a behavior that greatly increases their chance of diabetic retinopathy (Rydall, Rodin, Olmsted, Devenyi, & Daneman, 1997).

Sexual Orientation

Research generally indicates that homosexual men may be at greater risk for overall body size–weight dissatisfaction and its associated eating disturbances than are heterosexual men; however, the findings remain inconclusive in studies that have directly compared lesbians with heterosexual women (Beren, Hayden, Wilfley, & Grilo, 1996). Beren et al. found that lesbians, gay men, and heterosexual women did not differ on levels of body dissatisfaction; however, the three groups were more dissatisfied than were heterosexual men. They also found an effect of affiliation with the gay community for men—higher level of affiliation was associated with greater dissatisfaction. No relationship between the two variables was observed for the lesbian women. Beren, Hayden, Wilfley, and Striegel-Moore (1997) also conducted a multifaceted investigation of how lesbians' body image concerns relate to factors such as lesbian beauty ideals, sources of lesbian beauty ideals, conflict about beauty, stereotypes of lesbians' appearance, and lesbian feminine identity. They found that the lesbian beauty ideal includes factors of thinness and fitness. They also noted that there was a disparity between mainstream and lesbian ideals of weight and appearance.

Sexual orientation may also have an effect on adolescents' and teenagers' body image. In a study of 36,320 students, ages 12–20, homosexual male students were more dissatisfied than heterosexual male students, whereas homosexual female students were more satisfied than heterosexual female students (French, Story, Remafedi, Resnick, & Blum, 1996).

Ethnic and Cultural Effects

It's lunch time at the overflowing Hospital for Anorexia and Bulimia here, and hundreds of thin teenage girls cluster around rows of makeshift dining tables in the halls of this compound, where scales are forbidden and sizes are torn from all clothing. . . . The patients are part of an extraordinary problem in Argentina, where a pathology of thinness is sickening young girls at an alarming rate. The rate of anorexia and bulimia—also known here as fashion model syndrome—is three times higher than in the United States, and possibly the highest in the world, mental health experts say. ("A pathology of thinness," 1997, p. A14)

In our review of the large-scale surveys earlier in this chapter, there were several instances noted wherein samples of diverse ethnic identities were contrasted, in particular African-American and White samples. These findings along with the conclusions of recent investigations and reviews indicate that particular body image concerns are present in people of diverse ethnic backgrounds (Altabe, 1996, 1998; Caldwell, Brownell, & Wilfley, 1997; Crago, Shisslak, & Estes, 1996; Rolland, Farnill, & Griffiths, 1997; Striegel-Moore & Smolak, 1996; S. H. Thompson, Corwin, & Sargent, 1997; Wilfley et al., 1996). One result of this intense interest in ethnic background and body image is the realization that it is extremely important to use a broad range of measures to assess multiple components of body image because particular concerns vary across individuals of different ethnic–cultural identities (see Altabe, 1998, and chapter 2).

Surveys in other countries also support the supposition that body image problems are not limited to the United States. For instance, Button, Loan, Davies, and Sonuga-Barke (1997) found that 56% of the school girls in the south of England felt "too fat." In an investigation of 606 female and 315 male high school students in Australia, 25.5% of the normal weight girls and 6.1% of the normal weight boys rated themselves as overweight (Maude, Wertheim, Paxton, Gibbons, & Szmukler, 1993). Findings of body image problems and associations of body image disturbance with factors such as eating dysfunction, depression, and self-esteem are beginning to appear in the literature from a broad range of countries, including Norway, China, Italy, and Argentina (Davis & Katzman, 1997; Martinez & Spinetta, 1997; Santonastaso, Favaro, Ferrara, Sala, & Zanetti, 1995; Wichstrom, 1995).

A final line of research in this area is that of cross-country comparisons. For instance, Cogan, Bhalla, Sefa-Dedeh, and Rothblum (1996) compared 219 U.S. students with 349 students at a Ghanaian university on a variety of measures of body image and cultural ideals of body size. American women were more dissatisfied with their bodies than Ghanaian women; however, nationality did not affect men's scores. Country of origin did affect ideal body size beliefs for both men and women; students in the United States had a smaller female ideal (4.8, on a 1–12 scale) than did students from Ghana (mean of 5.9). It is interesting to note that there was no nationality difference on preference for male figure size, however, there was a gender effect, with women having a slightly smaller male ideal (5.2) than did men (5.45). A second cross-country survey was conducted by Lunner et al. (1998), who evaluated body satisfaction in Swedish, American, and Australian adolescents. They found that Swedish and American participants were equally dissatisfied but adolescents from these two countries were more dissatisfied than the Australian sample.

Summary: Surveys and Individual Differences

In isolation, the foregoing information tells us little about any clinical relevance of body image disturbance or even if individuals are particularly distressed because of an unhappiness with appearance. In the next few sections, we make the case for the importance of body image as a diagnostic variable for certain clinical disorders, such as eating disorders, and detail its role in the possible development of such clinical disturbances. Because traditionally most of the research and theorizing of body image has been in the area of eating disorders, we begin with a review of this research. This is followed by an examination of body dysmorphic disorder, wherein we find that there is a specific *Diagnostic and Statistical Manual of Mental Disorders–Fourth Edition* (DSM-IV; American Psychiatric Association, 1994) category in the somatoform disorders for a disorder of body image. Next, we consider the role of body image in obesity, individuals with disfigurements, cancer victims, and people with visual impairment. A person's avocation (e.g., ballet, avid suntanner) or athletic preference (e.g., gymnast, runner, or wrestler) may also place them at risk for the development of clinically important levels of body image disturbance. Finally, we review the "costs" both financially and emotionally of body image disturbance.

SO I AM DISSATISFIED . . . IS THAT A PROBLEM?

Research increasingly demonstrates that the answer to the question posed in this section's title is *yes*. As noted in our Introduction, in the 1980s Rodin, Silberstein, and Striegel-Moore (1985) referred to the dissatisfaction that women feel with their appearance as a *normative discontent*, a phrase that has been often repeated to capture the essence of a body image disturbance so prevalent among women that it should be considered a normal part of their life experience. However, *normative* should not be considered synonymous with *benign*. Although it would certainly be an overstatement to conclude that any person with a high level of dissatisfaction will necessarily develop an eating disorder, major depression, or body dysmorphia, emerging research suggests that we should be cognizant of the role of such body image problems as a possible precursor to clinical problems.

Eating Disorders

> I always thought I was fat. In high school everybody was thin and perfect. There was a lot of pressure to be beautiful. I wanted to look as slender and sleek as Kate Moss. I thought people like Cindy Crawford were overweight. (an 18-year-old girl, as quoted in Schneider, 1996, p. 73)

> It's hard to get girls if you're overweight. People look at you differently. . . . Sometimes I take diet pills. They're prescription. I haven't learned how to deal with it better. If I need to lose 10 pounds and need to do it fast, I'll take the diet pills. (a 17-year-old boy, as quoted in Schneider, 1996, p. 73)

For many years, body image has been thought to be essential to both understanding the etiology of eating disorders and strategizing optimal therapeutic interventions. Bruch (1962) considered it the most important pathognomonic feature of anorexia nervosa and felt that successful treatment of the eating disorder "without a corrective change in the body image" (p. 189) was likely to be short lived. Slade (1982) contended that it was the primary force behind both anorexia nervosa and bulimia nervosa. J. C. Rosen (1992) felt that the disordered-eating patterns and weight-control strategies of the individual with eating disturbance were secondary to issues of overconcern with body shape and weight, even noting that "it may be more appropriate to think of anorexia and bulimia nervosa as body-image disorders" (p. 171). J. K. Thompson (1992) agreed with J. C. Rosen and others in their belief that body image is primary in the development of eating disorders, not a secondary associate or epiphenomenon.

Perhaps supportive data for this argument are most powerful in the research conducted in the last few years on risk factors for the development of eating disorders. Several prospective studies indicate that body dissatisfaction is the most consistent predictor of the onset of eating disturbances. Cattarin and Thompson (1994), in a 3-year longitudinal study of female adolescents, found that body dissatisfaction predicted the onset of restrictive eating behaviors. Killen et al. (1996) at Stanford University School of Medicine studied 877 high school age girls for a 4-year period, evaluating factors that predicted "partial-syndrome" onset of eating disturbances. (Often in studies of adolescence, an indicator of some level of eating disturbance, such as partial syndrome, is used instead of *DSM-IV*-based criteria because of the low number of cases that actually develop into full-fledged cases of anorexia nervosa or bulimia nervosa.) Girls scoring in the highest quartile on a measure of weight concerns had the highest incidence (10%) of partial syndrome onset.

Graber, Brooks-Gunn, Paikoff, and Warren (1994) tracked 116 girls from young adolescence into young adulthood over a period of 8 years. They evaluated the role of several predictors of risk for eating disturbances during three time periods: young adolescence, midadolescence, and young adulthood. Level of body fat was found to be predictive of eating disturbance at all three epochs; body satisfaction was significantly related at the first two time periods. Recently, Stice and Agras (1998), in a sample of female adolescents followed for 9 months, found that not only did body dissatisfaction predict the onset of binge eating and purging but also that decreased body dissatisfaction predicted the remission of these bulimic behaviors. In a 4-year study of 543 female adolescents, Stice, Killen, Hayward, and Taylor (in press) found that body dissatisfaction predicted the onset of binge eating and purging.

These longitudinal studies certainly support the contemporary view that body image issues may be at the core of eating disorders (J. C. Rosen, 1992; J. K. Thompson, 1996b). Recent work with structural equation modeling and covariance structure modeling analyses indicates that body image disturbance may also mediate the connection between multiple other risk factors and eating disturbances. For instance, Veron-Guidry, Williamson, and Netemeyer (1997) found that eating-disorder symptoms were affected by the interaction of social pressure for thinness, negative self-appraisal, and negative affect but that body dissatisfaction mediated the relationship between the risk factors and eating disturbance. In a similar vein, J. K. Thompson, Coovert, Richards, Johnson, and Cattarin (1995) found that body dissatisfaction mediated the negative effect of teasing on eating disturbances. (Many of these studies also measured the influence of other factors, such as teasing and sociocultural pressures, on the development of body image; however, these issues are explored in subsequent chapters that deal specifically with theories of body image disturbance.)

A recent longitudinal study with adults sheds some unexpected positive light on the potential changes in body image and related eating-disorder symptoms over time. Heatherton, Mahamedi, Striepe, Field, and Keel (1997) followed 509 women and 206 men from 1982 when they were in college until 1992. On average, the women gained 4 lb (1.81 kg) and the men gained 12 lb (5.44 kg). However, as Table 1.7 reveals, women became more satisfied with their weight, whereas men became more dissatisfied. For instance, in 1982 49% of the women reported that they were "overweight" and in 1992, the figure had dropped to 25.4% (note also that in terms of objective overweight standards, the percentages are almost incredibly low, at 1.0% for 1982 and 4.2% for 1992). For men, however, 13.7% stated that they were overweight in 1982, and the figure increased to 24.4% for 1992. Similar findings are present for the desire to lose weight. As Table 1.7 indicates, women decreased on this variable from 82.1% to 67.9%, whereas men increased from 37.1% to 55.4%. Obviously, at least some of these differential sex changes are attributable to the objectively greater weight gain of the men (12 lb [16.32 kg] vs. 4 lb [5.44 kg]). Also note that the initial differences were quite large in 1982, and despite changes in the opposite direction on many of the variables, more men were still objectively overweight or obese (a combination equaling 10.2% vs. women's 6.4%) yet self-categorized themselves less frequently as overweight or obese (combination equaling 24.9% vs. 29.2%). These and other findings in the Heatherton et al. (1987) study, indicating that women's dieting, body dissatisfaction, and eating-disorder symptoms diminish over a 10-year period during early adulthood (including that rates of eating disorders dropped by more than half), "suggest[s] that maturing into adulthood and getting away from the enormous social influences that emphasize thinness . . . help women escape from chronic dieting and abnormal eating" (p. 123).

Until recently, research in the area of eating disorders focused almost exclusively on anorexia nervosa and bulimia nervosa; however, in recent years a new category—binge eating disorder (BED)—has gained enormous attention (W. G. Johnson & Torgrud, 1996). This disorder was not formally included as an eating disorder in the *DSM-IV* but is included in an appendix of disorders needing further empirical investigation. Unlike anorexia nervosa and bulimia nervosa wherein the presence of body image disturbance is a necessary criterion for diagnosis, BED has no such requirement. However, body image disturbances do appear to be present in this disorder, leading some researchers to suggest that "overconcern with weight and shape be further investigated as a diagnostic feature of BED" (Eldredge & Agras, 1996, p. 73).

In this section, we primarily focused on body image as a predictor of

TABLE 1.7
Changes in Overall Weight and Dieting Behavior: 1982–1992

| | Women | | | | Men | | | |
| | 1982 | | 1992 | | 1982 | | 1992 | |
	n	%	n	%	n	%	n	%
Weight group[a]								
Underweight	158	31.2	145	28.7	43	21.0	11	5.3
Average	342	67.5	328	65.0	157	76.6	174	84.5
Overweight	5	1.0	21	4.2	5	2.4	17	8.3
Obese	2	0.4	11	2.2	0	0.0	4	1.9
Self-categorization[a]								
Very underweight	1	0.2	2	0.4	1	0.5	0	0.0
Underweight	11	2.2	39	7.7	27	13.2	12	5.8
Average	230	45.5	317	62.5	148	72.2	142	69.3
Overweight	248	49.0	129	25.4	28	13.7	50	24.4
Very overweight	16	3.2	20	3.9	1	0.5	1	0.5
Desire to[a]								
Lose weight	417	82.1	346	67.9	75	37.1	114	55.4
Stay same	75	14.8	151	29.7	81	40.1	66	32.0
Gain weight	16	3.2	12	2.4	46	22.8	26	12.6

Note. From "A 10-Year Longitudinal Study of Body Weight, Dieting, and Eating Disorder Symptoms," by T. F. Heatherton, F. Mahamedi, M. Striepe, A. E. Field, and P. Keel, 1997, *Journal of Abnormal Psychology, 106*, p. 121. Copyright 1997 by American Psychological Association. Reprinted with permission.
[a]Significant difference for women and for men (using a chi-square analysis).

eating disturbances, with some mention of body image as a mediator between other risk factors and eating disturbances. As noted above, studies that evaluated certain risk factors as predictors of body image are a primary concern for us in later chapters on theoretical explanations for the development of body image disturbances. However, the importance of these findings just discussed, based on prospective studies that strongly indict body image issues as an etiological factor in the development of eating disturbances, cannot be underestimated: Treatment programs and prevention strategies for eating problems should begin to systematically target body image disturbances (Thompson, Heinberg, & Clarke, 1996).

Body Dysmorphic Disorder

At times, the dysphoria and disparagement that one feels from an aspect of one's appearance takes on such severity that it may constitute not an associate of another disorder (e.g., anorexia nervosa, bulimia nervosa) but may compose a discrete *DSM* disorder all its own. This is the case when the concern becomes "markedly excessive" and the "preoccupation causes clinically significant distress or impairment" (American Psychiatric Association, 1994, p. 468). The essential feature of this disorder is the gravity of a person's preoccupation with an aspect of his or her appearance: At times, the individual's concern seems out of line (excessive) with the degree of the appearance problem, but in some cases, objective evaluation might reveal the clear absence of any appearance deficit, yet the patient maintains a high level of distress over the "imagined defect in appearance" (p. 468). Consider the following case history, taken from Phillips (1996; our source for many of the illustrative cases included in this chapter):

> Sometimes I'd pick and pick with pins dipped in alcohol trying to get rid of the pimples and get the pus out. I'd pick at all kinds of things —little bumps, blackheads, any mark or imperfection. Sometimes I'd be up doing this at 1:00 or 2:00 in the morning, and then I'd fall asleep in class the next day, if I even went. Sometimes it would even bleed. I always felt terrible afterward. I'd make such a mess of my skin that I'd get totally hysterical. (a 22-year-old woman recalling the ninth grade, as quoted on p. 11)

Body dysmorphic disorder was once known by the term *dysmorphophobia*, which was introduced in 1886 by Morselli and literally meant "fear of ugliness" (J. C. Rosen, 1996a). The differential diagnosis of body dysmorphic disorder is often a confusing affair, and clinicians must always consider other disorders in their differential diagnosis, such as obsessive–compulsive disorder (OCD) and delusional disorder, somatic type. Body dysmorphic disorder is correctly chosen if the OCD is confined to appearance-related cognitions and behaviors, not other areas of concern (in which case a diagnosis of OCD might be warranted). If the preoccupation with the appearance defect is of "delusional intensity" (American Psychiatric Association, 1994, p. 468), indicating that the individual is unable to consider that they may be inaccurate regarding their own appearance perception, the diagnosis of delusional disorder, somatic type should be considered. Note also that the *DSM-IV* states that if the preoccupation is "restricted to concerns about 'fatness'" (p. 468) present in an individual with anorexia nervosa, body dysmorphic disorder should not be diagnosed. However, this bit of guidance is quite unclear—no mention is made of the case of concerns with body fat level in an individual with bulimia nervosa, and it is not clear if the term *fatness* is confined to an overall evaluation of weight or might apply to an excessive concern with an individual body site.

This is an important diagnostic question because surveys indicate that weight-related body sites are often the target of an individual's preoccupation. Table 1.8 contains the site of body dysmorphic disorder complaints from two surveys. Two weight-relevant body sites (thighs and abdomen)

TABLE 1.8
Type of Appearance Complaints in Patients
With Body Dysmorphic Disorder

Phillips et al. (1993)	Rosen et al. (1995b)
Hair[a] (63)	Thighs (38)
Nose (50)	Abdomen (35)
Skin[b] (50)	Breast size or shape (20)
Eyes (27)	Skin[b] (17)
Breast size or shape (20)	Buttocks (15)
Head—face shape (20)	Facial features (12)
Overall body build (20)	Overall weight (9)
Lips (17)	Scars (8)
Chin (17)	Aging (7)
Stomach (17)	Hair[a] (7)
Teeth (13)	Height (6)
Legs (13)	Hips (5)
Breasts—pectoral muscles (10)	Teeth (4)
Ugly face (10)	Arms (3)
Ears (7)	
Cheeks (7)	
Buttocks (7)	
Penis (7)	
Arms (7)	
Neck (3)	
Forehead (3)	
Facial muscles (3)	
Shoulders (3)	
Hips (3)	

Note. Numbers in parentheses are in percentages. Phillips et al.'s (1993) participants were 17 men and 13 women; J. C. Rosen et al.'s (1995b) participants were 54 women.
[a]Head and body hair. [b]Acne, blemishes, and wrinkles.

were the most often found in the J. C. Rosen, Reiter, and Orosan (1995b) survey—"overall weight," which may come closest to the fatness descriptor found in the *DSM-IV*, was the target of disparagement in 9% of his cases. Contrast this with the Phillips, McElroy, Keck, Pope, and Hudson (1993) data where the top categories are hair, nose, skin, and eyes, with the first item that is weight related (i.e., "overall body build") as the aspect of concern for only 20% of the sample. The differences in these two surveys may be related to two differences in the data collection. Phillips's sample contained men and women, whereas J. C. Rosen's sample evaluated only women. In addition, J. C. Rosen included only primary and secondary complaints, whereas Phillips's data contains all reports of appearance concerns. However, these data are useful indicators of the great range of appearance components that may form the excessive concern in body dysmorphic disorder patients.

A new form of dysmorphia has recently been described by Phillips, Pope, and colleagues, which they refer to as *muscle dysmorphia* (Pope, Gruber, Choi, Olivardia, & Phillips, 1997). Individuals with this form of body dysmorphic disorder may consider themselves small and physically weak when, in fact, they are quite muscular and large. These people may be bodybuilders who nonetheless score higher on body dissatisfaction than do others (Blouin & Goldfield, 1995). Pope et al. found that this type of body dysmorphic disorder also occurs in women (84% of the female bodybuilders they surveyed) and that the disorder, for both men and women, is associated with steroid use, subjective distress, and impaired social and occupational functioning.

Unlike the foregoing discussion of the large-scale studies of body dissatisfaction in a number of groups, there exists little prevalence data on body dysmorphic disorder because of a lack of large-scale, randomized surveys. However, it is possible that it may be underdiagnosed and undetected because of a lack of scientific and clinical interest, until the past few years. The pioneering work of Phillips (1996), whose book details numerous cases and the significant distress and depression associated with the condition, and J. C. Rosen (1996a), who has recently developed the first clinical interview for the assessment of the disorder, are two developments that have brought body dysmorphic disorder to the attention of researchers and clinicians. J. C. Rosen and Ramirez (in press) recently conducted a direct comparison of groups with eating disorders versus those with body dysmorphic disorder. J. C. Rosen's Body Dysmorphic Disorder Examination (discussed in more detail in chapter 2) was used as the primary measure of diverse body image concerns; it is interesting to note that the two groups did not differ on total scores on this measure. A grouping of individual items reflecting different aspects of body image disturbance revealed that the body dysmorphic disorder participants reported more avoidance of social activities and more negative self-evaluation; however, the groups did not differ on factors such as preoccupation with appearance (i.e., distress over being noticed), dissatisfaction with appearance, or body checking (i.e., inspecting one's appearance or comparing oneself with other individuals).

Obesity

> Just looking at myself in a store window makes me feel terrible. It's gotten so I am very careful not to look by accident. It's a feeling that people have the right to hate me and hate anyone who looks as fat as me. As soon as I see myself, I feel an uncontrollable burst of hatred. I just look at myself and say "I hate you, you're loathsome!" (Stunkard & Mendelson, 1967, p. 1296)

One of the most intriguing lapses in research until the past few years is the almost nonexistent database on obesity and body image (J. K. Thompson & Tantleff-Dunn, 1998). Early observations by Stunkard and colleagues (Stunkard & Burt, 1967; Stunkard & Mendelson, 1967) over 30 years ago of the body image concerns of obese individuals have only recently been accompanied by systematic work on body dissatisfaction as a severe and distressing consequence of this physical condition (J. K. Thompson, 1996a). Researchers are now considering the relevance of body image for understanding multiple dimensions of obesity, including etiology, assessment, and treatment.

For instance, research with children, adolescents, and adults documents the high levels of body dissatisfaction that occur in individuals who do not meet the societal ideal of weight and size (Faith & Allison, 1996; Friedman & Brownell, 1995). However, several factors may moderate the level of dissatisfaction felt by an obese or overweight person. For instance, level of binge eating and childhood onset of obesity are associated with greater disturbance (Cash, 1991; Stunkard & Mendelson, 1967), and women reported greater dissatisfaction than did men (Cash & Hicks, 1990). In addition, researchers now see the issue as much more complex than simply ascribing to the view that overweight persons must lose excessive weight before body image satisfaction improves. J. C. Rosen (1996b) has found that weight loss may not be necessary for body image improvements in obesity—a finding that argues for the potential benefits of treatment strategies for improving appearance satisfaction for overweight individuals, regardless of the success of their weight-management efforts. Attempts to alter acceptance of body shape, given the poor outcome of most obesity treatment efforts, is part of a more general movement among researchers and clinicians toward acceptance of the obese condition (Brownell & Rodin, 1994; Wilson, 1996). (An interesting twist to this issue comes from a recent finding that low levels of body dissatisfaction may predict a lack of weight loss in African American men and women; given the health ramifications of obesity, it might be argued that some degree of dissatisfaction is necessary to fully adopt and maintain the countless, daily changes necessary for long-term lifestyle change (Heinberg, Haythornthwaite, Rosofsky, McCarron, & Clarke, 1996).

Even when weight loss is accomplished, there is not necessarily a parallel improvement in body image. Cash, Counts, and Huffine (1990) found that individuals who had lost weight were no different in appearance evaluation than a currently overweight sample and were more distressed than a group of individuals who had never been overweight. *Vestigial body image* was the phrase they chose to describe such a residual view of one's appearance, even after objective changes in weight status. These two seemingly counterintuitive findings—body image enhancements in the absence of weight loss (e.g., the findings of J. C Rosen discussed in the previous paragraph) and residual body image disturbance consequent to weight loss—illustrate the complexity of the issue of body image and obesity and the necessity for much future research.

Certainly, we do know one thing: Individuals who are overweight suffer the "slings and arrows" of societal stigmatization. Prospective studies with adolescents indicate that elevated weight or body fat may be associated with hazardous social interactions, such as being teased about one's appearance, that lead to elevated levels of body dissatisfaction (Cattarin & Thompson, 1994; see also chapter 5). Additionally, there now exists a wealth of data cataloging the social abuse that being fat entails in U.S. society. J. K. Thompson, Coovert, Richards, Johnson, and Cattarin (1995), using covariance structure modeling in two samples of adolescents, found that teasing was a mediator between weight status and body dissatisfaction. Grilo, Wilfley, Brownell, and Rodin (1994), in a sample of adult obese patients, found that teasing about weight during adolescence was predictive of adult levels of appearance dissatisfaction. It is interesting to note that body size remains one of the few personal attributes (vs. ethnicity or disability) that many individuals still see as an acceptable target of prejudice. Movies, talk shows, sitcoms, and magazines provide abundant models for the disparagement of fatness. These injustices have led many researchers and activists to begin to develop measures designed to assess fat prejudice and interventions for modifying people's stereotypes and prejudicial behaviors (e.g., Cash & Roy, in press). This area is addressed in chapter 2, which deals with assessment and treatment issues.

In sheer numbers, the incidence of body image disturbances relating to obesity outranks all the other issues listed in this chapter. Surveys conducted indicate that over 58 million Americans are obese (Kolata, 1997). The *1996 Surgeon General's Report on Physical Activity and Health* notes that 4.7 million children (ages 6–17) are obese—this was 11% of the total school age population in 1996 (Centers for Disease Control and Prevention, 1996). Paradoxically, one positive result of this "fattening" of America entails the modification of fashion to fit this large group of consumers.

After many years of virtually neglecting large-size individuals, the industry is now creating large and fashionable clothing to meet the demand. In addition, at least one large fashion model, Emme Aronson, has begun to get a level of attention normally reserved for her underweight "supermodel" colleagues (Witchel, 1997).

Disfigurement

> If one compares the trajectory of development of a child who is born with a visible defect such as cleft lip, port wine stain, or cranial deformity, with that of a child who has a less visible defect, it is evident that the world does not impinge so directly. A family worries about a heart murmur, but strangers don't stare and question. (Bernstein, 1990, p. 135)

Individuals with some type of physical disfigurement have, from either congenital or acquired means, experienced extreme modifications in "normal" appearance. These objective physical conditions include craniofacial deformities, dermatological diseases (acne, psoriasis), oral–maxillofacial conditions, physical changes secondary to cancer, burn victims, and persons with port wine stains. The body image issues for these individuals vary widely, as might be expected from the immense heterogeneity of possible appearance disfigurements from so many diverse causes and conditions, but the degree of disturbance in body image is perhaps more severe than in any other category discussed so far.

In many of these cases, the dissatisfaction and distress associated with the appearance disfigurement is completely normal, not an overreaction to a minor defect as is the case so often with body dysmorphic disorder. Neither is their dysphoric response like that of the nondisfigured person who simply fails to meet his or her or society's expectations of an ideal. Rather, individuals with these extreme appearance alterations may be forced to live with conditions that are not malleable by psychological and, in many cases, surgical interventions. In addition, the social stigma and negative interpersonal reactions encountered on a regular basis by individuals with a type of disfigurement may be especially detrimental. As Macgregor (1990) noted with reference to facial disfigurement, these individuals deal with "naked stares, startled reactions, 'double-takes,' whispering remarks, furtive looks, curiosity, personal questions, advice, manifestations of pity or aversion, laughter, ridicule, and outright avoidance" (p. 250).

On the positive side, a great deal of research has been invested in recent years into methods to not only modify disfigurements through surgical procedures but also help these individuals cope with societal and interpersonal pressures and prejudices. In particular, Changing Faces (1996), a charity founded in 1992 and designed specifically for professionals working with the facially disfigured, has been a leader in the dissemination of research and development of intervention programs (see chapter 2 for more information about this program).

Visually Challenged Individuals

Visual impairment presents unique difficulties in body image formation—perception of one's own image is difficult or impossible, and an assessment of others' views and reactions to one's looks may also be hindered. Visual exposure to societal standards, particularly as conveyed through the media, may be eliminated or attenuated; however, verbal information may still have the potential to inform the visually challenged person of prevailing appearance standards. Little work has been done in this area; however, J. W. Pierce and Wardle (1996) recently reviewed the literature and compared 9- to 11-year-old blind children with controls on measures of self-esteem, body esteem, and parental views of the children's body size. Generally, levels of self-esteem and body-esteem were comparable for the two groups (although no statistical comparisons were conducted). Overall, parental views of their children as overweight had no effect on self-esteem; in fact, the children desired "a more robust stature, a bigger presence, and a feeling of weight which appeared to supersede any acquired negative attitudes to fatness" (Pierce & Wardle, 1996, p. 205).

Some of the comments of Pierce and Wardle's (1996) participants, however, indicate the unique appearance issues that this population often encounters. One noted that boys called her "buzzy eyes," and several mentioned some concern about their "white eyes." The children were also asked how they identified the body sizes of other persons. Forty-four percent used the individual's voice alone or in conjunction with other auditory information. For instance, high voices were associated with thinness and deep voices with fatness. The sound of the overweight individual's walk and of their breath after exertion were also used.

Athletic and Vocational Status

> Thinness was not always prized in ballet. Louise Fitzjames, a French ballerina of the mid-19th century, was depicted in a famous caricature as a dancing asparagus in a "Ballet of the Vegetables" and was described by one French critic as "having no body at all" and being "as skinny as a lizard or a silkworm". . . . Balanchine is credited with, or accused of, creating the concept of the ideal ballet body. Gelsey Kirkland has written that as a troubled young dancer at City Ballet in the late 1960s, she was told by Balanchine that he wanted to "see the bones." (J. Dunning, 1997, p. B8)

For many individuals, their chosen profession or hobby may place them at risk for body image disturbance. Because of the rigid weight and size requirements typically manifested by the fashion profession, female models have been at risk for many years. A. E. Fallon (1990), in her comprehensive review of the body size ideals in fashion over the past 100 years, noted that the ideal woman was 5 ft 4 in. (1.62 m) and 140 lb (63.05 kg) in 1894; by 1947, she was reduced to 125 lb (56.70 kg), and by 1975, she had grown to 5 ft 8 in. (1.72 m), but her weight had furthered declined to 118 lb (53.52 kg). Unfortunately, these "models" seem to influence U.S. standards of attractiveness; Nichter and Nichter (1991) found that adolescent girls described the "ideal girl" as a size 5, weighing 100 lb (45.36 kg) and reaching a height of 5 ft 7 in. (1.70 m; more on the role of a sociocultural model of body image disturbance is in chapter 3). Unfortunately, there is little empirical data on the body image of professional models. However, fashion merchandising majors do not appear to be at any greater risk for body dissatisfaction and eating disordered symptoms than do students who major in other studies (Petersons, Phillips, & Steinhaus, 1996).

Ballet dancers, gymnasts, male wrestlers, and horse jockeys are individuals who must also meet extreme weight demands, size demands, or both to be successful at their profession (Ryan, 1996). In a 2-year longitudinal study, body satisfaction and a measure of "drive for thinness" predicted the onset of eating-disorder symptoms in ballet students (Garner, Garfinkel, Rockert, & Olmsted, 1987). The particular physical problems, body image issues, and eating problems associated with the low-weight demands of being a gymnast were well catalogued by O'Connor and colleagues (O'Connor, Lewis, & Boyd, 1996; O'Connor, Lewis, & Kirchner, 1995; O'Connor, Lewis, Kirchner, & Cook, 1996). The dysfunctional eating and weight-loss habits of male lightweight football players, who must maintain a weight of no more than 158 lb (71.66 kg), were reviewed by dePalma et al. (1993) who found that 17% of the sample had used self-induced vomiting.

Williamson et al. (1995) have shown that the particular demands on the college athlete lead to excessive concern about size and weight, which, in turn, predict the level of eating-disorder symptoms. These researchers found that the combination of pressures for thinness, performance anxiety, and negative self-appraisal of athletic achievement predicted level of concern with appearance.

One does not have to be involved in a formal college or professional athletic training program to suffer the body image complications associated with participation. For instance, several studies indicate that even casual athletes are dissatisfied with their appearance and may be at risk for problems such as eating disorders. As noted earlier, bodybuilders may be at risk for body image problems (Pope et al., in press); Pasman and Thompson (1988) found that female runners also had higher levels of dissatisfaction than did controls (it is interesting to note that male runners were more satisfied than were male sedentary individuals). Related to these findings is research, briefly referred to in the Introduction, suggesting that the motivations for exercise may be primarily appearance related. Cash, Novy, and

Grant (1994) found that appearance/weight-management reasons, but not fitness–health, stress–mood, or socializing motives, were correlated with exercise frequency for women. McDonald and Thompson (1992) found that women ranked "weight" and "tone" as more important reasons for exercising than did men; however, there were no gender differences on other motivations, such as fitness, mood, health, attractiveness, and enjoyment. J. K. Thompson and Pasman (1991) found that the obligatory nature of the exercise, that is, exercising despite injury or other contraindications, was positively associated with level of body dissatisfaction.

Cancer

The emotional consequences of dealing with a diagnosis of cancer and, particularly, its treatment are not limited to depression and distress regarding long-term outcome and the physical status of an individual. In the case where surgical treatment, chemotherapy treatment, or both modify the appearance, body image issues emerge as a significant patient concern. This has been well documented in the case of breast cancer and the mastectomy surgery that is often the outcome of such a diagnosis as well as other cancers and their sequelae (Ghizzani, Pirtoli, Bellezza, & Velicogna, 1995; Madan-Swain, Brown, Sexson, & Baldwin, 1994). With reference to breast cancer, it has been suggested that one major reason for the use of breast-conserving therapy, as opposed to a mastectomy, is its effect on preserving the body image of the patient (Blichert-Toft, 1992; Glanz & Lerman, 1992). In a meta-analysis of 40 studies that evaluated the psychosocial outcomes of breast-conserving versus mastectomy surgery for breast cancer patients, the strongest effects were found for the measures of body image, indicating enhanced satisfaction, feelings of sexual desirability, and less shame and embarrassment regarding appearance for the breast-conserving procedure (A. Moyer, 1997). Intervention strategies also recommend a consideration of body image issues for the breast cancer patient (Fawzy & Fawzy, 1994; Mock, 1993).

Skin cancer is another type of cancer for which the effect of the disease may have serious consequences for one's appearance. As noted by Brody (1997) in the following excerpt, some types of skin cancer are on a sharp upward trajectory:

> Melanoma, the least common but most feared form of skin cancer, does not just happen out of the blue. Because of changes in fashion and behavior that occurred more than a half-century ago, someone born today is more than 12 times as likely to development melanoma as someone born in mid-century. The main reason for this explosive growth, as you may have guessed, is overexposure to sunshine. (p. B9)

Recent work in this area has begun to address strategies to understand the lack of use of sunscreen and intervene to increase its use. Body image appears to be one critical factor. For instance in a study of 15,168 Norwegian high school students, Wichstrom (1994) found that the value of appearance to the students was one of several predictors of sunbathing frequency. In a study of Australian adolescents, Broadstock and Gason (1992) found that a medium tan was rated as healthiest and most attractive; no tan was rated as both least attractive and healthy. Jones and Leary (1994) tested the effectiveness of a health-based message regarding the dangers of sun exposure versus an appearance-based message (which described the negative effects of tanning on appearance [wrinkling, scarring, etc.]). Participants who read the appearance essay were significantly more likely to use sunscreen than those who read the health essay.

Additionally, the role of smoking as it relates to one's body image, weight-management strategies, and cancer deserves mention in this section. Klesges and colleagues have conducted several investigations that support the connection between reticence to quit smoking and concern over postcessation weight gain (for a review, see Meyers et al., 1997). Meyers et al. found that weight-concerned participants were less likely to be abstinent at 1-, 6-, and 12-month follow-up periods.

THE "COSTS" OF BODY IMAGE DISTURBANCE

With the exception of evidence from surveys of cosmetic surgery (discussed shortly), it is virtually impossible to put a dollar amount on the total costs to society and the individual of body image disturbance. As noted earlier, there is a wealth of data linking body image problems to the onset and maintenance of eating disorders; therefore, we might get some idea of the clinical impact if we consider that the overall combined prevalence rate of anorexia nervosa (0.5–1.0%) and bulimia nervosa (approximately 3.0%) is around 3.5–4.0% of the population (American Psychiatric Association, 1994) and that mortality rates from these disorders range between 5% and 10% (Gilbert & Thompson, 1996).

Mortality rates are not currently available for body dysmorphic disorder; however as noted by Phillips (1996), severe depression (8% of individuals with body dysmorphic disorder) and hospitalization are frequently associated with this form of extreme body disparagement. She also described two cases that are illustrative of the financial costs of body dysmorphic disorder—one woman was over $10,000 in debt because of the expenses for clothing and wigs, and one man's hospitalizations, primarily for three suicide attempts, exceeded $100,000.

We noted earlier the societal prejudices against individuals who are overweight or obese. The psychological effects of cultural stigmatization of these persons and the associated harm to their body image were summarized nicely by Stunkard and Sobal (1995), who noted that "persons with disparagement of the body image view their bodies as grotesque and loathsome and believe that others can view them only with hostility and contempt" (p. 418). Certainly, in terms of sheer numbers, perhaps the total sum of psychosocial costs is composed disproportionately of the emotional pain of obese individuals (approximately 1/3 of the U.S. population is obese; e.g.,

TABLE 1.9
1996 Average Surgeon Fees: Cosmetic and
Reconstruction Procedures

Procedure	National average (in $)	Procedure	National average (in $)
Breast augmentation	2,784 (3,029)[a]	Fat injection	
		Head−neck	753
Breast lift	3,224	Trunk	812
Breast reconstruction		Extremities	823
Implant alone	2,546	Forehead lift	3,275
Tissue expander	4,175		(2,494)[a]
Latisimus dorsi musculature flap	5,136	Laser skin resurfacing	
		Full face	2,556
TRAM (pedicel) flap	6,559	Partial face	1,191
Microsurgical free flap	7,422	Liposuction (any single site)	1,710
		Male-pattern baldness	
Breast reduction in women	4,877	Plug grafts (per plug)	574
		Strip grafts (per strip)	825
Breast reduction in men	2,419	Scalp reduction (all stages)	2,457
Buttock lift	3,319	Pedicel flap (all stages)	3,072
Cheek implants	1,930	Tissue expansion (all stages)	2,787
Chemical peel			
Full face	1,513	Nose reshaping (primary)	
Regional	701	Fee for open rhinoplasty	3,104
Chin augmentation		Fee for closed rhinoplasty	2,997
Implant	1,334	Nose reshaping (secondary)	
Osteotomy	2,045	Fee for open rhinoplasty	2,907
Collagen injections	281	Fee for closed rhinoplasty	2,804
(per 1 cc injection)		Retin-A treatment (per visit)	109
Dermabrasion	1,536	Thigh lift	3,336
Ear surgery	2,262	Tummy tuck	3,795
Eyelid surgery			(3,832)[a]
Both uppers	1,580	Upper arm lift	2,539
Both lowers	1,622	Wrinkle injection	209
Combination of both	2,775		
Face lift	4,407 (4,783)[a]		

Note. TRAM = transverse rectus abdominus myocutaneous. Fees generally vary according to region of country and patient need. These fees are averages only. In general, fees do not include anesthesia, operating room facilities, or other related expenses. From *1996 Plastic Surgery Statistics*, by the American Society of Plastic and Reconstructive Surgeons, 1996, p. 9, Arlington Heights, IL: Author. Copyright American Society of Plastic and Reconstructive Surgeons 1996. Reprinted with permission.
[a]Averages for procedures performed specifically with an endoscope are reported in parentheses.

Kuczmarski, Flegal, Campbell, & Johnson, 1994). But it is not all due to the body image disparagement that flows from societal ostracism. Stunkard and Sobal reviewed evidence that there is a true financial toll from enhanced adiposity; in one survey, 16% of employers stated that they would not hire obese individuals under any circumstances, and an additional 44% noted that there would be some instances where the obesity would be a factor in employment. Gortmaker, Must, Perrin, Sobol, and Dietz (1993) evaluated the weight status of individuals in 1981 and subsequently assessed several social and economic indicators for the sample in 1988. They found that women overweight in 1981 as compared with nonoverweight women were, in 1988, 20% less likely to be married and had household incomes of $6,710 less per year. Overweight men were 11% less likely to be married; however, income was not significantly different from nonoverweight men.

We noted earlier the potential role of body image in explaining differences between individuals' suntanning frequency. If we only take the statistics of one type of cancer, melanoma, the potential stakes of excessive sun exposure are incredibly noteworthy. Recent data suggests that it is the fifth most common type of cancer in the United States and is the fastest growing, in terms of frequency of diagnosis. By the year 2000, it is expected that the lifetime risk will be 1 in 75 (it is interesting to note that this would put it in the same ballpark as anorexia nervosa). For 1997, the American Cancer Society predicted that 40,300 new cases would be found and 7,300 Americans would die of the disease (Brody, 1997).

Financial costs are more easily calculated, particularly when the procedure is elective cosmetic surgery. Table 1.9 contains some cost estimates from the most recent figures available from the American Society of Plastic and Reconstructive Surgeons (1996).

CONCLUSIONS

The goal of this chapter was to provide an overview of the vast scope of body image, hopefully removing it forever from its narrow confines within the field of eating disorders. In fact, the number of individuals with diagnosable eating disorders and concomitant body image disturbance is a small portion of the total population for which body image issues are problematic (in one sense or the other). For individuals with body dysmorphic disorder, body image is the central factor in a life obsessed with one's appearance. For obesity, personal dissatisfaction is exacerbated by societal sanctions. Persons of "excessive" weight have only recently begun to fight against a ready acquiescence to prevailing cultural mores. Other groups noted in this chapter, from those with visual impairments to sun worshipers, have body image issues particular to their situation yet integrally connected to their psychological well-being, physical well-being, or both.

2

AN OVERVIEW OF ASSESSMENT AND TREATMENT STRATEGIES

In this second background chapter, we focus on an overview of the assessment and treatment approaches that have received the most empirical evaluation and are the most commonly used for measuring and intervening for body image disturbance. We also examine the relatively new emphasis on antifat stigmatization strategies and measures and the recent shift in focus to prevention programs. As noted in the Introduction, there are a large number of definitions of different components of body image, and correspondingly, there are a plethora of measures available for assessing these subcomponents. In this chapter, we focus on measures that address the components of body image related to satisfaction, esteem, appearance evaluation, distress, anxiety, and related concepts. Measures of other dimensions, particularly cognitive and behavioral components, are addressed in subsequent chapters, which detail these perspectives from a more theoretical background.

We also follow this general strategy within the other chapters. Thus, for instance, social comparison measures are reviewed in the chapter in which we review a social comparison etiological model (chapter 4), and measures that index negative feedback regarding appearance are included in the chapter in which we explore the role of appearance feedback in the formation and maintenance of body image problems (chapter 5). As noted in the Introduction, this model fits with our overall goal of integrating theory and practice. In each of the chapters in the four theoretical sections of this book, a discussion of research background for each theoretical perspective is followed by a presentation of the measures useful for the clinical assessment of that factor for treatment purposes. We then examine treatment approaches for that particular risk factor or associated feature.

MEASURES OF SATISFACTION AND RELATED COMPONENTS OF BODY IMAGE

In this section, we selectively review some of the most widely used and psychometrically sound assessments. The great majority of these measures are self-reported, paper-and-pencil rating scales or questionnaires because this strategy appears to be the optimal method of indexing an individual's ratings of his or her own appearance. The measures discussed herein and in Table 2.1 have met minimal standards for reliability and validity and are frequently used by researchers in the study of body image.

Before beginning, however, we must offer a caveat related to our previous discussion of the multiple definitions of body image disturbance. Although we grouped the measures in this section based on their general homogeneity, that is, they measure satisfaction or a closely related feature of body image, future research may indicate that we may have erred in some instances. For instance, we do not include measures that assess a "preoccupation" with appearance, even though this may, at first glance, appear to be synonymous with "satisfaction." Cash (1994a) found that a measure of preoccupation was more closely related to scales assessing an "investment" in appearance (e.g., appearance orientation and appearance schemas). This investment dimension, which has also been referred to as an "importance" component, is distinct, at least in factor analytic studies, from a more affective dimension, which Cash (1994a) labeled as *evaluation/affect* (p. 1169). This example highlights the need for much more factor analytic work in this area (J. K. Thompson, Altabe, Johnson, & Stormer, 1994). It also reveals that future work may or may not support the inclusion of all of the measures in this chapter as reflective of a specific satisfaction, esteem, or related construct. With this qualification in mind, we now discuss some of the measures that we feel should form the basis of any initial assessment protocol.

Weight–Size Discrepancy

One of the simplest measures of overall weight satisfaction is to compare a person's "ideal" weight with their current weight, using the difference or discrepancy between the two levels as an indication of weight dissatisfaction. Another somewhat related approach involves using sche-

TABLE 2.1
Measures of Body Satisfaction and Related Concepts

Name of instrument	Author(s)	Description	Reliability 1, 2	Standardization sample	Address of author
		Figure ratings/silhouettes			
Figure Rating Scale	(a) Stunkard et al. (1983)	Select from nine figures that vary in size from underweight to overweight	(a) IC: na	(a) 92 normal male and female undergraduates	Albert J. Stunkard, MD University of Pennsylvania Department of Psychiatry 133 S. 36th Street Philadelphia, PA 19104
	(b) J. K. Thompson & Altabe (1991)		(b) TR: 2 weeks: ideal (male students, −.82; female students, −.71), self-think (male students, −.92; female students, −.89), self-feel (male students, −.81; female students, −.83)		
Contour Drawing Rating Scale	M. A. Thompson & Gray (1995)	Nine male and nine female schematic figures, ranging from underweight to overweight	IC: na TR: 1 week (self, .79)	40 male and female undergraduates	James J. Gray, PhD American University Department of Psychology Asbury Building Washington, DC 20016-8062
Breast/Chest Rating Scale	J. K. Thompson & Tantleff (1992)	Five male and five female schematic figures, ranging from small to large upper torso	IC: na TR: current (.85), ideal breast (.81), ideal chest (.69)	43 male and female participants	J. Kevin Thompson, PhD Department of Psychology University of South Florida Tampa, FL 33620-8200
None given	(a) Collins (1991)	Seven boy and seven girl figures that vary in size	(a) IC: na TR: 3 days (self, .71; ideal self, .59; ideal other child, .38; ideal adult, .55; ideal other adult, .49)	(a) 1,118 preadolescent children	M. E. Collins, HSD, MPH Centers for Disease Control and Prevention 4770 Buford Highway, NE Mailstop K26 Atlanta, GA 30341-3724
	(b) Wood et al. (1996)		(b) TR: 2 weeks (self, .70; ideal self, .63)	(b) 109 boys and 95 girls (ages 8–10)	

Table continues

TABLE 2.1 (Continued)

Name of instrument	Author(s)	Description	Reliability 1, 2	Standardization sample	Address of author
Body Image Assessment	Williamson et al. (1989)	Select from nine figures of various sizes	IC: na TR: immediately to 8 weeks (.60–.93), bulimics (ideal, –.74; current, –.83), obese (ideal ns; current, –.88), binge eaters (ideal, –.65; current, –.81)	659 female bulimic, binge eater, anorexic, normal, obese, and atypical eating-disordered participants	Donald A. Williamson, Ph.D Department of Psychology Louisiana State University Baton Rouge, LA 70803-5501
			Questionnaire measures		
Eating Disorder Inventory–Body dissatisfaction scale	(a) Garner et al. (1983) (b) Shore & Porter (1990) (c) K. C. Wood et al. (1996)	Indicate degree of agreement with nine statements about body parts being too large (7 items)	(a) IC: anorexic participants (.90), controls (.91), female participants (.91), male participants (.86) (b) IC: adolescents (11–18) (c) IC: children (8–10), girls (.84), boys (.72)	(a) 113 female anorexic participants and 577 female controls (b) 196 boys and 414 girls	David M. Garner, PhD c/o Psychological Assessments Resources, Inc. P.O. Box 998 Odessa, FL 33556
Color-A-Person Body Dissatisfaction Test	Wooley & Roll (1991)	Use five colors to indicate level of satisfaction with body sites by masking on a schematic figure	IC: .74–.85 TR: 2 weeks (.72–.84), 4 weeks (.75–.89)	(c) 109 male and 95 female participants 102 male and female college students, 103 bulimic participants	Orland W. Wooley, PhD Department of Psychiatry University of Cincinnati College of Medicine Cincinnati, OH 45267
Extended Satisfaction With Life Scale–Physical Appearance Scale	Alfonso & Allison (1993)	Rate general satisfaction with appearance on a 7-point scale (5 items)	IC: .91 TR: 2 weeks (.83)	Male and female undergraduates (n = 170)	David B. Allison, PhD Obesity Research Center St. Luke's/Roosevelt Hospital Columbia University College of Physicians and Surgeons New York, NY 10025

Body Mapping Questionnaire and Colour-the-Body-Task	Huon & Brown (1989)	67 female bulimic and 67 female control participants	IC: na TR: none given	Rate feelings (strongly dislike–strongly like) about 21 body regions, color red body sites "liked" and black body sites "disliked"	G. F. Huon, PhD Department of Psychology University of Wollongong, PO Box 1144 Wollongong, New South Wales 2500 Australia
Body Satisfaction Scale	Slade et al. (1990)	Women: undergraduate and nursing students, volunteers, and over-weight, anorexic, and bulimic participants	IC: range, .79–89 TR: none given	Indicate degree of satisfaction with 16 parts (three subscales: general, head, body)	P. D. Slade, PhD Department of Psychiatry and Department of Movement Science Liverpool University Medical School P.O. Box 147 Liverpool, L69 3BX England
Body-Esteem Scale	(a) Mendelson & White (1985) (b) D. R. White (personal communications, September 5, 1990)	(a) 97 boys and girls (ages 8–17), 48 over-weight and 49 normal weight (b) 105 boys and girls (ages 8–13)	(a) IC: split-half reliability (.85) (b) TR: 2 years (.66)	Report degree of agreement with various statements about one's body	Donna Romano White, PhD Department of Psychology Concordia University 1455 de Maisonneuve West Montreal, Quebec Canada H3G-1M8
Body-Esteem Scale Revised	Mendelson et al. (1998)	Adults and adolescents	IC: .81–.94	23-item scale with three subscales: Appearance, Attribution, Weight	Beverly K. Mendelson Department of Psychology Concordia University 7141 Sherbrooke Street Montreal, Quebec Canada H4B-1R6

Table continues

TABLE 2.1 (Continued)

Name of instrument	Author(s)	Description	Reliability 1, 2	Standardization sample	Address of author
Multidimensional Body Self-Relations Questionnaire—Appearance Evaluation Subscale	Cash (1995b, 1996, 1997)	7-item scale that measures overall appearance satisfaction and evaluation	IC: .88 for female and male participants	Over 2,000 male and female participants	T. F. Cash, PhD Old Dominion University Department of Psychology Norfolk, VA 23529-0267
Body Shape Questionnaire	P. J. Cooper et al. (1987)	34 items on one's concern with one's body shape	IC: none given TR: none given	Bulimic participants and several control groups	Peter Cooper, PhD University of Cambridge Department of Psychiatry Addenbrooke's Hospital, Hills Road Cambridge, CB22QQ England
Self-Image Questionnaire for Young Adolescents—Body Image subscale	Petersen et al. (1984)	Designed for 10- to 15-year-olds; 11-item body image subscale assesses positive feelings toward the body	IC: boys (−.81), girls (−.77) TR: 1 year (.60); 2 years (.44)	335 sixth grade students who were followed through the eighth grade	Anne C. Peterson, PhD College of Health and Human Development 101 Henderson Building Pennsylvania State University University Park, PA 16802
Physical Appearance State and Trait Anxiety Scale	Reed et al. (1991)	Rate the anxiety associated with 16 body sites (8 weight relevant, 8 nonweight relevant); trait and state versions available	IC: Trait: .88–.82 State: .82–.92 TR: 2 weeks, .87	Female undergraduate students	J. Kevin Thompson, PhD Department of Psychology 4202 Fowler Avenue University of South Florida Tampa, FL 33620-8200

Note. IC = internal consistency; TR = test–retest reliability.

matic figures or silhouettes of varying sizes, from thin (underweight) to heavy (overweight) and, again, taking the discrepancy between the individual's choice of their ideal figure versus their conception of the figure that matches their current size (J. K. Thompson, 1992, 1995; Williamson, Davis, Bennett, Goreczny, & Gleaves, 1989). Figure 2.1 contains an example of a figure rating scale and the differences between size ratings based on different instructions. For instance, in this study, participants made "current" size ratings using two different protocols—one based on a cognitive instruction (i.e., they were asked to rate how they "think" they look) and one based on an "affective" instruction (how they "feel" they look; J. K. Thompson, 1990). It is interesting to note that as Figure 2.1 illustrates, women feel larger than they actually think they look, emphasizing the point that an affective aspect of satisfaction may lead them to feel worse about their appearance (i.e., larger than they know, intellectually, to be the case).

Altabe and Thompson (1992) found that the affective–ideal discrepancy was more strongly correlated with eating disturbance than was the cognitive–ideal discrepancy. In fact, it has been found that the affective–cognitive discrepancy is significantly related to eating disturbance for both men and women and associated with low self-esteem for women (Altabe & Thompson, 1992; J. K. Thompson & Altabe, 1991). Therefore, when using this method of assessment, clearly specifying the two rating protocols—affective and cognitive—yields a more precise understanding of the emotional versus intellectual nature of the discrepancy. A larger affective than cognitive rating has implications for treatment, indicating that procedures such as the desensitization strategies (Cash, 1996, 1997), outlined later in this chapter, may be useful at decreasing the anxiety associated with one's body image. (See Table 2.1 for a list of schematic figure methodologies useful for determining discrepancy levels.)

Gardner, Friedman, and Jackson (1998) recently criticized some of the figural scales because of the lack of consistent size gradations between adjacent figures. For instance, they evaluated the Stunkard, Sorenson, and Schulsinger (1983) figures illustrated in Figure 2.1 and found that the proportional change from size 5 to size 4 was .100 whereas the change from size 4 to size 3 was .176 and the change from size 3 to size 2 was .03. For this reason, we suggest a consideration of the figures created by M. A. Thompson and Gray (1995), who constructed the adjacent figures to have similar differences in actual size (see Appendix 2A). It is important to note that figure rating scales have also been developed for children and adolescents (Collins, 1991; Tiggemann & Pennington, 1990; Veron-Guidry & Williamson, 1996).

Other schematic designs have been created to assess different aspects of physical appearance than overall body size satisfaction. J. K. Thompson and Tantleff (1992) were interested in upper torso satisfaction, particularly

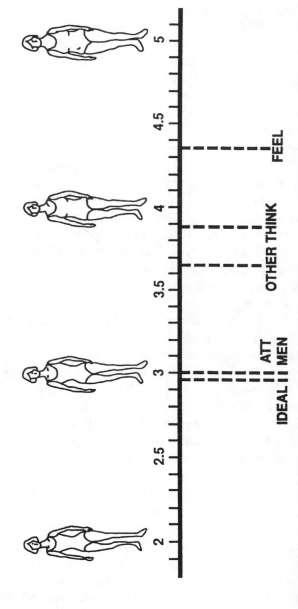

Figure 2.1. Size ratings based on different instructional protocols. IDEAL = rating of ideal figure; ATT MEN = rating of figure women believe is most attractive to men; OTHER = actual selection of female figure that men find most attractive; THINK = rating of figure that women think best matches their own figure; and FEEL = rating of figure that women feel best matches their own figure. From *Body Image Disturbance: Assessment and Treatment* (p. 11), by J. K. Thompson, 1990, Elmsford, NY: Pergamon Press. Copyright 1990 by McGraw-Hill. Reprinted with permission.

breast- and chest-size satisfaction, and developed the Breast/Chest Rating Scale for this purpose (see Appendix 2B). As expected, ideal size selections were larger than current size ratings, for both men and women. Furnham, Titman, and Sleeman (1994) also developed a scale of nine figures that vary only on degree of muscularity (see Appendix 2C).

Allison, Hoy, Fournier, and Heymsfield (1993) created a latitude of acceptance size rating that consists of the discrepancy between ratings of the thinnest and heaviest figure that participants would consider dating. We feel that this rating might also be used clinically by having clients consider an "acceptable" body size, as opposed to an ideal, as their goal. The acceptable-current size discrepancy index, in contrast to the ideal-current rating, should produce a smaller dissatisfaction level. Cachelin, Striegel-Moore, and Elder (1998) recently proposed a rating similar to the Allison et al. acceptability protocol, which they labeled *realistic body size*.

One potential problem with standardized figure rating procedures is that the sizes and dimensions reflected by the figures may not match that of individual clients, leading individuals to say "none of these shapes look like me." Computer programs that allow one to "change the size of . . . body parts independently" (Schlundt & Bell, 1993, p. 267) are useful for dealing with this problem. A second problem with the published figure rating scales is that the facial and hair features often appear Caucasian, which may make their use disconcerting or inappropriate with individuals of other ethnicities (J. K. Thompson, 1996a). K. C. Wood, Becker, and Thompson (1996) have advocated that these features be removed and did not find this to be a problem for participants. Koff and Benavage (1998) have similarly successfully modified the Breast-Chest Rating Scale to render it ethnically neutral.

Questionnaire Measures

Several questionnaire measures have also been constructed for measuring satisfaction. One of the most widely used is the Eating Disorder Inventory 2–Body Dissatisfaction subscale, which is a 9-item measure assessing satisfaction with weight-related body sites (waist, hips, thighs; Garner, 1991). Garner, Garner, and Van Egeren (1992) have constructed a statistical correction for this measure that adjusts for differences in body weight, allowing valid comparisons among diverse samples such as individuals with anorexia nervosa and overweight persons. The Body Areas Satisfaction scale of the Multidimensional Body Self-Relations Questionnaire (MBSRQ) is also a widely used index of body site satisfaction but also includes a reference to nonweight sites, such as height (T. A. Brown, Cash, & Mikulka, 1990). In addition, the Extended Satisfaction With Life Scale–Physical Appearance subscale measures satisfaction with several aspects of appearance (Alfonso, Allison, Rader, & Gorman, 1996). Several other measures of site-specific or overall appearance satisfaction are detailed in Table 2.1 (e.g., Slade, Dewey, Newton, Brodie, & Kiemle, 1990), along with information regarding reliabilities, standardization samples, and instructions for requesting materials from the test developers.

Some scales appear to measure both satisfaction *and* evaluation of the body, perhaps providing a more global assessment of a subjective aspect of body image disturbance (Feingold & Mazzella, 1996). The Appearance Evaluation scale of the MBSRQ is one of the most widely used measures of this type (T. A. Brown et al., 1990). This scale has been used extensively by many researchers and has one of the best available sets of normative data (see Appendix 2D and Cash, 1996, 1997). The Self-Image Questionnaire for Young Adolescents (SIQYA) also captures both evaluation and satisfaction and is one of the few scales appropriate for use with adolescents (Petersen, Schulenberg, Abramowitz, Offer, & Jarcho, 1984). Another measure used frequently by researchers and clinicians is the Body-Esteem Scale, which was recently revised for use with participants ranging in age from 12–25 (Mendelson, White, & Mendelson, 1998). The current edition of this measure is included in Appendix 2E. An analysis of the items in this questionnaire indicates its global assessment of evaluation and satisfaction.

Measures that supposedly assess concern or anxiety may be closely related to overall satisfaction and evaluation ratings and may be a useful adjunct to these measures. Reed, Thompson, Brannick, and Sacco (1991) developed the Physical Appearance State and Trait Anxiety Scale (PASTAS), which contains two subscales—Weight and Non-Weight—of eight items each. The Weight scale has items related to weight-related body sites, and the Non-Weight scale contains items such as lips, chin, and neck. One advantage of this test is that the trait scale can be used to assess a dispositional aspect of disturbance, that is, overall general level of body image anxiety, whereas the state measure can be used to determine day-to-day changes or even changes consequent to a within-session body image treatment intervention. (The trait version is contained in Appendix 2F; the state version is discussed more fully in chapter 9.)

Waist-to-Hips Ratio

A ratio between the sizes of certain body sites may provide useful data as an indirect indicator of satisfaction. The waist-to-hips ratio (WHR) is one such measure. A 1.0 on this measure indicates similar circumferences for both sites. Usually ratios are less than 1.0, reflecting the fact that one's hips are larger than one's waist. However, research on this measure is conflicting, with studies suggesting that high and low ratios are correlated with dissatisfaction (T. E. Joiner, Schmidt, & Singh, 1994; Radke-Sharpe, Whitney-Saltiel & Rodin, 1990). Of course, if both sites are "large," the measure may not be indicative of overall satisfaction. However, in individuals of average size, who have, for instance, much larger hips than waist (or no difference between waist and hips), it is possible that the measure may add important information to that ascertained from other satisfaction measures (as discussed above). Researchers in the area of objective ratings of attractiveness have made great use of this measure; indications are that a WHR of around .70 is preferred across a large number of diverse societies (see Furnham, Dias, & McClelland, 1998; and Furnham, Tan, & McManus, 1997). However, Tassinary and Hansen (1998) recently criticized the WHR measure, noting that "judgments of attractiveness . . . can be either unrelated or related, positively or negatively, to the WHR depending on waist size, hip size, and weight" (p. 150).

Interview Methods

Interview procedures, primarily developed for the study of eating disorders, may yield information useful for understanding the level of body image disturbance. For instance, two subscales of the Eating Disorder Examination (EDE) assess weight concern and shape concern—two factors closely connected to overall body satisfaction (Fairburn & Cooper, 1993). In this procedure, the scores are determined by 23 symptom ratings made by the assessor (see Williamson, Anderson, & Gleaves, 1996, for a review of this measure). The EDE has also been recently found to be useful, with some minor modifications in procedures, in the diagnosis of body image and eating problems in children and adolescents (Bryant-Waugh, Cooper, Taylor, & Lask, 1996).

Clinical Concerns

We are often asked to provide specific guidelines for the use of particular measures in the assessment of body image disturbance. This is a difficult task because the selection of a scale, procedure, or multiple measures depends to a large degree on the characteristics of the client. The use of any measure must be determined regarding its appropriateness for the diversity represented by the specific individual in terms of gender, ethnic background, age, and body size. Many measures have been validated only with Caucasian women, and they may not be suitable for use with overweight individuals (Faith & Allison, 1996; J. K. Thompson & Tantleff-Dunn, 1998) or individuals of a different ethnicity (J. K. Thompson, 1996a). Care should be taken also when selecting a measure for use with children or adolescents to ensure that normative and psychometric data is collected on that age range. For this reason, in Table 2.1 we include information regarding the validation sample and an address for contacting the authors of the different measures for more information regarding psychometrics and normative samples. We advocate that authors should be contacted for test information regarding the individual difference factors mentioned, such as gender and ethnicity, and that this data should be used to guide the selection of a measure for individual clients or research projects.

BODY DYSMORPHIC DISORDER EXAMINATION

In the case of extreme appearance disparagement, it seems only appropriate that a unique assessment tool has been developed. J. C. Rosen and colleagues have pioneered research on body dysmorphic disorder, not only in its treatment (discussed shortly) but also in the creation of a psychometrically sound instrument for assessing its multidimensional nature (J. C. Rosen & Reiter, 1996; J. C. Rosen, Reiter, & Orosan, 1995a). This measure should be considered whenever a clinician has indications, either from an interview or from an examination of some of the measures noted above that body dysmorphic disorder may exist (particularly if on some of the site-specific indices a client's disturbance seems excessive for a certain body part). The Body Dysmorphic Disorder Examination (BDDE) measures such body dysmorphic disorder aspects as "distressing self-consciousness, preoccupation with appearance, overvalued ideas about the importance of appearance to one's self-worth, and body image avoidance and checking behaviors" (J. C. Rosen et al., 1995a, p. 77).

The BDDE has two items that specifically address a dissatisfaction component: One focuses on overall appearance and the other on a site or specific body part dissatisfaction. The interview also has items that address multiple aspects and components of the complexity of body dysmorphic disorder, including several items devoted to behavioral features of avoidance and checking, an item for social comparison, and items related to receiving comments from others or being treated differently because of the appearance defect. Appendix 2G contains a list of the 34 items included on the BDDE.

TREATMENT APPROACHES

Two primary approaches for treating body image disturbance have received endorsement by way of controlled outcome studies and widespread use and acceptance from leading researchers and clinicians: cognitive–behavioral and feminist methodologies. Therefore, the essentials of these orientations receive our primary focus in the overview of tenets and tactics that follows shortly and in the extended exposition of techniques in subsequent chapters. We also deal briefly with new and emerging strategies at the end of this chapter. Treatments based on specific presenting risk factors are detailed in other chapters. For instance, in chapters 5 and 6, we offer several approaches based on handling interpersonal factors relevant to one's body image, such as teasing and feedback from romantic partners. In addition, following the accompanying overview of cognitive–behavioral and feminist approaches, we briefly examine image confrontation procedures, prevention programs, cosmetic surgery, methods designed to fight antifat prejudice and stigmatization, and exercise as an intervention to enhance body image.

Cognitive–Behavioral Strategies

Cash (1995b, 1996, 1997) and J. C. Rosen (1996a, 1996b) are the two leading figures in the development of cognitive–behavioral strategies. Their respective programs have extensive empirical evaluation and support and should be considered as a treatment option for a wide variety of clinical populations for which body image problems are relevant (J. K. Thompson, Heinberg, & Clarke, 1996).

Cash's (1995b, 1996, 1997) program consists of eight components. It is assumed that prior to engaging in such treatment, individuals are given a Comprehensive Body Image Assessment Questionnaire using many of the instruments described in this chapter and elsewhere in the book; Cash noted this as his first step in treatment. The second component is body image education and self-discoveries. The aim of this portion of treatment is to enhance the client's understanding of his or her body image through bibliotherapy, discussions with the therapist, and analysis of the body image assessment findings. Through an increasingly precise understanding of individual patterns and processes, the therapist and client set concrete, written goals for therapy (Cash, 1996).

The next component is body image exposure and desensitization. Clients develop relaxation skills and, in turn, use them to reduce and manage body image distress. Once this skill is well developed, a hierarchy is created and relaxation is paired with imagery in progressively more distressing body image situations. Clients then complete the hierarchy during an in vivo, full-length mirror confrontation.

The fourth step is identifying and challenging appearance assumptions. This phase of treatment targets body image assumptions and the problems produced by these maladaptive core beliefs about appearance. Homework assignments involve monitoring assumptions and beginning to question their veracity. These assumptions are more directly targeted in the fifth component, identifying and correcting cognitive errors. This section of therapy teaches patients to dispute negative appearance assumptions through audiotaping corrective thinking dialogues and keeping a diary (Cash, 1996).

The sixth component, modifying self-defeating body image behaviors, targets both avoidant behaviors and obsessive–compulsive patterns (e.g., frequent monitoring of disliked body parts). Hierarchies of each type of pattern are elicited, and clients are taught management strategies derived from stress inoculation training for each item on the hierarchy.

The seventh step involves the development of body image enhancement activities. The client completes a survey of various body-related activities (e.g., dancing), rates his or her feelings of mastery and pleasure derived from each, and completes a series of experiential exercises. Clients then select activities for mastery and pleasure to engage in regularly and are instructed to expand the number of positive body-related experiences. Finally, clients complete the eighth component, relapse prevention and maintenance of changes. Clients evaluate their progress, set future goals, and develop strategies for coping with inevitable high-risk situations and setbacks (Cash, 1996).

J. C. Rosen has also developed and described cognitive–behavioral interventions for body image distress and has discussed interventions specific to individuals with body dysmorphic disorder and obesity (J. C. Rosen, 1996a, 1996b, 1997). Like the previously discussed cognitive–behavioral body image therapy of Cash, J. C. Rosen has stressed the importance of psychoeducation, cognitive restructuring, and self-monitoring. However, J. C. Rosen's interventions place a greater emphasis on behavioral procedures, such as exposure to avoided situations and response prevention. In vivo exposure includes not only mirror confrontation but also graded exercises designed to combat avoidance of situations that cue body image distress (e.g., wearing form-fitting clothes, undressing in front of one's spouse, going to the beach in a bathing suit). Response prevention involves deliberate efforts to reduce behaviors related to inspecting, measuring, or correcting one's appearance (J. C. Rosen, 1996a, 1996b, 1997).

Researchers have long demonstrated the efficacy of cognitive–behavioral interventions for reducing distress related to body image. For instance, Dworkin and Kerr (1987) and Butters and Cash (1987) demonstrated the effectiveness of a cognitive–behavioral treatment for body image disturbance as compared with wait-list controls. J. C. Rosen, Saltzberg, and Srebnik (1989) examined the efficacy of cognitive–behavioral interventions compared with a minimal treatment group (cognitive–behavioral treatment without specific exercises for maladaptive body image cognitions, behaviors, and perceptions) and demonstrated significant reductions in size overestimation and in behavioral avoidance at a 2-month follow-up. J. Grant and Cash (1995) used Cash's (1991) body image cognitive–behavioral therapy and compared a self-directed program with a group cognitive–behavioral therapy. Equivalent therapeutic outcomes (decreased avoidance behaviors, increased satisfaction) for the two groups were sustained at a 2-month follow-up. These studies strongly suggest that cognitive–behavioral interventions have been shown to address the important facets of body image, including perceptual, subjective, and behavioral factors that influence psychosocial adjustment.

Cognitive–behavioral intervention for body image is the most empirically documented approach and has been used with female college students (Cash, 1996), obese persons (J. C. Rosen, 1996b), and individuals with body dysmorphic disorder (Neziroglu, McKay, Todaro, & Yaryura-Tobias, 1996; Rosen, 1996a). Unfortunately, it has not been applied to eating-disorder samples as often as might be expected, given its proven efficacy with these other clinical groups (J. K. Thompson et al., 1996).

In summary, cognitive–behavior therapy has been demonstrated to be an efficacious treatment for body image disturbance for a wide variety of populations. The next generation of studies should examine its usefulness with understudied populations (e.g., persons with eating disorders, children, persons with disfiguring injuries, men). (In subsequent chapters, we return to different components of the cognitive–behavioral approach, discussed in this section, for a more thorough analysis of how such techniques fit within a particular theoretical approach.)

Feminist Approaches

The feminist literature outlining treatment approaches for body image and eating disorders can be differentiated from cognitive–behavioral techniques in three primary ways. First, the feminist literature criticizes approaches that focus on treating body image problems by changing a woman's appearance (e.g., diet, exercise). Feminists have argued that rather than trying to encourage women to struggle to meet a cultural demand, therapists should help women accept and celebrate the bodies that they have (Bergner, Remer, & Whetsell, 1985). Stated more globally, many feminists believe that the only way to truly improve women's body image in general and reduce the epidemic of eating disorders among women is through the advocating of equality of the genders and the discouraging of the view that women are defined by their appearance (Dionne, Davis, Fox, & Gurevich, 1995). These authors argued that strategies designed to help women meet an extreme, culturally defined goal only perpetuate the inherent sexism of American culture and that the likely failure that women experience (i.e., long-term weight loss remains intangible for the vast majority of persons) only reinforces women's negative feelings about their bodies and themselves.

Second, feminist authors have different assumptions regarding psychotherapy. Feminist therapists typically eschew the traditional hierarchical doctor–patient relationship because of the belief that it only reinforces women's sense of dependency and helplessness. Instead, feminist therapy relies on an egalitarian relationship characterized by therapist self-disclosure, greater informality and nurturance, and patient advocacy (S. C. Wooley, 1995). Feminists have also preferred less intellectual interpretation and behavioral strategies in favor of experiential therapies, such as art, music, movement therapy, gestalt techniques, and psychodrama.

Finally, feminist interventions focus on different etiological factors that play a role in the development of body image disturbance. Primary among proposed etiologies is the role of sexual abuse in the later development of body disparagement and shame. Feminist treatment of sexual abuse expands beyond individual therapy to include family therapy, victim support services, confronting perpetrators, and possible social and legal interventions (S. C. Wooley, 1995). Other etiological factors that have received feminist analysis include physical abuse, inadequate fathering, differential treatment and expectations within families for sons and daughters, and the role of daughters in families as emotional care givers (S. C. Wooley, 1995).

In conclusion, feminist therapies differ in a number of ways from the other interventions discussed in this chapter. Studies comparing feminist treatments for body image with control groups or cognitive–behavioral approaches would provide important information on the benefits of this perspective (Kearney-Cooke & Striegel-Moore, 1997). The specific strategies used by feminist therapists are covered in greater detail at various junctures in the next eight chapters; in particular, chapters 7 and 8 contain an extensive analysis of this approach.

Video Confrontation Procedures

These strategies are generally designed to deal with the size overestimation component of body image disturbance. Usually, individuals are directly confronted with information that suggests that they may be inaccurate in their perception of their body size. For instance, Goldsmith and Thompson (1989) used chalk drawings on a blackboard to illustrate the disagreement between participants' estimates of their body dimensions and their actual sizes. Another strategy that has been used by researchers consists of directly confronting individuals with their often-emaciated image by way of feedback from a video monitor (e.g., Fernandez & Vandereycken, 1994). The success of these procedures and more details regarding their use are presented in chapter 10.

Prevention Programs

Prevention programs attempt to intervene with adolescents, and sometimes adults, prior to the onset of clinically severe body image disturbances. Generally, the findings from the few studies in this area lead to a mixed picture—awareness of nutrition knowledge and weight regulation can be increased, but modification of attitudes and behaviors reflective of body dissatisfaction and disordered eating have not been greatly affected (Franko & Orosan-Weine, in press; M. P. Levine, in press; Smolak, Levine, & Schermer, 1998, in press; J. K. Thompson et al., 1996). For instance, in the most recent study in this area, Smolak et al. (1998) were able to improve knowledge of nutrition, negative effects of dieting, and the possible causes of body fat, but overall body satisfaction for the fifth-grade sample was unaffected by the intervention. Smolak and Levine (1994) offered six specific goals for early intervention programs that deal especially with issues that might benefit body image problems. These components are contained in Exhibit 2.1.

Disconcertingly, two recent prevention studies indicate that early intervention may actually be harmful. Carter, Stewart, Dunn, and Fairburn (1997) tested a program designed to reduce eating restraint levels (i.e., dieting) in 46 thirteen- to fourteen-year-old girls. Unlike most earlier studies, their immediate postintervention analyses indicated a positive effect on knowledge and a decrease in eating and shape-related measures, specifically for a measure of restraint and shape concern. However, by their 6-month follow-up, shape concern was back to the baseline level and restraint score was higher than it was at baseline. The authors noted that the intervention, which was a cognitive–behavioral treatment program used successfully with adults, may have somehow encouraged the dieting behavior of vulnerable participants because of its emphasis on weight and shape concerns.

In a second prevention study, Mann et al. (1997) found that female college students who received an intervention—conducted by classmates who had recovered from eating disorders—that focused on the experiences of the therapists and provided information about eating disorders actually

EXHIBIT 2.1
Goals for Early Intervention Programs

1. Acceptance of diverse body shapes. This requires discussion of the causes of body size and shape and of prejudice against heavy people. It should also include, especially among older elementary schoolers, information concerning pubertal changes.
2. Understanding that body shape is not infinitely mutable.
3. Understanding proper nutrition, including the importance of dietary fat and of a minimum caloric intake.
4. Discussion of the negative effects of dieting as well as the lack of long-term positive effects.
5. Consideration of the positive effects of moderate exercise and the negative effects of excessive or compensatory exercise.
6. Development of strategies to resist teasing, pressure to diet, propaganda about the importance of slenderness, etc.

From "Toward an Empirical Basis for Primary Prevention of Eating Problems With Elementary School Children," by L. Smolak and M. P. Levine, 1994, *Eating Disorders: The Journal of Treatment and Prevention, 2,* pp. 301–302. Copyright 1994 by *Eating Disorders: The Journal of Treatment and Prevention.* Reprinted with permission.

produced an increase in eating-disorder symptoms. Mann et al. (1997) noted that their program may have "reduced the stigma" of eating disorders, thus "inadvertently normalizing them" (p. 215).

Cosmetic Surgery

Regardless of the increasing number of psychologists, psychiatrists, and other mental health professionals who advocate and provide psychologically based interventions for body image disturbance, it remains apparent that many more individuals receive "treatment" for their disparagement by way of the surgical strategy of plastic surgery. Table 2.2, Table 2.3, and Table 2.4 contain the latest available figures from the American Society of Plastic and Reconstructive Surgeons (1996), broken down by gender and type of procedure (reconstructive and cosmetic). It is interesting to note that despite the potential wealth that might accrue from such a large naturally occurring research pool, remarkably few researchers have evaluated the short- or long-term body image modifications that result from these procedures (Sarwer, Wadden, Pertschuk, & Whitaker, 1998). However, in one of only a few longitudinal studies, Cash and Horton (1990) found that 86% of their sample were happy with the physical results of the surgery 1 month after the procedure.

Recent research by Sarwer and colleagues has greatly enhanced our understanding of the relatively neglected area of body image and cosmetic surgery (Sarwer et al., 1998; Sarwer, Pertschuk, Wadden, & Whitaker, in press). For instance, Pertschuk, Sarwer, Wadden, and Whitaker (1998) completed the first investigation of body dissatisfaction in male cosmetic surgery patients, finding that these patients were more dissatisfied with the body site or feature for which surgery was sought but did not differ in overall appearance satisfaction from a normative control group of men. These findings were extended in their analysis of a sample of women seeking rhytidectomy or blepharoplasty to improve aging facial features— satisfaction with the site of concern was lower than for a control group, but overall satisfaction with appearance was higher than for the controls (Sarwer, Whitaker, Wadden, & Pertschuk, 1997).

In another investigation, Sarwer, Bartlett, et al. (1998) found that presurgery body dissatisfaction and symptoms of body dysmorphia, such as avoidance of social situations, were higher in breast reduction patients than in breast augmentation patients. This was an extremely important finding, as the authors noted along with an accompanying discussion (J. K. Thompson, 1998), because insurance reimbursement seldom covers reduction surgery for patients who are overweight (80% of the sample in Sarwer, Bartlett, et al.'s, 1998, investigation were overweight). Much of Sarwer and colleagues' work also has treatment implications from a psychological perspective when considering work with the "obsessive" cosmetic surgery pa-

TABLE 2.2
1996 National Plastic Surgery Statistics

Procedure	Plastic surgery procedures	
	Total[a,b]	%
Animal bites	12,366	0.6
Birth defects	29,214	1.5
Breast augmentation (augmentation mamma-plasty)	87,704 (3,425)	4.5
Breast implant removal[c]	14,379	0.7
Breast lift (mastopexy)	16,097	0.8
Breast reconstruction	42,454	2.2
Breast reduction	57,679	3.0
Breast reduction in men (gynecomastia)	6,045	0.3
Burn care	25,177	1.3
Buttock lift	774	d
Cheek implants (malar augmentation)	2,257	0.1
Chemical peel	42,628	2.2
Chin augmentation (mentoplasty)	4,797	0.2
Collagen injections	34,091	1.8
Dermabrasion	7,979	0.4
Ear surgery (otoplasty)	7,192	0.4
Eyelid surgery (blepharoplasty)	76,242	3.9
Facelift (rhytidectomy)	53,435 (3,617)	2.8
Fat injection	13,654	0.7
Forehead lift	22,864 (11,644)	1.2
Hand surgery	**153,581**[2]	7.9
Lacerations	**115,998**[4]	6.0
Laser skin resurfacing	46,253	2.4
Liposuction (suction-assisted lipectomy)	**109,353**[5]	5.6
Male-pattern baldness	4,042	0.2
Maxillofacial surgery	28,338	1.5
Microsurgery	21,337	1.1
Nose reshaping (rhinoplasty)	45,977	2.4
Retin-A treatment	74,382	3.8
Scar revision	50,952	2.6
Subcutaneous mastectomy	1,766	d
Thigh lift	2,114	0.1
Tummy tuck (abdominoplasty)	34,235 (490)	1.8
Tumor removal	**542,063**[1]	28.0
Upper arm lift (brachioplasty)	1,614	d
Wrinkle injection (fibril injection)	164	d
Other reconstructive	**146,470**[3]	7.6
Other endoscopic	2,214	0.1
Total	1,937,877	100%

Note. Top five procedures are in boldface, with superscript numbers designating the rank. From *1996 Plastic Surgery Statistics*, by the American Society of Plastic and Reconstructive Surgeons, 1996, p. 3, Arlington Heights, IL: Author. Copyright American Society of Plastic and Reconstructive Surgeons 1996. Reprinted with permission.
[a]All figures are projected based on a survey of American Society of Plastic and Reconstructive Surgeons (ASPRS) members only. ASPRS membership includes 97% of the plastic surgeons certified by the American Board of Plastic Surgery. Figures and percentages may not add up to 100% because of rounding. [b]Figures in parentheses indicate the number of procedures performed with an endoscope. These figures are also included in the totals for each procedure. [c]Includes implants originally inserted for both cosmetic and reconstructive purposes. [d]Less than 0.1%.

TABLE 2.3
1996 National Plastic Surgery Statistics: Reconstructive Procedures

Procedure	Plastic surgery procedures	
	Total	%
Animal bites	12,366	1.0
Birth defects	29,214	2.4
Breast implant removal	11,366	0.9
Breast reconstruction	42,454	3.4
Breast reduction	**57,679**[5]	4.6
Burn care	25,177	2.0
Hand surgery	**153,581**[2]	12.4
Lacerations	**115,998**[4]	9.3
Maxillofacial surgery	28,338	2.3
Microsurgery	21,337	1.7
Scar revision	50,952	4.1
Subcutaneous mastectomy	1,766	0.1
Tumor removal	**542,063**[1]	43.7
Other reconstructive	**146,470**[3]	11.8
Other endoscopic	2,214	0.2
Total	1,240,973	

Note. Top five reconstruction procedures are in boldface, with superscript numbers designating the rank. From *1996 Plastic Surgery Statistics*, by the American Society of Plastic and Reconstructive Surgeons, 1996, p. 4, Arlington Heights, IL: Author. Copyright American Society of Plastic and Reconstructive Surgeons 1996. Reprinted with permission.

tient, obese individuals, or samples who may have associated body dysmorphic disorder symptoms (Sarwer, 1997; Sarwer, Wadden, Pertschuk, & Whitaker, in press; Sarwer, Wadden, & Foster, in press).

Clinical considerations have also been targeted by Pruzinsky (1996), who suggested that a multidimensional psychological evaluation is useful in prescreening individuals for elective cosmetic surgery. Certainly, there may be cases, such as the existence of a body dysmorphic disorder or severe psychopathology, where such surgery is contraindicated. The assessment of a potential surgery candidate's social, psychological, and surgical expectations, along with other variables, could maximize the possibility that cosmetic surgery is indeed the treatment procedure of choice (Pruzinsky, 1996).

One thing is certain: Cosmetic approaches to modify appearance continue to push the envelope. For instance, a recent procedure consisted of bacterial toxin injections to paralyze certain facial muscles that "cause worry and squint lines, leaving smoother skin around the forehead and eyes" ("A toxic beauty," 1997, p. 82). The injections, marketed under the name Botox, cost between $500–$1,500 and last for 3–4 months. Dowd (1997) also catalogued some other recent procedures, including a hollow tube implanted in the lips to accentuate poutiness and fat extraction from the hips and buttocks, which is then frozen to be used later to smooth out

TABLE 2.4
1996 Gender Distribution: Cosmetic Procedures

Procedure	Procedures performed[a]		Total male patients		Total female patients	
Breast augmentation	87,704[2]	(12.6%)	0	(0%)	87,704[2]	(100%)
Breast implant removal	3,013	(0.4%)	0	(0%)	3,013	(100%)
Breast lift	16,097	(2.3%)	0	(0%)	16,097	(100%)
Breast reduction in men	6,045	(0.9%)	6,045[4]	(100%)	0	(0%)
Buttock lift	774	(0.1%)	28	(4%)	747	(96%)
Cheek implants	2,257	(0.3%)	319	(14%)	1,938	(86%)
Chemical peel	42,628	(6.1%)	2,557	(6%)	40,071	(94%)
Chin augmentation	4,797	(0.7%)	1,139	(24%)	3,658	(76%)
Collagen injections	34,091	(4.9%)	1,389	(4%)	32,702	(96%)
Dermabrasion	7,975	(1.1%)	1,539	(19%)	6,368	(81%)
Ear surgery	7,192	(1.0%)	3,357	(47%)	3,836	(53%)
Eyelid surgery	76,242[3]	(10.9%)	11,190[2]	(15%)	65,052[4]	(85%)
Facelift	53,435[5]	(7.7%)	5,051	(9%)	48,383[5]	(91%)
Fat injection	13,654	(2.0%)	906	(7%)	12,748	(93%)
Forehead lift	22,864	(3.3%)	1,922	(8%)	20,942	(92%)
Laser skin resurfacing	46,253	(6.6%)	3,992	(9%)	42,262	(91%)
Liposuction	109,353[1]	(15.7%)	12,184[1]	(11%)	97,169[1]	(89%)
Male-pattern baldness	4,042	(0.6%)	4,042	(100%)	0	(0%)
Nose reshaping	45,977	(6.6%)	10,859[3]	(24%)	35,118	(76%)
Retin-A treatment	74,382[4]	(10.7%)	5,666[5]	(8%)	68,715[3]	(92%)
Thigh lift	2,114	(0.3%)	14	(1%)	2,100	(99%)
Tummy tuck	34,235	(4.9%)	1,634	(5%)	32,601	(95%)
Upper arm lift	1,614	(0.2%)	88	(5%)	1,526	(95%)
Wrinkle injection	164	([b])	0	(0%)	164	(100%)
Total	696,904	100%	73,921	(11%)	622,982	(89%)

Note. Top five are in boldface, with superscript numbers designating the rank. From *1996 Plastic Surgery Statistics*, by the American Society of Plastic and Reconstructive Surgeons, 1996, p. 5, Arlington Heights, IL: Author. Copyright American Society of Plastic and Reconstructive Surgeons 1996. Reprinted with permission.
[a]Some procedures commonly considered cosmetic may actually be reconstructive and be subject to insurance reimbursement, depending on the patient's condition. Because of rounding for projections, male and female patient totals may not equal procedure total.   [b]Less than 0.1%.

wrinkles in the face. (For a fascinating historical review of cosmetic surgery, see Haiken, 1997.)

Antistigmatization and Radical Acceptance Procedures

Recently, several groups decided that it was time to fight societal prejudices, stereotypes, and discrimination against obese individuals. One such group is the National Association to Advance Fat Acceptance (NAAFA), which publishes a bimonthly newsletter devoted to this cause. For instance, the following excerpt is from one of their articles on the antifat messages in the film *The Nutty Professor*, starring Eddie Murphy:

> According to Executive Director Sally E. Smith, "The film reinforces the stereotype that fat people are gluttonous and perpetuates the myth that one must become thin in order to find romance, while in fact

fatness is largely a result of genetics and dieting history, and many fat people are in successful love relationships." While Murphy has repeatedly said in the media that the movie's moral is that fat people shouldn't be ridiculed, and that in the end, Klump opts for self-acceptance, Smith feels that moviegoers won't get the message. "Any moral contained in the movie gets lost in a string of fat jokes, and I think that most viewers will walk away with the sense that fat people are fair game. After all, there was a "moral" in the original version of "The Nutty Professor," but when people think of that movie, the first thing that comes to mind is not the moral, but of Jerry Lewis acting like a nerd." ("NAAFA denounces *The Nutty Professor*," 1996, p. 10)

Certainly, this issue is beginning to occupy not only the minds of individuals who are targets of such discrimination, who have begun to voice their displeasure, but also the minds of researchers and clinicians who now advocate intervention with patients to improve body image and with society to alter negative perceptions of the obese condition. A consequence of this shift is a rather heated debate between those individuals whose position is firmly based in the "antidiet" and "fat acceptance" camp versus professionals who continue to focus on the negative health risks associated with obesity and to advocate intervention (J. K. Thompson & Tantleff-Dunn, 1998). Brownell and Rodin (1994) reviewed this issue, with recommendations for careful selection and intervention, and tried to bridge the gap between various factions, noting that

> accepting one's body, as opposed to relentless pursuit of an unrealistic ideal, is likely to be important for the health and well-being of many individuals. Balanced against this is a growing concern with the high prevalence of obesity in American youth. (p. 787)

A few recent studies illustrate the trend toward developing measures and interventions to fight fat stigmatization. (See Cash & Roy, in press, for a more extensive historical review.) Lewis, Cash, Jacobi, and Bubb-Lewis (1997) developed the Antifat Attitudes Test, which is a 47-item measure with three factors: social/character disparagement, physical/romantic unattractiveness, and weight control/blame. They found that men held more negative attitudes than women. Myers and Rosen (1998) developed two questionnaires based on obese men's and women's detailed lists of stigmatization situations and coping responses. The analysis of this information resulted in a 50-item Stigma Situations Scale and a 99-item Responses to Stigma Situations Questionnaire. They found that more frequent exposure to stigmatization was associated with more severe obesity, coping attempts, and psychological distress.

In terms of treatment, B. E. Robinson and Bacon (1996) piloted an innovative group treatment for overweight women that focused on such issues as understanding the cultural origins of negative body image attitudes, redefining the meaning of beauty, reducing self-blame for weight, and responding more assertively to social maltreatment. They named their treatment the If Only I Were Thin program. Lewis et al. (1997) looked at the modification of antifat attitudes in a sample of 120 college students by exposing them to differential information regarding the basis of excessive weight. Participants received information suggesting that weight was due to biogenetic or behavioral factors. The latter informational condition led to greater blame assigned to individuals because of their body size.

Articles in the NAAFA newsletter often focus on first-person accounts and books devoted to maximizing fat acceptance. Information about NAAFA and related organizations that promote fat acceptance is contained in Exhibit 2.2.

Exercise

Although it is often neglected in reviews of strategies designed to modify body image, increasing physical activity levels, even more so than cosmetic surgery and psychologically based interventions combined, is the method many people use to enhance feelings about their physical appearance. In fact, evidence suggests that this approach may be beneficial. E.

EXHIBIT 2.2
Organizations That Promote Fat Acceptance

National Association for Advancement of Fat Acceptance
P. O. Box 188620
Sacramento, CA 95818

Fat!So?
Box 423464
San Francisco, CA 94142

Abundia
P. O. Box 252
Downers Grove, IL 60515

Ample Opportunity
P. O. Box 40621
Portland, OR 97240-0621

Council of Size and Weight Discrimination
P. O. Box 305
Mt. Marion, NY 12456

Largely Positive
P. O. Box 17223
Glendale, WI 53217

Largesse, the Network for Size Esteem
P. O. Box 9404
New Haven, CT 06534-0404

Fisher and Thompson (1994) directly compared exercise (a combination of aerobic and anaerobic activities) with the cognitive–behavioral program developed by Cash (1995b, 1996, 1997) and found that the two procedures were roughly equivalent in improving body image satisfaction in female non-eating-disordered college students. To date, no published study has replicated these findings. However, data from related research areas also supports the use of exercise as a possible method to improve body image.

For example, Koff and Bauman (1997) compared three different physical education classes—wellness, fitness, and sport skills—for their effects on a wide range of fitness, body satisfaction, and lifestyle behaviors for 140 female college students. Body image changes were reported for both the wellness and fitness classes but not for the sport skills class. Recent findings also indicate that exercise may benefit health status, even in the absence of weight loss (Blair et al., 1995; Gaesser, 1996). Of course, this information may not satisfy overweight clients who are narrowly focused on weight loss. However, we have found that discussing health benefits facilitates the adoption of a model of "multiple indicators" of success—weight loss may be one goal, but health, greater self-acceptance, and other byproducts of exercise are also important.

Miscellaneous Approaches

Recent interventions in the treatment area involve approaches for the unique needs of certain clients. For instance, individuals with facial disfigurements confront substantial interpersonal and social issues related to their condition; a charitable organization by the name of Changing Faces has been at the forefront of developing awareness and interventions for this population (see Exhibit 2.3). Other researchers are also focusing on the unique social interactional problems for the facially disfigured person (Macgregor, 1990; E. Robinson, Rumsey, & Partridge, 1996). Strategies for handling the teasing that is a significant problem for these individuals have also been noted (see Gerrard, 1991, and chapter 5).

EXHIBIT 2.3
Changing Faces

Changing Faces is a charitable organization devoted to research and treatment of facial disfigurement. They have, to date, over 14 books, booklets, and videos that address various aspects of this clinical area, including guides for parents, health professionals, and clients.
Contact information: Changing Faces, 1 & 2 Junction Mews, London W2 1PN, United Kingdom (e-mail: info@faces.demon.co.uk).

CONCLUSIONS

In this chapter, we provided a broad overview of assessment and intervention strategies. In subsequent chapters, we return to component parts of the treatment programs noted in this chapter for further explication in the context of specific risk factors and theoretical models. However, a few recommendations regarding assessment and treatment can be offered at this juncture. An assessment of the satisfaction–dissatisfaction component seems necessary for the great majority of cases for which body image disturbance is suspected. Treatment outcome studies strongly support the effectiveness of cognitive–behavioral approaches; however, multiple other strategies, particularly feminist methods, may be appropriate, depending on clinical presentation. Certainly, we need more research designed to compare different approaches for the treatment of body image disturbance. In the next eight chapters, we explore how an evaluation of theoretical models and factors thought to be crucial to the onset and maintenance of disturbance may contribute to the selection of specific assessments and treatments.

APPENDIX 2A
CONTOUR DRAWING RATING SCALE

Instructions: Participants are asked to rate their "ideal" figure and their "current" size. As noted in the text, it may be useful to consider other instructional protocols, such as "think" and "feel" ratings. The discrepancy between the ideal and current size is the index of body size dissatisfaction.

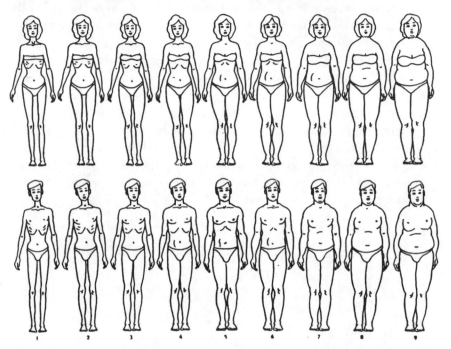

From "Development and Validation of a New Body Image Assessment Scale," by M. A. Thompson and J. J. Gray, 1995, *Journal of Personality Assessment, 64,* p. 263. Copyright 1995 by Lawrence Erlbaum Associates, Inc. Reprinted with permission.

APPENDIX 2B
BREAST/CHEST RATING SCALE

Instructions: Participants are asked to rate their "ideal" figure and their "current" size. As noted in the text, it may be useful to consider other instructional protocols, such as "think" and "feel" ratings. The discrepancy between the ideal and current size is the index of body size dissatisfaction.

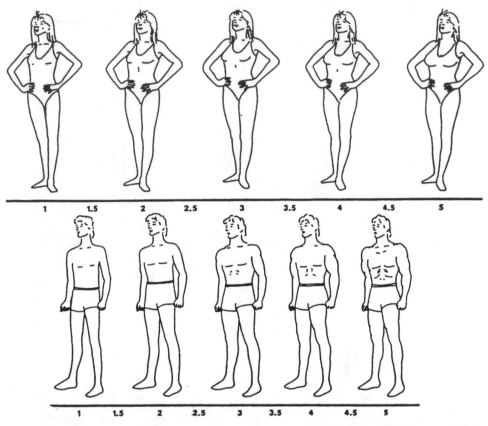

From "Female and Male Ratings of Upper Torso: Actual, Ideal, and Stereotypical Conceptions," by J. K. Thompson and S. T. Tantleff, 1992, *Journal of Social Behavior and Personality, 7,* pp. 349–350. Copyright 1992 by the *Journal of Social Behavior and Personality*. Reprinted with permission.

MUSCULARITY RATING SCALE

Instructions: Participants rate "ideal" and "current" figures from these sketches of nine female shapes, ranging from extremely anorexic to hypertrophic; for other potential ratings, see Furnham et al. (1994).

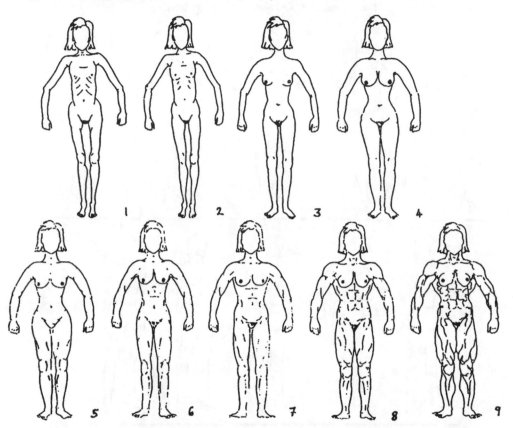

From "Perception of Female Body Shapes as a Function of Exercise," by A. Furnham, P. Titman, and E. Sleeman, 1994, *Journal of Social Behavior and Personality, 9,* p. 342. Copyright 1994 by the *Journal of Social Behavior and Personality.* Reprinted with permission.

APPENDIX 2D
BODY–SELF RELATIONS QUESTIONNAIRE:
APPEARANCE EVALUATION SUBSCALE

Instructions: Using the scale below, please circle the number that best matches your agreement with the following statements.

Definitely disagree	Mostly disagree	Neither agree nor disagree	Mostly agree	Definitely agree
1	2	3	4	5

1. My body is sexually appealing.   1 2 3 4 5
2. I like my looks just the way they are.   1 2 3 4 5
3. Most people would consider me good looking. 1 2 3 4 5
4. I like the way I look without my clothes. 1 2 3 4 5
5. I like the way my clothes fit me.   1 2 3 4 5
6. I dislike my physique.   1 2 3 4 5
7. I'm physically unattractive.   1 2 3 4 5

From the Multidimensional Body Self-Relations Questionnaire–Appearance Evaluation Scale, an unpublished scale by T. F. Cash. Reprinted with permission from the author. See Cash (1997) for more information.

APPENDIX 2E
BODY-ESTEEM SCALE FOR ADOLESCENTS AND ADULTS

Instructions: Indicate how often you agree with the following statements: Ranging from *never* (1) to *always* (5), circle the appropriate number beside each statement.

Never	Seldom	Sometimes	Often		Always	
1	2	3	4		5	

1. I like what I look like in pictures.	1	2	3	4	5
2. Other people consider me good looking.	1	2	3	4	5
3. I'm proud of my body.	1	2	3	4	5
4. I am preoccupied with trying to change my body weight.	1	2	3	4	5
5. I think my appearance would help me get a job.	1	2	3	4	5
6. I like what I see when I look in the mirror.	1	2	3	4	5
7. There are lots of things I'd change about my looks if I could.	1	2	3	4	5
8. I am satisfied with my weight.	1	2	3	4	5
9. I wish I looked better.	1	2	3	4	5
10. I really like what I weigh.	1	2	3	4	5
11. I wish I looked like someone else.	1	2	3	4	5
12. People my own age like my looks.	1	2	3	4	5
13. My looks upset me.	1	2	3	4	5
14. I'm as nice looking as most people.	1	2	3	4	5
15. I'm pretty happy about the way I look.	1	2	3	4	5
16. I feel I weigh the right amount for my height.	1	2	3	4	5
17. I feel ashamed of how I look.	1	2	3	4	5
18. Weighing myself depresses me.	1	2	3	4	5
19. My weight makes me unhappy.	1	2	3	4	5
20. My looks help me to get dates.	1	2	3	4	5
21. I worry about the way I look.	1	2	3	4	5
22. I think I have a good body.	1	2	3	4	5
23. I'm looking as nice as I'd like to.	1	2	3	4	5

From the Body-Esteem Scale for Adolescents and Adults, an unpublished scale by B. K. Mendelson, 1998. Reprinted with permission from the author. See Mendelson et al. (1998) for more information.

APPENDIX 2F
PHYSICAL APPEARANCE STATE AND
TRAIT ANXIETY SCALE: TRAIT

The statements listed below are to be used to describe how anxious, tense, or nervous you feel in general (i.e., usually) about your body or specific parts of your body.

Please read each statement and circle the number that best indicates the extent to which each statement holds true in general. Remember, there are no right or wrong answers.

Never	Seldom	Sometimes	Often	Always
1	2	3	4	5

In general I feel *anxious, tense,* or *nervous* about

1. The extent to which I look overweight	1	2	3	4	5
2. My thighs	1	2	3	4	5
3. My buttocks	1	2	3	4	5
4. My hips	1	2	3	4	5
5. My stomach	1	2	3	4	5
6. My legs	1	2	3	4	5
7. My waist	1	2	3	4	5
8. My muscle tone	1	2	3	4	5
9. My ears	1	2	3	4	5
10. My lips	1	2	3	4	5
11. My wrists	1	2	3	4	5
12. My Hands	1	2	3	4	5
13. My forehead	1	2	3	4	5
14. My neck	1	2	3	4	5
15. My chin	1	2	3	4	5
16. My feet	1	2	3	4	5

From "Assessing Body Image Disturbance: Measures, Methodology, and Implementation" (p. 80), by J. K. Thompson, in J. K. Thompson (Ed.), *Body Image, Eating Disorders, and Obesity,* 1996. Copyright 1996 by the American Psychological Association. Reprinted with permission.

APPENDIX 2G
ITEMS ON THE BODY DYSMORPHIC DISORDER EXAMINATION

1. Subject's description of the defect(s) in physical appearance.
2. Interviewer's rating of subject's physical appearance.
3. Presence of other types of somatic complaints.
4. Perceived abnormality of defect (extent to which subject believes the defect is common or rare).
5. Frequency of body checking.
6. Dissatisfaction with appearance defect.
7. Dissatisfaction with general appearance.
8. Frequency of seeking reassurance about appearance from other people.
9. How often subject experiences *upsetting* preoccupation with appearance.
10. Self-consciousness and embarrassment about appearance in *public* situations (e.g., city streets, restaurants).
11. Self-consciousness and embarrassment about appearance in *social* situations (e.g., at work).
12. How often subject thought other people were scrutinizing his/her defect.
13. Distress when other people pay attention to the defect.
14. How often subject received comment(s) from others about his/her defect.
15. Distress when other people comment about his/her appearance.
16. How often subject felt other people treat him or her differently due to appearance.
17. Distress when other people treat him or her differently due to appearance.
18. How important is physical appearance in self-evaluation.
19. Extent of negative self-evaluation in a non-physical sense due to appearance.
20. Extent of negative evaluation in a non-physical sense due to appearance.
21. Perceived physical attractiveness.
22. Degree of conviction in physical defect (rating based on several questions; if insight is poor, a separate assessment for delusional disorder somatic type could be appropriate).
23. Avoidance of public situations due to appearance (e.g., restaurants, restrooms, city streets).
24. Avoidance of social situations due to appearance (e.g., parties, speaking to authority figures).
25. Avoidance of close physical contact due to appearance (e.g., hugging, kissing, dancing close, sex).
26. Avoidance of physical activities (e.g., exercise or outdoor recreation) due to appearance.
27. How often subject camouflages or hides his or her appearance defects with clothes, make-up and so forth.
28. How often subject contorts body posture in order to hide the defect (e.g., keeping hands in pocket).
29. Inhibiting physical contact with others (changes body movements or posture during contact in order to hide defect, e.g., doesn't let partner touch certain body area).
30. Avoidance of looking at own body.
31. Avoidance of others looking at body unclothed.
32. How often subject compares his or her appearance to that of other people.
33. Remedies that the person has attempted to alter the appearance defect.
34. Appearance defect not accounted for by another disorder (separate examination to rule out other disorders, e.g., anorexia or bulimia nervosa, might be necessary).

From "Development of the Body Dysmorphic Disorder Examination" by J. C. Rosen and J. Reiter, 1996, *Behaviour Research and Therapy, 34*, pp. 765–766. Copyright 1996 by Elsevier Science. Reprinted with permission.

II

SOCIETAL AND SOCIAL APPROACHES

3

SOCIOCULTURAL THEORY: THE MEDIA AND SOCIETY

If we as a nation are obsessed with thinness—and I have yet to encounter anyone who disagrees with that statement—then it's safe to say that thinness has acquired a highly exaggerated status in assessing a woman's value. Obsession by its very definition is an expression of imbalance and disturbance. (W. C. Goodman, 1995, p. 13)

In PC game software . . . Barbie dominated the kids' bestseller list in 1997. (Barbie Fashion Designer and Barbie Magic Hair Styler were Numbers 1 and 2 on the top ten list; Lohr, 1998, p. D1)

It has already signed up 16,000 sales representatives in Moscow, St. Petersburg and the Siberian town of Perm and expects $30 million in revenue this year, up from $9 million in 1995. John Law, Avon's general manager in Moscow, says its long-term plan is to "sell a lot of lipstick." Ms. Kropf, the marketing executive, calls the country "Avon heaven." (Stanley, 1996, p. C16)

It was God who made me so beautiful. If I weren't, then I'd be a teacher. (Supermodel Linda Evangelista, as quoted in "Perspectives," 1997b, p. 27).

What's next, prenatal lipstick? (Alex Molnar, writer of *Giving Kids the Business: The Commercialization of America's Schools*, referring to a line of Barbie cosmetics geared at girls 6–9 years of age; as cited in "Perspectives," 1997a, p. 29)

Although a number of theoretical models have been proposed to account for body image problems, many researchers have noted that societal factors have a powerful influence on the development and maintenance of disturbance in Western societies (A. E. Fallon, 1990; Heinberg, 1996). This theoretical explanation has, perhaps, the strongest empirical support (Heinberg, Wood, & Thompson, 1995). A sociocultural theoretical model purports that current societal standards for beauty inordinately stress the importance of thinness (Tiggemann & Pickering, 1996) as well as other difficult to achieve standards of beauty (A. E. Fallon, 1990).

A sociocultural model emphasizes that the current societal standard for thinness in women is omnipresent and, unfortunately, often out of reach for the average woman. Indeed, although the average woman has become larger over recent years, evidence suggests that the ideal has become progressively thinner (Wiseman, Gray, Mosimann, & Ahrens, 1992).

In this chapter, we examine the evidence for a sociocultural theory of body image. Initially, the current ideal is described as well as the historical changes in society's expectations for thinness and beauty. The bulk of the chapter focuses on the research examining the influence of the mass media in communicating sociocultural expectations. This section is divided into research focusing on print media and television. Each of these divisions are further subdivided into a discussion of exposure to the media, evidence for a thin ideal, correlational studies, randomized experiments, and conclusions. Sociocultural influences on special populations are reviewed next, with emphases on men, children, minorities and acculturation issues, and disfigured populations as well as the evidence for weight prejudice. More comprehensive studies of the sociocultural model are evaluated. Finally, a review of sociocultural specific body image assessment and treatment is presented, followed by conclusions and future directions of research.

THE CURRENT SOCIOCULTURAL IDEAL

To ask what is beauty today is to come face to face with the changing definition of beauty. Perhaps more than any other time in history, we are preoccupied with, even confused by beauty: its power, its pleasures, its style, and its substance. Beauty may not be the most important of our values, but it affects us all; today more than ever, because we live in a Media Age where our visual landscape changes in seconds, and our first reaction to people is sometimes our last. Given this reality, the so-called "triviality" of beauty suddenly seems not so trivial after all. (Schefer, 1997, p. 9)

In Westernized American society, the equation of beauty with goodness and virtue (Franzoi & Herzog, 1987) has led thinness to become almost synonymous with beauty (Striegel-Moore, McAvay, & Rodin, 1986; J. K. Thompson, 1990). Comparably, researchers have found a complementary relationship with attitudes toward obesity. That is, whenever thinness is esteemed by a society, its opposite, obesity, is seriously denigrated (Rand & Kuldau, 1990; Rodin, Silberstein, & Striegel-Moore, 1985). Obesity is judged by America's weight-conscious society as unattractive and the "result of personal misbehavior" (J. C. Rosen, 1996b, p. 425). Although current societal ideals promote thinness, additional evidence suggests that women are pressured to achieve appearance goals that are inconsistent with thinness, namely, the possession of large breasts (J. K. Thompson &

Tantleff, 1992), or are somewhat contradictory to thinness, such as a muscular physique (Striegel-Moore, Silberstein, & Rodin, 1986).

In addition to endorsing a specific body shape, American society propagates other appearance-related myths. For instance, the sociocultural ideal has been resoundly criticized for erroneously informing individuals that body shape and weight are infinitely malleable. Unfortunately, one's *somatotype* (the body shape of an individual) often conflicts with society's prescribed ideal (Brownell, 1991). Although thinness is at least partially under an individual's control, many other socioculturally endorsed aspects of appearance, such as youth, height, and Caucasoid features, are less amenable to alteration (Heinberg, 1996). Thus, it has been hypothesized that although some changes may be possible through cosmetics or plastic surgery, sociohistorical changes favoring an aging population and expanding numbers of women of color will inevitably result in increasingly fewer women who are able to achieve the society's ideal. Perhaps, as a result, increasing numbers of women have reported significant body image discontent (Heinberg, 1996). This places culture and physiology in conflict (Brownell, 1991); judging from the normative degree of dissatisfaction with one's body among women (Cash & Henry, 1995), culture appears to be winning. Sociocultural pressure may also falsely promise that attaining the ideal will result in happiness, health, and self-esteem. Instead, the rewards may be less than expected, and the consequences of seeking the ideal and failing may lead to both psychological and physiological risks (e.g., weight cycling; Brownell, 1991).

Although the ideal figure has become thinner whereas the average woman's figure has become larger (Garner, Garfinkel, Schwartz, & Thompson, 1980), it appears that girls and women continue to accept the thinner societal ideal as a goal. Unfortunately, this ideal is pervasive among women of all ages. Collins (1991) found that expectations of thinness among girls may be evident as early as 6 or 7 years of age. As girls enter adolescence, they become more concerned with their appearance and the associated bodily changes and weight gain, continuing to adhere to the idealized societal standard (Freedman, 1986; Kelson, Kearney-Cooke, & Lansky, 1990). This adherence to a thin ideal continues into adulthood (A. E. Fallon & Rozin, 1985; Garner, 1997).

HISTORICAL CHANGES

In the 80's the shape changed again, this time to broad shoulders and noticeable breasts grafted unnaturally and sometimes surgically onto an emaciated frame. That women have reached the position of such an impossible aim which pulls them in opposite directions is interesting. (Raphael & Lacey, 1992, p. 294)

Throughout history, whenever ideals of feminine beauty have varied and changed in accordance with the aesthetic standards of the particular period of time, women have attempted to alter themselves to meet these ideals (Mazur, 1986). Idealized beauty has never been static. Although early cultures were likely to define as attractive a feminine appearance that was biologically associated with reproduction (e.g., wide hips), cultural influences have grown to be more influential than biological ones (A. E. Fallon, 1990). Indeed, there is no inherent biological value in a cosmetically altered nose or pierced ears. Rather, a number of historically sanctioned beauty ideals have been contradictory to biological determinism, such as bound feet, female circumcision, and skull deformations (A. E. Fallon, 1990). Even today, one can argue that some culturally endorsed beauty rituals are contradictory to optimum health (e.g., crash dieting, breast implants).

Historical factors are not the only influence on ideals of beauty. Cultural differences may play a significant role. For example, Nassar (1988) found that in non-Western cultures, thinness is not excessively valued and may even be devalued. He noted that in Chinese cultures, plumpness connotes affluence and longevity and Arab cultures associate greater body weight with female fertility (Nassar, 1988). Unlike current Western ideals, thinness is viewed by society as unattractive.

Further transcultural evidence is provided by Sobal and Stunkard (1989), who reviewed over 100 studies from both first- and third-world countries, examining the relationship between socioeconomic status and obesity in men, women, and children. They found a higher incidence of obesity in the lower classes of developed countries for women (not for men or children). However, in developing countries, a relationship occurred in the opposite direction—the higher the socioeconomic status, the higher the incidence of obesity (Furnham & Baguma, 1994; Powers, 1980; Sobal & Stunkard, 1989). Sobal and Stunkard noted that this fat ideal is the reverse of the Western thin ideal, especially among the higher socioeconomic groups. In reviewing transcultural data, McCarthy (1990) concluded that "all cultures that have eating disorders have the thin ideal. Further, no culture that does not have the thin ideal has eating disorders" (p. 210). Barber (1998), in an examination of published evidence from psychology, sociology, and anthropology, argued that where economic independence is possible for women, a thin ideal is favored. However, when women lack economic power, marriage is favored and the ideal is more likely to be curvaceous.

A brief review of the beauty ideal of Westernized cultures demonstrates the fluidity of sociocultural expectations (see Exhibit 3.1). Between 1400 and 1700, a fat body shape was considered sexually appealing and fashionable. The ideal woman was portrayed as plump, big-breasted, and maternal (Attie & Brooks-Gunn, 1987; A. E. Fallon, 1990). By the 19th

EXHIBIT 3.1
The Whys of Body Image Ideals

These are questions we hear from clients, colleagues, and friends at cocktail parties: Why is beauty so important for women? Why is thinness so valued in Western society now but not 100 years ago or in other parts of the world? (Consider the woman depicted in Figure 3.1A).

Certainly questioning the history of beauty ideals would be interesting, and the subject could be debated for quite some time. The difficulty is in testing various hypotheses using historical correlational data. We present these theories and the strength of the evidence supporting these ideas.

One theory of beauty ideals for women is based on economics. Barber (1995) explained the two economic strategies available to women. In societies that promote economic independence, women compete with men in the workplace. Looking more masculine (thinner, less curvaceous) makes them appear more competitive. In societies where economic independence for women is not possible, women must achieve their standing through the men they attract. Buss (1989) explained that as a biological organism, humans are driven to select mates who will give them the greatest likelihood of healthy, abundant offspring. So what is the best way for each sex to ensure the production and survival of many offspring? For men, a relatively young and healthy woman is most likely to produce more children (given that female reproductive years are limited by menopause). For women, a financially secure man will provide her with the most help.

Figure 3.1A. The beauty ideal from a different time in Western culture. The statue depicts Venus, the mythical goddess of love and beauty. Compare her proportions to the ideal figure of today. In a 1988 movie recreation (*The Goddess of Love*) of the Venus myth, Vanna White played the lead role. *Venus* attributed to Francesco Brambilla the Younger (circa 1580–1590). From the Andrew W. Mellon Collection, © 1998 Board of Trustees, National Gallery of Art, Washington, DC. Reprinted with permission.

Buss (1989) tested these ideas by evaluating individuals in 33 countries. Consistently across samples, men preferred younger mates. The trend was present but not quite as strong for women preferring older mates. In most countries, women placed a stronger value than did men on "good financial prospect" in mate selection. Men in turn placed a higher value on physical appearance than women did.

An example of a physical trait that signals youth and fertility is the waist-to-hip ratio. A smaller waist-to-hip ratio (more curvaceous) is generally preferred by men (Barber, 1995). Women have a smaller waist-to-hip ratio than do men beginning at puberty. The difference is so pronounced that it would be considered a secondary sex characteristic like breasts or male facial hair. Even more so, the low waist-to-hip ratio is partly

Exhibit continues on following page

EXHIBIT 3.1 (*Continued*)

determined by one's level of hormones, which is associated with less disease and decreased mortality and for underweight women associated with greater fertility. It is true that as both sexes age, they tend to deposit abdominal fat, making women more straight up and down. Thus, the waist-to-hip ratio is a good indicator for youth, health, and fertility. Being heavier and more curvaceous may be seen as useful to attract a mate for economic security.

As an illustration, look at Figure 3.1B. This is an impressionist painting of *Bather Arranging Her Hair* by Renoir. He was painting about and for the well-to-do of European society (Cole & Gealth, 1989). In that society, a woman's position was determined by marriage.

As another example, compare the Marilyn Monroe figure of the 1950s to the ideal beauties in the decades since then as women's economic and political power has grown. However, the problem in the logic of the economic theory is that the ideal for women as they gain economic power is not to look more masculine (more muscular and thicker) but to look more waiflike. It is the thin, young adolescent Twiggy look that has been idealized. This led Raphael and Lacey (1992) to conclude that the thin ideal is associated with a woman's conflicted feelings about her role. Echoing that sentiment, Nagel and Jones (1992) cited studies that indicate that in terms of gender role orientation, eating disordered women are the most conflicted (not the most feminine). The main idea is that a more economically independent woman is more threatening to a man; therefore, idealizing a more childlike female look can be a comfort. Alternatively, thinness could be a way for a woman to show that she has so much self-control and independence from

Figure 3.1B. The beauty ideal for women when economic security was primarily through marriage. Note her youthful look and low waist-to-hip ratio. *Bather Arranging Her Hair* by Auguste Renoir (1893). From the Chester Dale Collection, © 1998 Board of Trustees, National Gallery of Art, Washington, DC. Reprinted with permission.

men that she hardly needs to eat at all. These theories are speculative; however, Raphael and Lacey cited historical cases of eating disorders (from 10th and 19th century Europe) as occurring during other periods of change in the role of women.

EXHIBIT 3.1 (*Continued*)

Figure 3.1C. The image of women when spiritual asceticism is valued. Her clothing minimizes the importance of her body in the picture, but it is still clear how thin she is from her neck and hands. *Saint Margaret* attributed to Sassetta (circa 1435). From the Samuel H. Kress Collection, © 1998 Board of Trustees, National Gallery of Art, Washington, DC. Reprinted with permission.

The evidence supporting these ideas is correlational, which limits its strength. But these theories are also limited, in that they do not explain why there is pressure for thinness on men as well. Smuts (1992) presented a theory that was less gender specific, although again based on economic principles. For much of history, societies have struggled with getting enough resources to survive. Heaviness was a sign of wealth, possession of more than adequate resources. At times, as is the case now for most people in the United States, there is an abundance of food. Smuts argued that valuing thinness is a reaction to this abundance. Thinness becomes the way to show off one's wealth, as if to say "I'm so secure financially, I don't need to carry any extra weight." To support this idea, Smuts quoted historians and cited the example of the growth of fasting practices among women in religious orders during the time that they were experiencing economic growth. In reaction to the abundance around them, these women came to value asceticism and spirituality (see Figure 3.1C). One could draw the parallel for today's society stating that people react to abundance by valuing self-control and intellectual pursuits.

These ideas could be debated for quite some time. For the practitioner, its importance to recognize is twofold. First, beauty ideas are unstable. Second, cultures appear to attach meaning to the beauty ideals they hold, especially for women. These are cultural pressures everyone must face.

century, this had shifted to a more voluptuous, corseted figure, idealizing a more hourglass shape. In pre-World War I American society, the "Gibson Girl" was idealized as voluptuous but tall and slender, only to be replaced by the flat-chested flappers of the 1920s (Mazur, 1986). In response to this new ideal, women began wearing binding garments and following strict diets, leading to the first concerns by physicians regarding outbreaks of eating disorders (A. E. Fallon, 1990). In turn, this ideal was replaced in the 1930s with an emphasis on legs and bustiness, epitomized by Betty Grable (Mazur, 1986). During the 1950s, a more curvaceous form was propagated as idealized by Marilyn Monroe and *Playboy* magazine. This trend continued until the 1960s, with the onset of Twiggy and the emphasis on angular body shapes favored over curvaceousness. Although the fashion ideal has been altered to include large breasts and a more toned, muscular shape, the thin ideal has remained the epitome of beauty for the past 30 years (Striegel-Moore, Silberstein, et al., 1986).

RESEARCH BACKGROUND

Previous research has demonstrated that there has been movement away from a preference for an hourglass figure to a less curvaceous and angular body shape (Garner et al., 1980; Silverstein, Perdue, Peterson, & Kelly, 1986). The mean bust-to-waist ratio (representing curvaceousness by dividing bust size by waist measurement—the larger the ratio, the more curvaceous the model) of models appearing in *Vogue* and *Ladies' Home Journal* has dropped to below 1.3 since 1965 (although it was at its lowest in 1925), and a similar decline has been shown for bust-to-waist ratios among popular movie actresses (Silverstein, Perdue, Peterson, & Kelly, 1986). Examining data from Miss America Pageant contestants and *Playboy* centerfolds from 1959 to 1978, researchers found decreasing weight-to-height ratios, reduced curvaceousness, and increasing heights. More recent research (Wiseman et al., 1992) corroborates these past findings, for example, demonstrating that 60% of Miss America contestants and 69% of *Playboy* centerfolds from 1979–1988 had body weights 15% or more below expected weights for women their height. Wiseman et al. concluded that the majority of "ideals" in American society, based on their low body weight, meet one of the *Diagnostic and Statistical Manual for Mental Disorders–Fourth Edition* (American Psychiatric Association, 1994) criteria for anorexia nervosa (e.g., having a body weight that is 15% below expected weight).

Several studies also document media's changing ideals of women's bodies. In examinations of popular women's magazines, past research demonstrates trends toward increasing slenderness of models and increases in articles and advertisements addressing dietary issues (Garner et al., 1980; Silverstein, Perdue, Peterson, & Kelly, 1986; Silverstein, Peterson, & Perdue, 1986). Wiseman et al. (1992) updated these studies by tabulating the number of diet-for-weight-loss, exercise, and diet and exercise articles from 1959 to 1989 in leading women's magazines (*Harpers Bazaar, Vogue, Ladies' Home Journal, Good Housekeeping, Woman's Day,* and *McCalls*). Results demonstrated an overall increase in the emphasis on weight loss over the 30-year period. It is interesting to note that the proportion of exercise and diet–exercise references has increased, and from 1983 onward, the prevalence of exercise articles has surpassed that of diet articles (Wiseman et al., 1992).

Spillman and Everington (1989) demonstrated that not only has the ideal body type changed but so too have perceived behavioral characteristics associated with body types. Several decades ago, consistent research demonstrated stereotypical behavioral and personality traits associated with each of the three somatotypes. These studies suggested that *mesomorphic* (medium body build) body types were associated with the most favorable traits whereas the heavier *endomorphs* were associated with being socially aggressive, lazy, and unattractive and the thin *ectomorphs* were associated with being nervous, socially withdrawn, and submissive (Dibiase & Hjelle, 1968). However, in a study of university students during the 1980s, the ectomorph was associated with positive characteristics, such as attractiveness, degree of sexual appeal, and frequency of dating (Spillman & Everington, 1989). This somatotype was also selected by women as best representing who they wished to look like.

Clearly, correlational research demonstrates the changing ideal of beauty and thinness over time and the idealization of thinness in women in the current U.S. sociohistorical moment. However, longitudinal studies are necessary to demonstrate the effect of resultant changes in women's body images over time. Furthermore, individual differences in sensitivity to these changes has not been sufficiently explored.

Mass Media

> Cookie-cutter women forsake their personal beauty for images represented by models who pass us by as quickly as trends do. (Norma Kamali, as quoted in Schefer, 1997, p. 108)

Mass media are forms of communication that generate messages designed for very large, very heterogeneous, and very anonymous audiences (R. J. Harris, 1994). The media communicates to provide education, entertainment, socialization, and an opportunity for sponsors to advertise their products. Mass media is omnipresent in American and most Western societies but has been harshly criticized for playing a powerful role in communicating the thin standard to the average woman (Mazur, 1986). Long before the advent of electronic media or ready accessibility to print media, images of beauty were communicated through art, music, and literature. However, Freedman (1986) explained that whereas throughout history, beauty ideals have been modeled, the impact of today's visual media is different from the effect of the visual arts of the past. She noted that historically figures of art were romanticized as unattainable, but today's media blurs the boundaries between glorified fiction and reality (Freedman, 1986). Airbrushing, soft-focus cameras, editing, and filters may blur the realistic nature of media images even further. For instance, Lakoff and Scherr (1984) asserted that television and magazines exert an especially toxic influence because models in these mediums are seen as realistic representations of actual people rather than carefully manipulated, artificially developed images. Often media representations are not even of a singular woman. Rather, they are computer-merged images in which one model may provide the hair, another the face, and a third her figure. Even when exposed to a single image, women may fail to appreciate that models in print media or on television may spend many hours with clothes designers and professional hair and make-up artists for a single photograph and follow a rigidly controlled diet and exercise program (Heinberg, 1996; Stormer & Thompson, 1995). Although the average woman can afford neither the time nor financial investment necessary to achieve this look, individuals regard it as a realistic representation of feminine beauty and as an appropriate comparison target for what one should look like (Jasper, 1993; Lakoff & Scherr, 1984).

A recent *Psychology Today* survey indicates the degree of influence the mass media has in promoting the cultural ideal, at least for women (Garner, 1997). Of 3,452 women responding, 23% indicated that movie or television celebrities influenced their body image when they were young, whereas 22% endorsed the influence of fashion magazine models (Garner, 1997). In contrast, only 13% and 6% of men reported an influence of movie–television celebrities or fashion magazine models, respectively.

The influence of the mass media has long been theoretically implicated in the development of eating disorders (Garfinkel & Garner, 1982) and as the means of communicating patriarchal dogma (Wolf, 1990; see also chapter 7 on feminist perspectives). However, researchers have queried whether the media determine women's views of themselves or whether women themselves influence the media (Raphael & Lacey, 1992). Striegel-Moore, Silberstein, et al. (1986), in a review of risk factors for bulimia nervosa, criticized the media as a means of teaching women not only about the thin ideal but as providing maladaptive information on how to attain this idealized figure, "including how to diet, purge and engage in other disregulating behaviors" (p. 256). Silverstein, Perdue, Peterson, and Kelly (1986) countered the argument that the media only reflects the desires of the greater public by arguing that "even if it were true that the presentations of a thin standard of bodily attractiveness for women appear only when media decision makers believe many women desire such presentations, these decisions would still feed back to affect other women" (p. 531).

It is likely that the relationship between mass media and body image is complex, multiply determined, and bidirectional. A number of additional individual differences may potentiate (e.g., social comparison tendency) or buffer against (e.g., sexual orientation) mass media exposure. Furthermore, the mass media may be seen as just one of numerous modes of socialization, including peers, family, school, and athletics, which compliment one another to endorse ideals of thinness and attractiveness (M. P. Levine & Smolak, 1996). Although the thin ideal is not promoted solely by the media and may not even be originated by the media, the popularity and pervasiveness of television, movies, and magazines leads the media to be among the most influential and efficacious communicators of the thin ideal (Raphael & Lacey, 1992; Silverstein, Perdue, Peterson, & Kelly, 1986). In the following sections, we review findings with regards to body image as it relates to the print media and television. The two sections on print and television media are subdivided into examination of exposure, endorsement of the cultural ideal, correlational studies, randomized studies, and conclusions.

Print Media

> Anorexia nervosa seems to follow the subscriptions to *Vogue*. If *Vogue* gets to your country, anorexia nervosa will eventually follow. (McHugh, 1997, p. K4)

> Moss does have a look that's unearthly and feverish, like a tubercular young woman in a nineteenth-century novel. (Barbara Lippert referring to supermodel Kate Moss, as cited in Schefer, 1997, p. 103)

Although many investigators have examined the influence of the mass media more globally, a number of investigators have focused their investigations on print media, primarily teen and women's fashion magazines. Proponents of sociocultural theories as etiologically significant in the fostering of eating disorders have accused women's magazines of being propaganda for the desirability of the thin ideal (Wolf, 1990), and indeed evidence suggests that these magazines do endorse societal standards emphasizing thinness and beauty. For example, Nichter and Nichter (1991) found that adolescent girls related their ideal to the models found in teen fashion magazines. The girls quantified the ideal teenage girl as being 5' 7" (1.70 m), 100 pounds (45.35 kg), size 5, with long blonde hair and blue eyes. Clearly, very few teenage girls meet this unrealistic standard, and such aspirations may lead to body dissatisfaction. More important, given that this ideal's body mass index is less than 16, thus within an anorexic and *amenorrheic* (cessation of regular menstruation) range, clearly this ideal is a problematic comparison target.

Exposure. Evidence suggests that girls and women have high rates of exposure to print media. Subscription figures for 1993 demonstrate that over 2 million women subscribed to *Glamour* and 5 million to *Ladies' Home Journal* and 1.8 million teenage girls subscribed to *Seventeen* (Winklepleck, Restum, & Strange, 1993). A far greater number of readers may be exposed to these magazines by borrowing from friends or library or office access. For example, in a nationwide sample of teenage girls, 40% read *Seventeen*, 32% *Teen*, 30% *Young Miss*, and 20% *Sassy* (M. P. Levine & Smolak, 1996). Overall, 83% of teenage girls reported spending a mean of 4.3 hr a week reading magazines for pleasure or school (M. P. Levine & Smolak, 1996). M. P. Levine, Smolak, and Hayden (1994) found that approximately 42% of middle school age girls read fashion magazines on a frequent basis and rated them as a moderately important source of information about beauty and fitness. Seventy percent of those who read such magazines regularly endorsed them as an important source of beauty and fitness information (M. P. Levine, Smolak, & Hayden, 1994). A subgroup of 22% of the middle school girls who read fashion magazines regularly reported being very interested in emulating the models shown in these magazines. Given the significant number of women and girls exposed to print media, it is important to examine the content of these magazines and its relation to body image.

Evidence of a thin ideal. An interview study of 15-year-old girls suggested that print media were seen as a major force in the development of body image dissatisfaction (Wertheim, Paxton, Schutz, & Muir, 1997). Girls reported a comparison to models seen in these magazines, and their initial dieting experiences were triggered by diets found in these magazines. In a content analyses of the 106 pages of the April 1994 issue of *Teen*, Levine and Smolak (1996) found that out of 95 images of girls or women, all were thin, only two were African American, and only two could be interpreted as having moderately substantial waists or hips. In a similar type of content analysis, Andersen and DiDomenico (1992) examined the 10 most popular magazines read by women in the fall of 1987. Among these magazines, 57 diet advertisements or articles and 20 muscle development—toning ads or articles were published compared with 5 and 17, respectively, among the 10 magazines most read by men (Andersen & DiDomenico, 1992). The authors concluded that the 11 times greater prevalence of diet ads and articles reflects a dose-response effect of media exposure, paralleling the gender differences in the prevalence of body dissatisfaction and eating disorders (Andersen & DiDomenico, 1992).

Similar findings were demonstrated by the content analysis of Nemeroff, Stein, Diehl, and Smilack (1994) in an examination of traditional women's magazines (*Ladies' Home Journal, Good Housekeeping*), fashion magazines (*Cosmopolitan, Glamour*), and modern women's magazines (*New Woman, Ms.*) published during 1980–1991. Although the number of exercise articles per 6-month period was analogous for men's and women's magazines, the women's magazines published 13 times as many weight-loss articles and 6 times as many articles on beauty or improving one's appearance (Nemeroff et al., 1994).

In a recent study, Cusumano and Thompson (1997) surveyed college students for the level of readership of magazines and then coded the images contained in these periodicals to determine which magazines promoted the thinnest images. As Exhibit 3.2 illustrates, most of the magazines' images were in the lower range of the 9-point scale on the figural rating scale (see

EXHIBIT 3.2
Magazines by Mean Body Shape Rating

Magazine	Mean body shape rating
'Teen	1.86
Rolling Stone	2.00
Allure	2.29
YM (Young & Modern)	2.41
Mademoiselle	2.49
Newsweek	2.50
Health	2.50
Self	2.52
Vogue	2.54
Ebony	2.55
Entertainment Weekly	2.64
Details	2.65
Elle	2.70
New Woman	2.72
Fitness	2.84
Good Housekeeping	2.85
Cosmopolitan	2.92
Redbook	2.92
Shape	2.99
Prevention	3.00
Glamour	3.02
McCalls	3.17
Seventeen	3.19
Family Circle	3.32
Sports Illustrated	3.38
Woman's Day	3.41
Ladies' Home Journal	3.62
People	3.79
Essence	4.00

Body shapes were rated on a 9-point scale, with 1 representing the thinnest figure and 9 representing the heaviest figure. From "Body Image and Body Shape Ideals in Magazines: Exposure, Awareness, and Internalization," by D. L. Cusumano and J. K. Thompson, 1997, *Sex Roles, 37,* p. 710. Copyright 1997 by Plenum Publishing Corporation. Reprinted with permission.

Figure 2A.1 in chapter 2's Appendix 2A). Almost all of the magazines were in the 3 range, which is also typically the range that women select as their ideal body size.

It has also been suggested that mass media, particularly women's magazines, contribute to the development of body image disturbance and eating disorders by emphasizing the importance of beauty and external appearance in girls and women over more substantive issues, such as identity and independence (M. P. Levine & Smolak, 1996; Stice, 1994). For example, content analyses show that 45–62% of articles in teen fashion magazines focus on appearance and that only 30% or less of the articles focus on identity or self-development (Evans, Rutberg, Sather, & Turner, 1991; K. Pierce, 1990).

Correlational and descriptive investigations. In several correlational and survey studies, researchers have examined the influence of magazine consumption on body image and eating behaviors. For instance, Then (1992) found that 68% of women university students reported feeling worse about their physical appearance after reading women's magazines. Similarly, 33% of undergraduate women reported that fashion advertisements made them feel less satisfied with their appearance, and 50% reported that they wished they looked more like models in cosmetic advertisements.

In a large-scale survey conducted for *Psychology Today*, Garner (1997) asked both men and women how fashion models influenced their feelings about their own appearance. Twenty-seven percent of women versus only 12% of men always or very often compared themselves to models in magazines, and 28% of women and 19% of men carefully studied the shapes of models (Garner, 1997). However, when stratified on body image disturbance, 43% and 47%, respectively, of dissatisfied women compared themselves with or carefully examined the shape of models. Similarly, almost 67% of extremely dissatisfied women reported that thin models made them feel insecure about their weight and made them want to lose weight, and 45% reported feeling angry or resentful in response to such exposure (Garner, 1997). The greater prevalence of women versus men comparing themselves to models may be due to the greater likelihood that women will be judged on their appearance (see chapter 7 for a detailed discussion of this phenomenon by feminist theorists).

More compelling evidence is provided by M. P. Levine, Smolak, and Hayden (1994), who conducted a series of stepwise multiple regressions, predicting for age on body image and eating disorder behavior. These analyses revealed that the influence of magazine advertisements and articles on ideal shape and the girls' motivation to attain the ideal were highly correlated with weight-management behaviors, disordered eating, and a drive for thinness in adolescent girls ages 11–14 (Levine, Smolak, & Hayden, 1994).

It has also been hypothesized that the link with media exposure may be mediated by a third variable, such as a tendency to internalize messages regarding ideals for thinness and attractiveness (Heinberg & Thompson, 1995; Heinberg, Thompson, & Stormer, 1995). To investigate this hypothesis, Cusumano and Thompson (1997) assessed three aspects of sociocultural influence on appearance—print media exposure, awareness of societal ideals, and internalization of sociocultural messages—in a group of undergraduate women. As noted above, print media exposure was assessed by measuring the size of images in magazines actually read by the students. Awareness and internalization of societal values were measured with the Sociocultural Attitudes Towards Appearance Questionnaire (Heinberg, Thompson, & Stormer, 1995). These findings revealed that internalization was by far the most important correlate of body image disturbance. Thus, mere exposure and even awareness of societal pressures may not be sufficient to explain body image disturbance. Rather, individuals may vary with regards to their level of acceptance or "buying into" of the ideals propagated by the media.

Randomized experiments. As previously discussed, a number of studies suggest historical changes in the content of print media with regards to beauty, diet, exercise, and thinness (Garner et al., 1980; Silverstein, Perdue, Peterson, & Kelly, 1986; Wiseman et al., 1992) and the relationship between media exposure and body image (Garner, 1997; M. P. Levine, Smolak, & Hayden, 1994). However, only a handful of studies examined the immediate impact of exposure to mass media on body image. Waller, Hamilton, and Shaw (1992) found that participants with eating disorders demonstrated a significant increase in body size overestimation following exposure to photographs of models from popular fashion magazines. In a similar study, participants of varying levels of self-reported bulimic symptomatology were exposed to photographs of thin, average, and oversize models (Irving, 1990). Regardless of the severity of bulimic symptomatology, the participants who were shown photographs of thinner models reported lower levels of self-esteem and weight satisfaction than did participants who were shown photographs of larger models (Irving, 1990).

Although it appears clear that women with eating disorders are vulnerable to exposure to images of thin models, few experimental researchers have examined the effect of print media on normal weight, non-eating-disordered women. Stice and Shaw (1994) reported that a 3-min exposure to 12 photographs of models taken from popular women's magazines led to higher levels of depression, stress, guilt, shame, insecurity, and body image dissatisfaction than did similar exposure to photographs of average-size models. More recently, Kalodner (1997) examined the influence of photographs of thin models in a non-eating-disordered population of college men and women. She found that college women exposed to photographs of thin models from *Cosmopolitan* and *Vogue* magazines reported significantly higher levels of private body self-consciousness, body competence, and state anxiety (Kalodner, 1997). No effect was found for men. Thornton and Maurice (1997) exposed undergraduate women to 50 photographs of models for 8 seconds each. In comparison to a control condition, self-esteem was lower following exposure, whereas public self-consciousness and social anxiety remained unchanged. No differences were found for the effect of the exposure on varying levels of adherence to the attractiveness ideal (Thornton & Maurice, 1997). Although provocative, it is not clear whether there is a lasting effect on body image from media exposure or the mechanism between exposure and disturbance.

Summary. The previously reviewed research suggests that girls and women experience a significant rate of exposure to the print media, this source of information strongly endorses the thin ideal as well as proposes means of achieving it (e.g., diet, exercise) and that women, particularly those with eating disorder pathology, are vulnerable to increases in body image distress and general negative affect in response to this exposure. Future research is necessary to more fully examine the influence for exposure in non-eating-disordered women and teenage girls. In addition, it is not known whether changes following exposure are transitory or long lasting and whether some individuals are successful in challenging these media messages. On the basis of the available research, however, it would appear most useful to develop prevention and treatment strategies to help women combat problematic messages from print media.

Television

> On Fridays, everyone at work is talking about what was on *Friends* the night before. I wish I could watch but it just is too devastating to my self-esteem—all of those perfect looking, petite women—I would just hate my body after seeing it. (a 30-year-old, Caucasian woman in treatment for body image disturbance)

In the previous section, we demonstrated that individuals report significant exposure to the thin ideal and the importance of attractiveness through women's magazines. Television, however, is far more prevalent and accessible to most girls and women in American society.

Exposure. Almost without exception, every American household has at least one television, and in the average home, the television is on for over 7 hr per day (R. J. Harris, 1994). M. P. Levine and Smolak (1996) reported that children and adolescents spend more time watching television than in school; in fact, they engage in passive television viewing more than any other activity except sleeping. It has been approximated that the average person in the United States views over 35,000 television advertisements per year. Clearly, exposure to televised media messages can be said to be omnipresent.

Evidence for the thin ideal. A significant body of research suggests that television, like the print media, promotes the thin ideal. The vast majority of female characters are thinner than the average American woman. Indeed, fewer than 10% of women in television shows and commercials are overweight (Gonzalez-Lavin & Smolak, 1995; Silverstein, Perdue, Peterson, & Kelly, 1986). When television characters are overweight, they are often seen as fodder for humor or depicted as unattractive and undesirable. Similarly, overweight individuals in commercials are either "before" images in diet advertisements or targets of humor or disdain. Although still relatively rare, overweight men are two to five times more prevalent in commercials than overweight women (Kaufman, 1980; Silverstein, Perdue, Peterson, & Kelly, 1986).

These trends may be even more typical in television programs favored by younger women and adolescents. Gonzalez-Lavin and Smolak (1995) demonstrated that 94% of the female characters on programs favored by middle school age girls (e.g., *Beverly Hills 90210*) were below average in weight. Indeed, the girls' favorite characters were rated as at an average of 2.75 on a scale in which 4.5 represented the average woman (Gonzalez-Lavin & Smolak, 1995).

Like the literature examining the influence of magazines, content analyses demonstrate the prevalence of the thin ideal on television. Downs and Harrison (1985) studied over 4,000 commercials aired between 8:00 a.m. and 10:00 p.m. on the three major networks during 1 week of 1982. Some type of message touting the importance of appearance was found for every 1 out of 3.8 commercials, and 1 out of 11 commercials contained a direct message that beauty is an important and valuable attribute. Among commercials airing during Saturday morning cartoons, 14% related to enhancing one's appearance (Ogletree, Williams, Raffeld, Mason, & Fricke, 1990). Of these advertisements, the vast majority had a female announcer (91%) and were targeted to female consumers (86%).

Other researchers (Wiseman, Gunning, & Gray, 1993) tabulated the number of television commercials endorsing diet food or diet products aired on the three major American networks during the years 1973–1991. A highly significant increase in the number of both types of commercials was demonstrated, and the trend does not appear to be leveling off. Wiseman et al. (1993) concluded that currently "the pressure by the media to be thin and to diet is stronger than at any other time during the years 1973–1991" (p. 58).

Correlational investigations. Correlational studies indicate that exposure to television significantly relates to body image disturbance. M. C. Martin and Kennedy (1993) found that in a sample of 4th-, 8th-, and 12th-grade girls, a 2-item measure assessing their tendency to compare themselves with advertising models was negatively correlated ($r = -.48$) with self-reported physical attractiveness. Gonzalez-Lavin and Smolak (1995) found that number of hours of television exposure was unrelated to dieting and disordered eating behavior in middle school age girls. However, girls who watched more than 8 hr of television per week reported significantly greater body image dissatisfaction than girls with less television exposure.

Similar findings were demonstrated by Tiggemann and Pickering (1996). Measures of high school age girls' body image dissatisfaction and drive for thinness were examined along with reported television exposure during the previous week. Frequency of television exposure did not correlate with either body dissatisfaction or drive for thinness (Tiggemann & Pickering, 1996). However, it is interesting to note that amount of exposure to specific types of programs was related to dissatisfaction and drive for thinness. Specifically, exposure to soap operas and movies predicted body image dissatisfaction and exposure to music videos predicted drive for thinness, whereas amount of time spent watching sports was negatively correlated with one's body image dissatisfaction (Tiggemann & Pickering, 1996).

Thus, type of program watched, rather than mere television exposure, is an important variable to assess when examining media influences on body image. Individuals who endorse television as an appropriate source of influence regarding attractiveness may also be more vulnerable. Gonzalez-Lavin and Smolak (1995) found that middle school age girls who rated peers and television as important sources of information regarding attractiveness also reported greater body image dissatisfaction, use of weight-management techniques, and pathological beliefs about eating.

Similar findings were found for college age women using structural equation modeling (Stice, Schupak-Neuberg, Shaw, & Stein, 1994). Two-hundred and thirty-eight undergraduate women completed measures assessing media exposure, gender role endorsement, ideal body stereotype internalization, body dissatisfaction, and eating disorder symptomatology. Media exposure measured both how many fashion and health magazines participants had examined in the past month and the number of comedy, drama, and game shows they had viewed. Although the correlations between media exposure and body dissatisfaction and eating disorder symptomatology were only .10 and .25, respectively, the direct and indirect relations of these relationships, along with mediational variables, accounted for 43.5% of the variance in eating disorder symptomatology and 13.3% of the variance in ideal body stereotype internalization (Stice et al., 1994). Thus, in addition to a direct path between media exposure and eating disorder behaviors, media exposure leads to internalization of a slender ideal body shape, which in turn may lead to body dissatisfaction and eating disorder symptoms (Stice et al., 1994; see also the discussion in chapter 11 on integrative themes).

Randomized experiments. Although the vast majority of research evidence providing support for both the sociocultural theoretical model and impact of mass media are correlational in nature, a handful of controlled laboratory investigations have been conducted more recently and provide more convincing support for sociocultural theories. In one recent study, college age women viewed 10-min videotapes of commercials that either contained stimuli emphasizing societal ideals of thinness and attractiveness or contained neutral, non-appearance-related stimuli (Heinberg & Thompson, 1995). Results indicated that participants who viewed the videotape stressing the importance of thinness and attractiveness reported greater depression, anger, weight dissatisfaction, and overall appearance dissatisfaction than those given the neutral manipulation (Heinberg & Thompson, 1995). Furthermore, participants who possessed high dispositional levels of body image dissatisfaction showed increases in dissatisfaction with both weight and overall appearance following exposure to the experimental tape, whereas participants who had low levels of dispositional body image dissatisfaction had a reduction in state levels of both weight and appearance dissatisfaction following the exposure to the appearance-related video. All participants exposed to the neutral, control video demonstrated decreases in both weight and appearance dissatisfaction (Heinberg & Thompson, 1995).

Cattarin, Williams, Thomas, and Thompson (in press) recently extended this line of research. Similar to the findings of Heinberg and Thompson (1995) and Stice and Shaw (1994), results indicate that women viewing media images reflecting the current societal ideal reported greater increases in anger, anxiety, and depression; these findings were also moderated by dispositional levels of internalization of societal ideals for thinness and attractiveness (Cattarin et al., in press). (This study also contained a social comparison condition and, therefore, has relevance for a social comparison model of influence. See chapter 4 for a fuller discussion.)

These studies point to the importance of examining moderational and mediational effects. Although these results support the sociocultural theory of body image disturbance, it appears that only participants who are at the upper end of the continuum of body image dissatisfaction are particularly sensitive to the media exposure. This is analogous to findings of subgroups at risk with regard to print media exposure (Gonzalez-Lavin & Smolak, 1995). As more risk factors are identified, researchers will need to investigate how multiple risk factors are functionally interrelated.

Summary. As with the print media, clearly television is a pervasive, commonly used communicator of attractiveness standards. In addition, correlational studies suggest that exposure to television may lead to body image dissatisfaction and eating disorder symptomatology among girls and women. However, experimental studies suggest that particular groups of individuals (e.g., those with high dispositional levels of body image disturbance, those with higher internalization of societal ideals, or individuals who select certain types of television programs) may be at greater risk of body image dissatisfaction following media exposure. The vast majority of studies examining the influence of television are correlational in nature, and the direction of relationships is unclear. That is, it is not known whether exposure to electronic media is an etiological factor in body image and eating disturbance or whether these women choose to expose themselves to such images at a higher rate than their less distressed counterparts. Indeed, although most women are exposed to an inordinate amount of television and print media, not all exhibit body image dissatisfaction, and very few are likely to develop eating disorders or body dysmorphic disorder. Thus, future researchers should examine what biological, personality, social, and cognitive factors may place certain women at risk when exposed to the mass media.

Theories of Mass Media Influence

As outlined above, a vast amount of theoretical, correlational, and experimental evidence supports a link between the mass media and the communication of the thin and attractive ideal. However, little work expounds on the mechanisms by which the media actually influence women. Recently, M. P. Levine and Smolak (in press) explored various theories of mass media influence in the hopes of developing more efficacious primary prevention programs for individuals with eating disorders. They outlined two potential processes by which mass media contribute to the development of eating disorders among certain women. The first, the dual-pathway model, is based on the work of Stice and colleagues (Stice, 1994; Stice, Nemeroff, & Shaw, 1996; Stice et al., 1994). The dual-pathway model assumes that maladaptive messages in the mass media predispose individuals for bulimia nervosa when those messages are reinforced by family and peers and, when this occurs in the setting of low self-esteem, an unstable self concept and perceptions of being overweight. In addition, it is proposed that media influence may play a secondary role by "providing guidance concerning extreme dietary restriction, excessive exercising, and even purging" (M. P. Levine & Smolak, in press).

A second theory is derived from the work of M. P. Levine, Smolak, and colleagues (Levine & Smolak, 1992; Smolak & Levine, 1994, 1996; Smolak, Levine, & Gralen, 1993). This theory, the developmental transitions model, proposes that childhood predispositions, such as schematic beliefs about the importance of thinness, are developed and maintained by teasing and by family and peer modeling of weight concerns. In turn, these predispositions interact with simultaneous adolescent changes (e.g., weight increase at puberty, academic stress) within a context of social messages about the importance of thinness, the availability of dieting, and further teasing. These factors together predict the development of disordered eating (M. P. Levine & Smolak, in press).

Both theories appear to implicate not just the mass media but also concurrent pressures for slenderness from family and peers. This may help explain why primary prevention programs or treatment paradigms simply focusing on how to resist media influences have met with less than overwhelming results (M. P. Levine & Smolak, in press).

SPECIAL POPULATIONS

Historically, the larger body image literature as well as research focusing on sociocultural aspects of body image have focused on women. More recently, interest has grown in examining the influence of sociocultural ideals on a number of other populations. Studies examining children, men, minorities, disfigured individuals, and the evidence for weight prejudice are briefly reviewed.

Children

> Everybody feels like they are not good enough, not pretty enough, not skinny enough ... every time you open a magazine you always see beautiful people ... it is always blasted over TV about how ... you have to look good to be a good person. (a 15-year-old Australian girl, as quoted in Wertheim et al., 1997, p. 350)

Body image in children and adolescents has been well examined by a number of authors (see Heinberg, Wood, et al., 1995, for a review). However, far fewer researchers have examined sociocultural influences on children. Some researchers have examined media influences, particularly television, which were reviewed earlier in the chapter (Gonzalez-Lavin & Smolak, 1995; Ogletree et al., 1990). Several other researchers have examined sociocultural factors independent of mass media exposure.

Cultural notions about what is attractive and desirable are generally made before children enter school (Attie & Brooks-Gunn, 1987). Thus, children have learned a preference for athletic and lean body size before they have learned to read. Researchers have examined the influence of beliefs about thinness and likability among children (Oliver & Thelen, 1996). In a sample of third, fourth, and fifth graders, a belief that thinness will increase how much peers like them was a significant predictor of eating and body image concerns. This internalized belief about the importance of thinness was significant, whereas overt peer messages (e.g., teasing) did not predict eating behaviors or body image (Oliver & Thelen, 1996). Thus, even young children may be aware of the sociocultural pressures for thinness and against weight gain.

The influence of play in the socialization process and body image has also been assessed. For children, dolls that are socially acceptable and provide a tactile, tangible image of the body are a major representation of the body (Norton, Olds, Olive, & Dank, 1996). One of the most popular types of dolls, with over $1 billion in sales a year (and most criticized) is Mattel's Ken and Barbie (Norton et al., 1996). These dolls have been reproached because they reflect body ideals that are virtually impossible to attain. However, Mattel has said that the Barbie doll is an aspirational role model (Pedersen & Markee, 1991). Much of the discussion regarding Barbie has remained subjective; however, Norton et al. used *anthropometry* (the branch of anthropology that deals with the comparative measurements of the human body and its parts) and the rules of *allometry* (mathematical formulations used in anthropology) to scale the dolls to an adult height to determine the adjusted size dimensions that these dolls could assume. In turn, the dimensions for Barbie were compared with a cross-section of young

Australian women, models, and anorexic female patients. Ken's dimensions were compared with a cross-section of young Australian men and professional Australian football players. Z-score deviations were derived using these adult reference groups. Models yielded an average z score of -0.76, anorexic patients yielded an average z score of -1.31, and Barbie yielded a z score of -4.17 (Norton et al., 1996). This represents a probability of less than 1 in 100,000 women achieving Barbie's proportions—far from an "aspirational role model" (Norton et al., 1996). Ken's average z score was -2.1, with a corresponding probability of about 2 in 100.

The long-term effect of playing with these toys on children's developing body image is unclear. Studies examining the influence of sociocultural processes on children's body image remain largely correlational. Experimental investigations are necessary to further define the influence of the societal ideal and identify potential individual differences. Studies examining children also allow for longitudinal analysis. Unfortunately, studies exploring the long-term effects of media exposure on children have yet to be conducted.

It is interesting to note that in late 1997, in response to criticism from women's groups regarding Barbie's unrealistic body size, Mattel, Inc. announced the development of a new, more "realistic" Barbie who will have a "smaller chest, a larger waist, and smaller hips" (P. Davis, 1997, p. F1). Unfortunately, only 1 of the 24 new Barbies will have these new altered dimensions.

Men

> This month's cover image is a photo of an anonymous, bare-chested, well-built model whose shaving cream-covered face is partly obscured by his hand, as if he were halfheartedly trying to fend off the photographer. . . . It's rare to see a male model so clearly the object of the viewer's gaze; it's as if he were, well, a female model. (in reference to the June 1997 cover of *Men's Health* magazine; Handy, 1997, p. 87)

Perhaps because of body image's basis in the eating disorders literature, the vast majority of studies examining body image, particularly with regard to sociocultural influences, focuses on women. However, a few researchers are beginning to assess sociocultural pressures regarding men's physique and attractiveness. Shifting trends in the thin ideal as well as pressure to achieve that ideal have been well documented through archival research of print media marketed to women (Andersen & DiDomenico, 1992; Garner et al., 1980; Wiseman et al., 1992). In a recent study, Petrie et al. (1996) examined whether similar trends could be demonstrated by the two most popular men's magazines, GQ and *Esquire*. Article and advertisement content and male model body sizes were assessed during the period of 1960–1992. Linear trend analyses revealed that like those in women's magazines, the number of messages concerning physical activity and health have increased over time. However, in contrast to those in print media aimed at female audiences, messages concerning weight and physical attractiveness have declined since the late 1970s, and measurements of male model body sizes have not changed significantly since the 1960s (Petrie et al., 1996). Although pressures for thinness were absent for men, the authors hypothesized that the increasing pressure to be involved in fitness activity may lead to unhealthy body-changing practices (e.g., crash dieting, steroid use; Petrie et al., 1996).

Steroid use is one isolated area in the field of body image that has generally examined male samples. In a number of studies, researchers have examined steroid use prevalence, its relationship to body image, and the desire for weight loss or gain (Blouin & Goldfield, 1995; Drewnowski, Kurth, & Krahn, 1995; Schwerin et al., 1996). Investigations suggest that men who abuse steroids may be similar to women with eating disorders (Blouin & Goldfield, 1995). However, studies failed to examine the influence of sociocultural pressure on men's drive for a certain physique, exercise adherence, or steroid use.

Cash (1987, 1989, 1990a) has examined a rather neglected but important area in men's body image, namely, the impact of male pattern hair loss. Cash (1990a) noted that there is a long history of cultural symbolism associated with men's hair; however, over 30 million men in the United States and the majority of men over the age of 50 experience male pattern baldness. In one study, slides of age, race, and physically matched men were shown to both sexes (Cash, 1990a). The slide stimuli differed in baldness versus full hair. Generally, the balding men created less favorable initial impressions, including lower ratings of physical attractiveness, overestimations of age, and assumptions regarding less desirable personal and interpersonal characteristics (Cash, 1990a).

Men with male pattern baldness also reported a deleterious experience related to their body image changes. When nonbalding controls were compared with men having either visible male pattern baldness or considerable male pattern baldness, several important differences were demonstrated (Cash, 1987, 1989). Among men with male pattern baldness, significant levels of reported stress, distress, and coping efforts were reported for both the initial and cumulative effects of hair loss. Sixty percent of participants with considerable baldness reported negative social and emotional effects due to their hair loss; these results were even more pronounced in younger men, those with earlier onset of baldness, and those who were single and uninvolved in intimate relationships (Cash, 1989). When nonbalding men were asked to imagine their personal reaction to hair loss, the vast majority expected significant increases in negative emotions and social reactions, greater preoccupation with their hair, and greater behavioral efforts to cope with balding. Only 8% of nonbalding men indicated that they would not be bothered at all if they began to experience hair loss (Cash, 1987, 1989). Although a number of studies have been conducted on the body image of men with male pattern baldness, almost no data exists for the impact of societal ideals among men. Future descriptive, correlational, and experimental studies are clearly needed.

Minorities–Acculturation

> I don't hear that a lot [referring to a discussion of being fat]. I hang out with black people and they don't care—we don't worry if we're fat because we'd all be drawn away from that. We want to talk about what's going on, you know, about where we're going for lunch. We're not concerned with that. (a female African American adolescent quoted in Parker, Nichter, Vuckovic, Sims, & Ritenbaugh, 1995, p. 108)

Differences in body image, dieting, and eating disordered behavior among Caucasians and ethnic minorities have been demonstrated in children (Striegel-Moore, Schreiber, Pike, Wilfley, & Rodin, 1995), adolescents (Story, French, Resnick, & Blum, 1995), and adult women (Kumanyika, 1994; Rand & Kuldau, 1990; J. C. Rosen & Gross, 1987; Rucker & Cash, 1992). These differences have often been explained as due to differing cultural ideals of appropriate thinness (Altabe, 1996). For instance, African American women have been shown to have a greater window of acceptable weight, and African American women describing themselves as normal weight are significantly heavier than Caucasian women who believe they are normal weight (Rand & Kuldau, 1990; Rucker & Cash, 1992). Additionally, African Americans differ from Caucasians in the belief that weight is infinitely mutable and easy to alter (Kumanyika, 1994). However, a number of researchers have begun to look at different sociocultural influences among minorities and the influence of acculturation.

Although differing cultural standards among minorities is described as a potential buffer against eating disorders, some authors have suggested that the psychological effect on women of color judging themselves by the White American standard of beauty championed by society may lead to greater vulnerability to body image dissatisfaction and eating disorder symptomatology (Iijima Hall, 1995; Root, 1990). Racial identity attitudes have been demonstrated as significant predictors in body image among African American women. Women with pro-Black/anti-White attitudes demonstrate more favorable attitudes about their physical appearance (S. M. Harris, 1995). Similarly, women in the process of rejecting pro-White perspectives and immersing themselves in the Black culture reported satisfaction with specific body areas and more concern with engaging in health behaviors (S. M. Harris, 1995).

Differentiation has been made among minority populations born and raised in the United States and those with a shorter length of residence. It is hypothesized that individuals socialized in the American culture will be more likely to endorse and internalize a thin ideal than individuals socialized in another culture. For instance, non-Latina White women, Latina women born in the United States, and Latina women who immigrated after age 17 differed significantly in their selection of an ideal body type (Lopez, Blix, & Blix, 1995). Latinas, as a group, identified a heavier ideal body size compared with White women born in the United States. However, Latinas born in the United States identified an even smaller ideal body size than did their White counterparts, whereas those who immigrated chose a significantly larger ideal (Lopez et al., 1995).

In contrast, acculturation was not found to be related to the endorsement of the thin beauty ideal or eating disordered behavior among Asian American women (Yoshimura, 1995). Similarly, researchers examining an adolescent Mexican American population failed to find a relationship between acculturation levels and eating disorder symptomatology, self-esteem, body dissatisfaction, or thinness of ideal and attractive figures (G. W. Joiner & Kushubeck, 1996). Based on the latter two studies, body image disturbance and eating disorder pathology may no longer be an exclusively U.S. Caucasian phenomenon. Thus, even women with limited or recent exposure to the Western ideal may experience such difficulties. For instance, a recent study found that Ukranian women exposed to Western media (TV, movies, music, videos, magazines) had higher levels of internalization of sociocultural values regarding thinness; additionally, internalization was associated with higher levels of body dissatisfaction (Biloukha & Utermohler, 1997).

Disfigurement

A number of researchers have examined the impact of disfigurement on body image (Bernstein, 1990; Heinberg, Fauerbach, Spence, & Hackerman, 1997; Pruzinsky, 1992; Pruzinsky & Cash, 1990). Although the social impact of disfigurement is well established (Browne et al., 1985; Riva & Molinari, 1995; Tudahl, Blades, & Munster, 1987), little work examines the impact of sociocultural factors or social pressures on those with disfigurements. A similar paucity of literature exists on the body image of individuals with disabilities, which is discussed in the next section.

It has been suggested that sociocultural myths lead to prejudice toward facially disfigured persons. These myths include the myth of surgery (plastic–cosmetic surgery is a magic wand that can miraculously remove disfigurement and solve all other problems), the myth of ugliness (ugliness is a reflection of moral character or intelligence), and the myth of success (disfigurement rules out success in life; Partridge, 1996). Several theories have been offered to explain sociocultural pressures for bodily perfection as they relate to stigmatizing disfigured individuals (E. Robinson, Clarke, & Cooper, 1996). For instance, being confronted by someone who has a disability forces individuals to confront their own vulnerability. Similarly, because of the strong association made between health and good looks, people may fear that a disability is contagious. Finally, because interacting with others having a disability is a relatively novel experience, people may be uncertain as to how to behave (E. Robinson, Clarke, et al., 1996). The preceding myths support the importance of public education and social change rather than only focusing interventions on those with disabilities.

Researchers have also discussed the impact of media messages on individuals who are unable to meet the societal ideal. For example, Partridge (1990) discussed that early in childhood evil characters are portrayed as ugly (e.g., evil stepmother) whereas good characters are portrayed as beautiful (e.g., Snow White). This message continues in adult stories and films, often with an evil character displaying some type of deformity (e.g., Freddy Kruger in *Nightmare on Elm Street*).

An examination of body image among individuals with disfigurement is a relatively new, unexplored research area. As this review attests, little work examines the impact that sociocultural ideals and the mass media may have on individuals who fall far from the endorsed ideal of attractiveness or body shape. However, these individuals demonstrate significant heterogeneity in body image, and individual differences as well as the means of maintaining body image integrity should be explored.

Disabilities

As previously noted, individuals who do not meet the societal notion of "average" have generally been ignored in the body image literature. Although the Americans With Disabilities Act may have led to greater opportunities for persons with disabilities, little is known about the effect a disability may have on body image. In one study, Rybarczyk, Nyenhuis, Nicholas, Cash, and Kaiser (1995) examined body image disturbance perceived social stigma, and its relation to psychosocial adjustment in patients with leg amputations. The outcome was defined by a depression scale, a quality of life scale, and by a rating from the patients' prosthetists. Regression analyses indicated that subjective body satisfaction was a significant independent predictor for all three adjustment measures, even after controlling for such factors as age at time of amputation, time since amputation, site of amputation, self-report of health, and perceived social support (Rybarczyk et al., 1995). In addition, perceived social stigma was a significant independent predictor of depression, accounting for 18% of the variance in depression scores.

Theoretical accounts explain these findings as a reaction to "the myth of bodily perfection" (Stone, 1995). This myth pervades American society and states that everyone "can and should strive to achieve perfect bodies" (Stone, 1995, p. 413). Stone asserted that this myth encourages the definition of only a minority of the population as people with disabilities, leading those with hidden disabilities to hide in shame, and justifies treating people as "other." As discussed with regard to disfigurement, significant research is needed to better understand the needs of those with disabilities.

Weight Prejudice

A large amount of research suggests that just as thinness is valued and rewarded by the current society, its opposite, obesity, is abhorred and punished. It has been suggested that stigmatization of fatness is learned at a relatively young age (Attie & Brooks-Gunn, 1987; see Lerner & Jovanovic, 1990, for an excellent review). For example, kindergarten children express unfavorable personality characteristics about overweight people (S. C. Wooley & Wooley, 1983). Similarly, ethnically diverse first graders were assessed after viewing same-gender silhouettes representing various body types (Goldfield & Chrisler, 1995). Children were less likely to want to befriend an endomorphic (overweight) child (Goldfield & Chrisler, 1995). Prejudice against obese children has also been demonstrated in diverse samples of adults, including physicians, nurses, psychologists, physical and occupational therapists, and social workers (N. Goodman, Dornbusch, Richardson, & Hasdorf, 1963; Richardson, Goodman, Hasdorf, & Dornbusch, 1961). These professional adults rated obese children as less likable than children with a variety of physical handicaps, disfigurements, and deformities (N. Goodman et al., 1963; Richardson et al., 1961). Prejudice against obese persons has also been demonstrated among college students (Rothblum, Miller, & Garbutt, 1988; Tiggemann & Rothblum, 1988). Studies also suggest therapists' judgments differ when presented with case vignettes involving obese versus nonobese clients (Agell & Rothblum, 1991) and that very obese persons may suffer employment discrimination (Rothblum, Brand, Miller, & Oetjen, 1990).

Recently, a number of authors and interest groups (e.g., National Association to Advance Fat Acceptance, Inc.) have attempted to create a backlash against the assumption that thinness equals beauty and that obesity should be associated with negative. This has led to the development of Boycott Anorexic Marketing, which encourages consumers to boycott products that promote the thin ideal by using extremely thin models (see also chapters 1 and 2). More compelling, some theorists have suggested that this denigration of obesity is an example of prejudice that would be unacceptable if targeted toward any other group. W. C. Goodman (1995) noted that

> weight prejudice is a true form of bigotry in every sense of the word. Like racism, it is based on visible cues; i.e., the fat person is discrim-

inated against primarily because of the way she looks. Like anti-Semitism, it defines an entire group of people numbering in the millions within a narrow range of negative characteristics and behaviors. Like sexism, it elevates the status of one group of people at the expense of another. . . . In short, weight prejudice is a new twist on a timeless and ugly pattern of human social dynamics. (p. 7)

ASSESSMENT

Assessment of the sociocultural aspect of body image is still in its relative infancy. For many years, a major limitation in the literature was the unavailability of a measure to assess an individual's likelihood to be aware of and internalize the societally endorsed belief that thinness and attractiveness are important and vital for body image satisfaction. Although the prevalence of a societal ideal has been well documented (see Heinberg, 1996, for a review), individuals differ in their acceptance of this pervasive standard of attractiveness. One measure discussed earlier, the Sociocultural Attitudes Towards Appearance Questionnaire (Heinberg, Thompson, et al., 1995) was developed to assess women's awareness and acceptance of societally sanctioned standards of thinness and attractiveness. This measure has two distinct subscales measuring recognition and internalization of societal standards of appearance. Both subscales converge with other measures of body image and eating disturbance. However, regression analyses indicate that the internalization subscale significantly predicts body image disturbance and eating disordered behavior (Heinberg, Thompson, et al., 1995). A revision of this scale was recently developed by Cusumano and Thompson (1997). A copy of the Sociocultural Attitudes Towards Appearance Questionnaire can be found in Appendix 3A (female version) and Appendix 3B (male version). Details about this and other measures discussed in this section are contained in Table 3.1.

A few additional measures have also been developed to assess the influence of sociocultural factors in the development and maintenance of body image disturbance. For example, a semistructured interview has been used to assess participants' awareness of sociocultural pressures and the influence these pressures have had on their body image (Murray, Touyz, & Beumont, 1996). Stice and colleagues have developed a measure that assesses internalization of stereotypes of the ideal feminine figure (Stice et al., 1994; Stice, Nemeroff, & Shaw, 1996; Stice, Shaw, & Nemeroff, 1998; Stice, Ziemba, Margolis, & Flick, 1996). A copy of this instrument can be found in Appendix 3C. A measure assessing perceived sociocultural pressure to lose weight and have a thin body type has also been developed by Stice, Ziemba, et al. (1996) and is contained in Appendix 3D. Media modeling scales have also been developed (M. P. Levine, Smolak, & Hayden,

1994; Stice, Ziemba, et al., 1996), along with instruments to assess media consumption of magazines (Cusumano & Thompson, 1997; Stice et al., 1994; Strowman, 1996) and television (Stice et al., 1994; Strowman, 1996). Additionally, a measure has been developed to assess endorsement of the youth ideal in body image (Gupta & Schork, 1993), and one that assesses sociocultural aspects of amputation (Rybarczyk et al., 1995).

Although the sociocultural explanation has informed the development of a number of instruments, limitations are plentiful. For example, numerous measures focus on media "pressure," "consumption," and "internalization." However, these constructs lack clear definition, and their interrelationship has not been examined. Furthermore, the literature lacks multidimensional scales that include sociocultural elements or scales that assess an individual's ability to be critical of sociocultural messages. The addition of such instruments and items will help complete the assessment needs for this theoretical explanation.

TREATMENT

Treatment interventions designed to combat the negative influence of sociocultural pressure have been described for girls, female college students, and overweight adult women. For instance, Girls in the 90's is an eating disorder prevention program for preadolescent girls that provides girls with an understanding of societal pressures for thinness (S. S. Friedman, 1996). This program relies on role-play, movement, and art to help girls express their feelings and support one another (S. S. Friedman, 1996). Although well described, this intervention has not been empirically tested.

Because of the hypothesized importance of peers in prevention programs, Gleason (1995) developed an electronic bulletin board to help college women confront social pressure for thinness and attractiveness. Within 1 month of its development, this bulletin board became highly active with a number of women discussing the social and political aspects of body image (Gleason, 1995). Unfortunately, an assessment of efficacy has not yet been conducted.

Redefining standards of beauty has been identified as an instrumental aspect of the If Only I Were Thin treatment program for obese women (B. E. Robinson & Bacon, 1996). Because slimness was an unrealistic goal for most of the clients, they were taught about historical changes in the thin standard, effect of internalization of standards, and more diverse definitions of attractiveness. These goals were largely achieved through psychoeducation, cognitive restructuring, and guided imagery. Other treatment components included increasing daily activities, an examination of eating patterns, and assertiveness skills to confront the prejudice and discrimination faced by overweight individuals. The treatment program was com-

TABLE 3.1
Sociocultural Measures

Instrument	Author(s)	Description	Reliability 1, 2	Standardization sample	Address of author
Sociocultural Attitudes Towards Appearance Scale	Heinberg, Thompson, & Stormer (1995)	14 items assess recognition and acceptance of societal standards of appearance; two subscales: Awareness and Internalization	IC: awareness (.71), internalization (.88)	College students (344 female)	J. Kevin Thompson, PhD Department of Psychology University of South Florida 4202 Fowler Avenue Tampa, FL 33620-8200
Sociocultural Attitudes Towards Appearance Scale	Cusumano & Thompson (1997)	21 items assess recognition and acceptance of societal standards of appearance; two subscales: Awareness and Internalization	IC: awareness (.83), internalization (.89)	College students (175 female)	J. Kevin Thompson, PhD Department of Psychology University of South Florida 4202 Fowler Avenue Tampa, FL 33620-8200
Perceived Sociocultural Pressure Scale	Stice, Ziemba, et al. (1996)	8-point scale assessing perceived pressure from the media to have a thin body	IC: .87 TR: .93 (2 weeks)	125 high school and undergraduate students	Eric Stice, PhD Department of Psychiatry Stanford University 401 Quarry Road Stanford, CA 94305-5542
Ideal Body Internalization Scale–Revised	Stice et al., (1998)	10-item measure assessing agreement with socioculturally endorsed view of the ideal woman	IC: .88 TR: .59 (1 year)	218 high school students	Eric Stice, PhD Department of Psychiatry Stanford University 401 Quarry Road Stanford, CA 94305-5542
Media Exposure Survey	Strowman (1996)	Queries exposure to magazines and television at present and during senior year of high school	IC: female body image magazines (.71), male body image magazines (.35)	115 male and female undergraduates	Shelley Strowman, PhD 9 Carver Hill Court Natick, MA 01760

Scale	Citation	Description	Reliability	Sample	Contact
None	Murray et al. (1996)	Semistructured interview assessing awareness of ideals, perception of nature of ideals, perceived gender difference in ideals, and perceptions of influence of pressures	None reported	None reported	Sara Murray, PhD Department of Psychology Faculty of Arts and Sciences University of Western Sydney Macarthur, P.O. Box 555 Campbelltown, New South Wales 2560
Participant Magazine Assessment Tool	Cusumano & Thompson (1997)	Assesses time spent per month reading 69 selected magazine titles	None reported	175 female under-graduates	J. Kevin Thompson, PhD Department of Psychology University of South Florida 4202 Fowler Avenue Tampa, FL 33620-8200
Media Consumption Scale	Stice et al. (1994)	6-item scale assessing exposure to magazines and television over past 3 months	TR: .76 (3 weeks)	238 female under-graduates	Eric Stice, PhD Department of Psychiatry Stanford University 401 Quarry Road Stanford, CA 94305-5542
Amputation-Related Body Image Scale	Rybarczyk et al. (1995)	11-item scale assessing body image and related social concerns because of amputation	IC: .85	112 adults with a leg amputated	Bruce Rybarczyk, PhD Department of Psychology Rush-Presbyterian St. Luke's Medical Center 1653 West Congress Parkway Chicago, IL 60612
Model Emulation	Levine, Smolak, & Hayden (1994)	8-item scale assessing emulation of models on TV and in magazines	IC: .76	285 girls ages 10.87–15.56	Linda Smolak, PhD and Michael Levine, PhD Department of Psychology Kenyon College Gambier, OH 43022-9623

Note. IC = internal consistency; TR = test–retest reliability.

pleted by 47 women, and significant changes were demonstrated on fat phobia, activity level, depression, and self-esteem (B. E. Robinson & Bacon, 1996). However, no control group was present in this study.

Other researchers have described possible interventions specifically targeting the negative effect of mass media messages promoting the thin ideal (Jasper, 1993; Shaw & Waller, 1995). Suggestions include helping individuals be more selective in their use of the visual media, discouraging social comparison, and decreasing willingness to accept the media presentation of the ideal (Shaw & Waller, 1995). It is suggested that such interventions be preventative, should be conducted in adolescence or earlier, and should be part of the academic curriculum (McGill, Lawlis, Selby, Mooney, & McCoy, 1983).

Cash (1996) also emphasized the importance of psychoeducational procedures as part of his approach and provided information geared to promote a "rational view of the effects of objective appearance on people's lives" (p. 93) and to normalize their concerns (see also Cash, 1997). In addition, his treatment also focuses on identifying and challenging appearance assumptions, including strategies for combating sociocultural pressures regarding appearance. For example, a woman may believe that unless she looks like women in fashion magazines, she is fat and unattractive. Challenging and disputing this belief may involve education regarding the fabricated quality of print images, the relative rarity of the model's proportions, and the inappropriateness of such an individual as a comparison target. Modifying self-defeating body image behaviors is a further component of Cash's treatment protocol. This may involve canceling subscriptions to fashion magazines or deliberately engaging in more appropriate social comparisons.

We should note that both Cash's (1996, 1997) and J. C. Rosen's (1996a, 1996b, 1997) cognitive–behavioral strategies advocate identifying and challenging negative thoughts associated with a comparison with an unrealistic societal ideal; this type of cognitive procedure is one of the essential components of their program. Because it is specific to social appearance comparisons, which is the model reviewed in the next chapter, we delay our discussion of this treatment procedure until that section of chapter 4.

In a comparative study designed to assess the efficacy of psychoeducational procedures, Stormer and Thompson (1995, 1998) compared a control condition (health information) with an active treatment consisting of information on the thin ideal, history of changing ideals, and strategies for challenging these appearance assumptions. (See Exhibit 3.3 for a summary of this treatment.) Results indicated that only the experimental group showed significant decreases in appearance and weight-related anxiety and internalization of the sociocultural ideal (Stormer & Thompson, 1995, 1998). This study suggests that even a brief (30 min) intervention may be

EXHIBIT 3.3
Psychoeducational Program

Part A of the program focuses on issues pertinent to women.

Introduction (2–3 min)

The program first discusses the female beauty ideal that is presented in mass media and how it causes many women distress because they cannot live up to the very high standard. The presenter emphasizes that some women have no problem attaining this image but that many others have concerns about their own weight or appearance and overall self-satisfaction when comparing themselves with these media images. The introduction also discusses the pressures on women to be beautiful and thin, the prevalence of media images of the attractiveness ideal, and the definition of sociocultural factors (influences from the society in which one lives that can change the way one feels about himself or herself). Slides and examples from print media that promote the thin–attractive ideal are also presented.

History (2–3 min)

This is a brief presentation of the historical context of constrictive beauty ideals for women. It emphasizes that the current societal focus on thinness and attractiveness has evolved from earlier beauty practices that urged women to change their bodies to fit the current trend. Examples include foot binding, high heels (modern-day version of the same), corsets, breast implants, and other plastic surgery. Slides of examples are shown.

Body of Presentation: Part A (8–9 min)

This section focuses on current societal pressures toward female thinness that are promoted in the media and how these beauty images are often altered (either through the person's own cosmetic surgery or by changing the photograph itself), which makes the ideal an impossible one for most women to aspire to. (Pictures of women who are models for cosmetic surgery, examples of airbrushing to remove flaws, and a computer-shrunk picture of the experimenter are shown.) Participants are told that they might be aware of some of the image manipulations that occur in the media (that is not Julia Roberts's body on the *Pretty Woman* poster) but that they might be surprised at the lengths to which the media try to convince women that they need to fit this ideal. (Numerous other print media examples are shown.) Participants are confronted with facts after they see all the thin models: Less than 5% of women in America fit the body size and beauty ideal as presented in the media; the average model's body weight is approximately 30% under healthy weight as determined by normative tables; the average American woman is 5 ft 4 in. (1.63 m) and 142 lb (64.41 kg), where the average female model is 5 ft 9 in. (1.72 m) and 110 lb (49.90 kg). Information is also provided about the weight set-point theory and negative effects of dieting (i.e., weight naturally stays at a healthy point and dieting interferes with the body's normal processes, namely, digestion and metabolic activity, which can affect weight gain).

Part B of the program focuses on issues pertinent to men.

Transition (1–2 min)

At this time, the point is made that whereas women have dealt with these pressures for a long time, men have only recently begun to feel a strong focus

Exhibit continues on following page

EXHIBIT 3.3 (*Continued*)

on their appearance. Brief mention is made of men's powdered wigs and hosiery in the Renaissance and Victorian times; however the focus is on current images of men in the mass media that now present a male attractiveness ideal nearly as difficult to attain as the female ideal.

Body of Presentation: Part B (8–9 min)

In this part of the program, presenters show examples of current male images of attractiveness that are becoming more common in the mass media (i.e., the "Diet Coke guy," models in *GQ* and *Men's Health* magazines, movie stars such as Brad Pitt, Antonio Banderas, and Tom Cruise). Then information is presented detailing the difficulty involved for "average" men to look like these ideals, such as the enormous time commitment at the gym (often with dangerous steroid enhancement), rigorous attention to diet, and, more commonly, plastic surgery. The increasing incidence of male eating disorders is covered, as is the strong push that male executives are now getting to look and act younger to maintain their position in the business world. A focus is also made on the manipulation of male images in the media as well, using techniques similar to those used on female images.

Summary and Conclusions (1–2 min)

This segment wraps up the presentation by summarizing the main points that were covered: Female beauty ideals have a long history and are currently very hard for normal women to attain; media images select a very small range of the diversity of female body types to glorify, even those images are altered to look more perfect; and men are beginning to face some of the same appearance pressures that women have endured for a long time, leading to a higher incidence of body image concerns and eating disorders. Participants are reminded that these media images, although ever present, are not representative of what real Americans look like and that these appearances often do not reflect reality.

From Stormer and Thompson (1998).

efficacious in helping women improve their body image. If such information was disseminated more widely, the "normative discontent" of American women might be reduced.

M. P. Levine and Smolak (in press) outlined cutting-edge strategies for primary prevention of eating disorders that addressed sociocultural pressures. They suggested comprehensive programs that involve both the school and community to achieve the following: Use mass media to educate the public on the importance of eating disorders, promote personal and systemic changes targeting risk factor reduction, and enhance protective factors (M. P. Levine & Smolak, in press). By these means, they hope that the mass media can be transformed from a risk factor to a tool for advocacy and health promotion.

Other authors have suggested that treatment of the individual will not help resolve the social, political, and economic forces that support and sustain the unrealistic thin ideal (Hesse-Biber, 1996). Instead, a number of aspects of social activism should be endorsed. For example, Hershey's removed an advertisement for a chocolate bar that claimed "you can never be too rich or too thin" after a public interest group, Anorexia Nervosa and Associated Disorders, in concert with others, engaged in a letter-writing campaign (Jasper, 1993). Jasper suggested that women fight back against media-endorsed images by writing letters of complaint to the presidents of corporations whose advertisements are offensive and by occupying media time and space with alternative messages (e.g., press releases, television interviews).

Given the well-documented relationships among sociocultural influences, mass media, and body image disturbance, it is quite surprising that so few treatment interventions have been developed and empirically tested (Stormer & Thompson, 1995, 1998). Development of interventions and studies demonstrating their efficacy and comparing interventions to control groups are desperately needed.

CONCLUSIONS

The sociocultural explanation of body image disturbance is the most discussed and perhaps the most empirically validated of body image theories (Heinberg, 1996). An extant literature demonstrates the pervasiveness of the thin ideal, changes in ideal body shape over time, and the impact of the mass media on the body images of women. However, a complete explanation of the role of society in body image is lacking. Although all women in American society are presented the thin ideal through a variety of media, individuals fall on the continuum of normative discontent (Rodin et al., 1985), with some women reporting very little body image dissatisfaction whereas others develop extreme appearance disparagement.

The first generation of studies, those implicating the sociocultural explanation, has been sufficiently conducted. The next generation of studies needs to be conducted in two primary areas: (a) the identification of individual differences that moderate or mediate sociocultural pressures for thinness and attractiveness and (b) the development and demonstrated efficacy of treatment interventions designed to combat sociocultural pressures.

Living in a culture that promotes an almost unachievable ideal has been hypothesized to be a "setting condition" for the development of body image disturbance and eating disorder symptomatology (Heinberg, 1996; J. K. Thompson, 1992). Although this setting condition may be necessary, it is not a sufficient explanation. Rather, the interaction between the present sociocultural pressures and other theorized factors reviewed in this book may lead certain individuals to cross a threshold into disturbance. Furthermore, sociocultural pressures may be communicated not only through the mass media but also through family and peers. Integrative theories, such as those outlined by M. P. Levine and Smolak (in press), suggest that both eating disturbance and internalization of sociocultural ideals are multidetermined. Additionally, in this chapter, we identified a number of potential individual differences that deserve further consideration. Internalization of standards, social comparison tendency, and premorbid body image dissatisfaction may interact with cultural standards, resulting in significant body image disturbance. Personality variables may also be only partially responsible in moderating and mediating the influence of society. Demographic variables, such as ethnicity, somatotype, gender, age, and presence of disabilities, may interact with sociocultural processes. Further exploration and development of testable models are necessary to explore the complex influence of society and media on body image.

It is surprising that although the sociocultural explanation is well validated and accepted by body image researchers, so few have examined possible interventions. Preventative, psychoeducational programs for preadolescents should be developed as well as interventions designed for populations at risk. Interventions focusing on sociocultural aspects should be implemented into all body image and eating disorder treatments. For all types of interventions, efficacy should be empirically demonstrated, initially compared with a no-treatment control and later with other acceptable treatments. Finally, individual interventions alone will never fully be successful as long as society, as a whole, continues to accept an unhealthy, emaciated image as its ideal. Social activism may be necessary to truly prevent the majority of young girls from growing up hating their bodies and appearances.

APPENDIX 3A
SOCIOCULTURAL ATTITUDES TOWARDS APPEARANCE QUESTIONNAIRE–REVISED: FEMALE VERSION

Please read each of the following items, and circle the number that best reflects your agreement with the statement.

Completely disagree		Neither agree nor disagree		Completely agree
1	2	3	4	5

1. I would like my body to look like the women who appear in TV shows and movies.   1 2 3 4 5
2. I believe that clothes look better on women that are in good physical shape.   1 2 3 4 5
3. Music videos that show women who are in good physical shape make me wish that I were in better physical shape.   1 2 3 4 5
4. I do not wish to look like the female models who appear in magazines.   1 2 3 4 5
5. I tend to compare my body to TV and movie stars.   1 2 3 4 5
6. In our society, fat people are regarded as attractive.   1 2 3 4 5
7. Photographs of physically fit women make me wish that I had a better muscle tone.   1 2 3 4 5
8. Attractiveness is very important if you want to get ahead in our culture.   1 2 3 4 5
9. It's important for people to look attractive if they want to succeed in today's culture.   1 2 3 4 5
10. Most people believe that a toned and physically fit body improves how you look.   1 2 3 4 5
11. People think that the more attractive you are, the better you look in clothes.   1 2 3 4 5
12. In today's society, it's not important to always look attractive.   1 2 3 4 5
13. I wish I looked like the women pictured in magazines who model underwear.   1 2 3 4 5
14. I often read magazines and compare my appearance to the female models.   1 2 3 4 5
15. People with well-proportioned bodies look better in clothes.   1 2 3 4 5
16. A physically fit woman is admired for her looks more than someone who is not fit and toned.   1 2 3 4 5
17. How I look does not affect my mood in social situations.   1 2 3 4 5
18. People find individuals who are in shape more attractive than individuals who are not in shape.   1 2 3 4 5
19. In our culture, someone with a well-built body has a better chance of obtaining success.   1 2 3 4 5
20. I often find myself comparing my physique to that of athletes pictured in magazines.   1 2 3 4 5
21. I do not compare my appearance to people I consider very attractive.   1 2 3 4 5

APPENDIX 3B
SOCIOCULTURAL ATTITUDES TOWARDS APPEARANCE QUESTIONNAIRE–REVISED: MALE VERSION

Please read each of the following items, and circle the number that best reflects your agreement with the statement.

Completely disagree		Neither agree nor disagree		Completely agree
1	2	3	4	5

1. I would like my body to look like the men who appear in TV shows and movies.   1 2 3 4 5
2. I believe that clothes look better on men that are in good physical shape.   1 2 3 4 5
3. Music videos that show women who are in good physical shape make me wish that I were in better physical shape.   1 2 3 4 5
4. I do not wish to look like the male models who appear in magazines.   1 2 3 4 5
5. I tend to compare my body to TV and movie stars.   1 2 3 4 5
6. In our society, fat people are regarded as attractive.   1 2 3 4 5
7. Photographs of physically fit men make me wish that I had a better muscle tone.   1 2 3 4 5
8. Attractiveness is very important if you want to get ahead in our culture.   1 2 3 4 5
9. It's important for people to look attractive if they want to succeed in today's culture.   1 2 3 4 5
10. Most people believe that a toned and physically fit body improves how you look.   1 2 3 4 5
11. People think that the more attractive you are, the better you look in clothes.   1 2 3 4 5
12. In today's society, it's important to always look attractive.   1 2 3 4 5
13. I wish I looked like the men pictured in magazines who model underwear.   1 2 3 4 5
14. I often read magazines and compare my appearance to the male models.   1 2 3 4 5
15. People with well-proportioned bodies look better in clothes.   1 2 3 4 5
16. A physically fit man is admired for his looks more than someone who is not fit and toned.   1 2 3 4 5
17. How I look does not affect my mood in social situations.   1 2 3 4 5
18. People find individuals who are in shape more attractive than individuals who are not in shape.   1 2 3 4 5
19. In our culture, someone with a well-built body has a better chance of obtaining success.   1 2 3 4 5
20. I often find myself comparing my physique to that of athletes pictured in magazines.   1 2 3 4 5
21. I do not compare my appearance to people I consider very attractive.   1 2 3 4 5

For more information, see Cusumano and Thompson (1997).

APPENDIX 3C
IDEAL BODY INTERNALIZATION SCALE–REVISED

We want to know what you think attractive women look like. How much do you agree with these statements?

Strongly agree	Somewhat agree	Neither agree nor disagree	Somewhat disagree	Strongly disagree	
1	2	3	4	5	

1. Thin women are more attractive.	1	2	3	4	5
2. Tall women are more attractive.	1	2	3	4	5
3. Women with toned bodies are more attractive.	1	2	3	4	5
4. Slim women are more attractive.	1	2	3	4	5
5. Women who are in shape are more attractive.	1	2	3	4	5
6. Slender women are more attractive.	1	2	3	4	5
7. Women with long legs are more attractive.	1	2	3	4	5
8. Curvy women are more attractive.	1	2	3	4	5
9. Shapely women are more attractive.	1	2	3	4	5
10. Women who are taller are more attractive.					

From the Ideal Body Internalization Scale–Revised, an unpublished scale by E. Stice. Reprinted with permission from the author. For more information, see Stice, Ziemba, et al. (1996).

APPENDIX 3D
PERCEIVED SOCIOCULTURAL PRESSURE SCALE

Using the following scale, please circle the response that best captures your own experience.

Never	Rarely	Sometimes	Often	Always
1	2	3	4	5

1. I've felt pressure from my friends to lose weight.   1 2 3 4 5
2. I've noticed a strong message from my friends to have a thin body.   1 2 3 4 5
3. I've felt pressure from my family to lose weight.   1 2 3 4 5
4. I've noticed a strong message from my family to have a thin body.   1 2 3 4 5
5. I've felt pressure from people I've dated to lose weight.   1 2 3 4 5
6. I've noticed a strong message from people I have dated to have a thin body.   1 2 3 4 5
7. I've felt pressure from the media (e.g., TV, magazines) to lose weight.   1 2 3 4 5
8. I've noticed a strong message from the media to have a thin body.   1 2 3 4 5

From the Perceived Sociocultural Pressure Scale, an unpublished scale by E. Stice. Reprinted with permission from the author. For more information, see Stice, Ziemba, et al. (1996).

4

SOCIAL COMPARISON PROCESSES

The average fashion model is white, 5 feet 10 inches tall, and weighs 110 pounds. She is approximately 30 pounds less than the average American teenage girl, and almost 6 inches taller. Her looks are relatively rare, yet her image is so pervasive that it is difficult for girls to see themselves as anything but "wrong" in comparison. (Hesse-Biber, 1996, p. 96)

I have pictures of Kate Moss taped all over my wall at home. Everyone tells me I have anorexia, but she's still thinner than I am. If she looks too thin how come Johnnie Depp dates her? (a 16-year-old girl with anorexia nervosa)

I'm reinforcing the idea that I'm all right the way I am now and I'm trying to stop looking at women . . . not just women who are slim but women who are fat . . . [to] stop judging other people. (a New Zealand woman discussing self-acceptance as necessary for stopping dieting; Blood, 1996, pp. 112–113)

As discussed in the last chapter, sociocultural theories are the most accepted and widely investigated of etiological theories of body image disturbance. This theory purports that individuals, particularly women, are exposed to pervasive, culturewide ideals and expectations regarding what is deemed attractive. In Westernized culture, the societally sanctioned ideal is remarkably thin. Researchers have noted as well that the ideal also endorses attributes such as White skin, tall height, youth, physical fitness, and health (see Heinberg, 1996). Although widely discussed and investigated, the sociocultural explanation has been criticized for lacking an explanation for the heterogeneity of body image experiences. One can assume that all women are exposed to societal messages, at least to some extent. However, body image discontent occurs on a continuum, with some women relatively satisfied with their appearance whereas others may have extreme appearance disparagement (see chapter 1). More recently, individual differences have been identified and discussed as possible moderating variables between sociocultural pressure for thinness and attractiveness and body image distress (Heinberg, 1996). The model discussed in this chapter, social comparison theory, is a direct outgrowth of sociocultural theory. This theory proposes that individual differences in the tendency to compare oneself with others accounts for differing levels of body image disturbance within the context of a culture that endorses thinness and attractiveness.

RESEARCH BACKGROUND

Human beings engage in a relatively continuous self-evaluative process to examine their standing on numerous attributes. This tendency to gather information from which humans derive opinions about themselves is so innate as to be characterized as a drive state (Festinger, 1954). To develop a consistent and orderly impression of the self, humans reflect on their characteristics, strengths, liabilities, and capabilities. This self-examination process facilitates self-understanding and consistent, effective behavior. However, this information is not gathered in a vacuum. Festinger hypothesized that when a person is uncertain about a specific attribute, he or she will clarify his or her standing by examining the attribute with regard to objective sources of information or against direct physical standards. If these objective standards are not readily available, individuals will examine others as sources of comparison. The process of evaluating one's self in comparison with others in the social environment was the basis for Festinger's social comparison theory. This theory, in turn, has generated substantial research (Kruglanski & Mayseless, 1990; J. V. Wood, 1989); some of which suggests that social comparison may be a primary rather than secondary information-gathering phenomenon (Marsh & Parker, 1984; Ruble, 1983). That is, even when an objective standard is available (e.g., charts specifying healthy weights for a specific height), individuals may instead rely on their relative standing in their social environment to define themselves (e.g., weight of thinner friends).

Comparison Target

> I sent two models on a trip together to do bathing suits. One girl called me and said, "oh, my god, I wish I was her; she's got such a lean body with perfect muscle tone," and the other one called me up and said, "I was so ashamed of my figure, because she's so womanly." (Monique Pillard, as cited in Schefer, 1997, p. 89)

The selection of a comparison target is not a random occurrence. Rather, individuals exhibit some degree of volition in how and whom they select as comparison targets. D. T. Miller, Turnbull, and McFarland (1988) differentiated between universalistic and particularistic comparison targets. A *universalistic* comparison is determined by comparing oneself with a global comparison target on a specific attribute (e.g., for a woman, comparing her weight to that of other women). Conversely, one's *particularistic* standing is assessed by comparing with others who share a particular bond or identity (e.g., comparing her weight with women in her immediate peer group). Miller et al., in a series of five studies, found that individuals overwhelmingly preferred to compare themselves with distinctively similar others rather than with individuals that were nondistinctively similar.

Upward and Downward Comparisons

Your choice of a comparison target (i.e., who you compare yourself with) is also influenced by the target's relative standing in comparison with you on a particular attribute. Generally speaking, within any large comparison group certain individuals are inferior to you on the attribute of interest whereas others are superior. Comparisons are deemed *downward* when the target is inferior on the attribute of interest and are labeled *upward* when the target is superior (Kruglanski & Mayseless, 1990; J. V. Wood, 1989).

J. V. Wood (1989) suggested that individuals often make upward comparisons to improve themselves. For example, a female athlete may compare herself with someone who is more accomplished as a source of inspiration or motivation. However, the risk of such an upward comparison is that it may remind her of her own inferiority, a fact that can be threatening to her self-esteem. Recent research indicates that comparisons with others who are superior to oneself on the attribute of interest (upward comparison) are often associated with increases in emotional distress and decreases in self-esteem (Major, Testa, & Bylsma, 1991). J. V. Wood further elaborated that an upward comparison may be particularly threatening when the superior other is close or similar to the individual (particularistic, e.g., a close friend). Conversely, when the comparison target is dissimilar (universalistic, e.g., a stranger), their superiority on the attribute of interest may be deemed irrelevant.

In contrast to upward comparisons, downward comparisons may serve as a mechanism of self-enhancement (J. V. Wood, 1989). By comparing oneself with someone who is inferior on an attribute of interest, one may feel better about one's own standing. Indeed, when individuals experience misfortune, they often compare themselves with those who "are worse off" as a means of coping. A number of studies provide evidence that downward comparisons are common for individuals who perceive a threat from others. Pyszczynski, Greenberb, and LaPrelle (1985) conducted a study in which participants were told that they had received a low score on a test and were then given the opportunity to look at the marks of others. Participants showed an interest when they were told that others also did poorly but showed little interest if they thought that others had performed better than they had. It is hypothesized that this effect may be attenuated by a comparison with a more similar other.

Social Comparison and Body Image

A theoretical model using social comparison processes can be offered to explain how exposure to the sociocultural thin and attractive ideal leads to increased body dissatisfaction (Heinberg & Thompson, 1992b; Smolak, Levine, & Gralen, 1993; J. K. Thompson, Heinberg, & Tantleff, 1991). This theory assumes that individual differences in a tendency to compare oneself with others, engage in upward comparisons, or choose inappropriate comparison targets leads certain individuals to be more vulnerable than others to sociocultural appearance pressures. If the comparison or feedback is in terms of one's body—for example, teasing about weight or even ambiguous information that an aspect of one's appearance is unattractive— one's body image may be affected (J. K. Thompson, 1990; see also chapter 5). For instance, Striegel-Moore, McAvay, and Rodin (1986) found that women's level of comparing their own weight with other individuals was significantly correlated with body dissatisfaction. Since this early study, a number of investigators have examined the influence of social comparison on body image.

Correlational Studies

Studies examining social comparison theory in body image generally fall into one of two types: descriptive correlational studies and controlled experiments. Correlational studies generally measure the relationship between body satisfaction and individual differences in the tendency to compare one's body with others'. Correlational studies consistently find an association between social comparison tendencies and body satisfaction, suggesting that higher levels of comparison are associated with greater dissatisfaction (Heinberg & Thompson, 1992a, 1992b; J. K. Thompson, Heinberg, et al., 1991).

Even though the tendency to compare oneself with others has been shown to correlate with body image disturbance (J. K. Thompson, Heinberg, et al., 1991), identifying the target of those social comparisons has also been shown to provide further clarification of the social comparison process. Heinberg and Thompson (1992b) had male and female undergraduates rate the importance of six groups (family, friends, classmates, other university students, celebrities, and average U.S. citizens) as comparison targets for seven attributes (attractiveness, athletic ability, figure–physique, intelligence, confidence, fashion–clothes, and popularity). Table 4.1 contains the ratings for the different targets for two broad attribute dimensions—appearance (attractiveness, figure–physique) and nonappear-

TABLE 4.1
Statistics for the Rating of Importance for Six Target Groups

Target	M for appearance[a]		M for nonappearance[b]	
	Men	Women	Men	Women
Family	4.97 (2.26)	5.13 (2.45)	7.43 (2.02)	7.20 (2.34)
Friends	6.78 (2.06)	7.17 (2.06)	7.77 (1.56)	7.56 (2.00)
Classmates	6.25 (1.89)	5.90 (2.27)	6.57 (1.77)	6.69 (2.00)
University students	6.05 (2.00)	5.61 (2.20)	6.16 (1.97)	6.15 (2.03)
Celebrities	6.37 (2.89)	5.41 (2.80)[c]	5.03 (2.31)	4.27 (2.25)[c]
U.S. citizens	5.22 (2.07)	4.91 (2.23)	5.41 (2.02)	5.04 (2.15)

Note. The range of scores is 2–10. Standard deviations are in parentheses. From "Social Comparison: Gender, Target Importance Ratings, and Relation to Body Image Disturbance," by L. J. Heinberg and J. K. Thompson, 1992b, *Journal of Social Behavior and Personality, 7*, p. 339. Copyright 1992 by the *Journal of Social Behavior and Personality*. Reprinted with permission.
[a]Differences of friends were significantly greater than those of classmates. No differences were found among classmates, university students, and celebrities. However, differences of these three were greater than those of U.S. citizens and family. No significant differences were found between U.S. citizens and family.
[b]No differences were found between friends and family, but differences of both were significantly greater than those of classmates and university students. No significant differences were found between classmates and university students, although differences of both were significantly greater than those of U.S. citizens, whose differences were greater than celebrities.
[c]A significant gender difference was found for celebrities.

ance (intelligence, confidence). As these findings indicate, importance ratings for appearance were highest for the friends target, which was significantly higher than for classmates, other university students, and celebrities. In addition, these three groups were rated as more important than family and U.S. citizens. It is interesting to note that there was only one gender difference—male students rated celebrities as a more important comparison target than did female students. However, despite the general lack of gender effects in absolute magnitude of ratings, there were consistent gender differences in the correlations between the importance ratings and levels of body dissatisfaction and of eating disturbance. For female students, the importance rating for the appearance attributes was significantly associated with body dissatisfaction and eating disturbance, whereas there was no significant association for male students.

More recently, the social comparison with siblings—a particularistic comparison target—was explored. Rieves and Cash (1996) examined social–developmental etiological factors in women's body image, including appearance-related teasing, sibling social comparisons, and maternal modeling of body image attitudes and behaviors. One-hundred and fifty-two college-age women completed measures of body image and retrospective recall of the etiological factors of interest for childhood and adolescence. This recall included the Sibling Appearance Questionnaire, which asked participants to rate what type of effect, if any, their siblings' attractiveness had on how they felt about their own appearance while growing up (Rieves

& Cash, 1996). This rating was assessed for both childhood and adolescence.

Results of the study confirmed that each influence of sibling appearance at both childhood and adolescence explained significant variance in the women's present body image. More specifically, data revealed both upward and downward comparisons with the particularistic sibling target. A negative effect of siblings' appearance in childhood (i.e., a comparison with a sibling's appearance led to a negative effect on body image) was expressed by 19% of respondents. An additional 63% reported no effect, and 18% reported a positive effect (Rieves & Cash, 1996). The perceived effects of sibling's attractiveness were significantly related to an investment in the importance of appearance and body image dysphoria but not general evaluation of one's appearance or a preoccupation with or fear of being overweight (Rieves & Cash, 1996). Although not measuring frequency or importance of comparisons directly, the researchers concluded that having a more attractive sibling might foster unfavorable self-evaluations whereas self-appraisals of appearance may be enhanced by a less attractive sibling.

A related aspect of social comparison involves the perception of other individuals' investment in appearance and weight. For example, it has long been assumed that although women with eating disorders are preoccupied with weight and shape, they do not place prime importance on these aspects when evaluating others. Until recently, this assumption had not been empirically tested. Beebe, Hombeck, Schober, Lane, and Rosa (1996) showed female undergraduates a series of photographs of women and asked what aspects of the photo they first noticed as well as how the women in the photographs felt about themselves. Next, participants read scenarios in which women either overate or dieted and were asked to assess the women's feelings and likely weight fluctuation. Results demonstrated that women who placed a strong emphasis on their own body weight and shape (as measured by the Eating Attitudes Test) also emphasized these aspects when evaluating others. In addition, women emphasizing body weight and shape were more likely to attribute "fat" and "thin" feelings to the women in the photographs (Beebe et al., 1996). Finally, participants who focused on their own bodies and weight expected other women to feel negatively after overeating and positively after dieting (Beebe et al., 1996).

This study has important implications for social comparison and body image. Women with body image disturbance may not only engage in more social comparisons and rate them as important but may also believe that others give as much valence to weight and appearance concerns. Thus, even when women have significant body image dissatisfaction, the social comparison process may not only perpetuate feelings of inferiority but normalize an overemphasis on body and appearance concerns. Expectations that an overemphasis is typical may also make treatment interventions designed to counter irrational beliefs more difficult.

Randomized Experimental Studies

Controlled experimental designs have manipulated social comparison in the laboratory and have examined its effects on subjective body image. In these studies, participants are exposed to a comparison target (e.g., photographs of models, videotaped commercials), and any resultant changes in body image are measured. The majority of these studies examines body image immediately preceding and following mass media exposure (Heinberg & Thompson, 1995; Irving, 1990) and infers that a social comparison process has occurred. Although these studies were reviewed in the last chapter, those that specifically evaluated social comparison are discussed now.

In two experimental studies, researchers have examined social comparison in body image by directly manipulating the attribute, target of comparison, and feedback. Heinberg and Thompson (1992a) gave participants false feedback about their relative weight, leading half to believe they were thinner than average and half to believe they were heavier than average. In addition, half of each group was given feedback that was either particularistic or universalistic (i.e., either other students attending their university or the average person in the United States). It was hypothesized that individuals who were told that they were heavier than average would evidence greater disturbance than those who believed that they were much thinner and that this effect would be stronger for those who were told that they had a particularistic reference group for weight comparison (i.e., other students).

Unexpectedly, participants who compared themselves with more similar others reported greater body image anxiety and subjective dissatisfaction than did those who compared themselves with generic others, regardless of whether it was an upward or downward comparison (Heinberg & Thompson, 1992a). One possible explanation for this effect may be that the comparison process is in itself a threatening phenomenon. As J. K. Thompson, Heinberg, et al. (1991) suggested, a *generic* tendency (i.e., no specific target either upward or downward) to compare oneself with others is strongly related to levels of eating disturbance, body image dissatisfaction, and self-esteem. It can also be hypothesized that individuals tend to disregard either upward or downward comparisons with generic others because they judge the target group to be dissimilar and thus irrelevant (Heinberg & Thompson, 1992a). Although this effect was found for undergraduates, it is not known whether this finding would hold for other populations. For example, disfigured populations—for whom most comparisons would be upward—may not have access to a particularistic comparison group (i.e., other persons with disfiguring injuries).

Recently, Faith, Leone, and Allison (1997) attempted to replicate the association between social comparison tendencies and body dissatisfaction and to manipulate upward and downward social comparisons to assess their relevance to attitudinal body image. Male and female undergraduates were randomly assigned to an upward comparison, downward comparison, or control group. Using self-generated imagery, the students were asked to imagine someone of the same sex whom they considered much more attractive or well built than they were, someone whom they considered much less attractive than they were, or someone from a favorite movie or television program. Similar to the findings of Heinberg and Thompson (1992a), satisfaction levels did not vary as a function of the social comparison manipulation.

Cattarin, Williams, Thomas, and Thompson (in press) demonstrated a moderating effect of social comparison in the relationship between mass media exposure and transitory changes in body image. In this laboratory study, undergraduate female students were shown either a videotape containing commercials representative of the thin, attractive ideal or commercials with non-appearance-related messages. The instructional set for viewing the videotapes varied by group, such that individuals were told to compare oneself to the people in the video, told to pay close attention to the products advertised, or given neutral instructions (Cattarin et al., in press). A three-way interaction among instructional set, videotape, and time was found for appearance satisfaction. Women given the comparison instruction and who saw the appearance-related videotape reported greater decreases in appearance satisfaction than did the women in the other two groups (Cattarin et al., in press).

The previous findings suggest that although a tendency to compare relates to lower satisfaction levels, the designed manipulations fail to consistently elicit significant transitory changes. Perhaps a tendency to compare oneself with others is so pervasive that a singular upward or downward comparison is not salient enough to alter one's state body image. Thus, researchers should examine the effect of a longer or more personally relevant comparison manipulation. Additionally, it is unclear whether exposure to static stimuli, such as vignettes about a hypothetical person, photographs, or televised images, mirror the social comparisons that occur in everyday social interactions. One recent study offers some insight into the importance of personalized contact for comparison processes. C. M. Thomas and Thompson (1998) had a direct contact condition consisting of an interaction with an upward comparison target (a female confederate was preselected to meet the ideal in terms of attractiveness) and an indirect contact condition (the same confederate was observed by participants on video). Results indicated that the self-attractiveness ratings were more negatively affected in the live comparison condition.

Comparative Theoretical Studies

Recent interest has grown in comparing the relative contribution of competing theories to body image disturbance. Two recent comparative studies suggest the significant and independent predictive ability of social comparison. The relative importance of social comparisons and negative verbal commentary (i.e., teasing) in predicting variance associated with body dissatisfaction and eating disturbance was addressed by J. K. Thompson and Heinberg (1993). In this study, 146 female undergraduate students completed measures of eating disturbance, body dissatisfaction, self-esteem, depression, history of being teased about physical appearance, frequency of appearance comparison, and importance of various individuals as appearance comparison targets. Using multiple regression analyses, the researchers first entered the degree of self-esteem and depression into the regression equation to remove a general distress—negative affectivity variable from the analyses. With all predictors entered, the results indicated that specific teasing about weight—size, but not general appearance, was a significant and consistent predictor of body image dissatisfaction and eating disturbance (J. K. Thompson & Heinberg, 1993). In addition, the importance rating of others as comparison targets, but not general comparison frequency, predicted unique variance for both body dissatisfaction and disturbed eating behaviors (J. K. Thompson & Heinberg, 1993). Although the results fit with other data supportive of a developmental history of specific size—weight teasing as a possible cause of body dissatisfaction (see chapter 5), the significant role of comparison importance ratings adds a new dimension to the social comparison theory.

A recent comparative study provides even greater compelling evidence for the role of social comparison. Stormer and Thompson (1996) compared four theoretical factors: maturational status, negative verbal commentary, behavioral social comparison, and awareness—internalization of sociocultural pressures for thinness and attractiveness among 162 college women. Measures for each theoretical viewpoint were entered as predictors and regressed onto multiple measures of body image and eating disturbance. After variance associated with self-esteem and body mass index were parceled out, frequency of appearance comparison explained unique variance associated with several different measures of body image. In addition, frequency of appearance comparison explained more variance than did other predictors for all but two of the regressions. Finally, when a composite index of body image was assessed, frequency of appearance comparison accounted for 32% of the unique variance after self-esteem and body mass index were covaried (Stormer & Thompson, 1996). A similar pattern was found for the two measures of eating disturbance. The frequency of appearance comparison provided significant, unique variance in the prediction of drive for thinness and bulimic behavior. Again, social comparison provided more unique variance than did measures of maturational status, teasing history, or awareness–internalization of societal standards of thinness and attractiveness.

The role of social comparison as a possible mediational link among negative appearance-related feedback, body image, and eating disturbance was also recently examined (J. K. Thompson, Coovert, & Stormer, in press). Among an undergraduate female population, covariance structure modeling revealed that appearance-based social comparison mediated the relationship of appearance-related teasing to body image and eating disturbance. The authors concluded that the pernicious effects of social comparison may result from early teasing history, leading to greater vulnerability for body image and eating concerns (J. K. Thompson, Coovert, et al., in press). (These findings are discussed further in chapter 11.)

Self-Ideal Discrepancy Theory

Self-ideal discrepancy theory is another outgrowth of sociocultural theory. Like social comparison theory, it assumes that individuals become distressed when engaging in upward comparisons. However, rather than comparing oneself with another in the social domain, self-ideal discrepancy assumes that individuals compare their real selves with an idealized self. This theory purports that individuals are motivated to attain a match between their actual self concept and an internalized ideal (Cash & Szymanski, 1995). The discrepancy between an idealized body shape versus an actual one has been measured by a number of researchers. As noted in chapter 2, researchers have used assessment measures that consist of a comparison of one's actual perceived size on a schematic drawing versus a selected ideal size (A. E. Fallon & Rozin, 1985; J. K. Thompson, 1990). On the basis in part of these studies and of the importance of socioculturally endorsed ideal weights and appearances, Thompson proposed a self-ideal discrepancy hypothesis to explain the development and maintenance of body image disturbance.

This theory focuses on an individual's tendency to compare his or her perceived appearance with an imagined ideal or ideal other (J. K. Thompson, 1992). The result of such a comparison process may be a discrepancy between the perceived self and the ideal self (J. K. Thompson, 1990, 1992), and it is assumed by this theoretical model that the greater the discrepancy between one's perceived self and the perceived ideal, the greater the dissatisfaction. Recent research supports the hypothesis that a self-ideal discrepancy exists, that body image dissatisfaction and higher levels of eating disturbance of both genders are highly predictable from discrepancies scores, and that multiple-attribute discrepancies are incrementally additive (Altabe & Thompson, 1992; A. E. Fallon & Rozin, 1985; Jacobi & Cash, 1994; J. K. Thompson & Psaltis, 1988). Silberstein, Striegel-Moore, and

Rodin (1987) discussed the importance of this conceptualization and indicated that this discrepancy may be an etiological factor in "normative discontent."

Future Research

Research supports the emergence of appearance-based social comparison as a potentially influential theoretical model for understanding the development and maintenance of body image disturbance. Recent research also suggests that social comparison may play a mediational role between developmental factors and the later development of body image and eating disturbance (J. K. Thompson et al., in press). It is not known, however, why certain individuals, and particularly women, may be more likely to compare themselves on aspects of appearance. Could early teasing history or internalization of sociocultural factors lead certain individuals to engage in more frequent comparisons? Furthermore, it is not known why certain targets are more likely to be used for making upward comparisons. Finally, we could find no research that examined the influence of social comparison for individuals who are likely to be frequently making upward comparisons due to obesity, unattractiveness, disfigurement, or deformity.

ASSESSMENT

Since the interest in social comparison has increased in the body image literature, a number of brief instruments have been developed. Initially, these measures assessed a generic tendency to compare one's appearance with others'. However, more recent measures examine specific targets of comparison and specific attributes (see Table 4.2).

The Physical Appearance Comparison Scale (see Appendix 4A) is a very brief (5 items) measure of the degree to which individuals tend to compare their appearance with others (e.g., "In social situations, I compare my figure to the figures of other people"). High scores on this instrument have been shown to be strongly related to body image dissatisfaction and eating disturbance (J. K. Thompson, Heinberg, et al., 1991). Several similar scales have been developed since this initial instrument. Faith et al. (1997) developed the Body Image Comparison Scale, a 5-item scale that assesses attribute-specific comparison tendencies (e.g., the tendency to compare width of thighs). E. Fisher and Thompson (1998) recently developed the Body Comparison Scale, which assesses the frequency of comparison for multiple body sites (see Appendix 4B). As discussed at length earlier, Heinberg and Thompson (1992b) developed the Comparison Target Importance Rating, which asks participants to rate the importance of various targets (e.g., friend, celebrity) on specific attributes (e.g., appearance, intelligence).

TABLE 4.2
Appearance Comparison Measures

Instrument	Author(s)	Description	Reliability 1, 2	Standardization sample	Address of author
Physical Appearance Comparison Scale	J. K. Thompson, Heinberg, & Tantleff (1991)	5-item scale assessing tendency to compare one's own appearance to the appearance of others	IC: .78 TR: .72	80 female undergraduates	J. Kevin Thompson, PhD Department of Psychology University of South Florida 4202 Fowler Avenue Tampa, FL 33620-8200
Comparison Target Importance Rating	Heinberg & Thompson (1992b)	6-item list of comparison groups and rate the importance of target for seven attributes	TR: .68	189 female undergraduates, 108 male undergraduates	J. Kevin Thompson, PhD Department of Psychology University of South Florida 4202 Fowler Avenue Tampa, FL 33620-8200
Physical Appearance Comparison Scale–Revised	E. Fisher & Thompson (1998)	36-item scale measuring comparison of specific body sites and general comparison tendencies regarding appearance	IC: .95	2,171 male and female junior high, high school, and college students	J. Kevin Thompson, PhD Department of Psychology University of South Florida 4202 Fowler Avenue Tampa, FL 33620-8200
Comparison to Models Survey	Strowman (1996)	8-item measure assessing frequency of comparison to models on eight attributes	IC: men (.84) IC: women (.86), two factors	208 female undergraduates, 111 male undergraduates	Shelley Strowman, PhD 9 Carver Hill Court Natick, MA 01760

Instrument	Source	Description	Reliability	Sample	Contact
Body Image Comparison Scale	Faith et al. (1997)	5-item scale assessing frequency with which one engages in specific social comparison behaviors; includes one item from the Physical Appearance Comparison Scale	IC: .74, two factors	152 female undergraduates, 64 male undergraduates	Myles S. Faith, PhD Obesity Research Center St. Luke's/Roosevelt Hospital Columbia University College of Physicians & Surgeons 1090 Amsterdam Avenue New York, NY 10025
Body-Image Ideals Questionnaire	Cash & Szymanski (1995)	Rating of one's personal ideal and actual on 10 attributes related to weight–appearance and strength–importance of attribute	IC: .75 (discrepancy) IC: .82 (importance)	284 female undergraduates	Thomas F. Cash, PhD Department of Psychology Old Dominion University Norfolk, VA 23529-0267
Body-Image Ideals Questionnaire– Expanded	Szymanski & Cash (1995)	Rating of one's specific attributes from one's viewpoint and that of one's romantic partner based on "ideal" and "ought"	IC: .81–.95	143 female undergraduates	Thomas F. Cash, PhD Department of Psychology Old Dominion University Norfolk, VA 23529-0267

Note. IC = internal consistency; TR = test–retest reliability.

Finally, Strowman (1996) developed a Comparison to Models Survey (Appendix 4C).

Self-ideal discrepancy scores have long been assessed using standardized measures of body image, particularly figure rating scales (Heinberg, 1996; J. K. Thompson, 1990; see also chapter 1's Appendix 1A). For example, respondents are asked to select which figure best represents their current appearance and which best represents their ideal appearance. However, questionnaires for assessing a broad range of self-ideal discrepancies have recently been developed (Cash & Szymanski, 1995; M. L. Szymanski & Cash, 1995). The Body-Image Ideals Questionnaire allows participants to rate 11 attributes related to weight–appearance from a variety of reference points, including oneself and one's partner, on perspectives such as "ideal" and "ought" (Cash & Szymanski, 1995). Further information regarding the Body-Image Ideals Questionnaire (expanded version) may be found in Table 4.2 and Appendix 4D.

TREATMENT

Cognitive–behavioral treatment for body image disturbance has been well established as an efficacious means of improving body image disturbance and eating-disordered behaviors (e.g., chapter 2, this book; Cash, 1996; and J. C. Rosen, 1996a, 1996b). One of the most common and best empirically validated treatment strategies is the manualized cognitive–behavioral intervention developed by Cash (1997). An essential aspect of this treatment is the identification and successful challenging of cognitive errors of appearance.

Two of the cognitive errors identified relate to social comparison processes: the unreal ideal and unfair to compare. The *unreal ideal* refers to the use of a societal ideal as a standard of acceptable appearance. Feelings of dissatisfaction or being impossibly flawed occur as a result of comparing oneself with this unrealistically high standard of perfection. Automatic negative thoughts associated with this cognitive error include the following: "I'm too ugly (or short, or whatever) and therefore nothing about me is appealing" and "If only I looked like _____, I would be attractive and therefore happy."

A second cognitive error is termed *unfair to compare* by Cash (1991). It refers to a similar type of faulty, self-defeating thinking as the unreal ideal, except that one compares oneself with people who one encounters in everyday situations. Typically the comparison is very biased, and one compares one's appearance only with people seen as having those characteristics one would like to have (e.g., someone dissatisfied with being flat chested may compare herself with curvaceous women). Persons who think this way are also prone to spend a lot of time noticing others whom they regard as possessing the characteristic they desire; in contrast, seldom do they pay attention to persons with whom they would favorably compare (e.g., not noticing that some people are overweight or unattractive; Cash, 1991).

Patients are next taught to recognize these errors and associated negative thoughts and to begin to challenge them with more adaptive self-talk. With regards to the unreal ideal, counterarguments essentially challenge the comparison against some arbitrary and unrealistically perfect standard of appearance. The following statements are examples: "It might be nice if I wasn't 10 pounds overweight, but it is unrealistic to compare myself with a fashion model and criticize myself for not looking the same"; "I don't have to have a perfect-looking body to have a positive outlook on myself"; "Nobody but me is complaining that I don't look like a movie star"; and "I refuse to buy into this societal attitude that I need to be perfect looking to be happy." Counterarguments for unfair to compare include many of the same ones listed for the unreal ideal. However, the first step is to help patients realize what they are doing, that they just compared themselves in some respect with another individual and ended up feeling bad as a result. Corrective thinking may include the following statements: "Just because I think I am less attractive than that person does not mean that I'm bad looking"; "The fact that I like the way that person looks has nothing to do with the way I look"; "That person doesn't make me look bad; doesn't make me do anything. These unfair comparisons are making me feel bad"; and "Let me think of something about myself (special skill, talent, quality) that makes me compare well with other people."

Other writers have discussed treatment of social comparison in patients with low self-regard (Swallow, 1995; Swallow & Kuiper, 1988, 1992). Swallow indicated that the use of social comparison records is helpful in targeting which behaviors lead to decreases in self-regard. Individuals are taught to keep track of social comparisons, noting the context, target, comparison attribute, and affective consequence of each social comparison they make. On the basis of the outcome of these diaries, Swallow recommended a number of interventions, including (a) teach strategies that individuals can use to divert themselves from a self-focused state to a problem-solving state (e.g., shifting to considerations on how to improve one's appearance), (b) encourage individuals to behave like people with high self-regard and to seek out opportunities for downward comparisons, and (c) direct self-evaluative attention to other personal domains (e.g., athletic ability). In addition, if record keeping indicates that individuals seek out obviously advantaged others for comparisons (e.g., models), persons can be taught to identify advantaging factors and thus to discount their superiority (e.g., hair and make-up artists, airbrushing).

Treatment paradigms should also be developed to aid individuals who may be at a higher risk for making frequent upward comparisons. For example, body image concerns are quite frequent among obese persons (J. C. Rosen, 1996b). Although some degree of dissatisfaction may not be unrealistic, given an obese state, cognitive restructuring regarding the effect of an unrealistic ideal and comparison tendencies may help reduce the negative affect associated with these automatic thoughts. Similarly, individuals with disfigurements or deformities can be helped to engage in more realistic inner dialogues regarding the appropriateness of social comparison. For instance, counterarguments challenging a comparison against some arbitrary and unrealistically perfect standard of appearance may include the following: "It might be nice if I wasn't disfigured, but it's unrealistic to compare myself with someone without my injuries and criticize myself for not looking the same."

Future researchers should examine the efficacy of social comparison-relevant interventions and the potential benefit of matching these interventions with individuals who engage in frequent social comparisons or place inappropriate importance on comparing favorably with others. These interventions should also be examined in populations at risk, such as those with disfigurements.

CONCLUSIONS

The past 10 years have brought a new interest into the role of social comparison in the development, maintenance, and treatment of body image disturbance. In this chapter, we have attempted to provide an overview of this growing aspect of body image research. Studies demonstrate the relationship between a tendency to compare and body image dissatisfaction. Research examining the relative contribution of etiological theories to current body image satisfaction consistently demonstrates the powerful influence of social comparison (Stormer & Thompson, 1996; J. K. Thompson & Heinberg, 1993). However, this theoretical model is still in its relative infancy. Future research is necessary to evaluate individual differences in social comparison, to develop multidimensional instruments of social comparison, to investigate populations at risk, and to assess and further define treatment strategies.

In particular, the evaluation of at-risk populations, such as individuals who interact with an extremely thin particularistic reference group (i.e., dancers, gymnasts), is recommended. Additionally, researchers need to examine the effects of the inevitable upward comparisons that are part of being a member of certain subgroups (i.e., persons who are morbidly obese or disfigured). Techniques, such as those described in this chapter for countering appearance comparison tendencies, need to be further tested with these at-risk samples.

APPENDIX 4A
PHYSICAL APPEARANCE COMPARISON SCALE

Using the following scale, rate the statements below.

Never	Seldom	Sometimes	Often	Always
1	2	3	4	5

1. At parties or other social events, I compare my physical appearance to the physical appearance of others.　　1　2　3　4　5
2. The best way for people to know if they are overweight or underweight is to compare their figure to the figure of others.　　1　2　3　4　5
3. At parties or other social events, I compare how I am dressed to how other people are dressed.　　1　2　3　4　5
4. Comparing your "looks" to the "looks" of others is a bad way to determine if you are attractive or unattractive.　　1　2　3　4　5
5. In social situations, I sometimes compare my figure to the figures of other people.　　1　2　3　4　5

For more information, see J. K. Thompson, Heinberg, and Tantleff (1991).

APPENDIX 4B
BODY COMPARISON SCALE

For the items below, use the following scale to rate how often you compare these aspects of your body to those of other individuals of the same sex. Note: Please be sure that you read and respond to all of the questions according to how you would compare yourself to your same-sex peers.

Never	Rarely	Sometimes	Often	Always
1	2	3	4	5

1. Ears   1 2 3 4 5
2. Nose   1 2 3 4 5
3. Lips   1 2 3 4 5
4. Hair   1 2 3 4 5
5. Teeth   1 2 3 4 5
6. Chin   1 2 3 4 5
7. Shape of face   1 2 3 4 5
8. Cheeks   1 2 3 4 5
9. Forehead   1 2 3 4 5
10. Upper arm   1 2 3 4 5
11. Forearm   1 2 3 4 5
12. Shoulders   1 2 3 4 5
13. Chest   1 2 3 4 5
14. Back   1 2 3 4 5
15. Waist   1 2 3 4 5
16. Stomach   1 2 3 4 5
17. Buttocks   1 2 3 4 5
18. Thighs   1 2 3 4 5
19. Hips   1 2 3 4 5
20. Calves   1 2 3 4 5
21. Muscle tone of upper body   1 2 3 4 5
22. Overall shape of upper body   1 2 3 4 5
23. Muscle tone of lower body   1 2 3 4 5
24. Overall shape of lower body   1 2 3 4 5
25. Overall body   1 2 3 4 5

Use this scale to answer items 26–36.

Never	Rarely	Sometimes	Often	Always
1	2	3	4	5

26. I find myself thinking about how my nose is different than others'.   1 2 3 4 5
27. When I am with other people, I find myself comparing my complexion with theirs.   1 2 3 4 5
28. Being around people with firm, muscular arms makes me self-conscious.   1 2 3 4 5
29. When I compare myself with others, I compare their degree of muscle-tone with my muscle-tone.   1 2 3 4 5
30. When with others, I compare my thighs to those of my peers.   1 2 3 4 5

31. When I am with others, I compare my weight with theirs.	1	2	3	4	5
32. When I compare my weight with others, I feel that I am overweight.	1	2	3	4	5
33. I compare my physical appearance to the physical appearance of others.	1	2	3	4	5
34. When I see people who are overweight, I compare my body size to theirs.	1	2	3	4	5
35. I compare the attractiveness of my facial features with the facial features of others.	1	2	3	4	5
36. I compare how thin or overweight someone is more than I compare how muscular and in shape they are.	1	2	3	4	5

For more information, see E. Fisher and Thompson (1998).

APPENDIX 4C
COMPARISON TO MODELS SURVEY

Instructions: Please use this scale to answer the items below.

Never	Once in a while	About half of the time	Most of the time	Always
1	2	3	4	5

When you see models of your own sex in magazines, how often do you compare yourself to them

1. In general?	1 2 3 4 5
2. In terms of career success?	1 2 3 4 5
3. In terms of eating habits?	1 2 3 4 5
4. In terms of exercise habits?	1 2 3 4 5
5. In terms of happiness?	1 2 3 4 5
6. In terms of intelligence?	1 2 3 4 5
7. In terms of physical appearance?	1 2 3 4 5
8. In terms of popularity?	1 2 3 4 5

From "The Relation Between Media Exposure and Body Satisfaction: An Examination of Moderating Variables Derived From Social Comparison Theory," an unpublished doctoral dissertation (University of New Hampshire, Durham) by S. R. Strowman, 1996. Reprinted with permission from the author.

APPENDIX 4D
BODY-IMAGE IDEALS QUESTIONNAIRE (EXPANDED)

Each item on this questionnaire deals with a different physical characteristic. For each characteristic, think about how you would describe yourself as you *actually are*. Then think about how you *wish you were*. The difference between the two reveals how close you come to your personal ideal. In some instances, your looks may closely match your ideal. In other instances, they may differ considerably. On Part A of each item, rate *how much* you resemble your personal physical ideal by circling a number on the 0−3 scale.

Your physical ideals may differ in how important they are to you, regardless of how close you come to having them. You may feel strongly that some ideals embody the way you want to look or to be. In other areas, your ideals may be less important to you. On Part B of each item, rate *how important* your ideal is to you by circling a number on the 0−3 scale.

1. A. My ideal height is

0	1	2	3
Exactly as I am	Almost as I am	Fairly unlike me	Very unlike me

   B. How important to you is your ideal height?

0	1	2	3
Not important	Somewhat important	Moderately important	Very important

2. A. My ideal skin complexion is

0	1	2	3
Exactly as I am	Almost as I am	Fairly unlike me	Very unlike me

   B. How important to you is your ideal skin complexion?

0	1	2	3
Not important	Somewhat important	Moderately important	Very important

3. A. My ideal hair texture and thickness are

0	1	2	3
Exactly as I am	Almost as I am	Fairly unlike me	Very unlike me

   B. How important to you is your ideal hair texture and thickness?

0	1	2	3
Not important	Somewhat important	Moderately important	Very important

4. A. My ideal facial features (eyes, nose, ears, facial shape) are

0	1	2	3
Exactly as I am	Almost as I am	Fairly unlike me	Very unlike me

   B. How important to you are your ideal facial features?

0	1	2	3
Not important	Somewhat important	Moderately important	Very important

5. A. My ideal muscle tone and definition is

0	1	2	3
Exactly as I am	Almost as I am	Fairly unlike me	Very unlike me

B. How important to you is your ideal muscle tone and definition?

0	1	2	3
Not important	Somewhat important	Moderately important	Very important

6. A. My ideal body proportions are

0	1	2	3
Exactly as I am	Almost as I am	Fairly unlike me	Very unlike me

B. How important to you are your ideal body proportions?

0	1	2	3
Not important	Somewhat important	Moderately important	Very important

7. A. My ideal weight is

0	1	2	3
Exactly as I am	Almost as I am	Fairly unlike me	Very unlike me

B. How important to you is your ideal weight?

0	1	2	3
Not important	Somewhat important	Moderately important	Very important

8. A. My ideal chest size is

0	1	2	3
Exactly as I am	Almost as I am	Fairly unlike me	Very unlike me

B. How important to you is your ideal chest size?

0	1	2	3
Not important	Somewhat important	Moderately important	Very important

9. A. My ideal physical strength is

0	1	2	3
Exactly as I am	Almost as I am	Fairly unlike me	Very unlike me

B. How important to you is your ideal physical strength?

0	1	2	3
Not important	Somewhat important	Moderately important	Very important

10. A. My ideal physical coordination is

0	1	2	3
Exactly as I am	Almost as I am	Fairly unlike me	Very unlike me

B. How important to you is your ideal physical coordination?

0	1	2	3
Not important	Somewhat important	Moderately important	Very important

11. A. My ideal overall physical appearance is

0	1	2	3
Exactly as I am	Almost as I am	Fairly unlike me	Very unlike me

B. How important to you is your overall ideal physical appearance?

0	1	2	3
Not important	Somewhat important	Moderately important	Very important

From the Body-Image Ideals Questionnaire—Expanded, an unpublished scale by T. F. Cash. Reprinted with permission from the author. For more information, see M. L. Szymanski and Cash (1995).

III

INTERPERSONAL
APPROACHES

5

APPEARANCE-RELATED FEEDBACK

To 12-year-old Samuel John Graham, the start of middle school meant getting teased by kids again, detectives said. It meant being called fat again. Broward County [Florida] Sheriff's detectives said Samuel so dreaded the idea of walking into the first day of school at Parkway Middle School on Monday he got up in the middle of the night and hanged himself from a tree in the back yard of his Fort Lauderdale-area home. (Larrubia, 1996, p. B1)

A tennis fan who became a running gag for David Letterman after she was caught on camera with peach juice running down her chin is suing the comedian for ridiculing her.... Letterman showed the footage of Jane Bronstein, 54, at least six times between Sept. 5 and Sept. 20.... Letterman called her a "seductive temptress." Bronstein, a large woman, suffers from a thyroid condition and had childhood polio and two spinal fusions, her lawsuit said. ("Tennis fan sues Letterman," 1996, p. B2)

Constant teasing over a female officer's weight may have led to a fatal gunfight between two security officers.... At about 3:50 A.M., Virginia Rich, 51, and Canute Findsen, 43, drew their automatic pistols and shot each other to death.... Sgt. Patrick O'Toole wrote that Findsen had been teasing her "relentlessly" about her weight. ("Fatal gunfight," 1997, p. A5).

I had a sense that unless I was totally thin, my friends would tease me, or I wouldn't get a girlfriend. (Martin, 18, a male Argentine, who also noted that he feared swallowing because he thought his "saliva had too many calories"; "A pathology of thinness," 1997, p. A14).

Well, I don't know if it'll work, but I'd like to see kids stop teasing kids.... I would like to see that weird, different kid get a break because I was that kid. (Nicholas Cage, when asked what he'd like to say to children around the world; Persall, 1997, p. D1)

A wealth of research into appearance-related feedback supports the many anecdotal accounts that what others say to people can have a profound effect on their feelings. The clear-cut negative impact of receiving negative information about some aspect of one's appearance is one of the best supported areas in body image research. More important, researchers have not only investigated peer feedback but have also begun to address the contribution of appearance-related comments from parents, siblings, other family members, and other adults (e.g., coaches and teachers). The range of comments addressed by researchers is also quite broad, from supposedly "light-hearted" teasing to extremely pejorative comments that border on sexual harassment (or minimally meet our standard for appearance harassment, which is further addressed in chapter 8). Also it is now apparent that one does not necessarily have to verbalize an appearance-related comment—subtle gestures or "looks" that carry a message of an appearance-based critique may have a negative effect on the individual at the receiving end of such nonverbal communication.

RESEARCH BACKGROUND

Description and Prevalence

Surveys, correlational studies, and prospective (longitudinal) investigations support the role of appearance-related feedback as a critical factor in one's body satisfaction. Several large-scale surveys offer information from the past 20 years and are discussed prior to an examination of more sophisticated studies. Perhaps the most recent evidence comes from a *Psychology Today* survey (Garner, 1997), which was referred to earlier in chapters 1 and 3.

Several of the findings from that investigation of 4,000 men and women relate directly to the issue of feedback and body image. For instance, participants were asked, "What shaped your body image when you were young?" (Garner, 1997, p. 36). Forty-four percent of the women noted that "being teased by others" was a factor; 35% of men also claimed that this was a contributing factor. Some of the comments that readers sent in with their surveys illustrate the importance of this event in the development of body image. For instance, a 59-year-old man stated that "being teased when I was a child made me feel bad about my body for years and years" (p. 42). A 37-year-old woman noted that "no matter how thin I become, I always feel like the fat kid everyone made fun of" (p. 42).

In another descriptive study, Rieves and Cash (1996) evaluated 111 college women and asked them not only to name which aspect of their appearance was the target of teasing or criticism but also the specific perpetrator of the teasing. Table 5.1 contains some of their findings. Two targets, the face and head and weight, led the list as sites receiving teasing, at 45% and 36%, respectively. Surprisingly, the mid-torso region was not associated with any teasing instances. (This finding is likely an anomaly of

TABLE 5.1
Appearance Teasing—Criticism During Childhood and Adolescence

What was teased?[a]	%	Who were the teasers?	% ever	% worst
Face and head	45	Brother(s)[b]	79	33
Weight	36	Peers in general	62	28
Upper torso	19	Friends	47	16
Height	17	A specific peer	31	13
Clothes—attire	13	Mother	30	11
Hair	12	Sister(s)[b]	36	8
Lower torso	11	Father	24	6
General appearance	10	Other relatives	23	4
Hands—feet	3	Other adults	20	1
Mid-torso	2	Teachers	6	0
Muscle tone	1			
Miscellaneous	6			

Note. From "Social Development Factors and Women's Body Image Attitudes," by L. Rieves and T. F. Cash, 1996, *Journal of Social Behavior and Personality, 11*, p. 70. Copyright 1996 by the *Journal of Social Behavior and Personality.* Reprinted with permission.
[a]Percentages add up to over 100% because respondents may have been teased or criticized about more than one physical characteristic. [b]These percentages are based on only those respondents who had brothers or sisters.

the teasers' specific wording of comments—comments may not have included direct reference to the stomach but may have targeted this indirectly by including the word *weight* in the commentary.)

Cash (1995a) also found that 72% of women had such experiences and that the median duration was 5 years. In addition, these events were not rare: A total of 46% of the sample noted that they had been the target moderately often (26%), often (14%), or very often (6%). Seventy-one percent noted that the experiences had affected their body image; 70% reported that they think about the past experiences. Clearly, these events may have a long-lasting effect on the individual, a factor that we document further in the next section on associated features.

It is also interesting to note from Table 5.1 that the range of teasers is vast. Although peers in general make up the largest category (62%), family members are also frequent perpetrators, ranging from father (24%) to brother (79%). Friends also ranked near the top at 47%. Rieves and Cash (1996) allowed participants to pick their "worst" perpetrator—the champion in this rather distasteful category belongs to brother who was selected by 33% of the participants. Although this finding may not be a big surprise, the contrast between mother (11%) and father (6%) is somewhat unexpected.

Striegel-Moore, Wilfley, Caldwell, Needham, and Brownell (1996), in a large-scale study of factors affecting Black and White women's dieting and weight-loss practices, asked them about experiences of being "ridiculed" or "criticized" about their weight (by their mother or father) as a child or teenager. They tested 162 White women and 162 Black women.

The findings revealed that White women reported statistically higher levels than did the Black women on all three questions that addressed this issue. However, the actual means were not hugely disparate: For instance, the means for being ridiculed about weight were 2.2 for Black women and 2.5 for White women [1 (*never*) to 5 (*always*)]. This indicates that this negative experience is present in women of both ethnicities and may certainly have clinical indications for both Blacks and Whites. (These researchers did not investigate the relation between level of teasing and clinical measures of distress, such as depression; therefore, it is possible that although the Black women's overall level of ridicule was lower, a history of being ridiculed may be significantly associated with clinically important features. In the next section, this important issue receives an analysis.)

Relation to Body Image

An extensive database indicates that teasing is associated with body dissatisfaction and other clinically relevant dimensions. In one of the first studies in this area, Fabian and Thompson (1989), in a sample of 10- to 15-year-old female adolescents, found that teasing frequency and effect (degree of distress produced) were associated with higher levels of body dissatisfaction, eating disturbance, depression, and lower self-esteem. J. K. Thompson and Psaltis (1988) had female college students recall experiences of being teased and related these retrospective accounts to current levels of body dissatisfaction—both measures of teasing were significantly associated with current levels of body image. These findings were replicated by Cash (1995a) in a sample of female college students. The findings on teasing frequency and body image disturbance were also replicated by Rieves and Cash (1996) in another sample of college women and by Grilo, Wilfley, Brownell, and Rodin (1994) in a sample of obese adult women.

More recent findings—some of them from other countries—also support the connection between teasing and body image problems and offer some additional information into the complex nature of teasing. Wardle and Collins (1998) evaluated 766 girls (12–16 years of age) in London and Dublin, assessing the teasing that occurred in the home and school settings. Both forms of teasing were significantly correlated with body dissatisfaction; however in regression analyses, family-based teasing was a more important predictor than was school-based teasing. Lunner et al. (1998) assessed the frequency and effects of teasing, using the Perception of Teasing Scale (see Appendix 5A) in samples of Swedish, Australian, and U.S. adolescents. U.S. and Australian girls did not differ in frequency of teasing; however, the Australian sample had significantly higher levels on this measure than did the Swedish sample. None of the three groups differed on the effects of the teasing.

The above survey and correlational findings have been extended by the results from prospective and covariance structure modeling studies. Cattarin and Thompson (1994), in a 3-year longitudinal study, found that teasing predicted increases in body dissatisfaction. In addition, being overweight predicted which girls would receive negative feedback in the form of teasing. J. K. Thompson, Coovert, Richards, Johnson, and Cattarin (1995) used covariance structure modeling to test the directionality of relationships among teasing, weight status, body image, and eating disturbance. Teasing was found to be significantly associated with body dissatisfaction and eating disturbance, but perhaps more interesting was teasing's role as a mediator between degree of overweight and body image. Level of obesity was not directly related to body image; its effect was mediated through teasing. Specifically, only those individuals who were overweight and received teasing suffered negative body image effects.

Experimental Manipulation of Feedback

In a few recent studies, researchers have improved on the use of retrospective or survey methodology through the use of vignettes or videos of social interactions to assess reactions to appearance-related feedback scenarios. Kowalski et al. (1997) had male and female college students write two narratives: One involved an event in which they had been teased, and the other required that they describe an incident in which they had teased another individual. There was an interaction between sex of the narrator and the scenario for a measure of guilt: Women felt more guilt when they were the perpetrator rather than the recipient of the teasing comment; however, men's guilt level was the same for both vignettes. Furman and Thompson (1998) constructed a series of scenarios consisting of positive and negative social interactions, with half of the written vignettes focusing on appearance issues and half on abilities. Participants rated their mood and body satisfaction following an evaluation of the scenarios in which they were asked to imagine that the situation had happened to them. In addition, participants were blocked on level of dispositional body image dissatisfaction to determine the role of this as a moderator variable. The results revealed that individuals with high levels of dissatisfaction had the most negative changes in mood and body image after reading the negative appearance scenarios.

Tantleff-Dunn and Thompson (1998) constructed two video presentations of a social interaction between a male and female acquaintance: One of the videos contained several instances of verbal or nonverbal feedback that related to appearance (taken from the Feedback on Physical Appearance Scale; see Appendix 5B), and the other scale had non-appearance-related informational exchanges between the participants. In both cases, comments were directed at the female member from the male

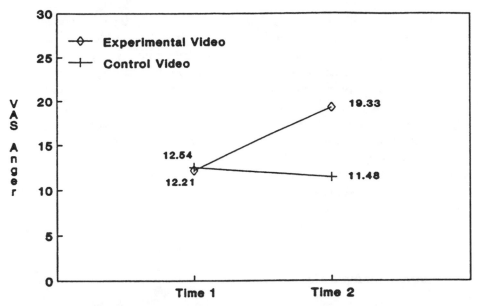

Figure 5.1. Interaction between video condition and time for anger level (Visual Analogue Scale [VAS], in millimeters). For more information, see Tantleff-Dunn and Thompson (1998).

member of the dyad. Participants who saw the videos rated their mood reactions to the vignettes. The results revealed that anger levels went up for the women who witnessed the appearance-related feedback video but not for the women who saw the control tape (see Figure 5.1). In addition, all participants, after viewing the videos, rated how negative they thought the experience had affected the female member of the dyad in the video. Participants with dispositionally high levels of body image anxiety thought the woman who received the appearance-related feedback was more negatively affected by this experience than the woman who was in the non-appearance-related interaction; however, individuals with low body image anxiety did not perceive any differences in the reaction of the woman in the video (see Figure 5.2). In actuality, the behavior of the woman in the dyad was the same, regardless of the condition. Tantleff-Dunn and Thompson conjectured that the women with high body image anxiety may have had a cognitive bias that affected their ratings of the woman's reactions. (More information is presented in chapter 10 on the issue of cognitive-processing models of body image disturbance.)

Methodological Issues

Particular methodological issues should be noted with regard to the research on appearance-based feedback. Because of the nature of the con-

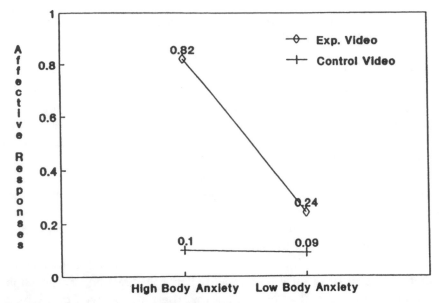

Figure 5.2. Interaction between dispositional anxiety level (high, low) and video for affective responses (Visual Analogue Scale, in millimeters). For more information, see Tantleff-Dunn and Thompson (1998).

struct, that is, relating one's own experiences of receiving negative commentary from others, the method of measurement is necessarily self-report and retrospective. Thus, it is difficult, if not impossible, to corroborate the information. One strategy could be to interview significant others, such as teachers, parents, or peers, to estimate the reliability of these self-reports. However, this is quite invasive and most likely would not be sufficient because these individuals might not be present for many of the negative experiences. In addition, it would be most difficult for external observers to rate the effects of such experiences of the recipient, even if they might add corroboration for the frequency.

Although the problems with retrospective recall information are somewhat problematic, many researchers in the field are partially satisfied that the findings are valid. First, prospective data show that teasing predicts an increase in body dissatisfaction over time (Cattarin & Thompson, 1994). Second, when the effects of non-appearance-based teasing (i.e., competency or abilities teasing) are factored out, the significant effects of appearance teasing remain (J. K. Thompson, Cattarin, Fowler, & Fisher, 1995). Finally, as noted above, in recent studies researchers have experimentally manipulated exposure to teasing or appearance-based scenarios and have found an immediate effect on participants' mood and body image. Therefore, although the methodology might be improved in future research in this area by, if possible, including methods to document the authenticity of teasing experiences, the extant data support the strong role of this as a factor in body image disturbance.

Theoretical Explanations

One of the most thorough discussions of theoretical perspectives on appearance-related commentary has been provided by Shapiro, Baumeister, and Kessler (1991). These researchers outlined a three-component model of teasing consisting of aggression, humor, and ambiguity. In their conceptualization, "neither unalloyed humor nor pure aggression" (Shapiro et al., 1991, p. 461) would qualify as teasing—teasing occurs only if these two means of social interaction are combined in a certain way. Only this combination produces ambiguity, which is often the source of confusion or displeasure on the part of the individual who is the target. One may have difficulty deciding if the reaction warranted is one of responding to a largely humorous intent or of an intent weighted in the direction of aggression. If the target interprets it as benign teasing, then all involved may have a good joke; however, if the interpretation is one of maliciousness, conflict may erupt. Of course, the source of the commentary may attempt to clarify the comment if a "misinterpretation" is made by the target. The validity of this "clarification," as judged by the target, determines the next step in the interaction. Common clarifiers are those many people have heard (or used), such as "I was just teasing" and "I didn't mean it."

Naturally, teasing without any humorous content is not actually teasing as we have defined it. An example might be an obvious or blatant insult, such as calling a person "hippo hips." For instance, a young boy with a disability may find little humor in the taunts directed at his prosthetic leg. Another appearance-related example, "Your clothes don't match," is devoid of humor, although it may or may not be considered insulting (unless the target is known for his or her strong investment in fashion). Alternatively, asking someone if they have "been dressing in the dark again" adds a bit of humor and conveys the same message regarding the person's sartorial sense.

Shapiro et al. (1991) found that as one might expect, most teasing is of a verbal nature, with the most commonly targeted aspects consisting of an individual's behavior or attribute (28%), comments on the individual's name or calling the person names (25%), and "simply laughing" (p. 462) at the individual (11%). Other verbal forms included sarcastic comments, facetious questions, and exaggerated imitation. They found that 9% of teasing events were nonverbal, including such behaviors as pointing, making faces, and generally annoying the person (e.g., adding a "kick me" sign to his or her back).

Shapiro et al. (1991) also found that the content of the teasing is consistent with the importance of this issue for body image. Physical appearance-related teasing occurred in 39% of the incidents reported by their sample and weight teasing occurred most frequently as the specific appearance target (33% of the total). Intellectual performance, physical abilities, and interest in the opposite sex were the subjects rated, in order, after appearance-based teasing events. It is interesting to note that girls were more likely than boys to report being teased about appearance (48% to 29%, respectively).

A characteristic of teasing that is not surprising is that the affective response of the target is usually highly predictable. In Shapiro et al.'s (1991) sample, 97% of elementary schoolchildren had a negative reaction when they were the target of teasing; among eighth graders, 78% had a negative reaction. Somewhat surprising is that the motives of teasers, who might be expected to sugarcoat their intentions, are often less than benevolent: 16% felt they were "playing, or joking around" (Shapiro et al., 1991, p. 463); however, 35% did it as a form of reciprocity (teasing back, after being a target); and 20% did it when in a bad mood or when disliking the target. Ten percent teased when they were aligned with a group that was engaging in the behavior. The 4% who engaged in the behavior as a form of flirting with the opposite sex only partially offset the large percentage of those with a negative intent. Clearly, the negative emotional reactions on the part of the recipient of teasing argue for some type of clinical intervention, which is addressed later in this chapter.

There is no simple explanation for helping one to understand the motivation of the teaser and the reaction of the individual who is the target of the commentary. Much of the research to date is descriptive and, as noted earlier, was designed to evaluate the connection between such commentary and clinical levels of body dissatisfaction, eating disturbance, and general psychological functioning. However, a few hypotheses have received attention. For instance, teasing may function as a means of establishing social dominance. Teasers are often described as bullies, however, they may also be the kid who is the funniest and most outspoken in the group (Shapiro et al., 1991). Both of these types of individuals have an elevated status or dominance in a group. Also supporting this idea is that the individuals who are often the brunt of teasing are those who may be of lower status, such as individuals deemed unattractive, less intelligent, and unpopular.

A second hypothesis is that teasing promotes conformity. Again as outlined by Shapiro et al. (1991), it may fall on the dominant teaser to enforce group norms through verbal feedback to the individual who doesn't "fit in." Wearing unstylish shoes, sporting an odd hairstyle, or simply being fat are appearance-related issues that may promote social feedback in the form of teasing—teasing that may be governed by its intention to inform the individual to make changes and conform to prevailing standards.

The reaction of the individual to being teased may not necessarily be determined solely by the specific behavior of the teaser. For instance, the target's previous history of being teased may be an important variable. In a series of studies, noted earlier, we have found that a previous history of being teased is associated with elevated levels of body dissatisfaction. Thus, it is likely that if one has developed a "sensitivity" to a particular issue (i.e., weight), as a function of previous weight-related teasing, future teasing events might be even more salient, producing an even stronger negative response. This is a tempting and logical premise; unfortunately, research has not been conducted to test the assumption.

One's attribution or inference regarding the teasing event is also a factor in the overall reaction. For instance, it is possible to make a subjective internal attribution (i.e., "I really am fat") that may produce a strong sense of dysphoria. Alternatively, one may eschew a personal dispositional tack and externalize the event (i.e., "He has problems if he thinks that's funny"). In addition, one might make a situational attribution, deciding that, for instance, because the comment was made during a party and most of the group were "kidding" each other, no malefaction was intended. Ready acceptance of the negative message versus targeting the lack of social skills on the part of the teaser illustrates the quite different potential effects of the same teasing event on the individual, which is moderated by a simple cognitive difference in attribution. To date, there appears to be no research on attributions of teasing and subsequent negative outcome. However, related to this hypothesis is research by Anderson, Miller, Riger, Dill, and Sedikides (1994) who found that individuals who internalize negative outcomes experience greater depression and loneliness.

A second dispositional trait that may be connected to teasing's negative effect is fear of negative evaluation. Wardle and Collins (1998) found that teasing from two sources—school and family—were both more damaging in girls with high fear of negative evaluation than in boys. C. M. Thomas, Keery, Williams, and Thompson (1998) recently developed a measure of fear of negative appearance evaluation (see Appendix 5C), which is significantly correlated with body dissatisfaction and a history of being teased. It would be interesting to determine if this concept is predictive of an individual's reaction to negative appearance-related vignettes, such as those discussed earlier.

Self-disclosure strategies may also have an impact on the effects of teasing. Vernberg, Ewell, Beery, Freeman, and Abwender (1995) found that many adolescents kept their experience of teasing a secret from other people, preferring to handle it on their own as opposed to seeking social support. Thirty-eight percent of girls and 46% of boys kept their experience of being teased from other people. Vernberg et al. found that this passive approach to handling the pain of teasing was associated with higher levels of loneliness.

Although several different processes have been offered as possible hypotheses to explain the negative effects of teasing and other types of negative appearance-related commentary, to date, little research has actually emerged to test the relative merits of the different explanations. One potentially fruitful approach might be to consider the behavioral and cognitive conceptualizations, which have been applied to posttraumatic stress disorder (Foa, Stekette, & Rothbaum, 1989). Clinically, the symptoms presented by many clients who have a history of a traumatic appearance-related teasing or an *appearance harassment* episode are similar in quality (if not quantity) to those of individuals who have had other traumatic incidents, such as physical assaults or accidents. The recall of such experiences is associated with extreme distress, and current events or situations that have cues similar to the original traumatizing experience cause anguish. Further work evaluating the commonalities among posttraumatic stress disorder and severe instances of appearance-related negative feedback is certainly recommended.

ASSESSMENT

Measures

In recent years, a wide variety of methods have been developed for the assessment of feedback from others regarding one's physical appearance. These measures range from empirically derived scales to interviews, and they have been used to target the influence of appearance-related feedback received from peers, romantic partners, siblings, parents, and other individuals. Although the measures have been developed and designed primarily for research purposes, many of them can be easily adapted for a variety of uses, including clinical assessment of clients with body image-related problems.

The Physical Appearance Related Teasing Scale (PARTS; J. K. Thompson, Fabian, Moulton, Dunn, & Altabe, 1991) was designed as a retrospective measure of teasing related to size, weight, and general physical appearance. This factorially derived scale consists of two subscales: 12 items dealing with weight/size-related teasing and 6 items pertaining to teasing about nonweight/general appearance-related issues. Each item requires participants to rate how frequently they were the targets of a teasing behavior while growing up. A psychometric evaluation with a sample of female college undergraduates suggests that both subscales have high internal consistency and test–retest reliability with that particular population. (See Table 5.2 for information about this scale and others discussed in this section.) In addition, the weight/size-related teasing subscale converges well with measures of eating disturbance, body image dissatisfaction, social comparison, depression, and self-esteem, whereas the general appearance teasing subscale is largely unrelated to these variables.

TABLE 5.2
Measures of Appearance-Related Feedback

Instrument	Author(s)	Description	Reliability 1, 2	Standardization sample	Address of author
Physical Appearance Related Teasing Scale	J. K. Thompson, Fabian, et al. (1991)	18-item scale assessing history of weight–size and general appearance-related teasing	(a) IC: weight–size scale, –.91; appearance scale, –.71 (b) TR: 2 weeks (weight–size, –.86; appearance scale, –.87)	Female undergraduates	J. Kevin Thompson, PhD Department of Psychology University of South Florida 4202 Fowler Avenue Tampa, FL 33620-8200
Perception of Teasing Scale	J. K. Thompson, Cattarin, et al. (1995)	12 items indexing general weight teasing and competency teasing	IC: general weight (.94), competency (.78)	227 female undergraduates	J. Kevin Thompson, PhD Department of Psychology University of South Florida 4202 Fowler Avenue Tampa, FL 33620-8200
Feedback on Physical Appearance Scale	Tantleff-Dunn et al. (1995)	8 items assessing appearance-related commentary (verbal and nonverbal)	(a) IC: .84 (b) TR: (2 weeks) .82	College undergraduates: 237 female students, 161 male students	Stacey Tantleff-Dunn, PhD Department of Psychology University of Central Florida P.O. Box 161390 Orlando, FL 32816-1390
Inventory of Peer Influence on Eating Concerns	Oliver & Thelen (1996)	30 items measure the frequency with which children receive negative messages from peers about their bodies or eating habits (Messages factor), the frequency with which children interact with their peers about eating or body-related issues (Interactions factor), and the degree to which children believe that being thin will increase their likability with peers (Likability factor)	IC: messages, .91; interactions/boys, .76; interactions/girls, .80; likability/boys, .88; likability/girls, .88	142 third graders and 122 fifth graders (both boys and girls) drawn from health classes at two elementary schools in a Midwestern community (predominantly middle socioeconomic status)	Mark H. Thelen, PhD Psychology Department University of Missouri—Columbia 210 McAlester Hall Columbia, MO 65211

Measure	Source	Description	Reliability	Sample	Author contact
Family History of Eating Survey	Moreno & Thelen (1993)	Scale compares parental concerns about child's weight with child's perception of parental concern; a modified version uses four items related to the number of times parents encouraged children to lose weight	IC: (based on four items) daughter's perception of mother's and father's encouragement to lose weight, .83 and .72, respectively; son's perception of mother's and father's encouragement to lose weight, .68 and .62, respectively	51 female and 49 male fourth graders enrolled in public schools in the Midwest from two-parent and single-parent families	Mark H. Thelen, PhD Psychology Department University of Missouri—Columbia 210 McAlester Hall Columbia, MO 65211
None given	Striegel-Moore & Kearney-Cooke (1994)	Parent survey developed as part of a 77-item questionnaire on body image; parent section includes questions about perceptions of their child's attractiveness and what parents had done to change their child's appearance			Ruth Striegel-Moore, PhD Department of Psychology Wesleyan University Middletown, CT 06459-0408
Aversive Experiences Interview	Vernberg et al. (1995)	Respondents indicate how frequently they were teased, hit or pushed, threatened with physical harm, or left out of a desired peer activity	IC: .36–.51 TR: Moderate stability over 6 months	130 early adolescents (65 boys and 65 girls), age = 13 years, in the public school system in Dade County, FL; ethnically diverse but predominantly middle socioeconomic status	Eric Vernberg, PhD Clinical Child Psychology Program University of Kansas 1122 West Campus Road Lawrence, KS 66045
Appearance Teasing Inventory	Cash (1995b)	Uses open-ended and Likert-scaled items that assess if participants have been teased or criticized about their looks and identifies the most prominent offender; participants also rate the frequency, distress, and effects on current body image and the frequency of current recollections of these incidents	None reported	11 (ages 18–39) and 152 (ages 17–35) female college students	Thomas F. Cash, PhD Department of Psychology Old Dominion University Norfolk, VA 23529-0267

Note. IC = internal consistency; TR = test–retest reliability.

The PARTS is limited in that its items do not specify whether the teasing targeted a large or small body size (thus, being teased for being under vs. overweight is not differentiated), and the scale does not identify the source(s) of the teasing. To address these limitations, Thompson and colleagues revised the PARTS, and a new scale, the Perception of Teasing Scale (POTS; J. K. Thompson, Cattarin, et al., 1995), resulted. The POTS consists of two factors: six items comprise the weight-teasing subscale, and five items make up the competency-teasing subscale. The POTS includes a non-weight-teasing (competency) subscale, and the items are worded so that identification of the specific perpetrator of the teasing is possible (by simply modifying the beginning of each question from *people* to the source of interest, i.e., *parents* or *peers*). For instance, Schwartz, Phares, Tantleff-Dunn, and Thompson (in press) were able to differentiate the role of mother versus father teasing by rewording the items on the POTS. The POTS was also expanded to assess the effect of teasing, that is, how upset the experience was to the individual. (See Appendix 5A for the POTS.)

The Feedback on Physical Appearance Scale (FOPAS; Tantleff-Dunn, Thompson, & Dunn, 1995) expands on the type of feedback captured by the POTS by including items that address a more subtle form of appearance-related communication. This 8-item, factorially derived measure was designed to assess the frequency with which physical appearance-related verbal and nonverbal external feedback is received. An expanded version of the FOPAS includes 18 additional items that were dropped after a factor analysis but are helpful for gaining more information about a specific individual's appearance-related feedback experiences. Standardized on a sample of college undergraduates, the FOPAS has high convergence with a variety of body image and eating disturbance measures for both male and female participants. The FOPAS can be found in Appendix 5B.

The FOPAS, however, has yet to be used with clinical samples, and the potential utility of the scale needs to be further explored by psychometric evaluation with more diverse populations, including children, and ethnically diverse samples. The FOPAS can easily be adapted for a variety of purposes and has been used to examine feedback received from romantic partners (Tantleff-Dunn & Thompson, 1995) and parents (Schwartz et al., in press). Because it is a brief, easy-to-read, self-administered scale, the FOPAS may be a good screening tool in working with clients who are dissatisfied with their appearance and may be adversely affected by the subtle forms of appearance-related feedback that may go unreported. The scale may be particularly helpful for cases in which subtle forms of feedback are not readily recognized (and thus not brought to the clinician's attention) yet have a detrimental effect on the client. For example, when asked directly "Do others tease or criticize you about your weight?" an individual may respond negatively, despite the fact that he or she continually receives constant updates on new diets from family members or friends.

Other researchers have also developed short questionnaire measures or used single-item Likert-scaled indices. For instance, M. P. Levine, Smolak, and Hayden (1994) developed a 5-item scale of family teasing and criticism. Striegel-Moore et al. (1996) used single items to evaluate whether women had felt ridiculed or criticized about weight during childhood and adolescence. One limitation with the POTS, FOPAS, and other questionnaire measures is that the items are rather specific and closed ended, thereby restricting the information gained about an individual's idiosyncratic teasing experiences. More open-ended interview techniques, although difficult to analyze psychometrically, may yield information not possible with the more standardized questionnaire measurement procedures.

For instance, Cash (1995a) developed the Appearance Teasing Inventory (ATI), which elicits both interview data and quantitative information on respondents' teasing history and its reported past and current emotional effects (see also Rieves & Cash, 1996). The ATI assesses the particular aspects of physical appearance that were targeted by the teasing–criticism as well as the frequency and duration of the negative commentary. In addition, respondents identify the most frequent perpetrators of the teasing–criticism. The ATI converges with the PARTS (described above) when an ATI index score of teasing–criticism frequency and effect is calculated. The potential benefit of adding the ATI to an assessment battery is that it permits a collection of more detailed information related to the type of feedback received (teasing vs. criticism) and its impact. Given the added information gained from the interview component of the measure, the ATI may be especially useful in working with clients who have rich and unique past teasing experiences.

Vernberg et al. (1995) used the Rejection Experiences Interview to obtain information about how frequently children were teased, threatened with physical harm, or left out of a desired peer activity. The interview was designed to be nonthreatening by wording interview questions in a way that normalized teasing experiences (e.g., "Sometimes kids will tease or pick on other kids; how often has someone teased or picked on you?"). The adolescents responded on a 5-point scale (from 1 = *never* to 5 = *very often*), and further queries regarding whether the adolescent reported teasing incidents to others followed. This type of interview may be particularly helpful for uncovering teasing experiences that children are frequently exposed to yet unlikely to report to adults.

Methodological Issues

In assessing an individual with body image disturbance, one needs to distinguish between past and current teasing–feedback experiences. It is conceivable that past experiences may have had a significant influence on the development of body image and should be addressed, but distinguishing previous incidents from present situations may facilitate identification of the most significant current influences that can be addressed in treatment. For example, a female client reported that her father used to tease her a great deal about her weight and referred to her as "chunk" (short for chunky). This had an extremely negative and lasting influence on how she felt about her appearance and how she believed she was perceived by men. Because she was unable to assertively deal with her father, she tended to complain to teachers and to her mother that the boys in school were giving her a hard time about her weight and calling her names. Even years later when in treatment for a problem with binge eating, the woman described her husband as being very critical of her appearance and prone to call her chunk when she overate. After working with the couple for a while, the counselor realized that although the husband was not as supportive as his wife would have liked, he actually did not make disparaging comments or even call her by that disturbing name; she tended to verbalize what she thought her husband was thinking on the basis of her previous experience of being teased by her father.

As found by Vernberg et al. (1995), many adolescents who were frequent targets of such unpleasant behaviors as teasing and harassment told no one about these negative events and they felt isolated and lonely. When the events were discussed, adolescents usually disclosed them to peers rather than parents and teachers. Perhaps having children complete some of these teasing–feedback assessment measures would keep adults informed about the aversive experiences the children may be enduring. Adults may underestimate the degree to which children and adolescents are exposed to such taunting; therefore, using some formal mode of assessment may give adults the opportunity to provide the children with support and to teach coping strategies for dealing with these inevitable experiences in youth. Vernberg et al. emphasized the need for special measures to facilitate reporting of such unwelcome feedback and actual bullying, such as confidential hotlines and direct questioning of victims.

TREATMENT

Although in many ways appearance-related feedback research is still in its infancy, some important implications for treatment are worth exploring. The most appropriate and effective ways for addressing teasing and its influence largely depend on the context in which it occurs. For this reason, we now examine treatment implications related to teasing in the family, schools, and a more general social context.

Interventions for Children

People are often unaware of the impact of their behavior, particularly when it involves giving feedback on physical appearance. What a parent may consider harmless teasing, for example, a daughter may consider highly critical and damaging to her confidence about her appearance. Therefore, it may be helpful to have all family members and significant others involved in both the assessment and treatment of body image-related problems, so that discrepancies between what family members think they are doing and saying and what receivers perceive can be illustrated. Particularly with children, it may be helpful to have siblings and parents made aware of the impact of their behaviors on the child. For example, one client, an obese 14-year-old, was brought by her parents to an eating disorders clinic for treatment following several failed diets and exercise programs. During the initial interview with the family, the parents insisted that they were only concerned about their daughter's physical health and that their desire for her to lose weight was not at all related to concerns about her appearance because she was attractive and had lots of friends. Their denial of investment in their daughter's appearance was particularly interesting and did not match information obtained from observing the family while they were in the public waiting area. The mother picked lint off her daughter's shirt while the father interrogated his daughter about why she was wearing that "oversized outfit that was not at all flattering." A focus of treatment for this family involved exploring the impact of such behaviors on their daughter's body image and consequent rebellion by overeating.

It is important to also consider that children can have quite an impact on their parent's body image through their teasing and commentary. One of us (Stacey Tantleff-Dunn) was recently in a women's dressing room at a department store and overheard a conversation between a mother and her young daughter. "You are getting so fat, Mommy!" the daughter exclaimed as her mother undressed. "I can't believe you are going to buy clothes now when you look so fat. Shouldn't you lose some weight first? I like you better when you are skinny." The mother replied very defensively, "I don't look that bad!" but then assured her daughter that "I'll lose weight, but I still need new pants now." After exiting the dressing room, the young girl was encountered and asked her age. She was only 8 years old and already remarkably articulate in providing rather hurtful feedback to her mother, who, incidentally, was only slightly overweight. The mother did not sanction her daughter's verbal behavior but rather acted as if it were appropriate. Certainly, parents can help their children learn that many types of appearance-related feedback are inappropriate and hurtful by both modeling appropriate behavior and discouraging children from using appearance-related comments in relating to others.

In working with children, psychologists might assess the impact of feedback from parents, siblings, and peers, so that intervention may be planned where appropriate. A great deal of teasing takes place in schools; therefore, it is important to consider ways of handling the teasing issue in this setting. Until recently, very few researchers have even examined bullying. Most schools see it as an inevitable part of the school experience and choose to ignore it (Smith & Sharp, 1994). Following three student suicides that resulted from teasing, however, Norway experienced an increase in public concern about bullying and began focusing on developing ways in which schools could effectively deal with the problem. In 1983, Norway launched a nationwide campaign against bullying throughout all the schools. Teachers were given videos for classroom discussion, and parents were sent advice on how to help their children deal with bullying. In a well-designed evaluation of the campaign's effectiveness, Olweus (1991, 1993) found that 2 years after the program had started, bullying decreased by approximately 50% for both male and female students on a variety of measures. Thus, school programs can be an effective way of addressing and preventing the difficulties that result from teasing and bullying experiences.

Recently, Sjostrom and Stein (1996) outlined ideas for dealing with teasing and bullying in the school system. The following guidelines are taken from their book on this subject:

(a) Help students differentiate among joking, teasing, and bullying. Joking may involve playing a joke on oneself or behavior that both parties find humorous, whereas teasing and bullying are often at others' expense and are hurtful.

(b) Have students assume the role of researchers in their own school. Collecting observational data on teasing may raise their awareness of the prevalence of these problems, and they can assess the roles of targets and bystanders. They can determine when behavior crosses the line from joking into hurtful teasing and bullying. This is also effective for helping students recognize the impact of teasing from a more objective vantage point.

(c) Role-playing can be used to teach students more about the roles of the bully or teaser, the target, and the responsibility of bystanders. Sjostrom and Stein recommended using examples from students' observations. One role-play as an example is the following scenario: "I feel bullied when people make fun of my zits and how fat I am." Students are asked to work in small groups to brainstorm different ways that the situation might be handled (e.g., clear up skin, ignore the kids, tell a teacher, agree with the teaser) and then present the various options in role-plays for the entire class. Following role-playing, it is important to engage students in discussions on the advantages and disadvantages of each response to the teasing–bullying scenarios.

(d) Explore ways that students might be able to intervene as a bystander, with teachers encouraging students to act courageously as bystanders. In a related activity, students are asked to write a statement of their personal principles in relation to bullying and teasing. The hope is that by encouraging creative, proactive responses to teasing and bullying by bystanders, the problems of harassment in school can be addressed at the student level. Particularly for young students who do not yet readily adopt the perspective of others, these activities may be effective for helping children develop greater sensitivity to the feelings of their peers.

Another activity included in this antibullying program is encouraging students to write their bullies letters in which they articulate the behaviors that are unacceptable, the ways in which these behaviors have hurt them, and the ways that they would like the bully to treat them differently. Toward the end of the lessons on bullying and teasing, students are encouraged to come up with ideas and plans for eliminating bullying and teasing in their school and to become an antibullying activist, informing their friends outside of class about what they have learned about teasing and bullying.

Interventions for Adults

Many clinicians share the sentiment that it is more effective for individuals to learn how to problem solve, enhance their interpersonal communication skills, and engage in assertiveness training than for them to focus on changing the behavior of others. This may be particularly relevant in the area of addressing the sometimes devastating effects of receiving negative appearance-related feedback. One cognitive strategy that we have found useful is to *reframe* the experience. One case involved a college student who felt that her cheeks were too wide—a belief that she traced back to incessant teasing by an uncle when she was a young girl. She had internalized his comments and no longer doubted the veracity of his statements. She was asked to reconsider the validity of his early remarks by considering that he may have lacked other ways of socially interacting with her. That is, she was asked to reframe the experience as a skills deficit on his part. This also led to a reduction in her anger toward him over the experience.

Other cognitive strategies may also be helpful. For example, it is important to force clients to "examine the evidence." There may be cases where the individual misinterprets an experience, leading to body dissatisfaction. For instance, one client was extremely self-conscious and upset about his increasing hair loss. When a female friend gave him a baseball cap, he assumed that this gesture meant that she was disgusted by his patchy hair loss and she felt that he should cover it up. In reality, the baseball hat was purchased as a gift at a recent game in which his favorite team won. Making individuals aware of a possible tendency to distort information and help them learn how to substitute their biased notions with more accurate, realistic interpretations of others' behavior is a useful cognitive strategy.

Some clients may benefit a great deal from recognizing the irrational beliefs that underlie the negative impact of appearance-related comments from others. Such beliefs as "I must look good to be liked" or "I must be attractive to everyone" may make receiving feedback on physical appearance especially painful. By identifying these beliefs, clients may be able to put the importance of their physical appearance in a more realistic perspective and consequently be less sensitive about others' evaluation of them. Thus, some of the cognitive restructuring strategies outlined by Cash (e.g., 1997) and J. C. Rosen (e.g., 1997; see also chapter 2) may be especially suited for individuals with teasing-related problems (see also chapter 10 for a discussion of cognitive strategies).

Behavioral strategies may also be useful. For instance, assertiveness training may be recommended for individuals who are disturbed by teasing and other forms of appearance-related feedback, yet these people do not make it clear to others that they are hurt by it and would like the behavior to stop. They may get angry with the perpetrator but feel unable or unwilling to prevent future incidents from occurring. Although clients do not have control over others' behavior, by not reacting in an assertive manner they may be inadvertently condoning the teasing and feedback from others. Many clients have stated that they actually partake in the process of poking fun at their own appearance, earning the reputation of being able to joke about themselves. Thus, it is important to teach people appropriate ways of honestly communicating their feelings about receiving comments about their looks or being teased. Through role-play and other assertiveness training techniques, clients can get practice responding to appearance-related feedback in more effective ways that will not exacerbate or prolong the problem. Some examples of potentially effective responses are the following:

(a) I know you may just be kidding around, but it really hurts my feelings when you tease me about my appearance.
(b) I would really prefer if you would avoid making comments about my physical appearance. They really make me uncomfortable.
(c) I wonder why it is that you need to joke so much about my weight.

For those clients who prefer snappier comebacks, one strategy is to have a witty retort at the ready for such instances. For example, one suggestion for handling unwanted weight-related commentary might be following comeback: "Why should I lose weight? So my body can be as narrow as your mind?" This is just one example that demonstrates the strategy of dealing with hurtful comments by hurting back. Although this approach may effectively prevent further comments or teasing, it may also damage interpersonal relationships and teach the perpetrator nothing about the impact of their behavior. (It may also contribute to escalation and further conflict.) Nonetheless, sometimes an attention-getting, witty response may make its point and protect one from having to deal with the pain of the original comment. Because of the potential negative effects on relationships, however, they should be used sparingly and with caution.

Going Global—Can Psychologists Affect Society?

Thus far, we focused on strategies to help the individual cope with negative appearance-related feedback from interpersonal sources. Certainly, another avenue is to target the media—a factor that drives social acceptance, indeed models such behavior on the part of perpetrators (J. K. Thompson & Heinberg, in press). As noted in chapters 1 and 2, clinicians and organizations (e.g., National Association to Advance Fat Acceptance [NAAFA]) have argued for greater acceptance of diversity in appearance and actually have targeted specific negative influences, such as NAAFA's denouncement of the fat jokes contained in the Eddie Murphy movie *The Nutty Professor* ("NAAFA denounces *The Nutty Professor*," 1996). Legal options are also available in the case when teasing becomes harassment (see chapter 8). Finally, the role of continued research in this area and the dissemination of findings to educators, parents, and professionals is crucial to inform the general public about the connection between negative feedback and body image problems.

CONCLUSIONS

Clearly, research strongly documents the important role of feedback from others in the formation and maintenance of body image disturbance. A number of measures are currently available for the assessment of this influence, and these may be quite useful additions to any clinical assessment battery for individuals who present body image issues. Treatment approaches, although yet to receive empirical testing, have been articulated and may augment the effects of the treatments noted in chapter 2. Certainly, many individuals in U.S. society, particularly overweight persons, are the target of negative feedback, and efforts to promote greater acceptance of the diversity of body shapes, sizes, and appearances is a laudable public policy goal.

APPENDIX 5A
PERCEPTION OF TEASING SCALE

We are interested in whether you have been teased and how this affected you.

First, for each question rate *how often* you think you were teased using the scale provided, *never* (1) to *always* (5).

Never		Sometimes		Very often
1	2	3	4	5

Second, unless you respond *never* to the question, rate *how upset* you were by the teasing, *not upset* (1) to *very upset* (5)

Not upset		Somewhat upset		Very upset
1	2	3	4	5

1. People made fun of you because you were heavy.	1 2 3 4 5
How upset were you?	1 2 3 4 5
2. People made jokes about you being heavy.	1 2 3 4 5
How upset were you?	1 2 3 4 5
3. People laughed at you for trying out for sports because you were heavy.	1 2 3 4 5
How upset were you?	1 2 3 4 5
4. People called you names like "fatso."	1 2 3 4 5
How upset were you?	1 2 3 4 5
5. People pointed at you because you were overweight.	1 2 3 4 5
How upset were you?	1 2 3 4 5
6. People snickered about your heaviness when you walked into a room alone.	1 2 3 4 5
How upset were you?	1 2 3 4 5
7. People made fun of you by repeating something you said because they thought that it was dumb.	1 2 3 4 5
How upset were you?	1 2 3 4 5
8. People made fun of you because you were afraid to do something.	1 2 3 4 5
How upset were you?	1 2 3 4 5
9. People said you acted dumb.	1 2 3 4 5
How upset were you?	1 2 3 4 5
10. People laughed at you because you didn't understand something.	1 2 3 4 5
How upset were you?	1 2 3 4 5
11. People teased you because you didn't get a joke.	1 2 3 4 5
How upset were you?	1 2 3 4 5

From "The Perception of Teasing Scale (POTS): A Revision and Extension of the Physical Appearance Related Teasing Scale (PARTS)," by J. K. Thompson, J. Cattarin, B. Fowler, and E. Fisher, 1995, *Journal of Personality Assessment, 65*, p. 157. Copyright 1995 by Lawrence Erlbaum Associates, Inc. Reprinted with permission.

APPENDIX 5B
FEEDBACK ON PHYSICAL APPEARANCE SCALE

Sometimes people say or do things that make us feel good, bad, or just more self-conscious about our appearance. Please read each item and rate how often you think you have been the recipient or target of such behavior. Using the following scale, circle the number that is closest to the amount that the behavior occurs:

Never	Seldom	Sometimes	Often	Always
1	2	3	4	5

The following items refer to experiences that make you feel bad about your body.

1. Someone suggested a gym to work out in.	1	2	3	4	5
2. Someone asked if you've gained some weight.	1	2	3	4	5
3. Someone suggested that you should dress differently.	1	2	3	4	5
4. Someone made some facial expression when looking at your body.	1	2	3	4	5
5. Someone watched closely what you ate.	1	2	3	4	5
6. Someone suggested a new diet that's available.	1	2	3	4	5
7. Someone called you "fatso" (or something similar).	1	2	3	4	5
8. Someone did not offer you dessert.	1	2	3	4	5
9. Someone said, "You look like you've lost weight."	1	2	3	4	5
10. Someone whistled at you.	1	2	3	4	5
11. Someone commented on your outfit.	1	2	3	4	5
12. Someone grabbed your rear end.	1	2	3	4	5
13. Someone said, "Something about you looks different, but I can't figure out what it is."	1	2	3	4	5
14. Someone asked if you were younger or older than you were.	1	2	3	4	5
15. Someone asked if you'd been dieting.	1	2	3	4	5
16. Someone suggested in a clothing store that you were a larger/smaller size than you were.	1	2	3	4	5
17. Someone grabbed your waist.	1	2	3	4	5
18. Someone gave you the "once over glance."	1	2	3	4	5
19. Someone asked if you've been exercising lately.	1	2	3	4	5
20. Someone suggested you should eat more.	1	2	3	4	5
21. Someone called you "bones," "slim," or something similar.	1	2	3	4	5
22. Someone asked you how much you weigh.	1	2	3	4	5
23. Someone avoided looking at you while you were undressed.	1	2	3	4	5
24. Someone never said anything good or bad about your body.	1	2	3	4	5
25. Someone watched what food you purchased at the store.	1	2	3	4	5
26. Someone focused comments on nonweight-related areas (i.e., hair, eyes).	1	2	3	4	5

From "Development and Validation of the Feedback on Physical Appearance Scale," by S. Tantleff-Dunn, J. K. Thompson, and M. Dunn, 1995, *Eating Disorders: The Journal of Treatment and Prevention, 3*, 341–342. Copyright 1995 by *Eating Disorders: The Journal of Treatment and Prevention*. Reprinted with permission.

APPENDIX 5C
FEAR OF NEGATIVE APPEARANCE EVALUATION SCALE

Never true	Rarely true	Sometimes true	Frequently true	Almost always true		
1	2	3	4	5		

1. I am concerned about what other people think of my appearance.   1   2   3   4   5
2. It bothers me if I know someone is judging my physical shape.   1   2   3   4   5
3. I don't care about other people's opinion of my appearance.   1   2   3   4   5
4. I worry that people will find fault with the way I look.   1   2   3   4   5
5. When I meet new people, I wonder what they think about my appearance.   1   2   3   4   5
6. I am afraid other people will notice my physical flaws.   1   2   3   4   5
7. I am unconcerned even when I know that my appearance is being evaluated.   1   2   3   4   5
8. I think that other people's opinion of my appearance is too important to me.   1   2   3   4   5

From the Fear of Negative Appearance Evaluation Scale, an unpublished scale by C. M. Thomas and J. K. Thompson. Reprinted with permission from the authors. For more information, see C. M. Thomas et al. (1998).

6

INTERPERSONAL FACTORS: PEERS, PARENTS, PARTNERS, AND PERFECT STRANGERS

One plastic surgeon tells of a man who, envious of a spouse's breast augmentation, demanded a new set of pectorals to keep pace. (E. Rosenthal, 1991, p. C1)

You're not a year older, you're a year more eager for plastic surgery. So says the Carvel Ice Cream Bakery, whose informal survey found that tucks and lifts and other forms of improvement on nature are high on the birthday wish lists of both men and women. But whereas women wished for plastic surgery for themselves, men wished for plastic surgery for their wives. ("A face lift?" 1997, p. D4).

A 19-year-old Pakistani girl came seeking a rhinoplasty. She had a slight hump, and felt that her nose was ugly. She had always felt unaccepted by her family, and her sisters had told her that she was ugly and would never get married. Her parents wanted to arrange a marriage abroad, with someone much older, an inferior to her in status, education and income, as they perceived this as being her only chance of marriage. She wanted a rhinoplasty in order to look attractive, so that she could avoid this marriage and be accepted by her family. She eventually had a rhinoplasty, but was dissatisfied with the result and the family issues remained unresolved. She underwent the arranged marriage. (Bradbury, 1994, p. 303)

It is almost impossible to explore influences on body image and the consequences of body image disturbance without thinking about interpersonal relationships. After all, when people express feeling self-conscious about their bodies, they are usually concerned about how their appearance will be evaluated by others; people who feel confident about their looks have often received compliments or other forms of feedback that contributed to their positive body image. Clinically, we have had numerous experiences with appearance-conscious individuals, and the interpersonal nature of their concerns invariably enters into the discussion of causal and maintaining factors. Simply pondering the answers to such questions as

175

"What if we were stranded on a desert island, would we care about how we looked?" or "If there were no men left on the planet, would women still pursue thinness?" is sufficient to emphasize the omnipresent influence of significant others.

The interpersonal nature of body image is underscored by the results of the *Psychology Today* national survey (Garner, 1997): 40% of women and 29% of men surveyed said that their partner's opinion of their appearance was a factor in fostering body dissatisfaction. Additionally, "relationships not going well" (Garner, 1997, p. 38) was cited by 24% women and 21% men.

In the previous chapter, we focused on the direct effects of feedback regarding appearance on one's self-image, with a focus on teasing or overt comments or criticism. In this chapter, we explore the rather indirect influence of others by examining such issues as their perceptions of physical appearance ideals and their modeling of behaviors reflective of personal body dissatisfaction.

RESEARCH BACKGROUND

Parental Influences

Although researchers (and more recently the media) have closely attended to the fact that cultural ideals have become unrealistically thin, there has been little emphasis on understanding the mechanism by which social pressures to achieve the ideal figure affect body image and eating disturbance (Murray, Touyz, & Beumont, 1995). Numerous sociocultural theories of the development of body image disturbance have been developed (see chapter 3), but we are still left with the question, Why do only some individuals become distressed about body-related issues when everyone is exposed to the messages and images present in virtually every form of media? Benedikt, Wertheim, and Love (1998) suggested that it may be important to look at "more immediate sub-cultural influences, such as parents, who may transmit sociocultural messages to their daughters" (p. 44). Parents may knowingly or unwittingly influence their children from infancy when their body image ideals and eating-related beliefs may even affect their feeding practices (Birch, 1990; Klesges et al., 1983; A. Stein & Fairburn, 1989).

Anecdotally, we know of mothers who only give their babies skim milk because they are concerned about them becoming "chubby," and we are aware of parents who appear to invest an extraordinary amount of time, energy, and money in their children's appearances. Perhaps these caring parents are simply reacting to and preparing their children for the realities of living in a society in which beauty is highly valued and rewarded. Nonetheless, do these behaviors communicate influential messages that weight and appearance are important for being accepted and loved? Do these behaviors foster the development of unhealthy body image and eating attitudes and behaviors? Fortunately, a number of research studies have been conducted to begin to shed light on the answers to these questions.

Two main modes of influence have been the subject of a limited but growing number of research studies: (a) the potential modeling effect that parents' own body image and eating behaviors may have on their children and (b) the influence of parents through their attitudes toward their children's weight, shape, and diet. To assess these influences, researchers have studied the families of patients with eating disorders, the children of mothers with eating disorders, and body image and eating behavior in noneating-disordered individuals.

Maternal Influences: Like Mother, Like Daughter?

When I first read the script I said, "I know this mother". . .. Once I asked my mother, "Was I pretty as a baby?" and the words out of my mother's mouth were, "All babies are pretty," and I said, "No, I mean me: was I pretty?" and she said: "What's pretty anyway? Look at what good it did your sister." I just remember those lines; they were very powerful to me, and we put them in the script because it seemed so very right. (Barbra Streisand referring to part of her inspiration for the screenplay for *The Mirror Has Two Faces*, as quoted in Weinraub, 1996, p. B4)

It really bothers me when my daughter eats chips and sweets because I can see that she is getting too heavy. I don't want her to go through what I went through being a fat kid. I tell her not to eat that way and I tell her that she's getting really fat because I love her and I want what's best for her. She'll thank me later. (the mother of a 12-year-old daughter)

Although researchers have explored the relationship between mother–daughter eating behaviors, the results have been inconsistent. Whereas some researchers have found significant relationships between mother–daughter concerns about diet and weight (Pike & Rodin, 1991; Hill, Weaver, & Blundell, 1990), other investigators have failed to find such a positive connection (Attie & Brooks-Gunn, 1989; Sanftner, Crowther, Crawford, & Watts, 1996; Thelen & Cormier, 1995). It seems that mothers may or may not have a modeling effect on their daughters' diet and weight concerns. One problem with the research linking mothers and daughters with respect to disordered eating is that many of the studies are correlational. For example, some researchers have found that the mothers of girls with bulimia are more likely to have encouraged their daughters to diet (Moreno & Thelen, 1993), are overconcerned with their own weight (Blitzer, Rollins, & Blackwell, 1961), and are more likely to have poor relationships with their daughters. But it is unclear whether these maternal factors play a causal role in the development of eating disorders or are a consequence of their daughter's eating disorders (Sanftner et al., 1996; Wonderlich, 1992).

Sanftner et al. (1996) noted the limitations in the studies on the mother–daughter link with regard to eating disorders, and they set out to further explore the relationship using a large sample (382) of ethnically diverse 9- to 15-year-old girls and their mothers. All participants completed the Eating Disorder Inventory or the Eating Disorder Inventory for Children, and mothers completed the Tanner Stages Questionnaire to rate their daughter's level of pubertal development. Participants also completed questionnaires that assessed height and weight history as well as eating and weight control habits. They found that the mother's dieting status, weight concern, body dissatisfaction, and bulimic behaviors were not significantly related to any of these variables for their prepubertal daughters, but for girls who were further along in their pubertal development, their mother's weight preoccupation was significantly correlated with their daughter's restrictive behaviors. Mothers' and daughters' body dissatisfaction scores were significantly correlated as well. Thus, before puberty, mothers and daughters do not resemble one another in terms of their body image and eating behavior, whereas significant relationships between mothers' and daughters' weight preoccupation, dieting, bulimic behaviors, and drive for thinness are found later in the daughters' pubertal development.

However, the issue is more complex than simply pinning the blame on the mother. Sanftner et al. suggested that the relationship between mothers' and daughters' behaviors later in puberty might reflect the developmental changes experienced by the daughters, including increased social pressure to behave in gender stereotyped ways. Wooley and Wooley (1985) have noted that mothers have experienced the same sociocultural pressures as their daughters and that these mothers may simply serve as the interpreters of societal standards and expectations. Mothers may also model the solutions they used to cope with the thinness- and appearance-focused values of their culture. Thus, it is possible that mothers and daughters are simply using similar means in their attempts to manage the challenges they are faced with as the female members of their culture (Sanftner et al., 1996).

Benedikt et al. (1998) hypothesized that the modeling effect may be moderated by the types of diet behaviors modeled (e.g., extreme vs. moderate) and by the degree to which mothers actively encourage their daughters to lose weight. Their results indicated that the daughters' moderate weight-loss attempts and body dissatisfaction were significantly associated with their mothers' desire for them to be thinner and encouragement to lose weight (daughters' weight was statistically controlled for). Strikingly, only 14% of the daughters in their sample were overweight, but 51% of the mothers reported that they encouraged their daughters to lose weight and 39% of the mothers wanted their daughters to be thinner. Moderate dieting and body dissatisfaction were not predicted by the mothers' own diet behavior and body image. Thus, at the moderate level, a mother's impact appears to be through direct encouragement, not modeling. However, in looking at more extreme diet behavior and body dissatisfaction, a mother's own dissatisfaction and use of extreme measures to lose weight did in fact predict her daughter's behavior. So although mothers did not actively encourage their daughters to crash diet and skip meals, they may have unintentionally modeled such behaviors. These findings may be an important key to prevention. Psychologists may need to encourage mothers to explore why they may want their healthy daughters to lose weight and show mothers that they may influence their daughters through both their own behavior and direct encouragement for their daughters to lose weight. Doing so may be an effective way of counteracting the potentially negative influence of societal messages to pursue thinness that are amplified by a mother's behavior.

In an effort to further delineate possible maternal influences, researchers have also examined mothers with eating disorders, a group arguably at greater risk for transmitting unhealthy messages about weight and appearance to their children. Lacey and Smith (1987) found that some women with bulimia nervosa were concerned about their babies being overweight and tried to reduce their weight, and A. Stein and Fairburn (1989) found that some mothers with bulimia nervosa were overly concerned with their child's size and had significant difficulty feeding their child. A. Stein, Woolley, Cooper, and Fairburn (1994) conducted an observational study of 1-year-old children and their mothers with eating disorders. They found that when compared with mothers without eating pathology, mothers with eating disorders expressed more critical and derogatory remarks during mealtime (mothers were mostly concerned about the infants making a mess), and the mothers exhibited greater need to control their child's food intake. It is interesting to note that the infants of eating-disordered mothers weighed less than the control infants. In a follow-up study, A. Stein et al. (1996) confirmed that infants of mothers with eating disorders were smaller (in both weight and height) for their age than those of a comparison group of mothers with postnatal depression. A. Stein and Woolley (1996) described five broad mechanisms through which parents with eating disorders may influence their children:

1. Parents' extreme attitudes on eating, weight, and shape may directly influence their children; parents' fear of fat may lead them to underfeed their children, or their overconcern with weight and shape may lead them to be overly critical of their children's appearance and eating habits.

2. Parents' eating disorders may interfere with general parental functioning; their preoccupation with body image and eating may interfere with their ability to respond to their children's needs.
3. Parents may model disturbed eating behavior; children may learn about restrictive dieting or binge eating and later mimic their parents' behavior.
4. Parents' eating disorders may relate to marital discord and other interpersonal problems that are known to have negative effects on children.
5. Parents with eating disorders may have genetic effects; some researchers have identified a genetic component to eating disorders.

Family Dynamics

As Phares (1992) argued, there has been a disproportionate focus on mothers and a failure to include fathers in studies aimed to investigate parental influences on the development of child and adolescent psychopathology. The areas of eating disorders and body image are somewhat guilty as charged: Many researchers have emphasized the role of mothers in shaping their daughter's body image and diet behavior perhaps because researchers have often assumed that fathers are generally less concerned with their daughter's appearance and are thus less likely to model dieting or to directly encourage their daughter to lose weight. Therefore, "mothers are often considered the root of their daughters' difficulties with food and are targeted as important foci of change in the treatment of eating disorders in young women" (Sanftner et al., 1996, p. 148). A growing number of researchers, however, have begun to include fathers in their investigations of parental influences on eating disorders and body image disturbance. For example, Moreno and Thelen (1993), Rozin and Fallon (1988), and Thelen and Cormier (1995) all included fathers in their studies on the relationship between parents' weight concerns and their children's weight loss, body image, and weight concerns. This is an important component of developing a fuller understanding of body image and eating disturbance. As Sanftner et al. suggested, by ignoring the role of fathers, psychologists may miss some of the important negative effects that fathers may have. In addition, possibly because of the popularity of the family systems approach for conceptualizing and treating eating disorders, the whole family has come into focus as an important component for understanding the etiology of eating disturbance.

Striegel-Moore and Kearney-Cooke (1994), for example, studied the relationship between parents' concerns about their own body image and their perceptions and attitudes about the physical appearance, eating, and exercise habits of their children. The results indicated that both mothers and fathers tend to place moderate importance on their children's physical attractiveness. A minority of parents reported that they criticized their children about their appearance, and a large majority of parents were satisfied with their children's appearance. The authors concluded that "it is normative for parents to view their children as physically attractive" (Striegel-Moore & Kearney-Cooke, 1994, p. 383). Mothers were significantly more likely than fathers to experience pressure by others to improve their child's physical appearance. Parents' efforts to change their children's appearances were mainly focused on improving temporary conditions like acne or engaging the child in widely available and accepted improvements like orthodontic treatment. Women reportedly praised children significantly more often about their physical appearance than did men, and parents of daughters reported higher levels of praising their appearance than did parents of sons. This finding supports the notion that parents tend to emphasize physical appearance in girls and athletic skills in boys (Rodin, Silberstein, & Striegel-Moore, 1985). Parents were not, however, more lenient about obesity in their sons than in their daughters, so there may be increasing pressure on sons to conform to appearance standards. There was an interesting effect of age in their results: Parents were increasingly less positive in the evaluations of their children with increasing age of the child. The change in attitude was observed well before adolescence, but adolescents received the least positive evaluations, the least praise, and the most criticism. Consistent with at least one other study (M. Fisher, 1992), the results failed to reveal a significant relationship between the parents' own body image and perceptions of their children's physical appearance and eating behavior. Rodin et al. did, however, find a strong relationship between parental dieting and the encouraging of children to diet.

In one of the first studies to examine the eating- and body image-related attitudes and behaviors of parents of elementary schoolchildren, Thelen and Cormier (1995) sought to determine whether mothers encouraged dieting more than fathers and whether daughters received and perceived receiving more feedback to lose weight than did sons. They were also interested in exploring the relationship between parent and child weight-related concerns. Using a relatively large sample of fourth graders and their parents, they found no significant correlations between parents' and children's dieting and the desire to be thinner. The authors noted that this might have reflected a lack of serious eating pathology in the sample that made assessment of parental modeling less effective. Nonetheless, they found an interesting discrepancy regarding mothers' encouraging their children to lose weight. Although the mothers in the study were no more likely to report encouraging their children to lose weight than the fathers were, both daughters and sons perceived more encouragement for weight control and loss from their mothers than their fathers. It may be that mothers are more direct in their feedback because of their own concerns about food and weight, or perhaps the children were more likely to perceive such encouragement from their mothers because they see their mothers as weight and diet conscious themselves. Alternatively, mothers may have been unable or reluctant to acknowledge providing such encouragement because of their own struggles and conflicts with weight-related issues. It was interesting that sons as well as daughters perceived pressure to control or lose weight—mothers appeared to be concerned with their son's as well as daughter's weight management.

More research to assess the relative influences of modeling and direct communication about weight and shape is needed to bridge the gap between the increasing number of conflicting findings. Although studies examining familial impact on body image are scarce, the families of eating-disordered patients have been widely studied in an effort to explore the etiology of eating pathology within the family context. This database may be instructive in forming future research on the issue of body image. Connors (1996) reviewed this growing body of literature and summarized the findings in a number of key areas, including the following:

(a) *Cohesion*. Families of women with eating disorders generally perceive lower cohesion in the family than do control families. More specifically, parents of children with eating disorders are viewed by their children as less empathic, less emotionally supportive, and less affectionate and warm than are parents of children without eating disorders (Steiger, Liquornik, Chapman, & Hussain, 1991). Patients with anorexia nervosa and bulimia nervosa tend to view their families as less nurturant and more neglectful (Humphrey, 1986). Studies that involve behavioral observations of these families are consistent with these perceptions: The families of patients with bulimia nervosa displayed little affection or support and were characterized as "withholding, depriving, and lacking in empathy" (Connors, 1996, p. 293). (Scalf-McIver & Thompson, 1989, also found that non-eating-disorder women's body dissatisfaction was significantly associated with low cohesion and high conflict in the participants' family environment.)

(b) *Support for autonomy*. Familial enmeshment, overcontrol, and lack of support for autonomy has been said to describe the families of patients with anorexia nervosa and bulimia nervosa. Humphrey's (1989) behavioral observations of these families revealed the tendency to ignore and negate their daughter's self-expression.

(c) *Communication and expressiveness*. Findings from a number of investigations of communication in eating-disordered families suggest that these families tend to have a lack of open expression and poorer communication than do control families.

(d) *Achievement expectations.* Stern et al. (1989) found that patients with eating disorders rated their families as more achievement oriented than did their own parents or controls.

In summarizing the findings on family interaction, Connors (1996) concluded that

> data from self-report and observational studies converge to describe a problematic family environment for women with eating disorders of all subtypes. Family relationships seem characterized by a preponderance of negative interactions such as blaming, belittling, and overcontrol and by a dearth of positively toned exchanges. Parental support, empathy, and nurturance seem lacking, as does open expression of feelings. (p. 295)

Much future work remains to be done on the role of parents and the body image concerns of their offspring. The wealth of data on families of individuals with eating disorders may provide useful instruction in methodology and hypotheses. It is interesting to note that little research has jointly evaluated parental and peer influences—Levine, Smolak, and Hayden (1994) is one notable exception, which we review after first turning our attention to the general issue of peers and body image.

Relationships Outside the Family

Peers

> I have a friend who's thin and gorgeous, and she's always commenting on how much she hates her body and I think, wow, if she thinks that about her body, what does she think of mine? (a 15-year-old girl, as quoted in Schneider, 1996, p. 67)

Although most people are taught the old adage that "beauty is in the eye of the beholder," research findings indicate that there is high consensus among individuals in evaluating the physical attractiveness of others (e.g., Burns & Farina, 1992). In fact, children as young as 3 years of age show agreement with adults in rating the attractiveness of their peers. If children agree on who is and is not attractive, it is likely that they, like adults, may engage in preferential treatment of attractive peers and discrimination of their less attractive counterparts. This may, in turn, lay the foundation for the development of negative body images and unhealthy attempts to try to increase attractiveness. Peer influences can be influential, particularly as children enter adolescence.

Oliver and Thelen (1996) explored children's perceptions of peer influences on body image and eating behavior. They examined a variety of potential peer influences, including the frequency with which children perceive interacting with peers in appearance-related activities (e.g., exercising, talking about and comparing their bodies) and the degree to which they believe that being thin will make them more likable with their peers. They found that third- and fifth-grader's perceptions of such peer influences were related to their body image and eating concerns. Girls were more likely than boys to believe that thinness increases likability, and the degree to which this belief was held was identified as a significant predictor of weight and body image concerns. Girls were also more likely than boys to report sharing body- and eating-related interactions with other girls. Although such interactions did not emerge as a strong predictor of body image disturbance in their study, a previous study of middle school girls found that such peer interactions about weight and diet may indeed become associated with girls' shape and eating concerns slightly later in their development (M. P. Levine, Smolak, Moodey, Shuman, & Hessen, 1994).

Because the belief that being thinner is associated with greater likability was a better predictor of disturbance than receiving feedback about appearance or engaging in body-related activities, it appears that peer influences may not be direct. Perceptions related to peer acceptance, which may be influenced by more direct messages and interactions, may be the more directly influential component. Particularly in the area of body image, a focus on identifying and exploring such beliefs about thinness may be an important area for both prevention and treatment of body image and eating disturbance in children.

The influence of peers may continue into later adolescence and early adulthood. Schwartz, Thompson, and Johnson (1981), for instance, found that college women who purge usually know another woman who purges whereas women who do not purge rarely know other women who do. In addition, women who have more dieting friends tend to have more eating-disorder symptoms themselves. Crandall (1988), in a study of university sororities, found that the degree of binge eating behavior among one's immediate peer group was related to the individual's own bingeing.

Friends, however, may be less concerned about one's physical attractiveness than one's family. M. A. Johnson (1989) studied variables associated with friendship among adults. He examined pairs of close friends, acquaintances, and nonfriends to determine the relative importance of such variables as proximity, similarity, personality, and physical attractiveness in ongoing relationships. He found that personality factors, such as friendliness and pleasantness and having similar backgrounds, interests, and values, were strong predictors of friendship whereas physical appearance was completely unrelated to friendship. However, this finding may have reflected social desirability—people may have been reluctant to acknowledge that attractiveness played a role in their friendships. Alternatively, physical appearance may have been perceived as less important once relationships were established.

In one of the only studies to evaluate both the effects of peers and parents, M. P. Levine, Smolak, and Hayden (1994), in a study of adolescent girls, included several measures of influence, including an index of the girl's perception of the dieting and body concerns of her peers, a measure of her perception of her mother's investment in thinness, and a measure of both parents' investment in the daughter's shape. Other measures addressed peer and parental overt criticism and teasing about weight (see chapter 5) and the role of the media in body image (see chapter 3). Levine, Smolak, and Hayden used regression analyses to determine the unique predictive effects of these measures for levels of body dissatisfaction and eating disturbance. As discussed earlier in chapters 3 and 5, the sociocultural (importance of beauty and fitness information from magazines) and feedback (teasing) measures explained most of the variance in these analyses. However, the peer dieting measure—the measure of interest for us in this chapter—was also a significant predictor of investment in thinness, weight-management strategies (i.e., restricting activities), and eating disturbance.

Romantic Partners

> "Yes, I admit it," he said, "your weight really bothers me. You are a lot heavier than when we first got married. You don't even look like the woman I fell in love with and *you* hate the way you look too." Then he turned to the therapist and said, "So no, I haven't been as interested in being intimate—her body disgusts me!" The client did not appear surprised by his candor and responded, "I know. I admit I look terrible right now, especially naked, but don't you still love me for me—for what's inside?!" (a married couple in therapy)

> I was dating a man five years younger than me, and I was worried about being older than him. I was afraid he wouldn't want me because I was older. Shortly after he found out I was five years older, he broke up with me. I wondered if that was why, and I started being preoccupied with my appearance after that—that I looked too old. (a woman with body dysmorphic disorder, as quoted in Phillips, 1996, p. 188)[1]

Another anecdote relevant to romantic partners was offered by Roth (1982), the essentials of which are summarized here: Geneen was having dinner with her date when he asked her, "Would you like me if you saw

---

[1]From *The Broken Mirror: Understanding and Treating Body Dysmorphic Disorder* (p. 16), by Katherine A. Phillips, New York: Oxford University Press. Copyright © 1996 by Katherine A. Phillips, MD. Used by permission of Oxford University Press.

me with no clothes on and you didn't like my body?" She instinctively responded, "Of course," and thought about previous relationships and how she tended to remember the connection she had with these men rather than their physical condition. Then Geneen returned the question asking if he would like her if he did not like her body. "No, I wouldn't," he responded and elaborated by sharing that this had been a concern of his for some time because he prefers women who are thinner than she is.

Perhaps one of the least explored, and yet from anecdotal accounts of friends, colleagues, clients, and other professionals, one of the most important interpersonal factors in determining body image, is that of the partner. The above examples illustrate, in at least two ways, the role of this factor: fears related to being negatively evaluated by one's partner and concerns about finding one's partner's body acceptable or pleasing. In fact, one common obstacle to initiating relationships is a lack of confidence in one's physical appearance (Scharlot & Christ, 1995), and people who are physically unattractive are indeed approached less often by others interested in beginning a relationship (Sprecher & McKinney, 1987). Perceptions of significant others' evaluations of people may have a particularly strong influence, yet body image within the context of romantic relationships has received surprisingly little attention in the literature. Romantic partners are, for most people, an important part of their life, and romantic relationships may have a great deal of impact on those involved in them. Considering the amount of time and range of activities shared by romantic partners, it is likely that their perceptions of one another influence self-evaluations. The potential detrimental influence that relationships may have on body image and eating disturbance was suggested in Lasegue's (1873) seminal description of anorexia nervosa, wherein he identified a conflict in heterosexual relationships as a precipitating factor (e.g., Scott, 1987). More recent work suggests that interpersonal stress increases the likelihood of binge eating (Polivy, Herman, Olmsted, & Jazwinski, 1984; Schlundt, Jarrell, & Johnson, 1983; van Buren & Williamson, 1988).

The role of body image in marital relationships has also been examined. Marriage has generally been associated with a lesser risk of certain disorders, such as depression, and it has been hypothesized that the link between marriage and improved health may be related to a helpful regulation of health behaviors by one's spouse. Both husbands and wives regularly attempt to influence their spouse's health behavior, and the types, frequency, and motivation for such influence appear to be similar across husbands and wives (Anders & Tucker, 1997). However, Anders and Tucker found that although both wives and husbands reported that their attempts to influence their partners were based on a concern for health rather than appearance, husbands had a stronger tendency to target health behaviors related to appearance. Their sample consisted of young, healthy couples, yet among the top three behaviors targeted by husbands was the desire for their wives to lose weight. These findings may partially explain the strong relationship between body dissatisfaction and marital dissatisfaction for women (Friedman, Dixon, Brownell, Whisman, & Wilfley, in press).

Mark and Crowther (1997) further explored the relationship between body image and relationship satisfaction among young, unmarried women involved in dating relationships. They also found that greater body dissatisfaction was associated with lower relationship satisfaction. In addition, they found that men's relationship satisfaction was significantly related to their satisfaction with their partner's shape whereas there was no such link for women. This finding supports previous studies in which men demonstrated greater emphasis on their partner's physical attractiveness than did women. For instance, Nevid (1984) found that men tend to focus more on physical appearance in choosing romantic partners than do women. S. Davis (1990) found that heterosexual men who place personal ads list physical attractiveness as the most desired attribute in a partner whereas heterosexual women tend to focus more on issues of financial and intellectual status. Feingold (1990) conducted meta-analyses of five research paradigms used to test the hypothesis that men place more emphasis on physical attractiveness than do women. He examined questionnaire studies, personal advertisements, correlational studies on attractiveness and popularity, research on couples, and experiments that manipulated physical attractiveness. The results across research strategies supported the hypothesis that more men than women value physical attractiveness. It is interesting to note that the effect was stronger for self-reports of preferences than for measures of actual behaviors (e.g., dyadic interactions).

Although many researchers have examined perceptions of opposite-sex figure preferences (to be discussed in the next section), the more personally relevant variable of perceptions of a romantic partner's opposite-sex ideal has received limited attention. Mark and Crowther (1997) found that women inaccurately perceive their partners' preferences for them. Women chose figures that were thinner than the figures actually preferred by their partners (see also A. E. Fallon & Rozin, 1985). Tantleff-Dunn and Thompson (1995) hypothesized that these perceptions play an important role in body image satisfaction because one's romantic partner is likely to be an influential source of feedback on appearance and individuals may be more concerned with meeting their partner's ideal than general societal standards. Therefore, Tantleff-Dunn and Thompson extended the research on figure rating discrepancies by studying romantic couples.

In Tantleff-Dunn and Thompson's (1995) study, romantic partners made a number of figure ratings, including perceived partner's ideal, perceived partner's rating of self, and actual rating of partner. Results indicated that the types of discrepancies that predicted body image disturbance were clearly different for the male and female partners. For female partners, a discrepancy between self-rating and perceived partner's ideal female size accounted for almost all of the variance associated with body satisfaction, eating disturbance, and overall psychological functioning. In contrast, the male partner's body image and eating disturbance was associated with a discrepancy between self-rating and their female partner's actual rating of her ideal male size. (See Table 6.1 for a summary of these findings.)

An interesting twist on the issue of body image in significant romantic relationships comes from research on the power and control issues in marriages in which a wife has an eating disorder. For instance, Root, Fallon, and Friedrich (1986) suggested that bulimia nervosa can be a wife's way of caring for her husband: She demonstrates having a major problem, making him look strong by comparison, and the couple can attribute any relational difficulties to the wife's eating disorder. Although there has not been clear empirical evidence to support this premise, P. Levine (1988) reported that a small sample of couples indicated that their marriage grew stronger as a result of an eating disorder. Body image disturbance may be subtler and provide less opportunity for a couple to fight together against an "enemy" than a clinical eating disorder. However, feeling dissatisfied, anxious, and distraught about weight and shape may ultimately lead to some of the same dynamics in romantic relationships.

Although there is not yet enough research on this to warrant many conclusions, we offer a few hypotheses to explain why an individual might encourage, perhaps unknowingly, their romantic partner's negative body image:

1. Encouraging a negative body image may help maintain power in the relationship: As long as the partner is not feeling good about his or her appearance, the significant other will not have to worry about him or her receiving the attention and propositions that could result in marital conflict.

TABLE 6.1
Comparison of Figure Ratings

Rating	Women	Men
Own ideal	2.94 (.58)$_e$	4.25 (.64)$_{a, b}$
Perceived partner's ideal other gender	3.10 (.71)$_{c, d, e}$	3.95 (.85)$_c$
Actual partner's ideal other gender	3.39 (.62)$_{b, c, d}$	3.98 (.77)$_c$
Perceived partner's rating of you	3.44 (.87)$_{a, b, c}$	4.17 (1.10)$_{b, c}$
Actual partner's rating of you	3.53 (.74)$_{a, b}$	4.07 (1.07)$_{b, c}$
Self	3.81 (1.01)$_a$	4.44 (1.39)$_a$

Note. Subscripts indicate significant differences between ratings within gender. Means that do not share a common letter are significantly different. For example, for men, Self and Own ideal ratings are larger than all other ratings. From "Romantic Partners and Body Image Disturbance: Further Evidence for the Role of Perceived–Actual Disparities," by S. Tantleff-Dunn and J. K. Thompson, 1995, *Sex Roles, 33,* p. 597. Copyright 1995 by Plenum Publishing Corporation. Reprinted with permission.

2. Fostering body dissatisfaction may help maintain self-image: As long as she, for example, lacks self-confidence about her looks, she may look at him less critically and he will appear more attractive to her (or will seem to be the "best she could do").

3. Encouraging a negative body image may help assuage fears that a partner will become overweight or stop taking care of his or her appearance as he or she becomes more comfortable in the relationship: If, for example, she feels unattractive, she may actively keep trying to improve her appearance.

4. Perhaps encouraging negative body image makes a partner feel needed: For example, if he is unhappy with his appearance, he may desire her acceptance and reassurances and will love her for accepting him despite his unattractive appearance.

Obviously, these dynamics are not only problematic in terms of body image but may also have a number of negative effects on the relationship, including increased conflict and decreased trust, intimacy, and sexuality.

Perfect Strangers

A friend of mine recalls the time a plastic surgeon came up to him at a party, looked at his nose and said, "You know, I can fix that." When my friend said, "No thanks," the plastic surgeon appeared to think my friend a little crazy. As normalizing technologies become more accessible, people are expected to be bothered by their "unusual" features and expected to want to fix them. (Dreger, 1998, p. B10)

As noted in chapter 5, the negative feedback that people receive regarding their appearance may emanate not from peers, parents, or partners but perfect strangers. Some information that people use from unknown, or barely known, individuals may not be as direct as a weight-related teasing comment, yet it may have a connection to body dissatisfaction. Certainly, it is almost impossible to disentangle this influence from its sociocultural context because much of this information regarding appearance ideals is modeled or communicated through various forms of media (see chapter 3). Even as children, humans internalize the messages and physical standards of society and then judge themselves against these standards (Lerner & Jovanovic, 1990). People develop a sense of how they should look with respect to a multitude of physical characteristics, and they continually evaluate themselves in terms of how disparate their actual appearance is from the long list of "shoulds" they have acquired (Jacobi & Cash, 1994).

The perfect stranger influence may be conceptualized as a stereotype of others' ideals, often referred to as "other men" or "other women"—an index of people's views of the figure and appearance preferences of others. Men and women appear to be influenced by their perceptions of what the opposite sex sees as ideal, yet they are rather inaccurate in their estimations of what others prefer: Women typically believe that men prefer a female shape that is both thinner (A. E. Fallon & Rozin, 1985) and larger busted (J. K. Thompson & Tantleff, 1992) than men actually prefer, and men falsely assume that women prefer a heavier, more muscular, and larger chested male physique than women actually prefer (A. E. Fallon & Rozin, 1985; Jacobi & Cash, 1994; J. K. Thompson & Tantleff, 1992). Jacobi and Cash found that men significantly distorted women's ideals for a male appearance on many attributes and that women also had a variety of misconceptions about men's preferences. Gettelman and Thompson (1993) even found that misconceptions exist as a function of sexual orientation: Gay men were thought to have more body dissatisfaction than they actually reported, and lesbians were perceived to be less dissatisfied than they actually were. (It is interesting to note that these misconceptions were held by heterosexual and homosexual individuals of both sexes.)

A long-standing theory in social psychology known as the *reflected-appraisal process* may assist in understanding the role of others in one's appearance. Cooley (1922) and Mead (1934) suggested that individuals try to see themselves from others' perspectives and that their social behavior is then largely guided by these perceptions so as to have desired effects on others (Deaux & Wrightsman, 1984). Research has traditionally been focused on understanding the importance individuals place on others' opinions of them rather than exploring the actual impact their opinions have (Hoelter, 1984), and studies examining the relationship between others' actual opinions and self concept have not found support for the influence of significant others.

Two studies illustrate the investigation of reflected appraisals. Hoelter (1984) looked at the different effects of parents, teachers, and peers on high school students' self concepts. The results supported the premise that significant others have different degrees of influence on one's self concept, but these differences vary with gender. Perceived appraisals of parents had a greater effect on male than female students, whereas perceived appraisals of peers had a larger influence on female students. Hoelter concluded that it is untrue that female students are more globally influenced by the perceived appraisals of others than are male students—such appeared to be the case only in reference to peers or friends. Felson (1985) found that elementary schoolchildren's perceptions of peers' evaluations of their attractiveness had a significant impact on their own self-evaluation. It is interesting to note that he found that others' actual appraisals had less impact than the children's rather inaccurate perceptions of these appraisals.

The role that others play in body image development led Burns and

Farina (1992) to propose a three-stage model for the influence of attractiveness on adjustment:

Stage 1: Varying levels of attractiveness create differential responses in other people.

Stage 2: Differential responses in others result in differential treatment of individuals as a function of their attractiveness.

Stage 3: Differential treatment results in differential adjustment. (p. 160)

As reviewed by Burns and Farina, one of the clearest examples of this process was demonstrated by the results of a well-known experiment by Snyder, Tanke, and Berscheid (1977), in which men were shown a picture of an attractive or unattractive woman with whom they would soon engage in a telephone conversation. Men had more positive expectations of the attractive woman (sociable, poised, humorous, etc.) than her unattractive counterpart (unsociable, awkward, etc.). Furthermore, judges who were unaware of the purpose of the experiment listened to the phone conversations and found the men to be more sociable, sexually warm, and interesting when they believed they were speaking with an attractive woman. These men were then seen as more attractive and confident themselves. Perhaps even more interesting was that the men's behavior seemed to influence the women's conversation: Judges who listened only to the female voices rated women in the attractive condition to be more animated and confident than women in the unattractive condition. Thus, men were influenced by beliefs about the woman's attractiveness, they treated the attractive and unattractive women differently, and the women responded with differential behavior.

Burns and Farina (1992) cited additional studies to support each stage of the model, demonstrating that both children and adults tend to attribute more positive characteristics to infants, children, and adults perceived as physically attractive. Studies show a desire to interact with a stranger increases as the attractiveness of the stranger increases (Zakin, 1983), and a plethora of data demonstrates that unattractive people are perceived as maladjusted or less competent than attractive people in a variety of ways. Attractive people are not just perceived more positively but are often treated more favorably than unattractive individuals (see chapter 1 on stigmatization of overweight individuals). Studies demonstrate parents' and teachers' preferential treatment of attractive infants and children: Attractive students' ideas were more readily accepted by their teachers, and some studies even suggest that unattractive children may be treated in a more punishing, potentially abusive manner than are attractive children. Differential treatment has also been seen in adult interactions, with more attractive adults receiving more attention, honesty, and other reinforcing behaviors from others. Studies on the role of attractiveness in dating show that attractive partners are "liked more, smiled at more, looked at more, stood closer to, talked to more, and thought about more after the interaction" (Burns & Farina, 1992, p. 166).

Interpersonal issues related to strangers or casual acquaintances may be particularly poignant for girls and women with eating disorders. Murray et al. (1995) took a unique look at interpersonal influences on body image using open-ended interviews to compare female individuals having eating disorders with female and male controls. They found that 48% of the total sample reported that members of the opposite sex affected their eating, exercise, and body satisfaction, with no significant differences between comparison groups. Significantly more patients than female controls reported that they were influenced by members of the same sex, and significantly more female controls than male controls reported being influenced by same-sex individuals. Female patients with eating disorders were more likely than female controls to report that other women influenced their eating behavior and body satisfaction and to indicate that they spent time discussing weight and diet. Male controls were significantly less likely than female controls to compare their bodies with or to notice the weight of same-sex others or to believe that members of the same sex influenced their eating behavior or feelings about their bodies. Male controls were, however, more likely to report that they wanted to look attractive to members of the opposite sex. It is interesting to note that some of the men in the study reported that their interactions with women were influenced by their awareness that weight is a sensitive subject for many women. A good example of their interview data that illustrates women's concerns related to evaluations of the opposite sex is the following response from a female patient with bulimia nervosa: "My husband likes slim women. If he sees a fat woman he'll say, 'isn't she fat?'. . . listening to men talking, you get the idea that to be acceptable you have to be slim" (Murray et al, 1995, p. 249).

Summary and Future Research

A case summarized in *Ladies Home Journal* (M. D. Rosen, 1997) nicely illustrates the pervasive impact of interpersonal influences:

> Sherry reported that she received mixed messages from her mother who would prepare her a very fattening meal and then sneer at her (commenting that she eats like a truck driver) for finishing it. In later years her husband Mark would complain that Sherry's lousy eating habits and weight problem were going to rub off on their young daughter. Mark justified his snide remarks about his wife's eating habits as a reflection of his sincere concern about her health. He also indicated that he didn't mean to make critical remarks about her weight and

feels that she tends to misinterpret his comments. He did, however, acknowledge that Sherry's weight is a "sexual turnoff." The couple was on the brink of divorce, held together only by their child. The focus of therapy was dealing with the lingering unresolved childhood issues that contributed to the lack of communication and closeness in their marriage and to Sherry's compulsive overeating. The therapist encouraged Mark to focus on his own issues rather than concentrating on Sherry's weight problem, and Sherry was encouraged to let Mark know when he says something that hurts her. (p. 2)

We have reviewed a wealth of research suggesting that the role of peers, parents, romantic partners, and strangers may have an impact on body image disturbance. However, we need much more research to facilitate our understanding of the complex influence of these and other interpersonal variables on the development and maintenance of body image problems. We hope that future researchers will test diverse components at work in the interpersonal model. In particular, it would be informative to determine whether different interpersonal factors are influential at different ages or in individuals who vary on ethnic background or social setting.

ASSESSMENT

As a result of the growing interest in interpersonal influences on body image, a number of new instruments have been developed to assess the appearance-, weight-, and diet-related attitudes and behaviors of parents, peers, and romantic partners. Most of these measures deal with the perceptions of interpersonal influence, but some involve direct assessment of significant others. A majority of these measures consist of relatively few questions and have not been empirically evaluated using traditional psychometric techniques. Some of the more comprehensive measures as well as instruments for which psychometric information is available are described here. Table 6.2 contains more information on these measures.

M. P. Levine, Smolak, and Hayden (1994) developed several measures that tap into the impact of peers and family members on a female adolescent's body image. Their Parental Involvement Scale measures a girl's view of the importance of her weight and size to her parents. The Mother Influence Scale assesses a girl's perception of her mother's own dieting and investment in being thin. The Peer Dieting Scale assesses a girl's perceptions of the level of interest her friends have in dieting, weight, and shape. These three scales are contained in Appendices 6A, 6B, and 6C, respectively. Rieves and Cash (1996) also developed a scale specific to the effect of one's sibling on one's appearance (Appendix 6D).

Oliver and Thelen (1996) created the Inventory of Peer Influences on Eating Concerns to measure children's perceptions of peer messages

TABLE 6.2
Interpersonal Measures

Instrument	Author(s)	Description	Reliability 1, 2	Standardization sample	Address of author
Body Exposure in Sexual Activities Questionnaire	Hangen & Cash (1991)	28 items measure physical self-consciousness and avoidance of body exposure in sexual situations; two subscales: Worry and Self-Consciousness (WSC) and Comfort With Body Exposure (CBE)	IC: .98 (total scale), .97 (WSC scale), .92 (CBE scale)	College age normal controls: 401 women and 129 men	Thomas F. Cash, PhD Department of Psychology Old Dominion University Norfolk, VA 23529-0207
None given	Pike (1995)	4 Likert scale items that measure concern with overweight and dieting among family and friends; separate scores for mothers, fathers, and so forth can be used to determine individual influences	IC: .74	410 adolescent girls in 9th through 12th grade in public and private suburban schools in the Northeast, primarily Caucasian, middle-class	Kathleen Pike, PhD Eating Disorders Unit Department of Psychiatry Columbia University College of Physicians and Surgeons, PI-98 722 West 168 Street New York, NY 10032
Maternal Attitudes Toward Physical Appearance	Rieves & Cash (1996)	Three adaptations of Cash's Multidimensional Body Self-Relations Questionnaire that index the daughter's perception of her mother's appearance evaluation, investment, and weight preoccupation	IC: .71, .85, .88	152 female college students (ages 17–35)	Thomas F. Cash, PhD Department of Psychiatry Old Dominion University Norfolk, VA 23529-0207
Social Pressure to Diet	Pike (1995)	Four-item scale designed to assess the extent to which individuals feel pressured by family and friends to lose weight	IC: .75	410 adolescent girls in 9th through 12th grade in public and private suburban schools in the Northeast, primarily Caucasian, middle-class	Kathleen Pike, PhD Eating Disorders Unit Department of Psychiatry Columbia University College of Physicians and Surgeons, PI-98 722 West 168 Street New York, NY 10032

Measure	Citation	Description	Sample	Reliability	Contact
Inventory of Peer Influence on Eating Concerns	Oliver & Thelen (1996)	30-items measure of the frequency with which children receive negative messages from peers about their bodies or eating habits (Messages factor), the frequency with which children interact with their peers about eating or body-related issues (Interactions factor), and the degree to which children believe that being thin will increase their likability with peers (Likability factor)	142 third graders and 122 fifth graders (both boys and girls) drawn from health classes at two public elementary schools in a Midwestern community (predominantly middle socio-economic status)	IC: messages, .92; interactions/boys, .76; interactions/girls, .80; likability/boys, .88; likability/girls, .88	Mark H. Thelen, PhD Psychology Department University of Missouri—Columbia 210 McAlester Hall Columbia, MO 65211
Sibling Appearance Questionnaire	Rieves & Cash (1996)	Rate, for each sibling, the effect of that person's appearance on their feelings about their own looks	152 female college students (ages 17–35)	(not reported)	Thomas F. Cash, PhD Department of Psychology Old Dominion University Norfolk, VA 23529-0207
Family History of Eating Survey	Moreno & Thelen (1993)	Scale compares parental concern about child's weight with child's perception of parental concern; a modified version uses four items related to the number of times parents encouraged children to lose weight	51 female and 49 male fourth graders enrolled in public schools in the Midwest from two-parent and single-parent families	IC: (based on four items) daughters' perception of mothers' and fathers' encouragement to lose weight, .83 and .72, respectively; sons' perception of mothers' and fathers' encouragement to lose weight, .68 and .62, respectively	Mark H. Thelen, PhD Department of Psychology University of Central Florida P.O. Box 161390 Orlando, FL 32816-1390
None given	Striegel-Moore & Kearney-Cooke (1994)	Parent survey that was developed as part of a 77-item questionnaire on body image; parent section includes questions about their child's attractiveness and what parents had done to change their child's appearance			Ruth Striegel-Moore, PhD Department of Psychology Wesleyan University Middletown, CT 06459-0408

Table continues

TABLE 6.2 (Continued)

Instrument	Author(s)	Description	Reliability 1, 2	Standardization sample	Address of author
Maternal Struggle With Weight and Dieting	Benedikt et al. (1998)	Mothers respond on a 5-point scale to five items dealing with their tendency to watch their weight and emphasize the importance of thinness; parallel items are administered to daughters to assess their perception of their mother's weight struggles	Correlations between mother and daughter responses were all significant but varied in strength from .23 to .51	89 Australian mother–daughter pairs (mostly White and Asian-Pacific backgrounds). Daughters' mean age was 15.9 years.	Eleanor Wertheim, PhD School of Psychology LaTrobe University Bundoora, Victoria 3083 Australia
Parent Involvement Scale Mother Influence Scale Peer Dieting Survey	M. P. Levine, Smolak, & Hayden (1994)	Three scales assess perceptions of parental and peer attitudes and behaviors related to weight and shape; the Parent Involvement Scale consists of four items that measure daughter's perception of how important slenderness is to her parents; the Mother Influence Scale consists of three items related to perceptions of mother's investment in her own appearance; the Peer Dieting Survey assesses perceptions of friends' interest in diet/weight/shape issues	IC: .73, .80	385 females in Grades 6 through 8, mean age of 13 years, primarily Caucasian	Michael Levine, PhD Linda Smolak, PhD Department of Psychology Kenyon College Gambier, OH 43022-9623

Note. IC = internal consistency; TR = test–retest reliability.

about eating- and appearance-related issues. The 30 items on this self-administered questionnaire tap into three main domains: peer messages (e.g., receiving negative messages from one's peers about one's body or diet), peer interactions (e.g., talking about eating- and appearance-related issues), and peer likability (e.g., believing that being thin will increase one's popularity with one's peers).

Pike (1995) created a questionnaire to assess familial and peer influences related to bulimic symptomatology. Four items on this scale measure perceptions of weight and diet consciousness of family members and friends. In addition, the Anorexia and Bulimia Within the Social Systems Questionnaire assesses the frequency of eating disorders among female family members, male family members, and friends. A 4-item Social Pressure to Diet Scale is also used to measure the extent to which individuals feel weight-related pressures by family members and friends and the degree to which these people encourage one to diet. Finally, a Bulimic Symptomatology Within the Friendship Network Scale is based on the participants' friends' self-reports on the measure of bulimia.

Striegel-Moore and Kearney-Cooke (1994) developed a parent survey that was part of a large *Psychology Today* reader survey on body image. Their subsection of questions targets the parent's perceptions of his or her child's physical attractiveness and the parent's attempts to alter his or her child's appearance. In addition, parents are asked about their own body image satisfaction and about the importance of physical appearance in their lives.

The Family History of Eating–Parent and Family History of Eating–Students Scales were developed by Thelen and Cormier (1995). On the parent version, the first question asks parents how many times they have gone on a diet, and the next four questions assess how often parents engage in behaviors related to encouraging their child to lose weight (e.g., telling your child that he or she weighs too much, keeping your child from eating foods that he or she likes so that he or she will lose weight, or telling your child he or she should exercise to lose weight).

Benedikt et al. (1998) also developed a scale to facilitate the assessment of mothers' weight and dieting concerns. The Maternal Struggle With Weight and Dieting Questionnaire consists of five items that tap into a mother's watchfulness of her weight and five parallel items that assess a daughter's perceptions of her mother's weight-related struggles. Benedikt et al. also incorporated a scale in which mothers and daughters indicate the frequency with which they engage in eight weight-loss strategies (e.g., crash dieting, using diet pills, exercising). In addition, a maternal encouragement to lose weight index involves asking mothers how often they encourage their daughters to lose weight and whether they prefer their daughters to be thinner. Parallel items assess a daughter's perceptions of her mother's preference for her to be thinner and encouragements for her to lose weight.

The Body Exposure in Sexual Activities Questionnaire (Hangen & Cash, 1991) is a 28-item self-administered questionnaire designed to specifically measure one's comfort with physical appearance during sexual encounters. It is interesting to note that for both sexes, negative body image (in general and in a sexual context) was significantly associated with reports of fewer sexual experiences in the recent past and with less sexual satisfaction. For women, body dissatisfaction was also associated with lower rates of orgasm and more sexual difficulties. Also both men's and women's level of body image avoidance in sexual situations was associated with lower sex drive. The questionnaire may be particularly useful when dealing with clients having sexual dysfunctions. Investigating the role that appearance-related anxiety might play in these clients' sexual problems may be an important component in the assessment and treatment of their condition. Obviously, no clear causal connection can be inferred, but it is plausible that individuals who are highly self-conscious about their physical appearance may restrict their sexual behaviors. Body image concerns may decrease their pleasure during sex by focusing their attention to perceived flaws in their appearance instead of their current physical experience. It is also conceivable that sexual difficulties in a relationship may lead partners to question their physical attractiveness, leading to heightened body image anxiety. This questionnaire is in Appendix 6E.

TREATMENT

As noted in chapter 2, the cognitive–behavioral programs developed by Cash (e.g., 1996, 1997) and J. C. Rosen (e.g., 1996a, 1996b, 1997) have received the most empirical validation from controlled outcome studies, which consistently show them to be highly effective in treating body image disturbance. It is interesting to note that although these programs contain components relevant to psychoeducational, cognitive, and behavior treatment strategies, no specific aspect of the program targets the interpersonal factor. Certainly, however, it is possible to adapt some of these approaches to include an interpersonal component. For instance, cognitive restructuring might be used to challenge a female patient's belief that she does not deserve to be treated with respect from her husband, simply because she is overweight. (See chapter 10 for a fuller discussion of cognitive strategies.)

In addition, as noted in chapter 3, much of the psychoeducational treatment focuses on the societal and sociocultural influences; however, this fits readily into our discussion of the perfect stranger and the often inaccurate stereotypical beliefs people have regarding others' ideal body sizes and appearance attributes. One experience with a student in one of our classes captures a strategy for using psychoeducational methods. She had a friend who was considering breast implants, a tactic she thought was not needed because she felt her friend was not in need of enhancement. Rather than argue with her friend, she took her to a local single's establishment and proceeded to interview strangers regarding their rating of her friend's breast size. The ratings were sufficiently positive to dissuade her friend from further consideration of this elective cosmetic surgery.

The exposure techniques advocated by Cash (1996, 1997) and J. C. Rosen (1996a, 1996b, 1997; and discussed more fully in chapter 9) may also be used within an interpersonal context. For instance, many body image avoidant behaviors are a result of anxiety regarding public scrutiny from sources that may run the gamut from parents to peers to strangers. By designing and implementing an effective in vivo exposure plan, therapists can assist many individuals to reduce their fears of exposure to others' negative evaluations.

Thus, in handling the interpersonal aspect of body image disturbance, therapists might first consider adapting the cognitive–behavioral strategies reviewed in chapter 2. However, these procedures may be neither sufficient nor appropriate, given the specific case. Additional strategies may be needed for addressing parental and peer influences on body image. For example, it may be useful to increase parents' awareness of their potential impact on their children's body image, not just their direct influence (e.g., encouragement to lose weight, teasing) but through modeling as well. Treatment for parents who are struggling with body image and eating disturbance themselves may be an important component of addressing a child's needs. Exploring the influence of siblings and other significant others who have contact with the child is also recommended.

In cases with romantic partners, couples therapy may be recommended. Clients may benefit enormously from the opportunity to open a communication line to discuss feelings, thoughts, attitudes, and fears related to physical appearance. They may be surprised to learn that their partners do not dislike their bodies, do not place as much importance on weight and shape as they believed, or both. Romantic partners may gain awareness of the ways they may unknowingly contribute to or maintain body image disturbance. Sex therapy might also be appropriate in some cases. Clients may benefit from exploring the ways in which sexual experiences both reflect and contribute to body image anxiety. For couples in which weight- and body-image-related issues have decreased intimacy and hampered sexual functioning, strategies for improving these aspects of their relationship can be developed. For example, a partner who reports no longer being attracted to a spouse because of a significant weight gain can be encouraged to find non-weight-related aspects of their partner's appearance that are sexually appealing. In addition, skills training videotapes or didactics could be suggested for couples coping with physical and weight-related difficulties that affect their sexual relations.

Feminist approaches may be particularly useful in cases where abuse has occurred (or is feared) or a clear power differential is problematic. (See a further discussion of feminist strategies in chapters 2, 7, and 8.) M. P. Levine (1994) suggested that it is important for men to take responsibility for learning about the struggle that women in U.S. society experience, to take action against the discrimination they face, and to protest the "violence against women in the form of restrictive diets, liposuction, and 'cosmetic' surgery" (p. 104). M. P. Levine contended that men can play an important role in preventing eating disorders by teaching other men and boys that "a Y-chromosome does not confer a proprietary right to publicly tease and otherwise criticize daughters, sisters, girlfriends, and even strangers about weight and shape" (p. 108). He emphasized the need for men to let the women in their lives know that they love them, regardless of their weight, and let their sons know that "weightism" and "sexism" are unacceptable. M. P. Levine also encouraged fathers to take extra care to support and remain close to their adolescent daughters as they experiment and begin to struggle with the appearance-related issues of entering womanhood. A. Stein and Wooley (1996), on the basis of their research and clinical experience, outlined a number of treatment guidelines for working with patients having eating disorders and their children. Some of their recommendations are pertinent to our discussion:

1. Examine the quality of parent–child interactions.
2. Observe meal times if possible. Expect some conflict to occur—it is normal for parents and children to work out conflicts at meal time, but look out for extensive conflicts.
3. Help parents recognize how their overriding concerns about weight and appearance may be contributing to conflicts with their children.
4. Work with parents to lessen their attention to and criticism of their children's body weight and shape if this is problematic.
5. Encourage the spouses of eating-disordered parents to provide support and get involved in feeding responsibilities.

Although the majority of studies reviewed in this chapter represent documentation of the negative impact that interpersonal relationships may have on body image, it is likely that positive social interactions have the potential to improve body image or at least facilitate coping with body dissatisfaction. Perhaps the most compelling way that parents, spouses, and friends can have a positive influence on body image is through the provision of social support. Although there are many definitions of social support, most definitions reflect a process in which interpersonal exchanges give people a sense of companionship, attachment, and acceptance. Different types of social support may be particularly effective in helping individuals cope with a variety of stressors. Two types of support, esteem and informational, may be particularly helpful for dealing with body image disturbance. Esteem support increases a person's self-esteem through compliments, social recognition, and demonstrating respect for the individual. Informational support is characterized by advice and guidance geared toward problem solving. Effective informational support for body image disturbance may involve informing an individual about the possibility of distorted perceptions of one's own and others' evaluations or sharing some of the psychoeducational data available regarding the media's strategies to manipulate the appearance of models (see chapter 3).

CONCLUSIONS

It is important to recognize the potential interpersonal influences on body image. It is not enough to simply focus on the overt influences, such as teasing and criticism, directed at an individual from such sources as parents, peers, or partners. We must also acknowledge the more subtle forms of influence through a variety of behaviors. Evaluating the attractiveness of others or gossiping about someone's weight fluctuations, for example, may seem harmless. However, these rather ordinary kinds of interactions may be subtle ways of communicating the importance placed on looks and create or exacerbate the body image anxiety of others. A great deal of evidence shows that sociocultural factors are important influences on body image. The data on interpersonal influences, however, underscore the need to consider the role that personal relationships play in an individual's acceptance and pursuit of cultural ideals that are often unrealistic, unhealthy, and impossible to achieve. Understanding more about interpersonal influences on body image may provide unique opportunities for developing effective interventions. Whereas it may be difficult to make any significant strides toward creating cultural changes, it is quite feasible to incorporate significant others in the efforts to both prevent and treat body image disturbance.

APPENDIX 6A
PARENT INVOLVEMENT SCALE

For each question, circle the number that you feel is true for you.

Read this carefully: Some of the following questions may not apply to you. For example your father (see 2) may live in another town and, therefore, you hardly ever see him. If the question does not apply to you, then place a check in the space for Not applicable.

If you do not live with your parents, let the word *parents* in the questions stand for the adult(s) who take(s) care of you.

---

1. How concerned is your *mother* about whether you weigh too much or are too fat or might become too fat? _____ Not applicable

1	2	3
Not at all important	Important	Very important

2. How concerned is your *father* about whether you weigh too much or are too fat or might become too fat? _____ Not applicable

1	2	3
Not at all important	Important	Very important

3. How important is it to your *mother* that *you* be thin? _____ Not applicable

1	2	3
Not at all important	Important	Very important

4. How important is it to your *father* that *you* be thin? _____ Not applicable

1	2	3
Not at all important	Important	Very important

From the Parent Involvement Scale, an unpublished scale by M. P. Levine, L. Smolak, and H. Hayden. Reprinted with permission from the authors. For more information, see M. P. Levine, Smolak, and Hayden (1994).

APPENDIX 6B
MOTHER INFLUENCE SCALE

For each question, circle the number that you feel is true for you.

Read this carefully: Some of the following questions may not apply to you. For example your mother (see 1) may live in another town and, therefore, you hardly ever see her. If the question does not apply to you, then place a check in the space for Not applicable.

If you do not live with your parents, let the word "parents" in the questions stand for the adult(s) who take(s) care of you.

Second Scale

1. How often is your *mother* on a diet to lose weight? _____ Not applicable

1	2	3	4	5	6
Never	Rarely	Sometimes	Often	Very often	All the time

2. How important is it to your *mother* that *she* be as thin as possible? _____ Not applicable

1	2	3
Not at all important	Important	Very important

3. How important is your *mother's* physical appearance (shape, weight, clothing) to her? _____ Not applicable

1	2	3
Not at all important	Important	Very important

From the Mother Influence Scale, an unpublished scale by M. P. Levine, L. Smolak, and H. Hayden. Reprinted with permission from the authors. For more information, see M. P. Levine, Smolak, and Hayden (1994).

APPENDIX 6C
PEER DIETING SCALE

Think of the kids who you go around with, that is, the kids you spend time with and whose friendship or opinions matter at least somewhat to you. If you do not have a lot of friends, think of the kids and groups who you would like to be friends with. Let us call these kids your "friends."

There are no right or wrong answers to these questions. We are interested in your opinion and your "sense" of how things are.

In answering the following questions, think only about your friends who are *girls*.

---

1. About how many of your friends would like to be thinner?

1	2	3	4	5
None	A few	About half	Most	All

2. How many of your friends are "on a diet" to try to lose weight or slow down weight gain?

1	2	3	4	5
None	A few	About half	Most	All

3. How often do you and your friends talk about weight, weight loss, and dieting?

1	2	3	4	5
None	Rarely	Sometimes	Often	Very often

From the Peer Dieting Scale, an unpublished scale by M. P. Levine, L. Smolak, and H. Hayden. Reprinted with permission from the authors. For more information, see M. P. Levine, Smolak, and Hayden (1994).

APPENDIX 6D
SIBLING APPEARANCE QUESTIONNAIRE

Please indicate below *each sibling*, male or female, that lived with you for 6 months or longer while you were between the *ages of 5 and 18.* This sibling may be of biological or adoptive relation to you, a stepbrother/sister, half brother/sister, etc. The key here is that this sibling, if any, lived in the same household as you for at least 6 months. You are asked what effect your sibling's physical attractiveness had on you while growing up. Be sure to make ratings for both childhood (before the onset of puberty) and your teen years (during and after the onset of puberty).

If you are an only child, check this blank __ and proceed to the next questionnaire.

List your siblings *from the oldest to youngest,* include yourself. Write "me" to indicate your position in the family. Indicate sex, current age, and the effect each sibling's physical attractiveness had on *how you felt about your looks* using the following scale.

1   Very negative effect on how I felt about my looks.
2   Mostly negative effect on how I felt about my looks.
3   No effect on how I felt about my looks.
4   Mostly positive effect on how I felt about my looks.
5   Very positive effect on how I felt about my looks.

| First name | Sex | Current age | Rate the type of effect your sibling's physical appearance had on how you felt about your appearance | | | | | | | | | |
			As a child					As a teenager				
_____	M F	_____	1	2	3	4	5	1	2	3	4	5
_____	M F	_____	1	2	3	4	5	1	2	3	4	5
_____	M F	_____	1	2	3	4	5	1	2	3	4	5
_____	M F	_____	1	2	3	4	5	1	2	3	4	5
_____	M F	_____	1	2	3	4	5	1	2	3	4	5
_____	M F	_____	1	2	3	4	5	1	2	3	4	5
_____	M F	_____	1	2	3	4	5	1	2	3	4	5

Now circle the *one* sibling's name whose physical appearance *most strongly influenced* how you felt about your physical appearance. If no sibling's appearance had an influence, check here □.

From the Sibling Appearance Questionnaire, an unpublished scale by L. Rieves and T. F. Cash. Reprinted with permission from the authors. For information, see Rieves and Cash (1996).

APPENDIX 6E
BODY EXPOSURE IN SEXUAL ACTIVITIES QUESTIONNAIRE

We are interested in the thoughts and behaviors that an individual may experience or enact during sexual encounters. Read each statement carefully and identify how characteristic it is of you and your experience using the following code:

Never	Rarely	Sometimes	Often	Always	
1	2	3	4	5	

1. During sexual activity I am constantly thinking that my partner will notice something about my body that is a turnoff.   1   2   3   4   5

2. During sexual activity I worry that my partner will find aspects of my physique unappealing.   1   2   3   4   5

3. During sexual activity I am aware of how my body looks.   1   2   3   4   5

4. During sexual activity something about the way my body looks makes me feel inhibited.   1   2   3   4   5

5. I am uncomfortable when undressed by my partner.   1   2   3   4   5

6. I prefer to keep my body hidden under a sheet or blanket during sexual activity.   1   2   3   4   5

7. I am comfortable with my partner looking at my genitals during sexual activity.   1   2   3   4   5

8. During sexual activity I worry that my partner will find my body repulsive.   1   2   3   4   5

9. During sexual activity I worry that my partner will think the size and shape of my sex organs are inadequate or unattractive.   1   2   3   4   5

10. When it comes to my partner seeing me naked, I have nothing to hide.   1   2   3   4   5

11. During sexual activity I have thoughts that my body looks sexy.   1   2   3   4   5

12. I don't like my partner to see me completely naked during sexual activity.   1   2   3   4   5

13. During sexual activity I expect my partner to be excited by seeing me without my clothes.   1   2   3   4   5

14. I prefer to keep certain articles of clothing on during sexual activity.   1   2   3   4   5

15. I am self-conscious about my body during sexual activity.   1   2   3   4   5

16. During sexual activity I worry that my partner will find the appearance or odor of my genitals repulsive.   1   2   3   4   5

17. During sexual activity I try to hide certain areas of my body from my partner's view.   1   2   3   4   5

18. During sexual activity I keep thinking that parts of my body are too unattractive to be sexy.   1   2   3   4   5

19. There are parts of my body that I don't want my partner to see during sexual activity.   1   2   3   4   5

20. During sexual activity I worry about what my partner thinks about how my body looks.   1   2   3   4   5

21. During sexual activity I worry that my partner could be turned off by the way parts of my body feel to his/her touch.   1   2   3   4   5

22.	During sexual activity it is hard for me not to think about my weight.	1	2	3	4	5
23.	I feel self-conscious if the room is too well lit during sexual activity.	1	2	3	4	5
24.	I am generally comfortable having parts of my body exposed to my partner during sexual activity.	1	2	3	4	5
25.	During sexual activity I enjoy having my partner look at my body.	1	2	3	4	5
26.	During sexual activity there are certain poses or positions I avoid because of the way my body would look to my partner.	1	2	3	4	5
27.	During sexual activity I am distracted by thoughts of how certain parts of my body look.	1	2	3	4	5
28.	Prior to or following sexual activity I am comfortable.	1	2	3	4	5

From the Body Exposure in Sexual Activities Questionnaire, an unpublished questionnaire by J. D. Hangen and T. F. Cash. Reprinted with permission from the authors. For more information, see Hangen and Cash (1991).

IV

FEMINIST APPROACHES

7

FEMINIST PERSPECTIVES

Feminism taught women to accept their bodies. Yet a quarter-century after *Our Bodies, Ourselves*, women ... are still desperately out of balance, obsessed with weight and dieting and food. Haven't we gotten anywhere? (O'Hanlon, 1997, p. 11)

This problem I have with my body image, it just makes me so angry. I've bought into society's message, yet it insults my feminist sensibilities. (a 33-year-old, Caucasian woman seeking treatment for body image disturbance)

Eating disorders constitute a major threat to women's health (American Psychological Association, 1996). Approximately 4.0% of adult women meet diagnostic criteria for anorexia nervosa (0.5–1.0%) or bulimia nervosa (3.0%), and another 2.0–4.0% experience a clinically significant eating-disorder syndrome that does not fully meet criteria for either (American Psychiatric Association, 1994; Fairburn & Beglin, 1990; Gilbert & Thompson, 1996). It is interesting to note that eating disorders appear to be almost exclusively a female phenomenon, with women constituting 90–95% of eating-disordered patients (American Psychiatric Association, 1994). As discussed in chapter 1, body image disturbance also appears to be significantly more prevalent among women than men. Given women's prevalence of dissatisfaction with their body and the negative psychological sequelae associated with body image disturbance, one could argue that such difficulties relating to body image pose a major threat to women's mental health.

As a consequence of these striking gender disparities, a number of theoretical explanations have been offered to explain the pandemic rates of body image distress among women. As the opening quotes assert, although women today enjoy greater independence and equality than women of past generations, far too many continue to be plagued by an inordinate concern regarding body shape and size. Has the Women's Movement truly made progress when the majority of women detest the very aspects of their figures that are female? To address these concerns, feminist approaches have received an increasing emphasis to offer new insights into the etiology and maintenance of body image disturbance.

At its most general, a feminist approach involves the belief that "women's attitudes toward, feelings about, and behaviors directed at influencing their bodies need to be understood within the context of Western philosophical, political and cultural history" (Striegel-Moore, 1995, p. 224). In essence, feminists assert that an important aspect of a woman's socialization in Westernized cultures is the equation of physical attractiveness with self-worth (Heinberg, 1996). In a society in which women are valued for their appearance, physical attractiveness has become the economy on which women barter (Wolf, 1990). As a result of being socialized in this environment, women have overidentified with their bodies, in turn leading a woman's self-esteem to be conditional on conforming to the prevailing norms for thinness and attractiveness (Bergner, Remer, & Whetsell, 1985).

There is significant diversity in feminist approaches to understanding body image disturbance (Striegel-Moore, 1995). In this chapter, we try to assimilate the wide-ranging approaches that constitute the feminist perspective. In a recent review of feminist explanations in the development of eating disorders, Gilbert and Thompson (1996) found that there are consistent themes in the literature; their article guides our present coverage. A number of these themes—culture of thinness, weight as power and control, and anxieties about female achievement–appearance—are also appropriate to the feminist body image literature and are used to organize our review of the literature in this chapter. In addition, the impact of gender role and sexual orientation on body image is reviewed. For each theme, the relevant theoretical viewpoint is discussed, followed by a review of the empirical literature and a discussion of future research implications. Finally, feminist assessment and treatment approaches for body image disturbance are reviewed.

RESEARCH INVESTIGATIONS FROM A FEMINIST VIEWPOINT

Feminist research methods purposefully depart from traditional research methods because of the belief that sexist bias is inherent in scientific research. Thus, research may be identified as feminist in perspective because of not only the context of the evaluation but also the methods used. A primary assertion of feminist research is that traditional research is not value free (Striegel-Moore, 1994). In psychology, feminists have "attempted to rescue women from the generic 'man' of traditional research and theory and to study the impact of gender on social, intellectual, and physical development" (S. C. Wooley, 1995, p. 294). In addition, feminists have worked to remove barriers for female researchers and research from a feminist perspective, have worked to eradicate sexist language from the literature, and have focused work on sexist practices that lead to distress in women (S. C. Wooley, 1995). Feminist researchers also eschew the hierarchical aspects of traditional research, favor more participant–observer paradigms, and value qualitative research over simple reliance on the scientific method. Thus, the articles reviewed in this chapter may vary significantly from studies described elsewhere in the book, relying more heavily on theoretical works than experimental designs.

The feminist perspective provides useful criticism for the status quo of psychological science. These debates have led to important and long neglected changes in women's health research. For example, the decision by the National Institutes of Health in the late 1980s to establish a policy mandating that women be included as participants in health research was one such outcome. Although an important step forward, many researchers continue to report less than full compliance with this policy (Rodin & Ickovics, 1990). In addition, the feminist influence has led to a continued increase in gender comparative research. Although often rejected because of perceived methodological difficulties, such comparative methods have a long history in neuroscience and physiology (Rodin & Ickovics, 1990).

In spite of these contributions, feminist research methods are often criticized or dismissed. For example, although provocative, feminist theories have been criticized for lacking an organized, theoretical framework, with clear and testable postulates. Furthermore, many of these theories remain largely untested by empirical studies. Finally, feminist research techniques may be susceptible to experimenter bias, depending on the manner of collecting qualitative data (Gilbert & Thompson, 1996). Because of these concerns, Peplau and Conrad (1989) have suggested that the categorization of research as feminist should not be dependent on the type of experimental methods, numbers, or statistics. Rather, *feminist inquiry* should be defined as any research that is relevant to the lives of women and demonstrates sensitivity to gender issues (Peplau & Conrad, 1989). In this chapter, however, we limit ourselves to reviewing studies that are self-identified as from a feminist viewpoint, provide empirical evidence for a feminist viewpoint, or are gender comparative. It is also important to note that feminist authors have criticized the eating disorders and body image literature for overemphasizing the experience of White, heterosexual women (B. Thompson, 1996) and those without disabilities (Stone, 1995). Indeed, much of the work cited below focuses on a limited female experience, as does the majority of supporting evidence. Clearly, additional research is needed to include a more all-encompassing view of women's bodily experiences.

FEMINIST APPROACHES: EMERGING THEMES

Culture of Thinness

> [The] single-minded pursuit of thinness and beauty has many parallels
> to a religious cult. In both cases a group of individuals is committed
> to a life defined by a rigid set of values and rules. Members of true
> cults frequently isolate themselves from the rest of the world and de-
> velop a strong sense of community. They seem obsessed with the path
> to perfection, which, though unattainable, holds out compelling prom-
> ises. In following their ideals, they usually feel that they are among
> "the chosen." (Hesse-Biber, 1996, p. 9)

In keeping with sociocultural theories of body image disturbance (see
chapter 3), feminists assert that women are vulnerable to the culture of
thinness, which permeates Western society (Gilbert & Thompson, 1996;
Nagel & Jones, 1992). Unfortunately, for women, this link between esteem
and appearance is often reiterated by society's view that a lack of attractiveness is considered to be more of a social liability for women than men
(Bergner et al., 1985). It has been suggested by a number of authors that
the culture of thinness arose as a means by which patriarchal society could
effectively subjugate women (Wolf, 1990; S. C. Wooley, 1995). Feminist
authors have argued further that the denigration of fatness and overvalua-
tion of thinness in American society constitute forms of sexism and
misogyny (L. S. Brown, 1989).

More than many other theorists, feminist authors have firmly held
the belief that cultural aspects of gender are the core to understanding and
treating body image and eating disturbances (S. C. Wooley, 1995). Feminists have asserted that dieting, eating disorders, and dissatisfaction with
one's body are seen as natural responses to pathological societal pressures
to be thin rather than as indicative of overt psychopathology. Because of
the widespread frequency of body image distress among women, Bergner
et al. (1985) have explained that body image in women is derived from
cultural influences and internalized cultural norms. The individual woman
internalizes these social values in the form of a negative cognitive schema,
which she interprets as self-generated and as objective reality (see also
chapter 10 on cognitive-processing models). Thus, negative self-evaluation
and feelings may superficially appear to be individual problems but instead
represent a toxic sociopolitical environment for women. The work of Bergner et al. and others (e.g., Kearney-Cooke & Striegel-Moore, 1997) suggests that cultural influences on gender may mediate the relationship between cognitions and body image disturbance.

Although a culture of thinness may be a relatively new phenomenon,
women have attempted to alter themselves, in accordance with the aesthetic standards of the particular period of time, to meet the varied and

changing ideals (Mazur, 1986; for a more complete discussion of historical changes in body image, see chapter 3). For many centuries, a round and curvaceous figure was seen as the ideal because it reflected women's maternal and nurturing nature (Gilbert & Thompson, 1996). However, as women's role in North America and Europe has become more liberated, less constrained, and more threatening to patriarchal society, women's preferred body shape has become more angular and restricted. For example, at the time of women's suffrage in the 1920s, a thin flapper appearance was promulgated. In the more conservative post-World War II era, women again returned to a more curvaceous ideal. However, again in the 1960s as women began to assert greater independence, a gaunt, girlish appearance came into vogue. This historical trend of greater restriction of body size during periods of a push for greater independence has led feminist researchers to identify women's body size as an accurate barometer of women's current position in society (Chernin, 1981). It has been further suggested that whereas in the 1960s, thinness was equated with independence and success, today it has become the defining criteria for feminine beauty (Kilbourne, 1994). To fail in the task of maintaining a thin physique, women risk being denigrated as lazy and ugly and a failure (Rothblum, 1994). Seid (1994) suggested that thinness has become a moral imperative, analogous to an earlier era's moral imperative for chastity (Lawrence, 1979).

The culture of thinness has persisted as the standard of feminine beauty since the 1960s. Feminist theorists have suggested that this shift in culture served as a means to dampen the enthusiasm of the Women's Movement and the potential freedoms it offered (Wolf, 1990). Society weakened the Women's Movement by instituting a culture of thinness that decreased women's self-esteem and refocused women's energies onto obsessive weight control and appearance goals.

According to this feminist perspective, the primary mode of communicating the culture of thinness is through the mass media. The media has a vested interest in maintaining this culture because of the money generated by women's insecurities regarding their appearance (Wolf, 1990). During the 1960s, as the Women's Movement began to include a large number of female consumers, American industry became threatened by the shift away from traditional feminine sex roles and stereotypes and the consequent spending habits. By reinforcing appearance concerns, the media ensured that women (who often control family finances) would freely spend on a number of appearance-related products. For example, data reported from the early 1990s suggest that U.S. society supported a $20 billion cosmetic industry, a $33 billion diet industry, and a $300 million cosmetic surgery industry (Wolf, 1990).

The media, together with society's pressures to suppress women by generating anxiety about women's appearance and attractiveness, have influenced even normal weight, non-eating-disordered women to be obsessed with food, weight, and appearance (Faludi, 1991; J. E. Martin, 1989). This pressure does not just serve to drive multibillion dollar industries or to make women insecure. Additionally, the glorification of waiflike, emaciated girls as the ideal woman is a further example of a patriarchal society's rewarding and idealizing the weak and incapable woman over the strong and independent one (Gilbert & Thompson, 1996). By displaying women who meet at least some of the diagnostic criteria for anorexia nervosa as society's ideal, patriarchal society promotes inferior, powerless women as perfection.

Empirical Support

The culture of thinness hypothesis is probably best supported by available data (Heinberg, 1996). As discussed in depth in chapter 3, a wealth of correlational data suggest the shift over the past 30 years from a curvaceous female standard of beauty to one that is more toned, taut, and angular (Garner, Garfinkel, Schwartz, & Thompson, 1980; Wiseman, Gray, Mosimann, & Ahrens, 1992). Highlights from this extensive literature are briefly discussed below. Archival studies examining the heights, weights, and measurements of Miss America contestants from 1979 to 1988 have found body weights 13–19% below expected weights for women their height (Wiseman et al., 1992). Wiseman et al. concluded that the majority of ideals in U.S. society, based on their low body weight, meet one of the *Diagnostic and Statistical Manual of Mental Disorders–Fourth Edition* (American Psychiatric Association, 1994) criteria for anorexia nervosa.

Similar studies also examine historical changes in the ideal body shape and document women's continued investment in conforming to the ideal represented by their particular sociohistorical era. In examinations of popular women's magazines, past research demonstrated trends toward an increasing slenderness of models and an increase in articles and advertisements addressing dietary issues (Silverstein, Perdue, Peterson, & Kelly, 1986; Silverstein, Peterson, & Perdue, 1986). Although cultural expectations for thinness still abound, women are increasingly offered exercise as an alternative, along with the expectation of a toned, muscular body. For example, Wiseman et al. updated the studies previously described by tabulating the number of diet-for-weight-loss, exercise, and diet and exercise articles from 1959 to 1989 for leading women's magazines. An overall increase was demonstrated for the emphasis on weight loss over the 30-year period. It is interesting to note that the proportion of exercise and diet–exercise references has increased and, from 1983 onward, the prevalence of exercise articles has surpassed that of diet articles (Wiseman et al., 1992).

Evidence exists in television as well as the print media for a culture of thinness. Wiseman, Gunning, and Gray (1993) tabulated the number of television commercials for diet foods, aids, and products and weight-loss programs for the years 1973–1991, demonstrating a steady increase in the prevalence of these advertisements. Although the ideal figure has become thinner while the average woman's figure has become larger (Garner et al., 1980), it appears that women continue to accept the thinner ideal as a goal. Furthermore, although the thin ideal is not promoted only by the media and may not even originate with the media, the popularity of television, movies, and magazines leads the media to be among the most influential and effective communicators of the culture of thinness (Raphael & Lacey, 1992; Silverstein, Perdue, Peterson, & Kelly, 1986).

Future Research

As previously discussed in this section and chapter 3, a wealth of data suggests a link between the culture of thinness, or sociocultural hypothesis, and body image disturbance. Messages endorsing a culture of thinness regarding one's ideal weight and appearance are communicated ubiquitously through the mass media and gender socialization. Nevertheless, individuals fall onto a continuum of dissatisfaction, with some individuals or groups of people reporting very little disturbance and others developing eating-disorder behaviors. Future researchers should explore these individual and group differences. The culture of thinness hypothesis has failed to describe the mechanism by which a society plays a causative role in the development of body image disturbance and eating-disorder behavior. For example, a number of mediating variables, such as social comparison, teasing history, or gender role socialization, may be necessary to sensitize women to the culture of thinness. The former two variables are discussed at length in chapters 3 and 5, whereas gender role socialization is reviewed more fully later in this chapter.

Because the mass media is hypothesized as an essential communicator and reinforcer of the culture of thinness, exposure to media influences deserves particular research attention. A number of researchers have demonstrated transient changes in body image following exposure to media presentations of cultural ideals (Heinberg & Thompson, 1995; Irving, 1990; Waller, Hamilton, & Shaw, 1992).

Few researchers have explored the etiological link between patriarchal dogma and a culture of thinness. Although scholars have noted that shifts in the female beauty ideal toward extreme thinness have occurred during periods in which women have achieved progress toward greater freedom, research has failed to directly link the culture of thinness, or its communication through the mass media, to the causes proposed by feminists (Striegel-Moore, 1995).

In one study, however, researchers have examined the effect of a feminist ideology on exposure to cultural messages about the importance of appearance and a thin body type. In a study using a random sample of 500 men and women from a midsize Western city, participants endorsing feminine ideals differed significantly from nonfeminists in mass media consumption (Lull, Mulac, & Rosen, 1983). For example, feminists with college degrees viewed an average of 95 min of television per day, whereas nonfeminists with the same education viewed 160 min of television per day. Additionally, feminists watched significantly more movies, cultural programs, science fiction, comedies satirizing social norms, and documentaries than did the nonfeminists (Lull et al., 1983). Thus, women who differ in their endorsement of feminist beliefs differ in their use of electronic mass media. It is unclear what effect, if any, this exposure to mass media may have on body image among feminists and nonfeminists.

Future researchers should examine individual differences in media exposure, consumption, and internalization and body image disturbance (Gilbert & Thompson, 1996; Heinberg & Thompson, 1995). Furthermore, longitudinal studies following girls' childhood through adolescence and into adulthood could examine variables that would predict their later enculturation of sociocultural ideals.

Although a culture of thinness is likely to be necessary, it may not be etiologically sufficient for the development of body image disturbance. The presence or absence of other factors may simply potentiate the effect of or serve to buffer one from the current societal climate (Heinberg, 1996). Integrative hypotheses should be developed and empirically tested to examine how these multiple factors interplay with the culture of thinness in the development of body image disturbance.

Weight as Power and Control

Other authors (Orbach, 1978a, 1978b; Szekely, 1989) believe that women, in their efforts to achieve control in their lives, define themselves by their appearance and body shape, something that is ostensibly under their control. Thus, by controlling their weight, women can experience a sense of control that is otherwise thwarted in other areas of importance (Dworkin, 1988). Paradoxically, in an effort to achieve a sense of control, women become complacent with society's pressures to focus on weight and appearance as the paramount issue in their lives (Orbach, 1978a, 1978b; Szekely, 1989). Thus, in a contradictory way, women gain a greater sense of power by surrendering to the culture of thinness.

Still other feminist theorists, such as Chernin (1981), have asserted that women's body image relates to the power differential between men and women, with men attempting to grow larger and more powerful whereas women attempt to grow smaller, more dependent, and invisible. Similarly, Wolf (1990) conceptualized periods of increased sociocultural pressure for thinness in women as a backlash against women's push for increased independence. According to this theory, women define their ideal weight according to their needs for power and control (Gilbert & Thompson, 1996).

Historically, feminist theorists have asserted that the thin body ideal became prevalent during the 1960s in response to society's glorification of pornographic images of women's bodies (Gilbert & Thompson, 1996). By developing a thinner and more androgynous body shape, women may have believed that they would escape sexual harassment and coercion (Wolf, 1990). Thus, an emaciated body type represents a rejection of society's objectification of women's bodies (McLorg & Taub, 1987) and helps protect anorexic women from sexual harassment, perhaps increasing their power and influence in the workplace (Wolf, 1990).

The weight as power and control theory relates to the issue of sexual abuse as a risk factor for body image disturbance. In a few studies, researchers have examined the relationship between childhood sexual abuse and the development of body image disturbance, with mixed results. (See chapter 8 for a full discussion of the effects of sexual abuse, sexual harassment, and inappropriate sexual commentary on body image.) Feminist theorists, however, have posited that sexual abuse may be a significant risk factor for eating disorders (Gilbert & Thompson, 1996). For example, Root (1991) suggested that eating-disorder behaviors are a posttraumatic response to sexual abuse among women. Because of the lack of control experienced by women with sexual abuse histories (C. L. Cole, 1985; Kearney-Cooke & Striegel-Moore, 1994), developing the somatotype of a child without secondary sexual characteristics may serve to remove physical and psychological reminders of the abuse. Therefore, for a sexual abuse survivor, minimization of sexuality may offer a greater sense of control.

Although both the culture of thinness and weight as control and power hypotheses suggest that women are at higher risk of body image disturbance, they are at odds as to the agent of the thin standard. The culture of thinness hypothesis suggests that culture imposes an unrealistically thin ideal on women, whereas the weight as control and power hypothesis suggests that women themselves, to achieve power and control, impose stringent standards of body type. That is, although women passively submit to society's demands according to the culture of thinness, the weight as power and control theory suggests that women actively use their weight to achieve specific ends (Gilbert & Thompson, 1996).

Empirical Support

Literature supporting a weight as power and control hypothesis tends to be anecdotal and theoretical rather than strongly empirical in nature. Consistent themes of control have been discussed in the eating disorders literature (Bruch, 1973; Selvini-Palazzoli, 1974; Stern, 1991; Sugarman,

1991; S. C. Wooley, 1991). These authors have suggested that eating disorders are a maladaptive attempt by women to assert greater control over their lives. Other empirical research demonstrates a relationship between a perceived lack of control over one's life and eating-disorder beliefs and behaviors (Ahmad, Waller, & Verduyn, 1994; Wagner, Halmi, & Maguire, 1987). Finally, McLorg and Taub (1987) found a correlation between eating-disorder behaviors and a reported strong rejection of society's view of women as sex objects. That is, women who reject society's objectification of women are more likely to have eating disorders because they feel more in control of their lives.

Also in contrast to the culture of thinness hypothesis is the feminist writings of B. Thompson (1996). She suggested that eating problems have little correlation with vanity or concerns with appearance. Rather, they often begin as "orderly and sane responses to insane circumstances" (B. Thompson, 1996, p. 106), mainly racism, sexism, homophobia, classism, and sexual abuse. For this reason, she and other feminist researchers use the term *problem* rather than *disorder*. She explained that eating problems are often mislabeled as individual pathology when they are actually physical and psychological responses to social injustice (B. Thompson, 1996).

Although there is mixed evidence that patients with eating disorders have a higher incidence of childhood sexual abuse, Connors and Morse (1993), Hastings and Kern (1994), and Pope and Hudson (1992) concluded that early sexual abuse is not a risk factor for eating-disorder behavior. Feminist researchers have noted, however, that in this mixed literature, null effects are more frequently found by male principal investigators than female principal investigators (Rice, 1996). Wonderlich (1992) has suggested that methodological limitations of past research prohibit a conclusive judgment about the issue. Striegel-Moore and Marcus (1995) also noted that the lack of definitive proof of a causal link should not "obscure the fact that a history of sexual abuse" (p. 448) has treatment implications. In spite of these debates, interest remains in the possible relationship among abuse history, eating problems, and body image disturbance (Hastings & Kern, 1994; see the next chapter for a fuller discussion of this issue).

Future Research

The weight as power and control hypothesis has been criticized as being difficult to evaluate empirically (Gilbert & Thompson, 1996). This theory does not provide an explanation as to why some women choose to control their weight to achieve power whereas other women do not. For example, are women dissatisfied because they have been unable to achieve the degree of thinness necessary to achieve sufficient power? Are women with anorexia nervosa more likely to espouse feminist ideology as part of their personal philosophy? It is also unclear whether women with eating disorders or body image disturbance have failed to control their lives in more adaptive ways or are under undue control by others.

To better answer these questions, future researchers should examine the following: the perceptions of personal control among women with body image disturbance, the extent to which women with body image disturbance come from controlling or domineering families and personal relationships, the extent of feminist ideology among women with body image disturbance and eating disorders, and coping mechanisms used by women with and without body image disturbance in experimental paradigms designed to mimic a lack of control. Although the weight as power and control hypothesis is theoretically compelling, it lacks the analysis that its competitor, culture of thinness, has received in the literature.

Anxieties About Female Appearance–Achievement

A third group of feminist writings and research can be organized regarding women's anxieties about pressures to achieve professionally or physically. For example, a number of authors have suggested that women currently face conflicting pressures to achieve academically and professionally, as equal competitors with men, whereas concurrently experiencing pressure to achieve an acceptable degree of femininity and beauty (Bruch, 1978; Franks, 1986; Garner et al., 1980). Thus, it is not enough for women to simply compete equally with men in academic and professional pursuits, but they must also achieve a high standard of thinness and attractiveness to be seen as successful (Dworkin, 1988; Gilbert & Thompson, 1996). Lawrence (1984) suggested that eating disorders represent an attempt to temper the negative stigma associated with successful women. Thus, the emaciated woman can be seen as successful, sufficiently feminine, and non-threatening (Lawrence, 1984).

Other feminist authors have argued that body image disturbance, dieting, and eating disorders represent anxieties about the feminine form (Chernin, 1981; Larkin, Rice, & Russell, 1996; Rice, 1996). Dieting allows women to return to their previous, less-threatening prepubescent body shape. For example, Chernin asserted that women with anorexia nervosa develop their emaciated form in an attempt to take up as little space as possible. This obsession relates to feelings of illegitimacy as an independent abstract form (Chernin, 1981). By taking on the physical shape of a girl, the woman with anorexia reduces her symbolic threat to a phallocentric society. Somewhat similar, feminists have suggested that as girls develop during puberty, they begin to feel anxious about their more rounded, curvaceous, feminine form (Larkin et al., 1996; Rice, 1996). For example, Larkin et al. suggested that the leering, teasing, and sexual harassment that young girls begin to experience as their bodies develop signify a need for them to be constantly vigilant about their appearance. They reported that "harassment reminds girls that they are always at risk, and many begin to take on an identity that may offer them more protection. For many girls, this means altering the locus of their violation: their bodies" (Larkin et al., 1996, p. 21). Dieting and eating disorders allow women to achieve safety and avoid humiliation by returning to a less feminine form. These authors also argued that rather than internalizing a culture of thinness to attract men, young women attempt to reduce their developing bodies in the hopes of reducing unwanted and unwarranted male attention.

Empirical Support

A relatively large number of studies suggest a relationship between disordered-eating behaviors and women's achievement aspirations. For example, Perlick and Silverstein (1994) drew on correlational evidence suggesting that women with eating disorders tend to increase problematic eating behaviors during temporal periods of high achievement stress (e.g., college graduation) and tend to view their mother's lives as limited because of their gender. A number of other studies suggest that a relationship among high aspirations for achievement, a preference for thinness, and bulimic behaviors exists (Silverstein, Carpman, Perlick, & Perdue, 1990; Silverstein & Perdue, 1988; Silverstein, Perdue, Peterson, Vogel, & Fantini, 1986). However, these findings have been criticized for failing to recognize important confounding variables (Gilbert & Thompson, 1996). For example, the prevalence of eating disorders increasing at a time of increasing achievement needs, such as college graduation, does not mean the two are causally linked. Rather, a third variable, such as increasing women's enrollment in college or increasing academic demands, may have led to more women experiencing pressures and relying on unhealthy methods of coping, such as eating-disorder behaviors. Similarly, high achievement aspirations and a preference for thinness may be confounded by such variables as socioeconomic status or personality variables, such as perfectionism.

Research examining clinical samples of eating-disordered patients shows support for the anxieties about the female achievement–appearance hypothesis. For example, Boskind-Lodahl (1976) found that women with anorexia might be rewarded for their appearance and passive behaviors but might also be criticized when achieving successes, particularly success in relation to male peers. Silverstein, Perdue, Wolf, and Pizzolo (1988) found that women with bulimic behaviors were more likely than other women to report family views of women in stereotypical, secondary roles: Their mothers were unhappy with their own careers, their fathers thought the respondents' mother was not intelligent, and male siblings were treated as the most intelligent sibling by their father.

Qualitative research also suggests a link between sexual harassment and body image problems. Feminist researchers examined the link in adolescents as part of a support group and journal exercise (Larkin et al., 1996). They found that adolescent girls became increasingly uncomfortable with their bodies as they received more attention from the opposite sex, often commenting that they wished they did not have such feminine physiques (Larkin et al., 1996). Again, this area is covered in more detail in chapter 8.

Future Research

Future research needs to examine the mechanism by which dual achievement orientations (professional and appearance) relate to the development of body image disturbance and eating disorders. Some women may simply focus on achieving in a singular domain. What differentiates these women from those who feel the need to be successful in both areas? Gilbert and Thompson (1996) suggested that longitudinal, experimental, and quasi-experimental research should examine how women with high achievement aspirations differ from those with a lesser need to succeed (e.g., college students vs. age-matched noncollege peers, women enrolled in more challenging majors or those dominated by men vs. those whose majors do not meet these criteria). Laboratory studies may also be helpful by generating transient changes in achievement anxiety (e.g., simulating a classroom environment).

Feminist analyses of anxieties about female achievement have also been criticized for overemphasizing the mother's role and the participant's perceptions of their mother over the influence of their father, other family members, and society (Gilbert & Thompson, 1996). Future research needs to examine this topic from a more balanced, multidimensional viewpoint. (However, as we noted in chapters 5 and 6, increasingly fathers are being evaluated as a contributing factor in their daughters' and sons' body image concerns.)

Theoretical Conclusions

Taken largely from the feminist eating-disorders literature, as the preceding review demonstrates, there is a considerable amount of diversity in feminist approaches. It has been suggested that this diversity more globally reflects the evolution of feminist scholarship (Striegel-Moore, 1995). That is, more recent scholarship has shifted away from describing women as victims of an oppressive culture toward acknowledging women's role in bodily preoccupation. Anxieties about female appearance–achievement and power and control theories both assume that women are capable of resisting, subverting, or consciously accepting cultural demands (Striegel-Moore, 1995). To date, integrative feminist theories have yet to be developed or such models proposed that would hypothesize the links between feminist theories and other explanations of body image disturbance.

HETEROGENEITY OF NORMATIVE DISCONTENT

As previously discussed, feminist theories focus almost entirely on the role of culture, society, and women's roles in the current sociohistorical moment as having a profound influence on the development of body image disturbance and eating disorders. However, these theories fail to fully explain the large heterogeneity of normative discontent among women in Western cultures. Normative discontent ranges on a continuum, with some women reporting relative satisfaction with their bodies and appearance and others developing eating disorders (Striegel-Moore, Silberstein, & Rodin, 1986). Given that all women are exposed to the culture of thinness and the stressors related to women's role in society, it is unclear how this heterogeneity develops. A number of studies, reviewed next, demonstrate a relationship between sex-role orientation (i.e., attributes traditionally associated with a specific gender; see Table 7.1) and body image disturbance. Perhaps certain women, because of their endorsement of more traditional feminine values, are at a higher risk for being dissatisfied with their appearance and body shape.

Implications of Sex-Role Orientation

Sex-role orientation is proposed as etiologically significant in the development of body image dissatisfaction. Murnen and Smolak (1997) recently conducted a meta-analysis of 69 studies that examined the connection among masculinity, femininity, and eating problems. They found a small, positive relationship between femininity and eating problems and a negative relationship between masculinity and eating problems. A number of other studies suggest that traditionally sex-typed women have lower body satisfaction than their more androgynous peers (Jackson, Sullivan, & Rostker, 1988; van Strien, 1989). In addition, the importance of the masculine component of gender role has been demonstrated. Androgynous and masculine women had more favorable body image ratings and more feminine men had unfavorable ratings in a physical fitness domain of body image (Jackson et al., 1988). Recently, authors have suggested that moderating variables may influence the relationship between gender role and body image (Borchert & Heinberg, 1996; C. Davis, Dionne, & Lazarus, 1996; C. E. Johnson & Petrie, 1995). For example, neuroticism has been shown to interact with both masculinity in women and femininity in men in predicting positive ratings of attractiveness (C. Davis et al., 1996). The authors demonstrated that the positive relationship between gender role

TABLE 7.1
Ratings of the Femininity Versus Masculinity of
Various Activities and Attributes

Task	N	M	SD
Female raters			
Knowledge of romance novels	276	1.54	.66
Needle threading	276	1.58	.67
Beauty aid knowledge	275	1.65	.59
Soap opera trivia	276	1.78	.63
Knowledge about fashion designers	276	2.01	.62
Fashion knowledge	276	2.23	.72
Diet knowledge	276	2.26	.72
Male movie star recognition	276	2.33	.74
Pricing groceries	274	2.36	.67
Knowledge about cooking utensils	276	2.47	.67
Ice skating knowledge	275	2.48	.61
Cooking knowledge	274	2.61	.63
Health knowledge	276	2.78	.50
Vocabulary knowledge	276	2.84	.42
Solving anagrams	180	2.91	.39
Music trivia	276	2.96	.22
Putting objects together	275	3.16	.43
Math knowledge	275	3.17	.49
Female movie star recognition	276	3.18	.74
Programming a videocassette recorder	275	3.19	.52
Computer knowledge	276	3.21	.50
Video games	276	3.29	.49
Knowledge about brand names of cars	276	3.55	.62
Baseball and basketball	276	3.62	.69
Checking oil in automobile	276	3.64	.70
Poker	276	3.68	.68
Sports trivia	274	3.85	.67
Knowledge about weight lifting	276	3.88	.65
Car trivia	274	3.98	.60
Knowledge about car racing	276	4.17	.57
Tool–construction knowledge	276	4.21	.67
Male raters			
Needle threading	97	1.58	.67
Knowledge of romance novels	97	1.59	.75
Beauty aid knowledge	97	1.65	.65
Soap opera trivia	97	1.74	.67
Knowledge about fashion designers	97	1.90	.77
Fashion knowledge	97	2.18	.68
Ice skating knowledge	97	2.40	.76
Pricing groceries	97	2.45	.68
Knowledge about cooking utensils	96	2.49	.70
Male movie star recognition	97	2.53	.74
Cooking knowledge	97	2.54	.72
Diet knowledge	97	2.58	.69
Vocabulary knowledge	96	2.88	.53
Health knowledge	97	2.92	.55

Table continues

TABLE 7.1 (*Continued*)

Task	N	M	SD
Male raters (continued)			
Solving anagrams	59	2.95	.43
Music trivia	97	2.97	.49
Math knowledge	97	3.23	.49
Female movie star recognition	97	3.24	.80
Computer knowledge	97	3.35	.58
Putting objects together	97	3.42	.61
Programming a videocassette recorder	97	3.46	.76
Video games	97	3.54	.60
Knowledge about brand names of cars	97	3.79	.71
Poker	96	3.90	.70
Baseball and basketball	97	3.99	.71
Checking oil in automobile	97	4.03	.71
Knowledge about weight lifting	97	4.10	.64
Sports trivia	96	4.10	.64
Car trivia	97	4.13	.77
Knowledge about car racing	97	4.23	.55
Tool−construction knowledge	97	4.43	.59

Note. Range: 1 (*feminine*)−5 (*masculine*). From *Body Image and Mood Changes in Competitive Interactions: Winning or Losing Against an Opposite-Sexed Peer on a Gender-Based Task*, by S. Gilbert and J. K. Thompson, 1998, unpublished manuscript, University of South Florida. Reprinted with permission from the authors.

and body image only exists at low levels of neuroticism. As neuroticism increases, the relationship diminishes (C. Davis et al., 1996). Thus, the confluence of personality factors and gender-role orientation may be necessary for body image dissatisfaction.

Gender-role discrepancy, rather than gender-role endorsement, may also be an important predictor. For example, C. E. Johnson and Petrie (1995) found that women without a discrepancy between their real and ideal gender identity reported fewer eating disorder symptoms, less concern with body shape, and higher self-esteem than those who reported a discrepancy, particularly if they desired to be more masculine. Thus, women who evidence more body dissatisfaction and eating disorder behavior may feel conflicted about society's incompatible demands to be masculine while maintaining ideal femininity (C. E. Johnson & Petrie, 1995). Borchert and Heinberg (1996) demonstrated similar findings for the body image of men but not for women. Among college age women, physical size, not gender-role discrepancy, predicted body image dissatisfaction. However, for men, in addition to physical size, falling short of their masculine ideal predicted a more negative body image (Borchert & Heinberg, 1996).

Glidden and Tracey (1989) demonstrated that tailoring treatment programs for body image and weight concerns to different sex-role attitudes could be beneficial. Women with nontraditional sex-role attitudes preferred interventions focusing on internal personal causes. Conversely, women who were more traditional preferred an intervention attributing weight issues to more external, sociocultural etiologies.

In a small group of studies, researchers have examined the influence of feminist ideology more specifically on body image dissatisfaction. For example, Kelson, Kearney-Cooke, and Lansky (1990) examined public body consciousness, private body consciousness, and body competence among undergraduate women. When the sample was stratified on the basis of feminist identification (i.e., an endorsement of "I am an active feminist" or "I am a feminist but I am not currently active in the Women's Movement"), significant differences were found for self-defined body competence. For feminists, a competent body correlated with feeling healthy and awareness of internal sensations. In contrast, for nonfeminists, a competent body correlated with concerns about appearance. The authors concluded that because feminists are aware of pressures on women to conform to standards of beauty, the feminists might redefine what is personally beautiful as outside of the ideal (Kelson et al., 1990).

More recently, Dionne, Davis, Fox, and Gurevich (1995) examined the influence of feminist ideology on the body image dissatisfaction of 200 Canadian women. Multiple regression analyses, controlling for age, body mass index, neuroticism, and physical activity level, found that the Physical Attractiveness subscale of the Composite Feminist Ideology Scale was negatively related to both general and specific measures of body dissatisfaction. However, the total score on this scale was not a significant predictor. Thus, a woman's feminist attitudes about appearance relate significantly to body image satisfaction, but overall feminist ideology does not (Dionne et al., 1995).

Finally, it may not be feminist identity or even traditional gender-role beliefs that is the most important correlate of body image. Cash, Ancis, and Strachan (1997) found that traditional gender attitudes regarding male–female social interactions, that is, "women with conventional expectations and preferences about gender roles in *male–female social relations* were more invested in their looks and, to a greater extent, had internalized societal standards for maladaptive assumptions about their physical appearance" (p. 441).

Implications for Gay and Lesbian Body Image Issues

Correlational studies examining sexual orientation suggest that lesbian women, who may be more likely to reject patriarchal ideals, have a better body image than their heterosexual counterparts (Gettelman & Thompson, 1993). In a sample of lesbians, gay men, heterosexual women, and heterosexual men, lesbians were the least concerned about physical appearance, whereas gay men and heterosexual women showed significantly higher concern for physical attractiveness (Siever, 1994). Lesbian women said that physical attractiveness was not important in their evaluations of their partners nor was it important to their partners. These findings are more striking when one considers that the lesbian women in the sample were significantly heavier and more dissatisfied with their weight than were the heterosexual women. Thus, although lesbians may weigh more and wish to lose weight, they do not express these concerns in dysfunctional attitudes and behaviors associated with eating disorders (Siever, 1994).

Similar results were found among adolescents. In a sample of students in Grades 7–12, heterosexual girls and boys were compared with girls and boys who self-identified as homosexual or bisexual (French, Story, Rema-fedi, Resnick, & Blum, 1996). Homosexual female students were more likely than heterosexual female students to report a positive body image (42.1% vs. 20.5%), although no significant differences were found for diet-ing, binge eating, or purging. Homosexual boys were more likely to report body image dissatisfaction, frequent dieting, and bingeing and purging. The authors explained that the lack of protective effect of homosexual orien-tation in girls for dieting and eating-disorder behavior was due to their young age (French et al., 1996). The authors hypothesized an interaction between time in the lesbian community and the buffering effect of sexual orientation. That is, only when lesbians become older, better enculturated into the lesbian and feminist culture, and more politically aware do lower rates of dieting and eating disorders develop.

More recent research, however, suggests that lesbian women do not significantly differ from heterosexual women on measures of body image (Beren, Hayden, Wilfley, & Grilo, 1996) or in the rates of bulimia nervosa (Heffernan, 1996). In fact, binge eating disorder is shown to be more prev-alent among lesbian women than heterosexual women (Heffernan, 1996). In one study, an affiliation with the gay community served as a buffering agent for body image in gay men. However, an affiliation with the lesbian community was unrelated to body image disturbance among lesbian women (Beren et al., 1996). This suggests that a possible rejection of a more pa-triarchal society may not protect women from the culture of thinness. B. Thompson (1996) suggested that lesbian women might feel pressure to maintain a thin, attractive appearance for fear of appearing too "butch" (p. 109). These results suggest that lesbians' alternative lifestyle may not be sufficient to undo the effects of growing up in a culture of thinness (Dworkin, 1988; Striegel-Moore, Tucker, & Hsu, 1990).

ASSESSMENT

One recent scale has been developed from a feminist perspective that offers a multifaceted assessment of body image from this model. McKinley (1995; McKinley & Hyde, 1996) developed the Objectified Body Consciousness Scale (OBCS; see Appendix 7A) using feminist theory regarding the social construction of the female body. This scale was based on the assumption that women vary in their tendency to view their bodies as objects "to be looked at" (McKinley & Hyde, 1996, p. 182). Based on theories related to objectified body consciousness and the experiences of undergraduate women, items were created to reflect three components of objectified body consciousness: body surveillance (women as constant external onlookers to their own bodies), control beliefs (women are responsible for how their bodies look and can control their appearance to comply with cultural standards), and internalization/shame (shame regarding the inability to measure up to internalized standards of feminine beauty).

The proposed items were given to 121 undergraduate women, and a factor analysis demonstrated the three predicted dimensions. Internal consistencies (αs) of the OBCS were moderate to high: Surveillance scale, .89; Body Shame scale, .75; and Control Beliefs scale, .72; the first two subscales were significantly negatively correlated with body esteem. In a second study, researchers validated the scale's use with a middle-age population; in a third study, they cross-validated the factor findings and demonstrated convergent validity with measures of body image, eating disturbance, and public body self-consciousness (McKinley & Hyde, 1996). The OBCS was recently used in two studies that examined its utility for men and examined mother–daughter body image issues (McKinley, 1997, 1998).

The Feminine Gender Role Stress Scale (FGRS; Gillespie & Eisler, 1992) measures the cognitive appraisal of stressors that are particularly salient for women and includes a subscale relevant to body image. Factor analysis of the FGRS reveals five independent factors: (a) fear of unemotional relationships, (b) fear of physical unattractiveness (e.g., rating stress of "being perceived as being overweight"), (c) fear of victimization, (d) fear of behaving assertively, and (e) fear of not being nurturant. The FGRS has been shown to distinguish participants with eating disorders from those with other psychiatric disorders and college women with eating disorders from normal college women (Martz, Handley, & Eisler, 1996).

Other measures used by feminist researchers, although not measuring body image directly, are briefly reviewed next. The Personal Attributes Questionnaire (Spence & Helmreich, 1978) and the Bem Sex Role Inventory (Bem, 1981) are frequently used measures that assess feminine, masculine, and gender-neutral characteristics. The Composite Feminist Ideology Scale (Dionne, 1992) was designed to assess the degree of a participant's agreement with the tenets of the Women's Movement. The scale contains seven subscales, including one measuring physical attractiveness.

A projective measure, the Draw-A-Person Test, has also been used to measure gender identity conflict. Silverstein et al. (1990) used this test to predict disordered eating. They found that women whose drawings suggested a pattern of wishing they had been born male were more likely than other women to report purging or frequent bingeing (Silverstein et al., 1990).

TREATMENT

The feminist literature on treatment interventions for body image disturbance criticizes most counseling approaches as being focused on changing a woman's appearance (e.g., diet, exercise) rather than helping her accept and celebrate the body she has (Bergner et al., 1985). Instead of focusing on individual treatment, feminist researchers have suggested that methods to improve a woman's body image are by generally advocating equality of the genders and discouraging the view that women are defined by their appearance (Dionne et al., 1995). Interventions focusing on excessive diet and exercise are doomed to failure and only serve to lower a woman's already fragile self-esteem.

Feminist therapy, in general, varies from traditional forms of psychotherapy in a number of ways. Feminists believe that traditional forms of psychotherapy perpetuate the androcentric hierarchy of society in the form of the doctor–patient relationship (S. C. Wooley, 1995). As a result, feminist therapies strive to minimize hierarchy and place the therapist and client in equitable roles. Such minimization of hierarchical roles may include self-disclosure on the part of the therapist, particularly if the therapist is a woman, in regards to shared experiences as women (S. C. Wooley, 1995). For example, a feminist therapist working with a female patient who is describing her own body image distress may share her experience of living in a culture of thinness, and together they can discuss alternatives for challenging the societal assumptions of an ideal weight and size. Feminists have also paid close attention to the ways that mental health treatment can unwittingly reinforce gender stereotypes. For instance, S. C. Wooley (1995) asserted that

> adjunctive pharmacotherapy and hospitalization, for example, often become destructive reenactments of family patterns in which male physicians, cast in the role of consulting experts to female therapists, recreate the daughter's experiences with a distant father whose opinions were valued over those of her more available but less respected mother. (p. 297)

Feminists may also include more experiential techniques, such as guided imagery, movement exercises, and art and dance therapy. For example, art therapy has also been discussed as a feminist mode of treating body image distress (Ellis, 1989). Such interventions involve using a mirroring process to recreate one's own reflection to counter the social context of a woman's image of herself. Although guided imagery is often used as part of cognitive–behavioral interventions, feminists have also used these techniques to empower women and help create more positive body images. For example, Kearney-Cooke and Striegel-Moore (1997) described the following guided imagery exercise:

> You begin to see a figure on the cliffs. You realize the figure is wise and compassionate, knows your body's story, and is behind you 100% in the change process. This could be a spiritual figure, a person you've known or read about, or one you create. Look at his or her face. Sense the kindness, gentleness. Feel the love and acceptance . . . . Now look to the sky and realize there is a screen in the sky where you can see new images of yourself. You are aware that this is your body, your life. You hear yourself talking to yourself in a more positive way. (pp. 302–303)

Other experiential techniques include free-associative writing regarding a problematic body part, stage performance, or psychodrama (Bergner et al., 1985; S. C. Wooley, 1995).

One quasi-experimental design examining feminist body image therapy has been described in the literature. Bergner et al. (1985) compared three feminist group-counseling treatments (visual, kinesthetic, and visual–kinesthetic) and described their research as conducted from a feminist perspective. Each treatment was 8 weeks long, with 8 women per group, and was led by M. Bergner and C. Whetsell. The female coleader was seen as a supportive role model who could validate the participants' experiences as women in a society valuing the culture of thinness. The male coleader was seen as important because he did not respond to the women simply on the basis of their appearance. All three groups used cognitive restructuring, homework, diary keeping, and group processing of content. However, the visual groups accessed and reframed thoughts and feeling through a visual-processing system (e.g., mirror confrontation), whereas the kinesthetic group reframed through a movement-sensation-processing system (e.g., a guided movement exercise). The third group combined these two. All three groups improved on measures of body image, and no differences were found among the groups.

CONCLUSIONS

Feminist theorists have long been successful in bringing the public's attention to a number of women's issues, such as domestic violence, reproductive freedom, and sexual abuse and assault. More recently, feminist attention has turned to the influence of society and women's roles in society as important aspects in the etiology of body image and eating disturbance. These insights provide essential information for a multidimensional analysis of women's experiences of their bodies. In this chapter, we attempted to organize feminist theories into recognizable themes and began to examine supporting studies and avenues for future research. Although the various themes differ in the degree of empirical support, all would benefit from a longitudinal analysis and examination of individual differences among women. B. Thompson (1996) has noted that feminist research focusing on women is an improvement over traditional research; however, studies generally focus on White, upper-class, well-educated, heterosexual women. The increasing rates of eating and body image problems among African Americans, lesbians, and other groups (Heffernan, 1996; Striegel-Moore, Schreiber, Pike, Wilfley, & Rodin, 1995) indicate the importance of investigating these individuals—research that is well underway (Beren, Hayden, Wilfley, & Striegel-Moore, 1997).

APPENDIX 7A
OBJECTIFIED BODY CONSCIOUSNESS SCALE

Strongly disagree			Neither agree nor disagree			Strongly agree	Does not apply
1	2	3	4	5	6	7	na

1. I rarely think about how I look. 1 2 3 4 5 6 7 na
2. When I can't control my weight, I feel like something must be wrong with me. 1 2 3 4 5 6 7 na
3. I think it is more important that my clothes are comfortable than whether they look good on me. 1 2 3 4 5 6 7 na
4. I think a person is pretty much stuck with the looks they are born with. 1 2 3 4 5 6 7 na
5. I feel ashamed of myself when I haven't made the effort to look my best. 1 2 3 4 5 6 7 na
6. A large part of being in shape is having that kind of body in the first place. 1 2 3 4 5 6 7 na
7. I think more about how my body feels than how my body looks. 1 2 3 4 5 6 7 na
8. I feel like I must be a bad person when I don't look as good as I could. 1 2 3 4 5 6 7 na
9. I rarely compare how I look with how other people look.
10. I think a person can look pretty much how they want to if they are willing to work at it. 1 2 3 4 5 6 7 na
11. I would be ashamed for people to know what I really weigh. 1 2 3 4 5 6 7 na
12. I really don't think I have much control over how my body looks. 1 2 3 4 5 6 7 na
13. Even when I can't control my weight, I think I'm an okay person. 1 2 3 4 5 6 7 na
14. During the day, I think about how I look many times. 1 2 3 4 5 6 7 na
15. I never worry that something is wrong with me when I am not exercising as much as I should. 1 2 3 4 5 6 7 na
16. I often worry about whether the clothes I am wearing make me look good. 1 2 3 4 5 6 7 na
17. When I'm not exercising enough, I question whether I am a good enough person. 1 2 3 4 5 6 7 na
18. I rarely worry about how I look to other people. 1 2 3 4 5 6 7 na
19. I think a person's weight is mostly determined by the genes they are born with. 1 2 3 4 5 6 7 na
20. I am more concerned with what my body can do than how it looks. 1 2 3 4 5 6 7 na
21. It doesn't matter how hard I try to change my weight, it's probably always going to be about the same. 1 2 3 4 5 6 7 na

22. When I'm not the size I think I should be, I feel ashamed.	1	2	3	4	5	6	7	na
23. I can weigh what I'm supposed to when I try hard enough.	1	2	3	4	5	6	7	na
24. The shape you are in depends mostly on your genes.	1	2	3	4	5	6	7	na

From "Women and Objectified Body Consciousness: A Feminist Psychological Analysis," a dissertation (University of Wisconsin—Plattesville) by N. M. McKinley, 1995. Copyright 1995 by Nita Mary McKinley. All rights reserved. Reprinted with permission.

8

SEXUAL ABUSE AND SEXUAL HARASSMENT

A 45-year-old woman wanted all her moles removed. She had been sexually abused by her brother, and felt a sense of shame which manifested itself in these marks . . . . She also felt the need to punish herself by going through extensive surgery. (Bradbury, 1994, p. 303)

The impact of sexual harassment on girls' and women's developing concept of their body and self has rarely been examined with the goal of expanding our understanding of weight and shape preoccupation. (Larkin, Rice, & Russell, 1996, p. 5)

In Petaluma, California, eighth grader Tawnya Brawdy had to run a gauntlet of boys gathered outside her school who would begin mooing as she approached. "It went on before school, during classes, in between classes and during lunch," says Tawnya, adding that her teacher told her she'd just have to put up with it . . . . Brawdy sued her district over "emotional distress" and collected $20,000 in an out-of-court settlement. (Adler & Rosenberg, 1992, p. 77)

There's a message underneath every picture of every model. The picture says "look at me, I don't mind, I'm available to you, I'm yours." Which is not the way things really are. Back here on planet earth, women don't like being stared at. (Eric Bogosian, as quoted in Schefer, 1997, p. 91)

In this chapter, we focus on some particularly traumatic and damaging experiences, which may have far-ranging effects on various facets of psychological functioning, including depression, self-esteem, eating disturbances, and body image (Rorty & Yager, 1996). These experiences include sexual abuse and sexual harassment as well as early or precocious sexualization of young girls. In addition, we maintain that *appearance harassment* —receiving inappropriately critical or pejorative comments related to aspects of one's appearance—may fit within this category of sexually related traumatic experiences (e.g., comments directed at the size of the breasts). Increasingly, researchers and clinicians are cataloging the often tragic consequences of abuse and harassment on body image and targeting as problematic a social milieu that allows girls to be sexualized (e.g., exposed to inappropriate sexually related conversations or media, such as pornography) or harassed about their appearance.

Much of this work, to date, focuses on the blatant disregard for the physical rights of others (i.e., physical sexual abuse) and sexual harassment. The effect of these traumatic experiences on eating disorders and body image is an ongoing and controversial area of investigation. In addition, some recent work in the area of covert sexual abuse has expanded the notion of abuse to include experiences that are similar in nature to early sexualization and appearance harassment events. We examine the emerging research background for these issues, along with assessment and treatment indications, in this chapter.

RESEARCH BACKGROUND

Methodological Debate

The area of sexual abuse and eating disorders is deemed one of the most important and contentious research venues in the entire field of eating and shape-related disorders (Pope & Hudson, 1995; Rice, 1996; see also chapter 7); thus, this seems like a good place to begin our discussion. The range of interpretations of the extant data has generated a good deal of heat and accusations. For instance, Rice (1996) has suggested the existence of sex bias in the conclusions of empirical studies in this area, stating that male investigators, as opposed to female experimenters, more often affirm that there is a minimal relationship between a history of sexual abuse and the development of eating disorders. At least part of this disagreement between parties may be related to different philosophies of research; as reviewed by Gilbert and Thompson (1996), feminist researchers may focus more on the individual experience and qualitative data than a simple quantitative statistical analysis of data (see also chapter 7). As noted by Rice (1996),

> the logic used by researchers to draw their conclusions decontextualized and objectified the women's experiences, treating the subjects as though simple cause/effect relationships governed their behavior and as if the introduction of one stimulus always led to the same response. (p. 204)

Authors of a feminist orientation have argued that their theoretical framework is necessary to understand the nature of victims' experiences and the connection between these experiences and subsequent psychological distress, including appearance-related shame and disparagement. Alternatively, Pope and Hudson (1995) took a fairly narrow, methodological tack and found the available studies lacking in sufficient empirical rigor to the point that "we cannot reasonably conclude whether childhood sexual abuse is, or is not, an etiologic factor in adult psychiatric disorders" (p. 363). Perhaps the most recent and neutral review was conducted by P. Fallon and Wonderlich (1997); their call for more "prospective longitudinal studies of children who have been abused" (p. 399) will hopefully be answered by researchers of different theoretical approaches.

The foregoing brief review illustrates how one must take great care with any analysis and the resulting conclusions that are drawn from research on sexual abuse. Keeping in mind that the data are inconclusive and that the "ideal" study—as described by Pope and Hudson (1995)—has yet to be conducted, we offer the following presentation of recent research findings on sexual abuse and body image, followed by a discussion of sexual harassment and sexualization.

Research Findings

As with the research on eating disorders, the findings on the role of sexual abuse and body image are conflictual. D. M. Moyer, DiPietro, Berkowitz, and Stunkard (1997) evaluated girls between 14 and 18 years of age who had been abused and compared them with a control group. The abused girls were less satisfied with their weight than the controls and had poorer self-esteem, higher depression, and more binge eating. It is interesting to note that after adjusting for all variables with the use of multiple linear regression, they found that childhood sexual abuse was not independently related to binge eating—the strongest relationships were for weight satisfaction, body mass index, and depression.

Tobin and Griffing (1996) evaluated 103 adult patients with eating disorders, finding that 41% reported a history of abuse. However, abused versus nonabused patients did not differ on body dissatisfaction. Unfortunately, a non-eating-disorders control group was not included in the study. In another study in which a nonabused sample was included, differences between abused and nonabused groups on weight dissatisfaction were also not evident (Zlotnick et al., 1996). To further complicate the picture, Waller, Hamilton, Rose, and Sumra (1993) found that women with recent abuse overestimated body size more so than did nonabused controls or women with early abuse.

An interesting and recurrent methodological issue in this research, which may account for some of the discrepancy of findings across investigations, is the extreme variability of what researchers define as *sexual abuse*. This can be illustrated by an analysis of the definition used in the studies just reviewed. For instance, Zlotnick et al. (1996) used a "questionnaire with behaviorally-defined items describing sexual abuse" (p. 130), and the specific nature of the behaviors ranged "from fondling of breasts to vaginal and/or anal penetration" (p. 130). Tobin and Griffing (1996) used a somewhat broader definition: "Sexual abuse was defined to include unwanted, physical contact and included such experiences as fondling and intercourse" (p. 145). Perhaps an even broader definition was used by D. M. Moyer et al. (1997); in their study, sexual abuse was defined as "any unwanted sexual activity (either noncontact or contact) regardless of the age differential between the perpetrator and the victim" (p. 24).

This issue of the variability of researchers' definition of sexual abuse not only plays a role in the interpretation of findings across studies but also reflects an unresolved diagnostic controversy in this area of investigation. Specifically, some researchers have argued that a quite restrictive definition should be consistently used by researchers (Hastings & Kern, 1994; Pope & Hudson, 1992), along the lines of that used by Rorty, Yager, and Rossotto (1994): "Subject manually stimulated perpetrator's genitals, subject orally stimulated perpetrator's genitals, perpetrator stimulated subject's genitals, perpetrator inserted object into subject's vagina or rectum, and perpetrator inserted penis into subject's vagina or rectum" (pp. 321–322). However, less invasive behaviors have also been found to be detrimental, and a continuum model may be one way of reconceptualizing the issue of sexual abuse.

The Continuum of Undesired Sexual Experiences

Obviously, the extremely abusive behaviors noted above should form the cornerstone of any investigation of sexual abuse; however, other events, often of a noncontact nature, may be important to assess. For instance, in one study, 27% of the participants reported unwanted sexual experiences that were not contained in the definition of sexual abuse used in that particular investigation (Palmer, Oppenheimer, Dignon, Chaloner, & Howells, 1990). Some of these undesired experiences may appear to be closer to the traditional notion of sexual harassment (or, as noted earlier, appearance harassment) or inappropriate sexualization (if conducted with an underage individual). For instance, Simpson and Ramberg (1992) described a woman who had developed an extreme aversion to sexual matters and had developed anorexia nervosa, possibly related to her experience of being called a "whore" by peers. As noted above, D. M. Moyer et al. (1997) included in their definition "any unwanted sexual activity (either noncontact or contact)" (p. 24). Examples of these experiences are being the target of sexually related teasing, being exposed to sexually related materials against one's will, being forced to undress while others watch, and receiving sexually laced comments or demeaning verbalizations about one's body. The experience of Tawnya Brawdy, which led this chapter, might fit the criteria of appearance or sexual harassment (evidently, the boys' "mooing" was related to the size of her breasts).

In fact, if some of these behaviors were perpetrated on individuals in the workplace, they might create a "hostile environment" and, thus, be illegal. Feinberg (1996) reviewed several examples of sexual behavior that could conceivably meet the definition of creating a hostile environment, including

> leering or unwelcome staring at physical attributes . . . repeated comments about a person's physical attributes . . . repeated sexually derogatory remarks insulting to a person's sex . . . dirty jokes told directly to an individual or told in the individual's general vicinity . . . making unnecessary physical contact . . . boasting of one's own physical attributes . . . subtle requests or obvious requests for sexual favors. (p. 78)

Weiner and Thompson (1997) conceptualized the broad range of abusive and harassing behaviors as fitting into the covert and overt dimensions and developed a scale to measure both of these concepts, the Covert and Overt Sexual Abuse Questionnaire. (This scale is contained in Appendix 8A and is discussed in more detail in the next section on assessment.) In this model, the traditional notion of physical sexual abuse is labeled *overt* and includes such invasive behaviors as forced intercourse, fondling, and similar traumatic experiences. The overt category forms one end of the continuum, whereas *covert* sexual abuse, including events such as undesired sexually related comments or unwanted exposure to sexually related material, fits at the other end of the spectrum.

Weiner and Thompson (1997) found significant correlations between both overt and covert indices of abuse and measures of body image, eating disturbance, depression, and self-esteem. They were also interested in determining, using regression analyses, if covert abuse added any predictive value beyond that explained by overt abuse. Using a conservative procedure, they first entered levels of social desirability, self-esteem, depression, and overt abuse in a regression designed to explain the variance associated with measures of body image and eating disturbance; on the last step, they entered the covert variable. For three of the six regressions, covert abuse still accounted for significant variance, beyond that of the other variables, on measures of body image anxiety, restrictive eating behaviors, and bulimic symptoms.

Research Background: Summary

Although not as extreme as the tragic physical violations that compose a historical definition of sexual abuse, covert abuse may yet be importantly related to the onset and development of body image problems. A goal of future researchers will be to articulate and measure a "continuum of sexual trauma" (Weiner & Thompson, 1997) and its association with body image and other psychological variables, such as self-esteem and depression. Also, it will be useful to explore whether certain types of specific events, contained within the broad overt and covert categories have a disproportionate role in producing psychological distress and body image disturbance. In addition to the emerging research that supports the further examination of covert abuse, the reports of persons who have been traumatized by these experiences support the importance of such future inquiry (see Exhibit 8.1).

THEORETICAL EXPLANATIONS

A number of hypotheses offer an explanation regarding the possible mechanisms whereby the experience of sexual abuse may lead to eating and shape-related clinical problems. A few of these specifically focus on body image issues; however, most of them do not differentiate between eating- and appearance-related sequelae of abuse. In addition, as might be expected, several of these explanations have a feminist orientation.

Finkelhor (1984) suggested that the abuse might lead to a negative reaction to issues of sexuality and femininity. Root and Fallon (1988) believe that these negative reactions may lead to eating-disturbed behaviors,

EXHIBIT 8.1
An Example of Appearance Harassment

The following excerpt is from One Spring, a poem illustrating a particularly brutal example of appearance harassment, from Leslea Newman's (1986) book, *Good Enough to Eat*:

> When the blue car slowed alongside me
> I took no notice
> until two faces leaned out the open window
> "Nice tits ya got there, Honey."
> "Hey, Sweetheart, shine those headlights over here."
> "Want to go for a ride?"
> I stopped,
> dazed as a fish thrust out of water
> into sunlight so bright it burns my eyes,
> I turn and walk away fast
> head down, arms folded,
> feet slapping the ground,
> "Nice ass, too," they call
> and then I hear laughter
> the screech of tires
> silence. . . .

From *Good Enough to Eat* (p. 9), by L. Newman, 1986, New York: Firebrand Books. Copyright 1986 by Firebrand Books. Reprinted with permission.

in an attempt at changing body shape, perhaps as a means of establishing control over powerlessness.

Pitts and Waller (1993; Waller, 1993) suggested that the self-critical nature of individuals with abuse is the dominant cognitive component connected with dysfunctional personality features and self-destructive behaviors. Tobin and Griffing (1996) found that the use of self-criticism was higher in abused than nonabused patients with eating disorders; however, these researchers did not assess the relationship between self-criticism and body image disturbance.

Fitting the views of Nathanson (1989) and Andrews (1995) into a working hypothesis, Rorty and Yager (1996) suggested that bodily shame along with a sense of worthlessness and self-loathing connect the experience of abuse with the development of eating and weight-related disorders. Although still not supported by empirical data, such shame may lead to "body image disturbance, in turn promoting attempts to change body size via dieting" (Rorty & Yager, 1996, p. 779).

It is virtually impossible to separate the theoretical explanations for the role of sexual abuse, harassment, and sexualization in the development of body image disturbance from a feminist view of such mechanisms. Striegel-Moore, Kearney-Cooke, and Wooley are three individuals who have offered a great deal of information regarding possible mechanisms of body image disturbance and possible treatment interventions (Kearney-Cooke & Striegel-Moore, 1997; Striegel-Moore, 1993, 1995; S. C. Wooley, 1995). Striegel-Moore (1995) suggested that there are two aspects of femininity that are critical in the development of body image and eating problems: Women's relational orientation makes them especially susceptible to the views and opinions of others, and femininity and beauty are closely linked attributes. Kearney-Cooke and Striegel-Moore emphasized the tandem issues of internalization and projection as key mediators in the development of body image. *Projection* refers to a process whereby such factors as "overwhelming internal states and/or interpersonal struggles" (Kearney-Cooke & Striegel-Moore, 1997, p. 297) are "projected" onto the body, leading the individual to attempt bodily changes, such as appearance modifications, as a means of changing his or her life—a process known as the "myth of transformation" (p. 297). Internalization is the process of incorporating into one's own body image the outcomes of external events, such as sexual abuse, that are traumatizing to the body. Kearney-Cooke and Striegel-Moore (1997) cited the following case of a 28-year-old woman with bulimia nervosa to exemplify their concept of internalization:

> She also described an image of her body as repulsive and dirty, which she attributed to a long-term incestuous relationship with an older brother, who told her that her genital area smelled bad. To overcome the shame, she developed elaborate rituals to keep her body and

clothes clean. Hers was a family in which joy was derived primarily from achievement (including the achievement of "looking good"), rather than from the security and warmth of human connections. This led to an obsession with her shape and weight, to the point that almost all feedback was filtered through the lens of the body. The attainment of the perfect body was a way to gain prestige and admiration within her family. (pp. 296–297)

Work on the theoretical nature of how various sexually related, undesired or unwanted experiences lead to body image problems is just beginning. Factors, such as self-criticism, control, shame, internalization, and projection, offer intriguing avenues for future empirical work. It is important to note that along with the continuum model presented in the previous section, some of these concepts have also been used to enlighten assessment and treatment strategies.

ASSESSMENT

Assessment of sexually related trauma is one of the most difficult tasks of the clinician or researcher. We mentioned the questionnaire developed by Weiner and Thompson (1997)—the Covert and Overt Sexual Abuse Questionnaire—and this is one method of assessing the range of abusive experiences as well as some aspects of sexualization, given that some items tap into these experiences (see Appendix 8A). Perhaps one of the most exhaustive and contemporary reviews of this issue was offered by P. Fallon and Wonderlich (1997), with relevance to eating disorders. Again, given the almost impossible task of separating body image from eating-related problems in the context of unwanted sexual experiences, we offer their guidelines for assessment and treatment of the traumatic sexual experiences of the eating-disordered patient.

In addition to questionnaire measures, P. Fallon and Wonderlich (1997) suggested that the interview contain a few questions that are general in nature, such as "paint a picture of your family in words—the ways people communicate with each other; the ways they express feelings, especially anger; and the closeness and/or distance between members" (p. 401). Specific questions regarding abuse are offered by P. Fallon and Wonderlich (1997):

> When you were a child, did anyone ever touch your breasts or genitals, or ask you to touch them in ways that made you feel uncomfortable, "dirty," or scared? Have you ever been threatened or physically forced into sex as a child or an adult? When you were a child or teenager, did your teachers or other adults ever question you about bruises you received from an adult? Have you ever dressed in such a way to hide bruises? (p. 401)

If the patient notes that abuse has occurred, other questions to follow up on this disclosure might include those noted in Exhibit 8.2. Although these and, of course, other interview questions are necessary for understanding the trauma and its aftermath, the last two questions in Exhibit 8.2—modified for our concern of body image—are especially important. Indexing the individual's affective reaction—particularly the bodily shame as a result of the violation and their own interpretation of any connection between the experience and subsequent body image problems—is critically important to not only the case conceptualization (and, thus, making sense of the symptoms for the client) but also treatment planning. For instance, the body image sequelae of the trauma experience may help explain certain dysfunctional behaviors. P. Fallon and Wonderlich (1997) considered certain "strategies" or "functions of the eating disorder" (p. 402) as ways to cope with the trauma, by distracting oneself from its residual guilt, anxiety, or depression.

For example in the case described above, as an illustration of internalization, the woman became obsessed with her body as a means of dealing with the shame associated with her brother's physical (and verbal) abuse of her body. Eating-disordered behaviors that run the gamut from starvation to binge eating (the latter possibly leading to obesity) may be related to the protective function of preventing one from further sexual abuse by making one "undesirable." Although it sounds like a cliché, we have seen many patients in therapy who, quite matter of factly, have stated that their excessive weight served the function of removing the possibility of sexual advances. (In a society of massive stigmatization of overweight individuals,

EXHIBIT 8.2
Interview Questions for the Client Who Discloses Sexual Abuse

1. What specifically happened?
2. Who did it? What was this person's relationship to you?
3. How did it begin?
4. What degree of force was used?
5. Were you or someone else threatened if you disclosed any information about it?
6. How long did it go on?
7. Did you tell anyone? If so, what happened?
8. How old were you?
9. Who else have you told?
10. How did it end?
11. Did it happen to anyone else?
12. Why do you think it happened?
13. What did you feel?
14. Do you feel that there is any connection to either the onset of your eating disorder or its current maintenance?

From "Sexual Abuse and Other Forms of Trauma" (p. 402), by P. Fallon and S. A. Wonderlich, in D. M Garner and P. E. Garfinkel (Eds.), *Handbook of Treatment for Eating Disorders* (2nd ed.), 1997, New York: Guilford. Copyright 1997 by Guilford. Reprinted with permission.

this might be one of the only positive aspects of this discrimination.) Clearly, the realization, on the part of client and patient, of links between the sexual abuse and resultant eating and body image disturbances may not be immediate but may emerge after several therapy sessions.

TREATMENT

Shame engendered by harassment and other incidents of oppression causes young women to disconnect, hide their bodies, and make themselves invisible. Shame reinforces the splitting of bodies from minds, while it compels young women to engage in relentless body criticism and improvement in an effort to bolster their shattered self-esteem. (Larkin et al., 1996, p. 19)

General feminist approaches to the treatment of body image disturbance were outlined in chapter 2 and were more fully developed in chapter 7. Some of these strategies have particular relevance for individuals who have been sexually abused. P. Fallon and Wonderlich (1997) suggested that the guided imagery procedures we discussed earlier (see also Kearney-Cooke & Striegel-Moore, 1997) may also be useful for the trauma victim, with the images from "early sexual experiences, the family house, the transition to puberty, and recent sexual experiences . . . employed to evoke connections between the abuse and the survivor's present feelings and eating patterns" (p. 404). Other experiential techniques, such as sculpting, drawings, evaluating old family photographs, and recounting experiences to other individuals, may also increase an understanding of how body image is shaped by abuse encounters.

Often memories of the abuse may inhibit the individual's adaptive functioning; therefore, specific strategies, labeled *adaptive containment* procedures, are indicated to deal with this posttraumatic aspect of the abuse (P. Fallon & Wonderlich, 1997). These strategies include thought-stopping techniques, relaxation exercises, distraction, increasing social support systems, and constructing a safety plan for use in high-risk situations, such as an encounter with a family member associated with previous abuse. Group and family therapies may also help in the management of bodily shame and related symptoms of body image disturbance.

Larkin et al. (1996) focused their treatment program on young girls and women who were sexually harassed. They used focus groups that encouraged participants to describe their abusive experiences. Their goals included helping the young girls and women make the connection between the harassment and their body image and move their "shame . . . to anger and self-loathing to greater acceptance" (Larkin et al., 1996, p. 21). Their approach suggests self-consciousness-raising, with the goal of giving participants tools to empower themselves. Such tools include alternative images of women that emphasize nonconformity to prevailing ideals, the sharing of stories of resistance and empowerment, a focus on the need to feel proud of one's body and self, encouragement of the importance of connections among women, and a strong investment in one's acceptance of one's body and self.

CONCLUSIONS

In this chapter, we explored the pernicious role of sexual abuse, harassment, and sexualization in body image. Although researchers still debate the specific influence of childhood abuse on the development of eating disorders, there is no doubt that these types of experiences occur and have ramifications for how an individual views his or her body. We are just beginning to focus on the full range of abusive experiences; a continuum model, with its inclusion of covert forms of abuse, may illuminate the effect of sexual harassment, appearance harassment, and inappropriate sexualization on the developing body image. Unfortunately, as noted by Kearney-Cooke and Striegel-Moore (1997), there has been little empirical evaluation of the strategies used for treating body image problems resulting from various types of sexually abusive experiences; this will be a key challenge for future research in this area.

APPENDIX 8A
COVERT AND OVERT SEXUAL ABUSE QUESTIONNAIRE

For items 1–12, please think about your life before you were 16 years old. For items 13–25, consider your entire lifetime. This survey is completely anonymous. Do not put your name anywhere on these pages. Please refer to the following scale when answering questions:

Never	Rarely	Sometimes	Often	Always
1	2	3	4	5

How often did this happen to you?

1. Did anyone make teasing comments about your developing body?   1 2 3 4 5
2. Did anyone stare at your body in a sexual manner?   1 2 3 4 5
3. Did anyone ever tell you sexually explicit or dirty jokes or stories, particularly when you were the object of the joke?   1 2 3 4 5
4. Did anyone talk to you about their sexual frustrations, problems, or activities?   1 2 3 4 5
5. Did anyone seem overly jealous or ask too many questions about boyfriends or what you did on dates?   1 2 3 4 5
6. Did anyone show you pornographic material (magazines, books, pictures, movies, etc.)?   1 2 3 4 5
7. Did anyone suggest that you wear sexually revealing clothing?   1 2 3 4 5
8. Did anyone visually "inspect" your body?   1 2 3 4 5
9. Did anyone "undress you with their eyes"?   1 2 3 4 5
10. Did anyone ask you out on dates just because of your looks or body development?   1 2 3 4 5
11. Did anyone make you look at your nude body or genitals in a mirror?   1 2 3 4 5
12. Did anyone comment about how sexy you looked?   1 2 3 4 5
13. Has anyone ever forced you to undress and stand nude in front of them?   1 2 3 4 5
14. Has anyone ever forced you to undress and stand nude in front of others?   1 2 3 4 5
15. Have you ever been upset by someone exposing his or her genitals?   1 2 3 4 5
16. Has anyone ever tried or succeeded in having any kind of sexual intercourse with you against your wishes?   1 2 3 4 5
17. Has anyone ever tried or succeeded in getting you to touch his or her genitals against your wishes (besides anyone already included)?   1 2 3 4 5
18. Has anyone ever forced you to perform oral sex on him or her against your wishes?   1 2 3 4 5
19. Has anyone ever performed oral sex on you against your wishes?   1 2 3 4 5
20. Have you ever been the victim of a rape or attempted rate?   1 2 3 4 5

21. Some people have experienced unwanted sexual advances by someone who had authority over them, such as a doctor, teacher, employer, minister/priest, therapist, policeman, or much older person. Did you ever have any kind of unwanted sexual experience with someone who had authority over you, at any time in your life?   1   2   3   4   5

22. In general, have you narrowly missed being sexually assaulted by someone at any time in your life (other than what you have already included)?   1   2   3   4   5

23. Have you ever been in a situation where there was violence or threat of violence, where you were also afraid of being sexually assaulted (other than what was already included)?   1   2   3   4   5

24. Has anyone ever threatened harm to yourself or someone else if you ever told about a sexual advance or sexual activity that had taken place?   1   2   3   4   5

25. Has anyone ever told you that no one would believe you or love you if you told about a sexual advance or sexual activity that had taken place?   1   2   3   4   5

From "Overt and Covert Sexual Abuse: Relationship to Body Image and Eating Disturbance," By K. E. Weiner and J. K. Thompson, 1997, *International Journal of Eating Disorders, 22*, pp. 281–283. Copyright 1997 by John Wiley & Sons, Inc. Reprinted by permission of John Wiley & Sons, Inc.

V

BEHAVIORAL, COGNITIVE, AND INTEGRATIVE APPROACHES

9

BEHAVIORAL ASPECTS OF DISTURBANCE: CONDITIONING, CONTEXT, AND AVOIDANCE

Even though I live on the coast, I haven't been to the beach in three years. The last time I went, people stared at me the whole day. But that wasn't the worst—my daughter was so embarrassed about my weight that she didn't want to be seen around me. When I tried to build sand castles with her, she told me to go away. (a 40-year-old overweight client)

Behavioral theory has been used to explain the onset and maintenance of a variety of different clinical problems. From a behavioral viewpoint, the situational factor is paramount in understanding body image disturbance. The term *context* is frequently used to define the importance of the specific environment or situation and its effect on body image. Although there are traitlike properties to body image (i.e., a "general" dispositional level of satisfaction), there are also situational or contextual aspects, meaning that one's overall level of satisfaction is affected by the specific environment one is thrust into or the people that one encounters on a daily basis. Thus, one's disturbance at any point may be the net effect of one's baseline level of dispositional trait dissatisfaction and the context within which one finds oneself.

A behavioral model, as might be expected, also focuses on the precipitating event or trauma that may have been crucial to the onset of the disorder. In this book, we have mentioned many such critical events, from sexual abuse to verbal teasing, and these instances fit well into a behavioral *classical conditioning* explanation. Consider the following account:

I started worrying about my skin when one of my friends in high school called me "pizza face". . . . I know he was only kidding, but it stuck in

251

my mind. I started feeling very self-conscious about my skin. (a male adult, as quoted in Phillips, 1996, p. 39)[1]

The onset of this person's symptoms was traced to an aversive life experience. We explore this issue of critical situations associated with body image disturbance throughout this chapter. In addition, behavioral avoidance is also a common feature of body image disturbance, consisting of a refusal to enter into situations or seek environments that might accent the appraisal of one's body by others. This symptom may reach an extreme, almost agoraphobic-like level—such avoidance may characterize the behavior of individuals with extreme body disparagement or body dysmorphic disorder. The following description is by a woman in her mid-30s, as described by Phillips (1996):

> My sister and grandmother started buying my clothes and food. I started spending my entire day in my parents' house. Sometimes I watch television, but mostly I walk back and forth between the bedrooms on the third floor, thinking about how ugly I look. When relatives come over, I stay upstairs and don't see them. I don't even see them on holidays like Thanksgiving. I feel overwhelmed and hopeless and out of control. Sometimes I panic and think "I can't tolerate this. I'm going to die. I have to kill myself. I wish I could be put to sleep." (p. 41)[2]

These avoidant characteristics fit into an *operant conditioning* model. Together, the classical conditioning explanation of critical life events and the operant conceptualization of behavioral avoidance are the two components that form the cornerstone of a behavioral etiological–maintenance model. This model has a rich history in behavioral psychology and was originally presented as the two-factor theory by Mowrer (1960). Recent theoretical work and research on this model as a method of understanding clinical anxiety-related disorders maintains its stature as a dominant model for behavioral psychology (e.g., McAllister & McAllister, 1995) and, thus, provides the grounding for our own conceptualization of body image disturbance.

This approach was outlined in a classic article by Giles in 1988. He described a 28-year-old woman, under treatment for bulimia nervosa, whose body image problems seemed rooted in a specific traumatic conditioning experience in the sixth grade:

> I overheard two of the boys talking about me. They said they would like me if I wasn't so fat. They made fun of my thighs. The other kids started making fun of me, too. "Pat, Pat, your belly's fat," they would

---

[1]From *The Broken Mirror: Understanding and Treating Body Dysmorphic Disorder* (p. 39), by Katherine A. Phillips, New York: Oxford University Press. Copyright © 1996 by Katherine A. Phillips, MD. Used by permission of Oxford University Press.
[2]*Ibid*, p. 41.

say. I would go home in tears. I begged my mother not to make me go to school. After that year, I couldn't talk to any boys my age. I became extremely shy. I went all through high school and most of college with extreme fear of other people, especially men. (Giles, 1988, p. 145)

Giles's (1988) explanation to this young woman of the development and maintenance of her body image problems succinctly captures the essence of the two component behavioral model—traumatic conditioning event and subsequent avoidance:

> Human beings are quite adept at learning fear. They can learn fear by receiving frightening information about something or by suffering trauma. For example, many people become afraid to drive after having an accident. And I believe that you learned to be afraid of your body from those experiences in the sixth grade. You have learned to be anxious about being criticized or rejected. It is a phobia, really, a phobia about weight gain that has its basis in social disapproval. . . . Once a phobia has been learned, it tends to remain indefinitely until an effective treatment for it is implemented. In the meantime, the fear is avoided. The driving phobic refuses to drive. The height phobic refuses to go to the top of tall buildings. The snake phobic moves off the farm. And the weight phobic diets. (p. 145)

Giles (1988) went on to describe how a program consisting of systematic desensitization and assertiveness training was successful at reducing his patient's conditioned fear of observing herself in the mirror and hearing critical comments about her body. This procedure, as noted in chapter 2, has become one of the main ingredients of the cognitive–behavioral program developed by Cash (1995b, 1996, 1997) and J. C. Rosen (1996a, 1996b, 1997) and is further discussed later in this chapter.

With this introduction to a behavioral–contextual conceptualization, we now turn to an examination of recent research in this area. First, some rather descriptive information is discussed linking certain "critical" events to the onset of body image disturbance. From the behavioral–contextual model, these experiences are seen as traumatic conditioning events, along the lines of a classical conditioning paradigm discussed above. We then examine how avoidance, as a natural consequence of these experiences, develops in many individuals, perpetuating the problem of anxiety associated with aspects of physical appearance. Next, recent research supporting the importance of the context or situation as a factor in disturbance is addressed, followed by our usual review of assessment methods and treatment strategies.

RESEARCH BACKGROUND

In a sense, many of the chapters in this book have detailed negative body-image related experiences within the framework of other models of disturbance. For instance, negative feedback regarding appearance (chapter 5) and sexual harassment and abuse (chapter 8) are quite traumatic experiences that have been empirically linked to the onset and development of body image problems. These and other circumstances that have as their sequelae a negative body image have as their common ingredient an anxiety that is paired with an aversive life event. Descriptions of such events have been presented throughout this book, and these anecdotes along with those just presented in the previous section form a useful framework for the model discussed in this chapter.

Perhaps no one has put as much energy into cataloging these sorts of critical events as has J. C. Rosen and colleagues. He and his students have annotated literally hundreds of such episodes, as recalled by his students and patients (J. C. Rosen, Orosan-Weine, & Tang, 1997). They have also ordered them into 19 specific categories, such as (a) physical activity (experiencing an embarrassing moment related to weight during some sports or physical activity), (b) clothing (not fitting into good-looking clothes), and (c) architectural barriers (e.g., not fitting into airplane or movie seats). J. C. Rosen et al. found that a larger number of critical experiences were predictive of symptoms of body image disturbance, as assessed with Rosen's Body Dysmorphic Disorder Examination (see chapter 2). Exhibit 9.1 contains a complete listing of the 19 critical event categories, along with examples for each experience.

As noted earlier, the behavioral–contextual model emphasizes a situational analysis of body image, which is quite different from a traditional trait formulation (Altabe & Thompson, 1995). The great majority of researchers in this field have used questionnaire measures that assess a more stable, dispositional notion of body image disturbance. J. K. Thompson, Penner, and Altabe (1990) found that only 1 out of 40 body image assessment methods included an option for the assessment of a "state" component of disturbance. Recently, however, researchers have shown that one's self-image may be quite malleable and subject to modification, given even slight changes in factors such as the specific instructions given to participants for rating self-image, food intake, and environmental variables.

For instance, in a series of studies, Thompson and colleagues found that body size estimates (the perceptual aspect of disturbance) and subjective ratings of current size (using figure rating scales) tended to be larger if affective instructions (how you feel) were used instead of cognitively based instructions (how you think you look; J. K. Thompson, 1991, 1992; J. K. Thompson & Dolce, 1989; see also chapter 2). Food intake also has an immediate effect on judgments of body image. McKenzie, Williamson, and Cubic (1993) found that participants with bulimia, but not controls, selected a larger current body size (from a series of silhouettes) after consuming a candy bar and soft drink. J. K. Thompson, Coovert, Pasman, and Robb (1993), in a series of three studies, manipulated the "perceived ca-

EXHIBIT 9.1
Critical Experiences in the Development of Body Image

Category	Example
Self-esteem	Think I'm good at things
	Accept myself for who I am
	Have supportive relationships with other people
Social comparison	Comparing how other people look in a bathing suit to how I look
	Have friends who are better looking than me
	Being around others who were accepting of their appearances
Media	Reading fitness magazines
	Reading magazines about beauty and fashion
	Seeing fat people treated negatively in the media
Family values and attitudes	Message from parents to accept the way you are
	Parents not able to discuss sex
	Negative attitudes by parents toward overweight persons
	Parent with a negative attitude toward his or her own appearance
Peer of familial competition	Pressure to look a certain way
	Competition among peers to look more attractive than one another
Eating disorder	Knew someone who had an eating disorder
	Had problems overeating or being out of control with food
Puberty	Developing physically earlier than my peers
	Getting attention from others when started developing breasts
	Experienced a big change in height or weight during puberty
Sexual attention	People whistling or honking at me
	Walking to a bar or party and people checking me out
Physical activity	Played team sports as child or teenager
	Exercise regularly
	Experienced an embarrassing moment in sports or physical activity due to my weight
Acceptance/rejection	Asked out on dates
	Rejected because of my appearance
	Seeing someone succeed because of his or her looks
Weight and body size	Fat when younger
	Skinny when younger
	Lost a lot of weight once or more often
Clothing	Not fitting into good looking clothing
	Wore hand-me-downs as a child
	Had fashionable, nice clothes growing up
Verbal feedback about my appearance	Positive comments about my appearance or weight
	Advice from others on my appearance or weight

Exhibit continues

EXHIBIT 9.1 *(Continued)*

Category	Example
Parent's physical appear-ance	Family members overweight
	Parent's weight or body shape changing a great deal with age
	Seeing parents not fitting in clothes
Dieting	Tried to gain weight
	Always on and off diets
Teasing	Called nicknames about my appearance
	Teased about my clothes
	Teased in school about my appearance
Physical conditions	Experienced accident that changed physical appearance
	Had a major operation
	Stretch marks from pregnancy
Abuse/assault	Sexually abused as a child
	Physically abused as a child
	Raped
Architectural barriers	Not fitting into seats in a theater, restaurant, airplane, bus, or car

From "Critical Experiences in the Development of Body Image," by J. C. Rosen, P. Orosan-Weine, and T. Tang, 1997, *Eating Disorders: The Journal of Treatment and Prevention, 5,* pp. 196–198. Copyright 1997 by Taylor & Francis. Reprinted with permission.

loric content" of meals by telling participants that a milkshake was either high or low in calories. In actuality, the milkshakes were identical; however, participants who thought they had consumed the high-calorie foodstuff increased their levels of size overestimation when compared with the low-calorie group.

Randomized experimental studies that force a social comparison with the appearance of others also demonstrate the fluid nature of body image. For instance, simply giving female college students incorrect information about the "normativeness" of their size may lead to changes in their self-report. Heinberg and Thompson (1992a) told half of a sample that they were thinner than average and half that they were larger—in actuality they were all within the range of normal, yet the "larger" group evidenced immediate increases in dissatisfaction. Studies of this type using stimuli for comparison such as print or TV ads with attractive models consistently support the notion that one's self-image is due to change with minimal notice. (See chapters 3 and 4 for a fuller discussion of the sociocultural and social comparison literatures.)

Even having participants imagine themselves in different situations produces changes in ratings of body image. Reed, Thompson, Brannick, and Sacco (1991), using the State scale of the Physical Appearance State and Trait Anxiety Scale, found progressively increased anxiety when one imaged oneself alone at home, walking across a college campus, and walking on a beach in a swimsuit. Haimovitz, Lansky, and O'Reilly (1993) replicated these findings using a measure of body satisfaction and situations varying from a beach scenario to "trying on bathing suits in the dressing room of a department store" (p. 77).

Cash (1994a) feels that the contextual events might interact with a preexisting dispositional trait to produce negative emotional states regarding appearance. For instance, if one encounters a situation, such as appearing in a swimsuit at the beach, this might prime a body image *schema* if one has high levels of dispositional investment in appearance. This priming may lead to anxiety or dysphoria regarding one's self-image, which may, in turn, produce "adjustive, emotion-regulating actions" (Cash, 1994b, p. 133), such as dieting, or even an immediate withdrawal from the situation (e.g., the beach) to reduce the negative emotion. More information on this schematic model is contained in chapter 10, and this issue is revisited in chapter 11 on integrative models. For now, it is important to note that state body image disturbance is certainly a function of the particular context in which one finds oneself, but it also may be due to the added component of a dispositional tendency, that is, an easily primed body image schema.

ASSESSMENT

There are several methods of obtaining information related to critical events, contextual factors, and actual behavioral avoidance of body-related activities and situations. As we noted earlier, the existence of a wide range of possible critical events indicates that this component of the assessment must necessarily be idiographic, with the goal of arriving at the discrete experience of the individual client. An open-ended, hypothesis-testing interview, as is often done in the initial stages of assessment, is one method. Augmenting this procedure with J. C. Rosen et al.'s (1997) survey of body image experiences may optimize the possibility of ascertaining any and all relevant experiences. This somewhat structured interview asks clients to identify "what specific things such as events, time periods, places, people or things about a person have an impact, positive or negative, on how people think and feel about their body or physical appearance" (Rosen et al., 1997, p. 194).

Self-monitoring of contextual factors by the client is also a good way to corroborate interview information. J. C. Rosen and Cash (1995) offered the Body Image Diary as one means for collecting this type of self-recorded data (see Appendix 9A). This particular scale allows for the assessment of activators of disturbance, associated beliefs (see also chapter 10), and the consequences of the experience, along with ratings for the intensity of the episode and its duration.

Table 9.1 contains information on several questionnaire measures that

TABLE 9.1
Behavioral Measures

Instrument	Author(s)	Description	Reliability 1, 2	Standardization sample	Address of author
Body Image Avoidance Questionnaire	J. C. Rosen et al. (1991)	Indicate the frequency with which one engages in body image-related avoidance behaviors	IC: .89 TR: 2 weeks, .87	145 female undergraduates	James C. Rosen, PhD Department of Psychology University of Vermont Burlington, VT 05405
Physical Appearance Behavioral Avoidance Test	J. K. Thompson, Heinberg, & Marshall (1994)	Approach own image in a mirror, from a distance of 20 ft; SUDS ratings and approach distance are dependent measures	IC: na TR: none given	Female undergraduates	J. Kevin Thompson, PhD Department of Psychology University of South Florida 4202 Fowler Avenue Tampa, FL 33620-8200
Mirror Focus Procedure	(a) Butters & Cash (1987) (b) Keeton et al. (1990)	Look at oneself in a three-way mirror and then rate one's level of discomfort	(a) IC: na (b) TR: none given	Undergraduates with elevated body dissatisfaction	Thomas F. Cash, PhD Department of Psychology Old Dominion University Norfolk, VA 23529-0267
Feelings of Fatness Questionnaire	Roth & Armstrong (1993)	Rate extent to which one feels "thin–fat" for 61 situations; two scales: Troubles (38 items), Satisfactions (23 items)	IC: Troubles, .96; Satisfaction, .98 TR: none given	132 female undergraduates	David Roth, PhD Sheppard Pratt Hospital 6501 North Charter Street P.O. Box 6815 Baltimore, MD 21285-6815
Situational Inventory of Body Image Dysphoria	Cash (1994b)	Rate how often one experiences negative feelings (never, always, or almost always) for a total of 48 situations	IC: men, .96; women, .96 TR: 1 month; men, .87; women, .86	College student normal controls: 110 men and 177 women	Thomas F. Cash, PhD Department of Psychology Old Dominion University Norfolk, VA 23529-0267

Note. IC = internal consistency; TR = test–retest reliability.

index a state aspect of body image. For instance, the Physical Appearance State and Trait Anxiety Scale's State scale allows for the measurement of body image anxiety for weight and nonweight sites by requiring participants to rate anxiety levels "right now" (Reed et al., 1991). This measure is contained in Appendix 9B. The Situational Inventory of Body-Image Dysphoria (see Appendix 9C) is a scale that asks participants to rate the frequency of negative feelings about 38 different situations, including eating, exercise, and intimacy (Cash, 1994b). It is important to note that this measure has received validation on female and male samples.

The Visual Analogue Scale (see Appendix 9D) has been developed for the measurement of a state component of body satisfaction. With this assessment strategy, persons simply mark a spot on a 100-mm line to indicate their level of satisfaction. The score is computed by measuring the distance from the left end of the continuum. We have found this measure quite sensitive to fluctuations in body satisfaction in experimental studies (Heinberg & Thompson, 1995) and have used it for self-monitoring purposes to track clients' changes in satisfaction over days and across situations outside of the therapy setting.

Measures of behavioral avoidance in conjunction with the Critical Events Interview and state assessments afford a well-rounded evaluation of the contextual factors. Butters and Cash (1987) developed the mirror exposure method, whereby participants rate their level of subjective units of distress while evaluating themselves in front of a mirror. J. K. Thompson, Heinberg, and Marshall (1994) expanded on Butters and Cash's mirror exposure methodology by developing the Physical Appearance Behavioral Avoidance Test, which involves the progressive confrontation of one's image in a mirror, beginning at a distance of 20 ft (6.10 m), and approaching in 2-ft (0.61 m) increments. The subjective units of distress ratings are measured, but the actual measure of avoidance is when an individual refuses to approach the mirror. Winfield and Thompson (1997) modified the procedure, to obtain higher levels of avoidance, by instructing participants that judges behind a one-way mirror were rating each participant's appearance.

The only psychometrically evaluated questionnaire measure of avoidance is the Body Image Avoidance Questionnaire (see Appendix 9E) developed by J. C. Rosen, Srebnik, Saltzberg, and Wendt (1991). This measure is a self-report scale of avoidance and contains the following subscales: Clothing, Social Activities, Eating Restraint, and Grooming/Weighing. It is important to note that J. C. Rosen et al. found that individual ratings of avoidance of these body-image-related activities and situations were significantly correlated with roommates' ratings of the individuals' behaviors. Cash (1997) also recently offered a questionnaire measure that contains an assessment of avoidant "practices," such as a tendency to avoid being photographed or engaging in any activity that will "mess up" one's appearance, such as swimming; avoidance of "places" in which appearance is emphasized, such as clothing stores; avoidance of certain "people," that is, individuals who are attractive; and avoidance of certain "poses," such as smiling if one is concerned about the appearance of one's teeth.

The importance of these measures as an adjunct to other assessment strategies noted throughout this book cannot be overestimated. Trait measures may form the beginning basis for a determination of severity of disturbance and may even be sufficient for diagnosis of body dysmorphic disorder. However, in selecting specific idiosyncratic treatment interventions for the individual client, the measures discussed in this chapter may yield information of even greater relevance. For instance, state measures might be used, in session, during a role-play in which the client is asked to engage in an interaction with the therapist, simulating a seemingly important contextual factor (e.g., an interaction with a partner, a party). An evaluation of the immediate change in body-related satisfaction may verify the client's self-report of the distress, with regard to body image, produced by the event. In addition, state measures are ideal for assessing change, week to week, once treatment interventions have begun.

TREATMENT

Several of the treatments that compose the cognitive–behavioral strategies reviewed in chapter 2 are relevant for the conditioning and contextual factors covered in this chapter. First, without a doubt, the mirror exposure method is an excellent approach for conditioned anxiety associated with certain aspects of appearance. As we have noted throughout this book, there is a wealth of evidence that body image anxiety is elevated in individuals with body image concerns and cognitive–behavioral programs are effective at reducing this anxiety (e.g., E. Fisher & Thompson, 1994). The construction of an individually relevant hierarchy, followed by imaginal exposure and then an in vivo mirror exposure method, is one of the first steps of Cash's (1996, 1997) program and directly targets the anxiety that has become paired, possibly as a consequence of negative body image events, with one's appearance. Specific steps for the mirror exposure method by Cash (1997) are listed in Exhibit 9.2.

A second major component of both Cash's and J. C. Rosen's cognitive–behavioral program that has relevance for this chapter is their strong reliance on techniques designed to counter avoidant behaviors and appearance-related rituals. In vivo exposure techniques are used for the avoidance problem, and response prevention is used to stop repetitive checking behaviors. For instance, J. C. Rosen (1996a) described several strategies used by his patients, including

EXHIBIT 9.2
The Steps of the Mirror Exposure Method

1. Put your mirror in a place like your bathroom or bedroom where you'll have privacy during your sessions. For this method, don't sit in your normal relaxation spot; however, you may want to start out there while you get highly relaxed and then go stand in front of the mirror, at a distance of about 3 (0.91 m) or 4 ft (1.22 m).
2. Begin with the physical attribute listed at the bottom of your ladder. First prepare yourself by standing in front of the mirror with your eyes closed and visualizing this body area in your mind's eye for about 15 s.
3. Then, shift back to your relaxed mental state and let it deepen for a few moments.
4. Next, directly look at this body area in the mirror for about 15 s, then close your eyes and deepen your relaxation for a while.
5. Open your eyes and view this area for a little longer—about 30 s. Again, shut your eyes and continue to relax.
6. Then, look at the body area in the mirror for 1 full minute and relax afterward.
7. After mastering this, move up one rung.
8. Again prepare by mentally visualizing this body area for 15 s, followed by a brief period of relaxing.
9. Open your eyes and view this body area in the mirror for 15 s, then relax.
10. Next, look at it for 30 s before relaxing.
11. Then view it for 1 full minute, followed by relaxation.
12. In this systematic way, move up one rung at a time, successfully climbing your "ladder of distress" until you've reached the top.
13. Use a helpsheet to record your experiences after each session.[1] Always conclude each session with calming imagery and diaphragmatic breathing —never end on a negative note.
14. Don't try to progress too quickly up the ladder. Climb only one or two rungs each time. Take three or four separate sessions to make it all the way to the top. Begin each session on the rung that you successfully reached in the session before.
15. After mastering the mirror exposure method, carry out a final victory session in which you view each area for 1 full minute while actively maintaining a mellow, pleasant state of body and mind.

[1] See Cash (1997) for more information on helpsheets.
From *The Body Image Workbook: An 8-Step Program for Learning to Like Your Looks* (pp. 76–77), by T. F. Cash, 1997, Oakland, CA: New Harbinger. Copyright 1997 by New Harbinger Publications (www.newharbinger.com). Reprinted with permission.

wearing a form-fitting outfit instead of baggy clothes, undressing in front of a spouse, not hiding facial features with hands or combed-down hair, dressing to reveal scars, exercising in public wearing workout clothes, showering at the health club rather than home, drawing attention to appearance with more trendy clothes, accentuating a distressing feature (e.g., eyebrows) with makeup or not wearing makeup at all, standing closer to people, and trying on clothes or makeup in stores and then asking sales clerks for feedback. (p. 162)

Marks and Mishan (1988) also described a series of five patients who benefited from exposure-based techniques. One case involved a woman who believed that her face and lips were too red—she repeatedly avoided foods that might moisten her lips and used pale lipstick. She frequently checked her complexion and the coloring of her lips in a mirror. Her treatment consisted of asking her to enter many different social situations, while requiring her to do things to bring attention to her lips, such as eating juicy fruits or leaving bits of toothpaste on her lips. (Some of these exposure techniques might appear to be somewhat cruel to patients. Such strategies are always based on a clear rationale that emphasizes the notion of extinguishing conditioned fears related to appearance. Clients usually find that even obvious appearance "defects," accentuated by such techniques as leaving toothpaste on lips, go unnoticed by most people.)

Appearance-related rituals and compulsions are attacked by response prevention exercises. Such body inspecting behaviors include repeated viewings in mirrors (often taking an inordinate amount of time), measuring the dimensions of body parts, pinching body fat (e.g., testing the size of one's waist or hips), repeatedly reapplying make-up, compulsively combing then rearranging hairstyles, and so on. Another type of checking behavior involves asking for reassurances repeatedly from other individuals. For instance, a person might ask his or her spouse multiple times "how does this look," to the point of producing frustration in the partner and possible conflict in the relationship. One other type of checking was covered in chapter 4 on social comparison and is the tendency to compare one's own appearance with that of others, typically someone more attractive.

Preventing these behaviors might involve such tactics as removing scales from the house, covering mirrors, leaving the make-up kit at home, allowing only two changes of clothes prior to leaving home, and having an agreement with one's partner that he or she will not respond to reassurance requests (i.e., an extinction program). Cash (1997) gave a variety of strategies for obstructing, delaying, or restricting rituals. For instance, one quite reasonable strategy for someone who simply cannot eliminate reassurance seeking consists of "rationally rationing rituals." Using this procedure, the individual might allow oneself three such reassurance requests per day, to be used at one's dispensation but not to exceed the limit. Over time, the person might also gradually reduce to two requests per day, with an ultimate goal, of course, of elimination.

One of the interesting and seemingly paradoxical aspects of these treatments is that exposure and response prevention may indicate antithetical approaches. Consider the case of excessive social comparison. In one case, when a female client is around more attractive people, she feels more personal body dissatisfaction, and this negative affect leads her to avoid situations that involve exposure to attractive others. In a second case, another female client repeatedly seeks out situations with beautiful people so that she can check her own appearance against theirs. The first case is a classic case of avoidance, the second, a common case of checking (or a sort of internalized reassurance seeking—"I think I look as good as she does"). Certainly, the same behavior, social comparison, is at the root of two different aspects of a behavioral component of dissatisfaction. In the first case, obviously, we want to decondition the avoidance, so exposure is indicated. In the second case, exposure seems to be problematic because it leads to reassurance seeking; therefore, we want to increase avoidance of the situation, at least temporarily, until such exposure no longer leads to excessive social comparison. Of course, the ultimate goal is for clients to be as comfortable as possible, even in difficult situations that might produce appearance comparisons while keeping checking behaviors (i.e., reassurance seeking) to a minimum.

CONCLUSIONS

Traumatic conditioning events and the subsequent avoidance of body-related situations that such experiences engender constitute two hallmark components of body image disturbance. Critical events may consist of any type of negative body-focused experience, ranging from the casual comment by a stranger to sexual abuse by a family member. Avoidance of social situations, wherein the appearance may be viewed or scrutinized by others, is a particularly distressing symptom for many individuals. Assessment and treatment of these factors is essential to the clinical management of individuals with body image disturbance. Desensitization and in vivo exposure methods are the two primary behavioral treatment strategies. These methods are a major component of the empirically validated cognitive–behavioral programs developed by Cash (1995b, 1996, 1997) and J. C. Rosen (1996a, 1996b, 1997) and should be considered for anyone presenting clinically with body dysmorphia or less severe body image concerns.

APPENDIX 9A
BODY IMAGE DIARY: A-B-C SEQUENCE OF
BODY-IMAGE EXPERIENCES

Activators (triggering events and situations):

_____

_____

_____

Beliefs (thoughts and perceptions of the situation):

_____

_____

_____

_____

_____

Consequences (emotional TIDE):

Types of emotions: _____

Intensity of emotions (0–10): _____

Duration of the episode: _____

Effects of the episode on your behavior: _____

_____

_____

From "Learning To Have a Better Body Image," by J. C. Rosen and T. F. Cash, 1995, *Weight Control Digest, 5*, p. 414. Copyright 1995 by J. C. Rosen and T. F. Cash. Reprinted with permission.

APPENDIX 9B
PHYSICAL APPEARANCE STATE AND
TRAIT ANXIETY SCALE: STATE

The statements listed below are used to describe how anxious, tense, or nervous you feel *right now* about your body (use the following scale)

Not at all	Slightly	Moderately	Very much so	Exceptionally so
0	1	2	3	4

Right now, I feel anxious, tense, or nervous about

1. The extent to which I look overweight.		0 1 2 3 4
2. My thighs.		0 1 2 3 4
3. My buttocks		0 1 2 3 4
4. My hips.		0 1 2 3 4
5. My stomach (abdomen).		0 1 2 3 4
6. My legs.		0 1 2 3 4
7. My waist.		0 1 2 3 4
8. My muscle tone.		0 1 2 3 4
9. My ears.		0 1 2 3 4
10. My lips.		0 1 2 3 4
11. My wrists.		0 1 2 3 4
12. My hands.		0 1 2 3 4
13. My forehead.		0 1 2 3 4
14. My neck.		0 1 2 3 4
15. My chin.		0 1 2 3 4
16. My feet.		0 1 2 3 4

From "Assessing Body Image Disturbance: Measures, Methodology, and Implementation" (p. 80), by J. K. Thompson, in J. K. Thompson (Ed.), *Body Image, Eating Disorders, and Obesity*, 1996. Copyright 1996 by the American Psychological Association. Reprinted with permission.

APPENDIX 9C
SITUATIONAL INVENTORY OF BODY-IMAGE DYSPHORIA

At various times and in various situations, people may experience negative feelings about their own physical appearance. Such feelings include feelings of unattractiveness, physical self-consciousness, or dissatisfaction with one or more aspects of one's appearance. This questionnaire lists a number of situations and asks how often you have feelings about your appearance in each of these situations.

Think about times when you have been in the situation and indicate how often you have had any negative feelings about your physical appearance in that situation. Use the 0–4 scale provided to indicate how often you have negative feelings about your physical appearance in each of the following situations.

There may be situations on the list that you have not been in or that you avoid. For these situations, simply indicate how often you believe that you would experience negative feelings about your appearance if you were in the situation.

Please answer accurately and honestly. There are no right or wrong answers, and your responses are anonymous and confidential.

Never	Seldom	Sometimes	Often	Always
0	1	2	3	4

How often do you have negative feelings about your appearance?

1. At social gatherings where I know few people	0	1	2	3	4
2. When I look at myself in the mirror	0	1	2	3	4
3. When I am the focus of social attention	0	1	2	3	4
4. When people see me before I've fixed up	0	1	2	3	4
5. When I am with attractive persons of my sex	0	1	2	3	4
6. When I am with attractive persons of the opposite sex	0	1	2	3	4
7. When someone looks at parts of my appearance that I dislike	0	1	2	3	4
8. When I look at my nude body in the mirror	0	1	2	3	4
9. When I am trying on new clothes at the store	0	1	2	3	4
10. When I am exercising	0	1	2	3	4
11. After I have eaten a full meal	0	1	2	3	4
12. When people can see me from certain angles	0	1	2	3	4
13. When I am wearing certain "revealing" clothes	0	1	2	3	4
14. When I see attractive people on television or in magazines	0	1	2	3	4
15. When someone compliments me on my appearance	0	1	2	3	4
16. If I'm dressed differently than others at a social event	0	1	2	3	4
17. When I get on the scale to weigh	0	1	2	3	4
18. When I think someone has ignored or rejected me	0	1	2	3	4
19. When anticipating or having sexual relations	0	1	2	3	4
20. If my friend or partner doesn't notice when I'm "fixed up"	0	1	2	3	4
21. When I'm already in a bad mood about something else	0	1	2	3	4

22. When the topic of conversation pertains to appearance   0   1   2   3   4
23. When I think about how I looked earlier in my life   0   1   2   3   4
24. When I haven't exercised as much as usual   0   1   2   3   4
25. When someone comments unfavorably on my appearance   0   1   2   3   4
26. When my clothes don't fit just right   0   1   2   3   4
27. When my partner sees me undressed   0   1   2   3   4
28. When I see myself in a photograph or videotape   0   1   2   3   4
29. When I think I have gained some weight   0   1   2   3   4
30. When I think I have lost some weight   0   1   2   3   4
31. When somebody else's appearance gets complimented and nothing is said about my appearance   0   1   2   3   4
32. When I hear someone criticize another person's looks   0   1   2   3   4
33. After I get a new haircut or hairstyle   0   1   2   3   4
34. If my partner touches me in body areas that I dislike   0   1   2   3   4
35. When I think about what I wish I looked like   0   1   2   3   4
36. When I am not wearing any make-up   0   1   2   3   4
37. When I recall any kidding or unkind things people have said about my appearance   0   1   2   3   4
38. When I think about how I may look in the future   0   1   2   3   4
39. When I have my photograph taken   0   1   2   3   4
40. If my hair isn't fixed just right   0   1   2   3   4
41. If my partner doesn't show sexual interest   0   1   2   3   4
42. When I am with people who are talking about weight or dieting   0   1   2   3   4
43. When I am with a certain person (Specify whom: _____)   0   1   2   3   4
44. At particular times of the day or evening (Specify when: _____)   0   1   2   3   4
45. During particular times of the month (Specify when: _____)   0   1   2   3   4
46. During particular seasons of the year (Specify when: _____)   0   1   2   3   4
47. During certain recreational activities (Specify which: _____)   0   1   2   3   4
48. When I eat certain foods (Specify which: _____)   0   1   2   3   4
49. Any other situation? _____
50. Any other situation? _____

From the Situational Inventory of Body-Image Dysphoria, an unpublished scale by T. F. Cash. Reprinted with permission from the author. For more information, see Cash (1994b).

APPENDIX 9D
VISUAL ANALOGUE SCALE

No Weight/Size |————————| Extreme Weight/Size
Dissatisfaction   Dissatisfaction

No Overall |————————| Extreme Overall
Appearance   Appearance
Dissatisfaction   Dissatisfaction

Instructions: Participants mark their level of disturbance on the 100 mm line. The distance from 0, measured from the left in millimeters, indicates the level of distress.

From "Assessing Body Image Disturbance: Measures, Methodology, and Implementation" (p. 81), by J. K. Thompson, in J. K. Thompson (Ed.), *Body Image, Eating Disorders, and Obesity*, 1996. Copyright 1996 by the American Psychological Association. Reprinted with permission.

APPENDIX 9E
BODY IMAGE AVOIDANCE QUESTIONNAIRE

Circle the number that best describes how often you engage in these behaviors at the present time.

Never	Seldom	Sometimes	Often	Always	
0	1	2	3	4	

1. I wear baggy clothes.	0	1	2	3	4
2. I wear clothes I do not like.	0	1	2	3	4
3. I wear darker clothing.	0	1	2	3	4
4. I wear a special set of clothing (e.g., my "fat clothes").	0	1	2	3	4
5. I restrict the amount of food I eat.	0	1	2	3	4
6. I only eat fruit, vegetables and other low calorie foods.	0	1	2	3	4
7. I fast for a day or longer.	0	1	2	3	4
8. I do not go out socially if I will be "checked out."	0	1	2	3	4
9. I do not go out socially if the people I am with will discuss weight.	0	1	2	3	4
10. I do not go out socially if the people I am with are thinner than me.	0	1	2	3	4
11. I do not go out socially if it involves eating.	0	1	2	3	4
12. I weight myself.	0	1	2	3	4
13. I am inactive.	0	1	2	3	4
14. I look at myself in the mirror.	0	1	2	3	4
15. I avoid physical intimacy.	0	1	2	3	4
16. I wear clothes that will divert attention from my weight.	0	1	2	3	4
17. I avoid going clothes shopping.	0	1	2	3	4
18. I don't wear "revealing" clothes (e.g., bathing suits).	0	1	2	3	4
19. I get dressed up or made up.	0	1	2	3	4

From "Development of a Body Image Avoidance Questionnaire," by J. C. Rosen, D. Srebnik, E. Saltzberg, and S. Wendt, 1991, *Psychological Assessment, 3*, p. 37. Copyright 1991 by the American Psychological Association. Reprinted with permission.

10

COGNITIVE-PROCESSING MODELS

A female client comes in for a therapy session and says, "I was doing great after our last session, eating went okay, didn't think too much about my body, had fun with my friends, but by Thursday I felt awful, wanting to binge; it just got worse and I've been down ever since." "What happened Thursday?" the therapist asked, knowing some event must have triggered a downturn. "Oh, I don't know. Nothing really." (a woman in her mid-20s)

The client in the above example is correct; she is not aware of what event triggered the downturn or how that event was processed in a dysfunctional way, confirming her negative body image beliefs. These effects often occur outside of awareness but can be quite powerful. Sometimes it is useful to look at the immediate thought patterns that occur on a day-to-day basis for individuals with body image disturbance. That is the subject matter for cognitive theorists and therapists: How the habitual ways people think perpetuate pathology. In this chapter, we undertake a review of one of the fastest growing areas in the field of body image: cognitive-processing models of disturbance. We organize our presentation around three areas of cognition: processing related to the self, social situations, and general information. With each set of findings, we examine how the data aid the understanding of body image. Once we have built a theoretical understanding, we use it to talk about cognitive assessments and interventions. Reviewed in this context is how day-to-day events are perceived, judged, and interpreted in a way that leads to emotional, mental, and behavioral consequences. We also see how the cognitive paradigm has renewed interest in the area of body size perception. The application of the cognitive paradigm to body image disturbance is relatively new, and the conclusions presented here may require modification within the next decade. However, we hope that the information will provide a framework for organizing this fast-growing area of research.

AN OVERVIEW OF THE MODEL

Figure 10.1 depicts a current cognitive model of body image schema, and Exhibit 10.1 defines the relevant terminology for this model. The arrows in the figure are meant to show what might happen in the mind of an individual as he or she encounters body image-related information. In this model, the body image schema is defined as an organization of information about one's physical self. It can tend toward an overall negative or positive valence, such that every time an individual activates the schema in response to external events, he or she feels generally positive or negative. The body image schema is not physically separate from other areas of cognition. More likely, other large cognitive structures, such as the self, can become dominated by appearance-related characteristics. Alternatively, as with the mental encyclopedia, interconnections between factual knowledge (e.g., the word *chocolate*) and self-related meanings (bad-girl food) are built. The main hypothesis here is that the presence of a large negative body image schema affects the normal input, storage, and retrieval processes of the mental encyclopedia. Such an effect could be facilitatory as the body image schema speeds up the processing of relevant information. Alternatively, the effect could be inhibitory as the emotional consequences of the schema-relevant information use up mental resources.

Social information-processing biases develop to support and confirm set-in beliefs about the body and self. Thus, an individual who thinks negatively about his or her body assumes that others judge him or her harshly along the same dimensions and interpret others' behaviors on the basis of that belief. In a case of severe body image disturbance, body-related themes dominate one's cognition. This pattern may exist in individuals with eating disorders.

For example, consider how shameful many eating-disorder clients feel about their body. It is only in understanding the relationship between body image and the sense of self that one can understand why body dissatisfaction can feel like personal failure. Compare the individual in the above clinical example with those individuals who can recognize that they are overweight but dismiss it, similar to a reminder from a dentist to floss. Consider another example of social information-processing bias. Imagine a person facing the end of a romantic relationship. Although most people ending a relationship might blame the breakup on some mistake in action or words, or even some fault in their personality, the individual with body image disturbance would likely believe the relationship failure was due entirely to his or her own physical flaw. As another example, imagine if we had a window into the mind of a woman with an eating disorder as she is faced with a meal. We could watch the interplay among the mental encyclopedia (recognize food as French fries, access nutritional informa-

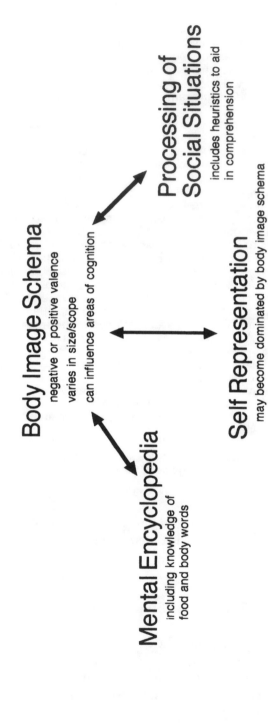

Figure 10.1. A body image schema and its relation to other areas of cognitive processing.

EXHIBIT 10.1
Glossary of Cognitive Terminology

Bias—This refers to the way in which prior expectations or beliefs affect how someone thinks about current events. For example, a person with depression might have a negative bias, which results in an excessively pessimistic view of a poor grade in school—this is an example of an interpretive bias. On a more basic level of cognition, prior beliefs may affect how information is attended to and selected for further processing; this is attentional bias. Bias is also used to describe the cognitive contribution in perceptual accuracy tasks. Although they share the same term, these biases refer to different cognitive processes.

Cognitive structure—This term refers to the way in which various beliefs and attitudes become organized in the mind. If one component of the structure is activated, the rest may also be aroused. For example, a woman with an eating disorder may have interconnected attitudes toward herself, her body, and food. Thinking about a fattening food may arouse negative feelings about herself.

Facilitation—This refers to the effect different variables can have on accuracy or speed of information processing. Expertise for a domain of knowledge is believed to facilitate judgments. Consider the speed at which champion chess players can play their game.

Interference—As the opposite effect of facilitation, this term refers to the way in which knowledge in a domain can cause a decrease in task performance.

Information processing—At the core of the cognitive model, the information received by people's senses undergoes a series of steps in becoming their thoughts and perceptions. To understand people is to understand those mental steps. It is analogous to the software that drives a computer.

Schema—An organization of beliefs and attitudes in the mind, a form of cognitive structure, a set of expectations about events said to have the power to influence speed, consistency, and recall of schema-relevant information.

Self-discrepancy—This is a specific type of self belief in which one aspect of the self is in conflict with another. For example, a woman might believe that her actual body weight does not meet her ideal body weight. At any one time, a specific discrepancy may or may not be activated.

Mental encyclopedia—This refers to the storage of world knowledge in memory and implies an organization and method of encoding the retrieval of information.

Accessibility—As the state of a set of beliefs or a schema, this is "prestimulus preparedness for activation" (Higgins & Brendl, 1995, p. 219).

---

tion, recognize as fat food), the body image schema ("I'm fat, I should be thinner"), and the self ("That's a bad-girl food").

RESEARCH BACKGROUND

To understand exactly how the model works, we need to review the experimental literature. Again, we organize our discussion around three general areas: self-related cognition, social cognition, and processing relating to the mental encyclopedia. Remember that much of the recent literature focuses on weight-related body image, but we can extrapolate to an understanding of general body image. Let us begin by looking at some models used to study self-related cognition in body image.

Self-Related Cognition

One early model of body image, based in self-schema theory, is that of Markus, Hamill, and Sentis (1987). In their view, individuals develop a self-schema through the experience of being labeled a particular way (e.g., through a verbal comment; see chapter 5). Thus, an individual may have been called "fatty pants" as a child and will continue to self-label himself or herself as "fatty." With repetition, the individual becomes faster and more efficient at seeing herself or himself as fat, until the point that a minimal time is spent considering the label and "fat" itself is an automatic thought in response to a variety of situations. The schema for fatness becomes so ingrained that the individual consistently self labels himself or herself as fat and resists any counterinformation. Such a person would be described as *schematic* for fatness. A person without these characteristics would be described as *aschematic*. (Some evidence shows that the exact words are encoded and reiterated.)

In an empirical test of these ideas, Markus et al. (1987) found that individuals schematic for fatness were faster when asked to decide if heavy silhouettes were like them than they were to decide if thin silhouettes were like them. Aschematic individuals showed no difference in judgment time. Thus, we see evidence for the quick ability of weight-schematic participants to see themselves as fat. Unfortunately, the group difference was not seen for responses to the words *fat* and *thin*, which led the authors to question whether any female American students could be aschematic for body weight. (This is an important point to consider when trying to discriminate typical from pathological body image cognition.) They also found that weight-schematic individuals were slower at responding to food words, a finding they had difficulty explaining but that fits in well with some later theories (see a discussion of the Stroop interference effects below).

Another model for understanding self-related cognition in body image is Higgins's (1987) self-discrepancy model. In this framework, the self is construed as containing many selves. An individual's perception of her or his actual self and ideal self would be two examples. Selves such as the ideal self and ought self are called *guides*. There are also standpoints on the self, such as one's own view or one's perception of one's parents' view. If all these different selves were pretty similar, that is, one saw oneself as close to one's ideal and close to perceived parental expectations, one would be a happy person. However, if any of these selves were discrepant, it would arouse feelings particular to that kind of discrepancy. According to self-discrepancy theory, an actual–ideal discrepancy is associated with depressive emotions, whereas an actual—ought discrepancy is associated with anxious emotions (Strauman & Higgins, 1987).

In several empirical studies, researchers have confirmed that self-discrepancies are related to body image and eating disturbance. For example, Strauman, Vookles, Berenstein, Chaiken, and Higgins (1991) found that general self-discrepancies (all aspects of self) were correlated with body dissatisfaction and eating-disorder symptoms. Forston and Stanton (1992) found that appearance-related actual—ideal discrepancy was associated with bulimic symptoms. Additionally, they found that individuals' reports of their mother's actual—ideal discrepancy for their children were also associated with bulimic symptoms.

This model helps explain how situational triggers lead to increases in symptoms. A main tenet of self-discrepancy theory is that if an event activates any aspect of an individual's self-discrepancy, then the emotion associated with that kind of discrepancy is aroused. In Strauman and Higgins's (1987) study, individuals were asked to complete sentences about other people, but these statements contained trait words that the individuals had previously indicated were discrepant for them (the traits were specific to the individual, e.g., intelligence). The act of completing those sentences triggered the emotion associated with that discrepancy. Similarly, Altabe and Thompson (1996) found that discrepancy-related emotions could be triggered with magazine pictures illustrating various body image traits.

Thus, we have a model for understanding how day-to-day events trigger mood changes. Self-discrepancy would predict that an individual with a self-discrepancy about his or her nose who also happens to see a news item about noses will have his or her self-discrepancy activated, leading to a negative emotion. A related tenet of self-discrepancy theory is the concept of chronically accessible cognitions (Higgins & Brendl, 1995). For individuals with chronically negative cognitions, the negative self beliefs are always active. Such a state has been related to depression (Segal, 1988).

Social Information-Processing Biases

Every day individuals are faced with numerous social situations that need interpretation. To understand the scope of the task, you could imagine that you are visiting another culture where you know the language but none of the customs. Imagine how difficult it would be to understand social interchanges.

Investigations of how people handle this information-processing load indicate that they use heuristics or interpretational biases based on their knowledge and beliefs (Williamson, 1996). Biases are part of normal thinking. Kahneman and Tversky (1973) were among the first researchers to consider heuristics in information processing. One of their experiments involved asking research participants to estimate which was greater, the number of words in the English language that begin with the letter k or those that have k in the third position. Nowadays, people could use a computer and program it to analyze an entire dictionary. If we had to do it ourselves, we would not read an entire dictionary. Instead, we would try to think of words that have k in those two positions. It turns out to be easier to think of words that begin with k (kitchen, kangaroo) than those with k in the third position (make, take). We would be likely to say that k-beginning words are more common than words with k in the third position. However, the opposite is true by a factor of 3:1. The strategy, called the *availability heuristic*, that is, using what comes easily to mind, was a lot faster than reading the dictionary but also fallible.

Consider another example of the availability heuristic. Suppose you read in the newspaper about an outbreak of food poisoning. Later in the day, you begin to feel ill. Because you just read it in the paper, you might think you have food poisoning, but your symptoms could have many causes. However, if there are cases of food poisoning in your area, it could be pretty adaptive to worry about your own symptoms that way. If you attribute your symptoms to a more statistically common cause, you may get a lot sicker before you get appropriate treatment. Thus, a heuristic may not be accurate, but it could be an effective information-processing strategy. In summary, biases are part of everyday thinking.

Investigating the role of heuristics in body image disturbance, Jackman, Williamson, Netemeyer, and Anderson (1995) compared the interpretations of weight-preoccupied and asymptomatic women for appearance- and health-related sentences that could be interpreted either positively or negatively. Participants were asked to recall these sentences. As expected, weight-preoccupied women recalled the appearance-related sentences as negative but did not show a bias for control sentences (see Exhibit 10.2 for an example). The authors concluded that the weight-preoccupied

EXHIBIT 10.2
An Example of the Ambiguous Sentence Task

Original: "After exercising for hours at a health club, you get a glimpse of the shape of your hips as you pass by the mirror."
Negative disambiguation: "After exercising for 2 hours at a health club, you get a glimpse of your large hips as you pass by the mirror."
Positive disambiguation: "After exercising for 2 hours at a health club, you get a glimpse of your toned hips as you pass by the mirror."
Negative control: "After swimming laps, you realize that you will never lose the weight you gained."
Positive control: "After swimming laps, you realize that you are beginning to lose weight."

From "Do Weight Preoccupied Women Misinterpret Ambiguous Stimuli Related to Body Size?" by L. P. Jackman, D. W. Williamson, R. G. Netemeyer, and D. A. Anderson, 1995, *Cognitive Therapy and Research, 19,* p. 345. Copyright 1995 by Plenum Press. Reprinted with permission.

women showed an information-processing bias that was consistent with their negative view of their own body. In a similar study, Cooper (1997) compared the interpretations of ambiguous interpersonal situations by eating-disordered individuals with those of symptomatic individuals. Persons with eating disorders coded events as weight related under two conditions: if the event was negative and self-relevant (i.e., primarily affected the individual) or if the event was positive and other relevant (i.e., affected someone else). In the latter case, an example might be someone else receiving compliments on his or her appearance—such an event was labeled *weight related* for Cooper's sample. Jackman et al. and Cooper speculated that these interpretation biases were self-reinforcing both in maintaining the biased view and the disordered eating and shape-related behaviors.

One aspect of social information bias is the interpretation of ambiguous information. Other steps in the processing of social information include selectively attending to and recalling the information. These processing steps were the subject of an investigation by Tantleff-Dunn and Thompson (1998). Participants viewed a video that depicted a conversation between a male and female actor, interspersed with weight- and appearance-related comments (see the excerpt in Exhibit 10.3). Participants high in trait body image anxiety reported that the female actor in the video reacted negatively. Those people low in body image anxiety saw her reaction as less negative. Thus, the social perception of high body image anxiety participants was negatively biased.

Wood, Altabe, and Thompson (1998) constructed a series of ambiguous appearance- and non-appearance-related sentences (the Commentary Interpretation Scale; see Appendix 10A), which were rated on a scale ranging from very positive to very negative. Body dissatisfied women rated the appearance sentences as more negative than they did the control sentences. Satisfied women rated the appearance sentences more positively and as more similar to control sentences. As with Tantleff-Dunn and Thompson (1998), it appears that individuals with high body image dis-

EXHIBIT 10.3
An Excerpt of Appearance-Related Comments From a Videotaped Conversation Between Two College Students

---

Female student: "Well, I can get it [calculator] back to you later—will you be around?"

Male student: "No, but I won't need it tonight . . . so have you heard about that new gym that just opened across from the University?"

Female student: (shakes her head no.)

Male student: "It's awesome . . . they come up with a personalized training program for you, they have all kinds of aerobics and good machines, . . . you should look into it. Do you work out?"

From Tantleff-Dunn and Thompson (1998).

turbance are more negative in their perceptions of ambiguous social phenomena, such as interactions and verbal comments.

Body Image and the Mental Encyclopedia

Perhaps some similar processes hold true for the processing of general information. A useful model for understanding this latter information processing is the mental encyclopedia. The mental encyclopedia can be illustrated as follows.

What do most people think about when they see the word *bread*? It is a fairly common word and a fairly common item that most people experience on a daily basis. It is probably safe to assume that most people have a large entry in their mental encyclopedia associated with the word *bread*, filled with types of breads, nutritional information, recipes using bread, and so forth. The encyclopedia notion is a metaphor for the organization in memory of an individual's knowledge.

What about individuals with weight-related body image disturbance? Does the experience of scrutinizing one's diet as part of the emotionally laden experience of body image disturbance change what happens when an individual sees the word *bread*? In what way might it change? Does the heightened importance of food information to a person with body image disturbance make him or her even more efficient at recognizing the word *bread* (called a *facilitation effect*)? Alternatively, do the negative emotions associated with that disturbance slow one down when processing the word *bread* (*interference effect*)?

The Stroop paradigm attempts to address these questions. This paradigm is based on the work of Stroop (1935), who studied interference effects with common words. Research participants were shown color names that were either consistent (the word *red* written with red ink) or inconsistent (the word *red* written in blue ink). When asked to name the ink color, the inconsistent information slowed the participants down.

Recently, the Stroop has been applied to the study of body image and eating disorders. In this application, the hypothesis is that symptomatic individuals will exhibit increased interference from body-image-themed words when compared with asymptomatic individuals. For example, Fairburn, Cooper, Cooper, McKenna, and Anastasisades (1991) showed that participants with bulimia were slower than asymptomatic participants on the color naming of weight-related words—a finding replicated by Cooper and Fairburn (1992) in their study of individuals with anorexia nervosa. However, some studies suggest that the modified Stroop paradigm does not clearly discriminate eating-disordered individuals from asymptomatic individuals (Perpina, Hemsley, Treasure, & de Silva, 1993). (For a complete review of the Stroop in eating-disorders research, see Huon, 1995.)

In other paradigms, researchers have investigated interference and facilitation effects in perception and attention (see Table 10.1). J. P. Newman et al. (1993) found that individuals with eating disorders or high body image concern were slower to decide if a string of characters were letters or numbers if the trial was preceded by body shape-related words. The authors hypothesized that the motivational significance of these words would use mental resources that otherwise would be available to complete the task.

The resource limitation explanation predicts that if the task was to identify the body-related words, the individual with high body image concern would do better because more resources were allocated. von Hippel, Hawkins, and Narayan (1994) used such a paradigm. Individuals were asked to identify familiar food-relevant words. Eating-disordered individuals were faster at this task. We can begin to generate a general principle: The presence of a dominant body image schema facilitates processing of body-related information and interferes with the processing of other information.

However, there may be some caveats. Rieger et al. (1998), using a visual probe procedure, found that individuals with eating disorders showed facilitation for negative body-shape words but inhibition for positive words. Similarly, Freeman et al. (1991) found that eating-disordered patients selectively attended to disliked body parts whereas asymptomatic participants looked at the whole image of themselves. Thus, the valence of the information is important; there may be a bias toward negative body-relevant stimuli.

Another issue that was originally raised with the Stroop paradigm is that of emotional arousal. Altabe and Sanocki (1996) used a visual search paradigm to investigate the efficiency of search for thin and heavy figure targets. Automaticity of search occurs if the task is fairly easy but breaks down when the task is increased in difficulty. In the study, body image disturbance was associated with less automaticity, even though the task was body relevant. Some evidence shows that emotional arousal from viewing the figure stimuli may have caused the interference.

We can conclude that body image disturbance is associated with the altered processing of body-relevant information. Perhaps the most careful statement is that this processing is deeper or more involved rather than a facilitation or interference across tasks. These processing paradigms give an indication of how the information in the mental encyclopedia might interfere with day-to-day information processing. It might be helpful to know how this information is organized. Research using repertory grids may inform this discussion.

The repertory grid task is based in part on Kelly's (1955) personal construct theory. His idea is that individuals act like scientists and try to develop theories to explain their world. A body image schema becomes an explanatory mechanism for understanding events. For example, an individual with body image disturbance has a weight-related framework for

TABLE 10.1

Effects on Cognitive Processing of Body- and Eating-Related Information

Paradigm	Cognitive process	Effects of body image disturbance	Study
Visual probe detection procedure	Attentional bias	Eating disorders show a facilitation for negative shape words and an inhibition for positive shape words	Rieger et al. (1998)
Perceptual identification	Word perception	Individuals with anorexia tendencies were faster at the identification of familiar relevant food words	von Hippel et al. (1994)
Letter–number identification	Character perception	Individuals with eating disorders and body image disturbance were distracted by relevant information preceding a letter-string identification task	J. P. Newman et al. (1993)
Stroop task	Color identification	Eating disturbance and body image disturbance were associated with the inhibition in color recognition of relevant words (not a consistent result)	Huon (1995)
Visual search	Automaticity of search figures	Body image disturbance was associated with less automaticity in a figure search	Altabe & Sanocki (1996)
Eye gaze	Selective attention	Eating disorders were associated with more attention to disliked body parts	Freeman et al. (1991)

understanding the world. "People fall into two categories: thin or fat" could be one belief. To assess an individual's construct system, one simply needs to present him or her with a set of people (me as I am now, mother, friend, me in the future, etc.) and ask what is most similar or different about any two of those people.

There are many formats for such an assessment. For example, Butow, Beumont, and Touyz (1993) compared individuals having an eating disorder with asymptomatic individuals who completed the repertory grid task. In this task, individuals indicate from their belief system what is different about two constructs from a standard set. For example, the stimulus constructs might be "me now" versus "me as I'd like to be," and the participants might respond "thinner" or "happier." Someone might also rate a popular person and an unpopular person as differing in thinness, thus popularity, "me as I'd like to be," and thinness would be closely intertwined constructs for that individual.

Butow et al. (1993) used the outcome of an open-ended repertory grid study to create a standardized personal construct test for eating-disordered samples (see Appendix 10B) to compare eating-disordered individuals with controls. In applying this standardized assessment, they found that the symptomatic group used the characteristics "concern about weight," "control," and "virtue" in a more extreme way (very high or low Likert ratings were applied). These participants were also more likely to use fewer characteristics, suggesting that their schema was more simple, rigid, and organized around thin–fat, good–bad, and control–no control. The repertory grid results suggested that the body image schema is a simplistic and extreme view, focusing on weight and good–bad dimensions. It also suggested that one's self-schema and body schema can become intertwined.

Summary: Research Background

On the basis of the review of empirical literature, we can begin to list the types of cognitive distortions associated with body image disturbance. From the literature on self-related cognition, we examined the concept of a *schema*, an organization of knowledge that affects the processing of new information. High schematicity speeds processing and makes it more consistent (Markus et al., 1987). Part of one's self-knowledge may be an abstract notion of an ideal self as suggested by the repertory grid and self-discrepancy paradigms. The research from the latter shows that the thinking involved in the self–ideal comparison can lead to negative emotions. A negative information-processing bias can also be seen with the interpretations of social information related to body image.

When we think about the cognition of an individual with body image disturbance, we think about two types of effects. First, an interference effect, as observed in the Stroop, is when individuals with body image disturbance process appearance-related information even when it takes resources away from the task at hand. J. P. Newman et al.'s (1993) results suggest that the interference persists for a brief period. However, if the task is to process information within the domain of body image, those individuals with body image disturbance are often fast, efficient, and consistent; this is the facilitation effect. The reason, according to Markus (1977), is that they have a schema, a preorganization of information that facilitates the processing of body image information. This facilitation serves to make these individuals efficient at confirming negative self beliefs. They may react emotionally to this information and have trouble processing other information. Thus, the mind of persons with body image disturbance is primed to react with a negative body image schema and to see many day-to-day events as confirming this distorted set of beliefs.

Finally, we have seen that the body image schema itself becomes interconnected with positive qualities, such as goodness and virtue—a connection first noted by Vitousek and Hollon (1990). An asymptomatic individual might say, "yes, I'm unhappy with my body, but it is not that important." A person with body image disturbance might say, "I gained weight. I'm a bad person. I feel awful." Thus, an individual with body image disturbance may think badly about his or her body in response to a variety of situations, confirming the negative beliefs about his or her body. That negative view dominates even the sense of self as a whole. We refer to this mental state of an individual with body image disturbance as the *hurricane effect.*

The Hurricane Effect

All of us have lived in Florida and like anyone in making metaphors, we draw from what is around us. Thus, we liken the progression from body dissatisfaction to disturbance as similar to the formation of a hurricane. A hurricane may start when waves of storm activity come off the coast of Africa and cross the Atlantic Ocean toward the eastern United States. If conditions are right, the storm becomes more organized, which means that instead of blotches of wind and rain, the energy of the storm becomes unidirectional in a circular pattern. As storms strengthen, they draw in more energy and become more organized in their unidirectional force. That force is what makes a hurricane so much more powerful than an isolated storm.

A similar pattern arises with the body image schema in eating disorders. Before someone develops the disorder, maybe he or she has some weight self-discrepancy or a few weight-dominated heuristics in social information processing—a few isolated thunderstorms of cognitive disturbance. If conditions are right, the areas of disturbance become more organized into a pattern or system of disturbed cognitions, hence, a schema. At its most severe, all thinking becomes dominated by the powerful schema. It is fast moving and powerful, and other patterns of thought have difficulty taking hold. Perhaps what will be shown in future research to discriminate pathology is not any one process but the pervasiveness of distorted body image cognition.

ASSESSMENT

In this section, we review the existing assessment instruments for the cognitive component of body image. These instruments fall into two categories. The first includes those that assess the typical cognitions of an individual with body image disturbance. The second category involves assessment techniques that allow for the assessment of self and body schemas from the individual's own perspective. Let us consider each instrument for the type of information it can yield and how it fits with the cognitive model presented above. (Table 10.2 contains more information about these scales.)

Sometimes it is useful to learn if a particular client experiences some of the typical cognitions associated with body image disturbance and eating disorders. An example is the Body-Image Automatic Thoughts Questionnaire (Cash, Lewis, & Keeton, 1987). This questionnaire assesses the frequency of specific thoughts about physical appearance, such as "I am comfortable with my appearance." Similarly, the Modified Distressing Thoughts (Clark, Feldman, & Channon, 1989) addresses the typical thoughts associated with a weight-related body image disturbance. Respondents rate these thoughts along several dimensions, including frequency and emotional intensity.

Two of the assessment instruments follow more directly from the self-representation models. The first, the Appearance Schemas Inventory (Cash & Labarge, 1996) assesses beliefs about the importance of physical appearance. It is based in part on Markus's (1977) *self-schema* definition, which includes a focus on the importance rating for a particular dimension. This inventory is particularly useful when trying to work on the treatment goal of deemphasizing the importance of appearance. With many clients, it may be easier to increase the importance of other aspects of the self rather than changing their body dissatisfaction.

Another instrument for the assessment of self-representation is the Body-Image Ideals Questionnaire–Expanded, which assesses self-discrepancy (M. L. Szymanski & Cash, 1995). Participants rate 11 appearance traits from four standpoints: both ideal self (likes, preferences, shoulds, expectations) and ought self from one's own and romantic partner's perspective. Respondents rate the extent to which they meet each of those expectations. For example, facial features in the spouse ought context may be rated as "exactly as I am," whereas chest size in the own ideal context may be rated as "very unlike me." The expanded version of this questionnaire is useful in assessing self-discrepancy in a quick closed-ended format in contrast to the longer Physical Appearance Discrepancy Questionnaire described below. Both instruments address self-discrepancy, which is particularly useful in addressing the cognition—emotion connection. Remember that ideal guides have been empirically related to depression emotions and ought guides to anxious emotions. From a clinical perspective, it is also a useful instrument in terms of addressing the social aspect of body image schema—that is, perceptions of others' judgments.

Another instrument for assessing the social cognition is the Commentary Interpretation Scale (see Appendix 10A). In this scale, individuals rate the positive—negative valence of neutral statements. The Commentary Interpretation Scale assesses the social information-processing bias described earlier. In the clinical context, the Commentary Interpretation Scale can help start a dialogue about biases in interpreting social commentary.

In clinical settings, it is often important to understand how individuals view themselves in their own particular environment. This clinical goal is well served by the open-ended measures derived from cognitive research into self-representation. For instance, a measure based on self-representation is the Physical Appearance Discrepancy Questionnaire (Altabe & Thompson, 1995), which is based on the Self-Discrepancy Questionnaire (Strauman & Higgins, 1987). Individuals are asked to name the traits associated with their actual self view and to indicate the extent to which they possess the trait on a 4-point scale. They do the same for their ideal self or other selves, such as the ideal from the mother's standpoint or the cultural ideal. Each of these guides is compared with the actual rating by using a set of scoring rules, resulting in a numerical discrepancy score. As a whole, the Physical Appearance Discrepancy Questionnaire helps to detail the specific physical appearance traits that are significant for the individual as well as provide a numerical rating of the extent of the discrepancy. It may be particularly useful for groups or individuals for whom weight is not a central body image concern (e.g., for cross-cultural research, see Altabe, 1998). Appendix 10C contains the format, scoring rules, and a case example of this measure.

Another measure that assesses body image as a form of self-representation is the Body Weight and Shape Self-Schema (see Appendix 10D). K. F. Stein and Hedger (1997) developed the Body Weight and Shape Self-Schema on the basis of Markus's (1977) self-schema theory. Participants consider five trait characteristics that refer to weight-related traits (slim, fit, athletic, fat, and out-of-shape). Each trait is rated on a 5-point scale for three dimensions: self, future self, and possible future self.

TABLE 10.2
Measures of Body Image Cognition

Instrument	Author(s)	Description	Reliability 1, 2	Standardization sample	Address of author
Bulimia Cognitive Distortions Scale—Physical Appearance Subscale	Schulman et al. (1986)	Indicate degree of agreement with 25 statements that measure physical appearance-related cognitions	IC: (.97; for entire scale)	55 outpatient bulimic women ages 17–45 and 55 normal women ages 18–40	Bill N. Kinder, PhD Department of Psychology University of South Florida 4202 Fowler Avenue Tampa, FL 33620-8200
Body-Image Automatic Thoughts Questionnaire	(a) Cash et al. (1987) (b) Cash (personal communications, April 11, 1990)	Indicate frequency with which one experiences 37 negative and 15 positive body image cognitions	(a) IC: (.90) for bulimic and normal participants for both positive and negative subscales (b) TR: 2 weeks (positive scales: males −.73; females −.71) (negative scale: males −.84; females −.90)	33 bulimic women inpatients and 79 female undergraduates	Thomas F. Cash, PhD Department of Psychology Old Dominion University Norfolk, VA 23529-0267
Appearance Schemas Inventory	Cash & La-Barge (1996)	14 items assess "core beliefs or assumptions" about appearance: three subscales: Vulnerability, Self-Investment, and Appearance Stereotyping	IC: .84 TR: .71	College student normal controls: 274 women	Thomas F. Cash, PhD Department of Psychology Old Dominion University Norfolk, VA 23529-0267
Body-Image Ideals Questionnaire	Cash & Szymanski (1995)	Rate one's personal ideal and actual rating on 10 attributes related to weight/appearance and strength/importance of attribute	IC: discrepancy, .75 IC: importance, .82	284 female undergraduates	Thomas F. Cash, PhD Department of Psychology Old Dominion University Norfolk, VA 23529-0267
Body-Image Ideals Questionnaire—Expanded	M. L. Szymanski & Cash (1995)	Rate one's specific attributes from own viewpoint and that of romantic partner based on "ideal" and "ought"	IC: .81–95	143 female undergraduates	Thomas F. Cash, PhD Department of Psychology Old Dominion University Norfolk, VA 23529-0267

Measure	Source	Description	Reliability	Sample	Contact
Body Weight and Shape Self-Schema	K. F. Stein & Hedger (1997)	Two 5-item scales that measure current and possible weight-related self-schemas		79 girls	Karen F. Stein, PhD School of Nursing University of Michigan 400 North Ingalls Ann Arbor, MI 48109-0482
Commentary Interpretation Scale	K. C. Wood, Altabe, & Thompson (1998)	16-item scale measuring the negativity of interpretation of neutral statements; contains Appearance Comment and General Comment subscales	TR: .72	Female college students	J. Kevin Thompson, PhD Department of Psychology University of South Florida 4202 Fowler Avenue Tampa, FL 33620
Modified Distressing Thoughts Questionnaire	Clark et al. (1989)	24-item scale containing anxious-, depression-, and weight-related thought statements; individuals rate each statement for frequency and emotional intensity	IC: anxious total, .92; depression total, .97; weight total, .98 TR: anxious total, .63; depression total, .69; weight total, .78	42 bulimic and 20 anorexic clients, 165 student nurse controls	D. A. Clark, PhD Department of Psychology University of New Brunswick Bag Service 45444 Fredericton, New Brunswick Canada E3B 6E4
Physical Appearance Discrepancy Questionnaire	Altabe & Thompson (1995)	Based on Higgins's discrepancies questionnaire; indicate the physical appearance traits associated with one's actual ideal and cultural ideal self		108 male and female college students	Madeline Altabe, PhD Department of Psychology University of South Florida 4202 Fowler Avenue Tampa, FL 33620
Repertory Grid for Eating Disorders	Butow et al. (1993)	Expands on prior method from George Kelly by focusing on eating situations and weight-related themes	na	53 anorexic, 45 bulimic, 65 restrained eater, 68 control participants	Dr. Phyllis Butow Medical Psychology Unit Department of Psychiatry Endocrinology and Cancer Medicine Royal Prince Alfred Hospital New South Wales, Australia 2006

Note. IC = internal consistency; TR = test–retest reliability.

The future scales may be especially informative and may provide unique clinical information for a client who feels hopeless about his or her body image.

The Body Weight and Shape Self-Schema Scale and Physical Appearance Discrepancy Questionnaire are assessment strategies that focus on the self. The repertory grid method (discussed earlier) looks at the main themes by which individuals view the world. Butow et al. (1993) developed a format appropriate for assessing body image disturbance. Individuals were given an open-ended repertory grid test. This test took the form of asking what is different about elements such as me and mother. (Other formats might use different "people" elements and ask for either similarities or differences.) Butow et al.'s results led to the development of an assessment of the typical constructs used by eating-disordered individuals for people and eating situations (see Appendix 10B).

This assessment may aid the clinician in understanding how individuals see themselves and others in relation to body image and personality dimensions. One would expect that psychotherapy for an individual with body image disturbance might lead to a more positive view of the self and others and a more differentiated view (i.e., one that was less focused on appearance dimensions).

TREATMENT

Treatment of body image problems almost always involves some type of cognitive intervention. As noted in chapter 2, cognitive restructuring is a critical component of the programs used by Cash and J. C. Rosen. Very often clients have self-schemas that are dominated by physical appearance traits. This can be evidenced in self-descriptions as well as journal entries. The client can be motivated by a need to prove his or her worth by making his or her body look good. The therapist may notice that the client with body image disturbance has a view of the self that is dominated by physical appearance traits and, in turn, associates body image ideals with "good" person values. In the social realm, the person discounts positive social feedback. For example, a client may think that those who give appearance compliments have ulterior motivations. Distortions in the mental encyclopedia realm may include categorization of some foods as "bad foods." Some common cognitive symptoms are presented in Exhibit 10.4.

Certainly, many of the measures noted in the assessment section are useful to detail the specific cognitive errors and biases that may form the basis for cognitive restructuring. Cash (1997) has also pinpointed 10 problems in this venue, which he labels as *arguable assumptions* (see Exhibit 10.5). For instance, one of these assumptions is "the first thing that people will notice about me is what's wrong with my appearance." These and other

EXHIBIT 10.4
Cognitive Symptoms Observable in the Clinical Setting

Area of cognition	Symptom
Sense of self	Negative view of self related to one's body image
	View of self dominated by appearance traits
	Periods of depression following negative body image experiences
	Self-talk mimics early feedback ("fatso kid")
	Examination of hated body parts lasts longer in mirror
	Association of thinness with goodness
Social interaction	Mind reads that others are thinking negatively of one's appearance
	Avoids social situations
	Discounts positive social feedback
	Believes failures are related to negative appearance
Mental encyclopedia	Emotionally ladened body and food words
	Automatic activation of body image schema in response to cues in environment
	Narrowing of attention to body-related matters

maladaptive assumptions might be challenged in the usual cognitive manner by helping the client evaluate the evidence for the assumption and then creating a more rational statement about people's first impressions.

Cash (1997) has also developed a list of eight common cognitive body image distortions (see Exhibit 10.6). One of these is the "beauty or beast" view, which is a dichotomous view of one's appearance as either excellent or awful. Again, cognitive strategies are helpful, consisting of correcting such extremist views and replacing them with a more moderated stance.

The following is an example of the use of restructuring. A client states that "my husband won't take me out because of my weight." As the ther-

EXHIBIT 10.5
Arguable Assumptions

1. Physically attractive people have it all.
2. The first thing that people will notice about me is what's wrong with my appearance.
3. One's outward physical appearance is a sign of the inner person.
4. If I could look just as I wish, my life would be much happier.
5. If people knew how I really look, they would like me less.
6. By controlling my appearance, I can control my social and emotional life.
7. My appearance is responsible for much of what has happened to me in my life.
8. I should always do whatever I can to look my best.
9. The media's messages make it impossible for me to be satisfied with my appearance.
10. The only way I could ever like my looks would be to change them.

From *The Body Image Workbook: An 8-Step Program for Learning to Like Your Looks* (p. 84), by T. F. Cash, 1997, Oakland, CA: New Harbinger. Copyright 1997 by New Harbinger Publications (www.newharbinger.com). Reprinted with permission.

EXHIBIT 10.6
Body Image Distortions

1. Beauty or beast	5. Mind misreading
2. Unfair to compare	6. Misfortune telling
3. The magnifying glass	7. Beauty bound
4. The blame game	8. Moody mirror

From *The Body Image Workbook: An 8-Step Program for Learning to Like Your Looks* (pp. 105–116), by T. F. Cash, 1997, Oakland, CA: New Harbinger. Copyright 1997 by New Harbinger Publications (www.newharbinger.com). Reprinted with permission.

apist processes this, it becomes clear that this assumption is based on the social information bias that "other people judge me harshly because of my appearance" or the self belief that "I am shameful because of my size." The therapist could challenge those beliefs directly in the session by asking the client to examine the evidence that supports the belief.

Alternatively, the therapist and client could create an experiment to challenge the assumption. In this example, the alternative explanations for the husband's behavior could be that he has been wanting to stay home more because of factors in his life or perhaps he is reacting to her negative affect and discomfort with herself. The client and therapist decide that she is to plan and initiate an evening out. Such an action will test her beliefs. If all goes well, the client will return with new information about herself. It is important to process this new information thoroughly because individuals tend to discount information inconsistent with their schema. In addition, they tend to be negatively biased in their processing of social situations. It may even be useful for the therapist to recall these incidents to the client in a later session. Another good follow-up to this assignment would be to ask the client to monitor her thoughts relating to this belief.

Cognitive restructuring builds new cognitive structures, with some specifically within the body image domain and some as new connections relating to the self and social realms. If body image disturbance is like a hurricane, then restructuring it is like a cool air mass descending on the hurricane and dissipating its energy.

PERCEPTUAL THEORIES: A RECONCEPTUALIZATION

Research Background

Most historians of body image disturbance agree that modern interest can be traced to two events: Bruch's (1962) descriptions of girls with anorexia nervosa who maintained their "fat" appearance, despite an emaciated state, and Slade and Russell's (1973) seminal investigation of size perception in individuals with anorexia nervosa—their findings were indicative of a greater perceptual overestimation for the clinical groups as compared with non-eating-disordered controls. Subsequently, the great majority of research, for the next 10–15 years, on the general phenomenon of body image actually focused narrowly on the size perception component of disturbance.

However, in the late 1980s and early 1990s, there was what amounted to a paradigm shift away from perceptual work and toward a greater focus on the subjective experience of the individual's "satisfaction" along with a focus on the risk factors and models that we identified in much of this book. There are at least three reasons for this shift in attention: (a) findings showing that this supposed "perceptual" type of body image is, in fact, affected by a number of situational and experimental factors (e.g., the level of ambient illumination, specific type of instructional protocol, and food intake; e.g., J. K. Thompson, 1992, 1996a; J. K. Thompson & Dolce, 1989); (b) research showing that subjective ratings of appearance satisfaction are more strongly related to clinical variables, such as eating dysfunction, self-esteem, and depression (Altabe & Thompson, 1992); and (c) conflictual evidence regarding whether overestimation was specific to eating-disordered individuals (Penner, Thompson, & Coovert, 1991; Williamson, Cubic, & Gleaves, 1993).

In the past decade, work by Gardner and colleagues (see Gardner & Bokenkamp, 1996), using signal detection methodology, has reenergized the study of perceptual processes of body image disturbance. The basic goal of this method is to separate sensory from nonsensory factors. *Sensory*, in the case of size perception, refers to the responses of the visual system (retina, visual cortex); *nonsensory* refers to other inputs in the mind that help to interpret the visual input (see Figure 10.2). Through a mathematical analysis of the correct responses and errors in a visual detection task, two measures emerge: *sensory sensitivity*, which is the ability to detect the sensory stimulus, and *response bias*, which is the tendency to interpret the stimulus in a distorted way.

For example, an individual shown a barely detectable flash of light may or may not be willing to guess that the light was present (for a more detailed explanation, see Appendix 10E). In the case of size estimates, individuals' attitudes, beliefs, and thoughts affect their willingness to perceive an image of themselves as normal or distorted. As illustrated in Figure 10.2, the signal detection approach (or integrative model) more generally recognizes the separate inputs of sensory and cognitive factors into perception. This view contrasts with older bottom-up models that conceptualize perception as purely a sensory challenge (i.e., accuracy), with cognitions and beliefs occurring separately and later. It is important to emphasize that although a perceptual distortion may be due to cognitive (nonsensory) factors, it is still a preconscious process; for the individual, the image appears distorted to him or her.

When Gardner and others (e.g., Gardner, Martinez, & Sandoval,

Bottom Up Model

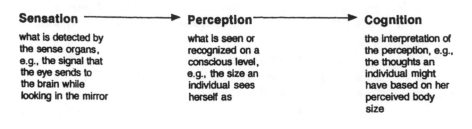

Sensation ———————————→ **Perception**———————————→ **Cognition**

what is detected by
the sense organs,
e.g., the signal that
the eye sends to
the brain while
looking in the mirror

what is seen or
recognized on a
conscious level,
e.g., the size an
individual sees
herself as

the interpretation of
the perception, e.g.,
the thoughts an
individual might
have based on her
perceived body
size

Integrative Model

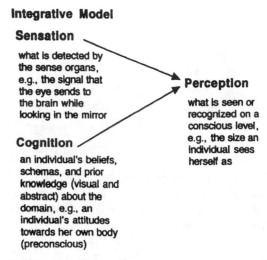

Sensation

what is detected by
the sense organs,
e.g., the signal that
the eye sends to
the brain while
looking in the mirror

Perception

what is seen or
recognized on a
conscious level,
e.g., the size an
individual sees
herself as

Cognition

an individual's beliefs,
schemas, and prior
knowledge (visual and
abstract) about the
domain, e.g., an
individual's attitudes
towards her own body
(preconscious)

Figure 10.2. The relationship between perceptual and cognitive processes.

1987; Gardner & Moncrieff, 1988; and L. A. Szymanski & Seime, 1997) applied the signal detection approach (or its variant, the adaptive probit estimation technique; see Appendix 10E) to the body perception domain, the results are generally consistent. Gardner and Bokenkamp (1996) have concluded that "it is the nonsensory factors which account for the overestimation in body size" (p. 11). By the nonsensory factors, they specifically mean affective and cognitive variables. For example, Gardner and Moncrieff found that participants with anorexia nervosa were as good as normal controls in detecting size differences; however, anorexic participants were more likely to report an image of themselves as distorted.

These findings call into question the interpretation of previous research using simpler methodologies of size overestimation assessment, such as requiring participants to adjust their video image to fit an internal standard of size matching (see J. K. Thompson, 1992, 1996b). One must conclude that perception is altered for certain groups in certain situations but only for cognitive and affective reasons (not sensory deficits).

Smeets (1997) further explored the issue of the origin of distorted perception. In reviewing research in the area of imagery, she concluded that size perceptions, like other images, are constructed. One is able to imagine things one has never seen. When one recalls what one has seen, one often inserts nonexistent details based on one's expectations. Size perception, too, can be constructed on the basis of attitudes and beliefs. An exploration of perception can help us understand these cognitions.

In an example of this approach, Gardner, Gardner, and Morrell (1990) examined the body image of physically and sexually abused children. Sexually abused children were more likely to say that an image of their appearance was distorted, whereas physically abused children were more likely to report self-images as nondistorted. Nonabused children showed neither bias. In another study, Gardner, Sorter, and Friedman (1997) found that parental weight concerns were related to a bias in children's body size perception. It may be useful to investigate further what implications a distorted self-perception (bias) has for reacting to other social and interpersonal factors.

From a treatment perspective, the signal detection approach implies that a range of therapy modalities may affect perception beyond those perceptual treatment approaches normally used to modify overestimation levels (e.g., confronting individuals with the inaccuracy of their estimations). We might expect instead that strategies outlined throughout this book, such as the affective (i.e., desensitization, exposure), cognitive, and feminist strategies, will result in improvements in perceptual accuracy. Thus, it is still useful to review assessments and treatments associated with size overestimation.

Assessment

Assessment of body size estimation has been reviewed extensively elsewhere (Smeets, 1997; J. K. Thompson, 1990, 1992, 1996a). There are two general types of methods (see Table 10.3). The first category is body site estimation techniques, where individuals indicate the size of specific body sites, such as the waist, as if they were viewing themselves in a mirror. An alternative method is the whole-image technique, where individuals can manipulate the width of a video or photographic image of themselves. For both these techniques, perceptual accuracy has been estimated using the following formula: ([perceived size − actual size]/actual size) × 100. One of the problems with this method is that a smaller person would show greater overestimation for the same size error (e.g., 1.50 in. [3.81 cm]). Recently, Smeets, Smit, Panhuysen, and Ingleby (in press) have revised this formula. They have proposed the Body Perception Index, which takes into account actual size.

Two recent innovations in technology also improved the assessment

TABLE 10.3

Measures of Size Estimation Accuracy

Instrument	Author(s)	Description	Reliability 1, 2	Standardization sample	Address of author
Adjustable light beam apparatus	(a) J. K. Thompson & Spana (1988) (b) J. K. Thompson (1990)	Adjust width of four light beams projected on wall to match perceived size of cheeks, waist, hips, and thighs	(a) IC: .83 TR: immediate, .83–.92; 1 week, .56–.86 (b) IC: .75	(a) 159 female undergraduates (b) 63 female adolescents (10–15) years old	J. Kevin Thompson, PhD Department of Psychology University of South Florida Tampa, FL 33620-8200
Body image detection device	(a) Ruff & Barrios (1986) (b) Barrios et al. (1989)	Adjust width of light beam projected on wall to watch perceived size of specific body site	(a) IC: .91, .93 TR: 3 weeks (bulimics, .82–.87; controls, .72–.85) (b) IC: .21–.82 TR: 3 weeks, .34; 4 weeks, .94; 7 weeks, .37	(a) 20 normal and 20 bulimic undergraduates (b) Female undergraduates	Billy A. Barrios, PhD College of Liberal Arts Department of Psychology University of Mississippi Oxford, MS 38677
Movable caliper technique: visual size estimation	(a) Slade & Russell (1973) (b) Slade (1985) (c) Ben-Tovim & Crisp (1984), Ben-Tovim et al. (1990)	Adjust distance between two lights to match perceived size	(a) IC: anorexics, .72–.93; controls, .37–.79 (b) IC: anorexics, .72; controls, .63 (c) TR: 2 weeks, .79–.95	(a) 14 female anorexics and 20 female postgraduates and secretaries (b) Anorexics (c) Normal females	(a) Peter Slade, PhD Department of Psychiatry and Department of Movement Science Liverpool University Medical School Ashton Street, P.O. Box 147 Liverpool L69 3BX, England (b) David I. Ben-Tovim, PhD Department of Psychiatry Repatriation General Hospital Daws Road, Daw Park South Australia, 5041

Method	References	Description	Reliability	Samples	Contact
Image marking procedure	(a) Askevold (1975) (b) Barrios et al. (1989) (c) Gleghorn et al. (1987) (d) Bowden et al. (1989)	Indicate one's perceived size by marking two endpoints on a life-size piece of paper	(b) IC: .25–.62 TR: 3 weeks, .17; 4 weeks, .33; 7 weeks, .14 (c) TR: immediate, .72–.92 (d) TR: 1 day, .38–.85	(b) College females (c) Bulimics, normal females (d) 12 anorexics, 12 bulimics, 24 controls	Finn Askevold, PhD Psychosomatic Department Oslo University Hospital Oslo, Norway
TV-video method	(a) Gardner et al. (1987) (b) Gardner & Moncrieff (1988)	Adjust the horizontal dimensions of a TV image of oneself to match perceived size	(a) IC: na TR: None given	(a) 38 normal and eating disordered adults (b) Normal and anorexic females	Rick M. Gardner, PhD Department of Psychology University of Colorado at Denver P.O. Box 173364 Denver, CO 80217-3364
Distorting video-camera	(a) Freeman et al. (1984) (b) Brodie et al. (1989)	Adjust a video image varied from 60% larger to 25% thinner	(a) IC: Front profile, .62 TR: 7–22 days (frontal; bulimics and anorexics, .91; controls, –.83) (b) IC: .56–.84 TR: 4 days, .17–.70	(a) 20 eating-disordered females (bulimics and anorexics and 20 normals) (b) Female controls	Richard J. Freeman, PhD Department of Psychology Simon Fraser University Burnaby, British Columbia Canada V5A 1S6
Distorting photograph technique	(a) Glucksman & Hirsch (1969) (b) Garfinkel et al. (1978) (c) Garfinkel et al. (1979)	Indicate one's size by adjusting a photograph that is distorted from 20% under to 20% over actual size	(a) IC: na (b) TR: 1 week (anorexics, –.75; controls, –.45) (c) 1 year (anorexics –.70; controls, –.14)	(a) Obese patients (b) Anorexics and controls (c) Anorexics and controls	David M. Garner, PhD c/o Psychological Assessment Resources, Inc. P.O. Box 998 Odessa, FL 33556

Table continues

TABLE 10.3 (Continued)

Instrument	Author(s)	Description	Reliability 1, 2	Standardization sample	Address of author
Distorting video technique	Touyz et al. (1985)	Indicate one's size by adjusting photograph that is distorted by 50% under to 50% over actual size	IC: na TR: Immediate, .82; 1 day, .63; 8 weeks, .61	Anorexics and bulimics	S. W. Touyz, PhD Department of Clinical Psychology Westmead Hospital Westmead 2145 New South Wales, Australia
Distorting television method	Bowden et al. (1989)	Photograph distorted by video camera to 50% over and under actual size	IC: na TR: 1 day, .92	Anorexics, bulimics, and controls	J. K. Collins, PhD School of Behavioral Science Macquarie University North Ryde, New South Wales Australia 2113
Distorting mirror	Brodie et al. (1989)	Distorting mirror (thinner–fatter images)	IC: .61–.92 TR: 4 days, .34–.84	29 female university students	Dr. D. A. Brodie School of Movement Science University of Liverpool P.O. Box 147 Liverpool L69 3BX, England
Video distortion method	Probst et al. (1998)	Adjust a life-size image projected onto a screen with a video camera	IC: Anorexia nervosa patients, .94–.97; bulimia nervosa patients, .88–.99; controls, .90–.96 Test–retest: anorexia nervosa patients, .87–.90; controls, .56–.81	53 anorexia nervosa patients, 38 bulimia nervosa patients, and 36 controls	M. Probst University Center St. Joseph Leuvensesteenweg 517 B-3070 Kortenberg Belgium

Note. IC = internal consistency; TR = test–retest reliability.

of body size estimation. Probst, Vandereycken, Vanderlinden, and Van Coppenolle (1998) developed a video distortion method, with a life-size projection screen on which participants view their image as they adjust it to match the experimenter's instructions for rating protocol (i.e., feel, think, ideal). Probst et al. found significant correlations between the estimate and questionnaire measures of body image dissatisfaction, which were higher than those detected in many previous studies. It would be interesting to compare this procedure with other techniques to determine if the confrontation with a life-size image somehow produces a different subjective response, enhances the reliability of ratings, or both. Another new measure is the Anamorphic Micro, a computer program that allows for the manipulation of photo images, so that the individual can appear thinner or heavier and view simultaneously images resulting from different ratings, such as ideal and feel (J. O. Thomas, 1998).

Treatment

Treatment strategies that consist of forcing individuals to confront their images, as a means of modifying specific size overestimation, have received periodic evaluation over the past 30 years. The first such use of a video confrontation method was in a study by Gottheil, Backup, and Cornelison (1969), who initially filmed a female 17-year-old responding to questions about her anorexia nervosa. Later she was shown this film and asked questions about her response to viewing her own emaciated image. Positive effects of this procedure were found; however, because it was combined with other treatments, such as psychotherapy and diet modification, no specific attribution of the changes to the size confrontation methods could be made.

Biggs, Rosen, and Summerfield (1980) found that the viewing of a 4-min video (participants with depression or anorexia nervosa and controls were tested) had negative effects on the self-esteem of the anorexic group whereas there were no changes on this variable for the other groups. Unfortunately, no body image measures were included in the assessment. More recently, Fernandez and Vandereycken (1994) had anorexic patients view a film of their bodies clothed in a dark bikini; afterward, the patients experienced their bodies as thinner and more active on the basis of their responses to a semantic differential scale. A variation on the confrontation methodology was used by Gardner, Gallegos, Martinez, and Espinoza (1989), who gave obese and normal weight participants the task of self-adjusting their own images, either with or without the presence of a mirror, in a test of the accuracy of estimation. Both groups were found to be more accurate with the presence of a mirror.

Norris (1984) found that simply allowing anorexic and bulimic participants to evaluate their image in a mirror led to an increased accuracy of estimation of a subsequent test of size accuracy. Following up on Norris's methodology, Goldsmith and Thompson (1989) found that a combination of mirror and verbal feedback increased accuracy. Non-eating-disordered participants who overestimated their body size were given 3 min to evaluate their image in a mirror and were then shown their degree of overestimation by lines drawn on a chalkboard representing their estimates and the actual dimensions of body sites (cheeks, waist, hips, and thighs). These participants improved significantly in accuracy over a control group.

Whereas treatment approaches focused on improving perceptual accuracy may create short-term improvements, the effects may not last. In fact, as we noted earlier in the discussion of the sensory detection research, any observed changes in perceptual accuracy may actually be modifications in the affective or cognitive aspects of one's body image. Because research increasingly supports the view that the nonsensory component of size perception is at the core of the symptom, it may be that other treatments could be just as useful. Thus, cognitive–behavioral and feminist strategies may be the treatment of choice for size overestimation symptoms. It is interesting to note, however, that virtually no comparative work has tested the efficacy of perceptual exposure treatments versus other treatments noted throughout this book.

Summary: Perceptual Theories

Perceptual aspects of disturbance, once nearly defining the field of body image, fell into disfavor for several years but are now being reexamined within a cognitive framework. Reviewing Figure 10.2, we observe that cognitions are essential, even for what might appear to be a simple process—perception. It seems more complicated at first, but the role of cognitive variables in day-to-day perception may be at the heart of what perpetuates body image disturbance for affected individuals. People respond to the environment they perceive and construct, or as Gardner and Bokenkamp (1996) noted, affected individuals "respond to the image they see in the mirror as though it were a fat person" (p. 11).

CONCLUSIONS

It has been about a decade now that researchers have begun intensively to use cognitive paradigms to study body image. Research has led us to a new understanding of how individuals react to day-to-day events in a way that reinforces their disorder. This is the case in the example at the beginning of this chapter. Assessment techniques have proliferated. Cognitive treatments developed for other disorders are being modified for body image disorders with success. Renewed meaning is being derived from the perceptual accuracy literature of decades past. The use of the cognitive paradigm is a promising proposition.

From the research, we have learned some of the specific ways that body image disturbance affects information processing. Body image appears to act like a form of self-representation. Personal and physical appearance values can become intertwined. Emotions relating to self-discrepancies can be activated.

Body image also appears to be a cognitive structure capable of affecting early information processing, perception, and attention. The effect appears to be primarily facilitatory for body image-relevant contents. Valence and emotional arousal may be mediating factors, and future research will likely reveal more specific information about these early processes.

Clearly from the literature, the presence of a body image disturbance is associated with interpretive biases for social information. General social situations are interpreted as appearance related, and appearance-related situations are interpreted more negatively. These biases are likely self-reinforcing: The more individuals make negative appearance interpretations, the more likely they are to continue to view the world in those terms.

The same may be said of many of the self-related cognitive processes: The more one refers to oneself as fat or ugly, the more likely the thought will come to mind. That is what is meant by accessibility or, in the more extreme case of nearly continuous activation of negative thoughts, *chronic accessibility*. The hurricane model is speculative but is meant to capture the idea that not only are individual cognitive distortions self-reinforcing, but they also reinforce each other, gather strength from each other, and block the formation of healthier thinking processes.

The assessment strategies developed thus far are able to assess typical cognitive distortions, social interpretive biases, and body image self concept. The standardized repertory grid, in particular, can help to understand how clients see themselves, others, and their own body image. In addition, the tools may be useful for monitoring the progress in treatment. Many are also good therapy tools because they reveal cognitive biases that the client is usually not aware of. Subsequently, traditional cognitive therapy techniques, such as challenging the beliefs and testing the assumptions, can be brought to bear. Cognitive restructuring can help to build new connections between self values and physical appearance beliefs, thus quieting the cognitive storm. Other therapy modalities may affect cognitive distortions as well.

The next decade of cognitive applications will likely bring to researchers more insight into the internal workings of body image schema. We have seen that to be especially true with perceptual accuracy studies. With the aid of the cognitive paradigm, we can better understand percep-

tual accuracy of body image disturbance, the form of disturbance that ini-
tiated the modern study of body image.

The cognitive paradigms are exciting, powerful, and complex. It is
easy to get caught up in them. We must continue to measure the utility
of these paradigms against the standard: Does it yield information that
would help us to understand more about body image disturbance? So far
the self models and social bias studies have aided our understanding.
The Stroop paradigm, taken by itself, does not yield any new information.
However, looking at it along with other interference and facilitation paradigms, we can learn something about the status of general information. It
will be particularly interesting to learn more about what factors mediate
facilitation and interference relative to the body image schema.
Cognition–emotion relationships, which also came up in relation to the
self concept, are a relatively unexplored area of body image cognition.

Whatever the direction the next decade takes, we will learn more
about what happens in the mind as individuals process moment-by-
moment events. Whatever the historical cause of body image disturbance
(feminist issues, social feedback, etc.), it is a disorder that exists and is
maintained by processes that occur in a flash of a second. Such is the legacy
of the cognitive paradigm.

APPENDIX 10A
COMMENTARY INTERPRETATION SCALE

Please imagine that you are hearing each of the following comments or questions from a friend. Rate each item according to how positively or negatively you would interpret it.

Very positive	Somewhat positive		Neutral	Somewhat negative		Very negative
1	2	3	4	5	6	7

Examples:

A. You did a great job on that project.   _____

(If you responded *1* for this item, it would mean you think this would be positive to hear from a friend.)

B. Would you do me a favor?   _____

(If you responded *5* for this item, it would mean you think this would be somewhat negative to hear from a friend.)

You are hearing each of the following comments or questions from a friend.

1. Did you study for that test?   _____
2. You have an unusual look about you.   _____
3. You're so talkative.   _____
4. Are you going to eat all of that?   _____
5. If you put in more effort, I'm sure you'd be very successful.   _____
6. I didn't even recognize you!   _____
7. You seem unusually witty today.   _____
8. Are you wearing any makeup?   _____

You are hearing each of the following comments or questions from a *male* friend.

9. You sure did ask a lot of questions in class today.   _____
10. Did you hear about that new diet?   _____
11. You're so sensitive.   _____
12. It would be healthy for you to work out.   _____
13. Are you stressed out about school?   _____
14. You're very muscular.   _____
15. You're acting like a different person these days.   _____
16. Did you get some sleep last night?   _____

From the Commentary Interpretation Scale, an unpublished scale by K. C. Wood, Altabe, and Thompson. Reprinted with permission from the authors. For more information, see K. C. Wood et al. (1998).

APPENDIX 10B
ASSESSMENT OF PERSONAL CONSTRUCT SYSTEM
QUESTIONNAIRE: SELF AND OTHERS

Choose one of the following people to describe:

me as I'd like to be	an admired person	a thin person I know
me now	mother	me much fatter
me as I will be in a year's time	father	me much thinner
	a pitied person	a fat person I know

Rate that person along the following dimensions:

A.   Heavy in weight   Light in weight

   1   2   3   4   5

B.   Attractive appearance   Unattractive in appearance

   1   2   3   4   5

C.   Normal   Abnormal

   1   2   3   4   5

D.   Self-confident   Not self-confident

   1   2   3   4   5

E.   Strong in character   Weak in character

   1   2   3   4   5

F.   Healthy   Unhealthy

   1   2   3   4   5

G.   Concerned about weight   Unconcerned about weight

   1   2   3   4   5

H.   Good   Bad

   1   2   3   4   5

I.   Has abilities   Lacks abilities

   1   2   3   4   5

J.   Extroverted   Introverted

   1   2   3   4   5

K.   Happy   Sad

   1   2   3   4   5

From the Assessment of Personal Construct System Questionnaire, an unpublished questionnaire by P. Butow. Reprinted with permission from the author. For more information, see Butow et al. (1993).

APPENDIX 10C
PHYSICAL APPEARANCE DISCREPANCY QUESTIONNAIRE: FORMAT, SCORING RULES, AND A CASE EXAMPLE

The purpose of this questionnaire is to find out about your beliefs about your own physical appearance. You will be asked to describe attributes (physical appearance traits) that you actually have and those you ideally would like to have. Please list a minimum of four attributes per page.

Trait	Extent (1–4)

Please list the physical appearance attributes of the type of person you believe you actually are now.

1. _____ _____
2. _____ _____
3. _____ _____
4. _____ _____
5. _____ _____
6. _____ _____
7. _____ _____
8. _____ _____

For each physical appearance attribute above, rate the extent to which you believe you actually possess the trait, using the following scale.

Slightly	Moderately	A great deal	Extremely
1	2	3	4

Trait	Extent (1–4)

Please list the physical appearance attributes of the type of person you believe you would ideally like to be (i.e., wish, desire, or hope to be).

1. _____ _____
2. _____ _____
3. _____ _____
4. _____ _____
5. _____ _____
6. _____ _____
7. _____ _____
8. _____ _____

For each physical appearance attribute above, rate the extent to which you believe you would ideally like to possess the trait, using the following scale.

Slightly	Moderately	A great deal	Extremely
1	2	3	4

Trait	Extent (1−4)

Please list the physical appearance attributes of the type of person your society/culture would ideally like you to look like.

1. _____ _____

2. _____ _____

3. _____ _____

4. _____ _____

5. _____ _____

6. _____ _____

7. _____ _____

8. _____ _____

For each physical appearance attribute above, rate the extent to which your society/culture would ideally like you to possess the attribute, using the following scale.

Slightly	Moderately	A great deal	Extremely
1	2	3	4

SCORING RULES

The goal of scoring is to assess the extent to which the participants' ideal differs from their actual appearance. The focus is on the ideal list as it compares with the actual trait list. Use the following scoring guidelines in the order of priority given below. Begin by comparing the ideal trait list with the actual trait list. At least four traits must be on the ideal list. If there are fewer than four traits, do not score. Note however that "compound" ideals such as "long brown hair" would count as two different traits (i.e., long hair and brown hair).

The Nondiscrepancy Rule

If the ideal trait exactly matches an actual trait (the same word or a synonym and the same extent number), score it as −2.

actual list: blue eyes, 3   *ideal list:* blue eyes, 3 = score of −2

The Value Discrepancy Rule

If the ideal trait is the same as or a synonym of an actual trait but differs in extent number take the absolute value of the difference in extent numbers.

actual list: blue eyes, 4   *ideal list:* blue eyes, 2 = score of 2

The Opposing Discrepancy Rule

If the ideal trait is the exact opposite of an actual trait, score it as 4, regardless of extent numbers. Also consider different hair color and different eye color to be opposites.

actual list: fat, 4   *ideal list:* thin, 4 = score of 4

The Relative Discrepancy Rule

A term usually stated with a suffix of *er* indicating a desire for more of this trait is called a relative discrepancy. A desire for less of a trait would fall into this area as well. Examples include taller, thinner, and more muscular. To score these, take the extent number of the ideal trait.

actual list: tan, 2   *ideal list:* tanner, 3 = score of 3
actual list: nothing   *ideal list:* lighter hair, 2 = score of 2

The Ambiguous Discrepancy Rule

If the trait listed on the ideal list is not a synonym or antonym of a trait listed on actual list, but clearly describes the same trait, this is scored as 2.

actual list: medium height, 3   *ideal list:* tall, 4 = score of 2

For each trait on the ideal list, try to apply one of these rules. If none of the rules apply to an ideal trait, score it as 0. Then add up the total for that ideal list. This is the discrepancy score.

A CASE EXAMPLE: AN 18-YEAR-OLD FEMALE CAUCASIAN AMERICAN

Actual Trait	Extent	Own ideal Trait	Extent	Score	Cultural ideal Trait	Extent	Score
Short	2	Tall	1	4	Tall	2	4
Overweight	3	Slim	2	4	Slender	2	4
Redhead	4	Redhead	4	−2	Redhead	2	2
Freckled	4	Freckled	4	−2	Freckled	0	4
Fair skinned	3	Fair skinned	3	−2	Tan	3	4
Larger than average frame	2	Average frame	2	2	Average frame	2	2
Total discrepancy				4			20

From "Body Image Disturbance: Advances in Assessment and Treatment" (pp. 102–106), by M. N. Altabe and J. K. Thompson, in L. Vandecreek, S. Knapp, and T. L. Jackson (Eds.), *Innovations in Clinical Practice: A Source Book* (Vol. 14), 1995, Sarasota, FL: Professional Resources Press. Copyright 1995 by Professional Resources Press. Reprinted with permission.

APPENDIX 10D
BODY WEIGHT AND SHAPE SELF-SCHEMA SCALE

For each of the following, please indicate "how much does it describe you *now*?"

		Not at all	A little	Somewhat	Quite a bit	Very much
A.	Slim	1	2	3	4	5
B.	Physically fit	1	2	3	4	5
C.	Athletic	1	2	3	4	5
D.	Too fat	1	2	3	4	5
E.	Out-of-shape	1	2	3	4	5
F.	Ugly	1	2	3	4	5
G.	Good looking	1	2	3	4	5

For each of the following, please indicate "how do you think it will describe you in the *future*?"

		Not at all	A little	Somewhat	Quite a bit	Very much
A.	Slim	1	2	3	4	5
B.	Physically fit	1	2	3	4	5
C.	Athletic	1	2	3	4	5
D.	Too fat	1	2	3	4	5
E.	Out-of-shape	1	2	3	4	5
F.	Ugly	1	2	3	4	5
G.	Good looking	1	2	3	4	5

For each of the following, please indicate "how *likely* is it that it will describe you in the *future*?"

		Not at all	A little	Somewhat	Quite a bit	Very much
A.	Slim	1	2	3	4	5
B.	Physically fit	1	2	3	4	5
C.	Athletic	1	2	3	4	5
D.	Too fat	1	2	3	4	5
E.	Out-of-shape	1	2	3	4	5
F.	Ugly	1	2	3	4	5
G.	Good looking	1	2	3	4	5

Note that these items were selected from the more extensive list of this scale. Psychometrics are based on the full version. From the Body Weight and Shape Self-Schema Scale, an unpublished scale by K. F. Stein. Reprinted with permission from the author. For more information, see K. F. Stein and Hedger (1997).

APPENDIX 10E
THE SIGNAL DETECTION APPROACH

As the main concept in signal detection, perception is not a simple sensory task because all the sensations people receive from their sensory organs are noisy and imprecise. Consider the following example.

You get off an airplane into a crowded terminal. You have landed in a strange city after a long flight. You are walking toward the baggage claim when you hear, "Groeaugthlinns." Is someone calling your name? Is someone calling for someone else? Or are your ears still clogged from the change in air pressure? Consider how likely you are to perceive the sound Groeaugthlinns as your name if you are expecting to meet someone in the terminal. Being "biased" by your prior knowledge or expectation is not an error or problem; it is part of the natural course of perception. Signal detection is all about separating the expectation—bias component from the sensory sensitivity of the system.

What if you were interested in disentangling the sensory from the nonsensory components for body size perception? You wonder, Are anorexic people truly unable to sense the change in their bodies? Has their experience with focusing on their body made them hyperaware of the slightest change in their body? If so, this might reflect sensory differences. Or do they expect their body to look distorted and ugly? Or maybe they expect to see the body they had when they were heavier. If so, this might reflect bias—expectation differences.

So you decide to undertake a signal detection analysis. This analysis is based on the probability graphs depicted in Figure 10E.1. Remember that any information perceived occurs against a background of noise that can be misconstrued as a target stimulus (e.g., the challenge of the airport situation). Similarly, noise alone could be perceived as a stimulus. Consider line A as the probability distribution for when there is no stimulus or distortion. In the absence of distortion, sensing some distortion happens with a certain frequency. In the presence of distortion, sensing distortion is a more probable occurrence. Thus, there are two probability distortions: one for when a signal is present and one for when a signal is absent. A signal-present distribution has a higher sensation strength. The difference between the peak of the two curves, the most common sensation in the presence of the stimulus, is the best estimate of the sensory sensitivity of the system. It is referred to as d' (d prime). The more difficult the perceptual task, the more minimal the sound or distortion, the greater the overlap between the distributions, and the lower the d'. Because of the overlap in distribution, it is unclear for the perceiver which sensation strength is associated with the stimulus. It is a guessing game. Perhaps the person is very willing to perceive an image as too wide because of his or her beliefs. If so, he or she would tend to put the criterion fairly low in relation to the sensation strength. Maybe another individual prefers to be very sure before saying an image of himself or herself is distorted. His or her criterion would be higher. The criterion is sometimes referred to as β (Beta).

Thus, we have a general idea of the relationship between stimulus strength and sensation strength. We can see how sensitivity and bias measures may be derived. Let us look at some data from Gardner (1996; see Figure 10E.2). In this figure, participants were shown images distorted to be thin, heavy, and normal. They were asked to respond with "too thin" or "too wide." The graph shows the relationship between the actual distortion (computer generated) and the "too wide" judgments made by the participants.

Clearly, first it is not an easy sensory task with perfect sensitivity; that might look like the left of Figure 10E.3. In this figure, if the image was distorted 0%, 1%, or 2%, the participant would never report too wide; but at the magic 4%, threshold, the participant would always perceive the distortion. We know that because sensations occur in a background of noise, this scenario would never

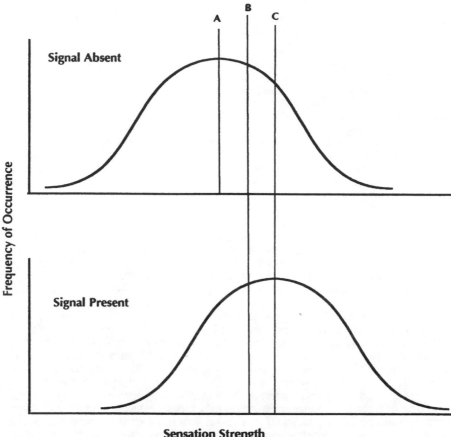

Figure 10E.1. Probability graphs showing the relationship between sensory activity level and frequency of occurrence. For example, Point A in the upper graph represents the average sensation strength an individual would experience when there is no signal present. Individuals must decide at what sensation strength they will respond, "yes, there was a signal." The "yes" point corresponds to Point B in the figure and is also called the criterion. Note that there are errors wherever the criterion is placed (consider the area to the right of Point B on the signal absent graph and to the left of that point on the signal present graph). The placement of the criterion represents the individual's bias in judging stimuli. The difference between the means of the two distributions, A and C, is the sensitivity of an individual's system to the stimulus. For a strong stimulus (e.g., a bright light, a figure distorted 25%), the distributions of the two graphs would have minimal overlap, high sensitivity, and few errors. To the extent that a stimulus is barely more potent than the background sensory noise, the graphs would overlap, sensitivity would be low, and errors would result wherever the criterion was placed.

happen. However, the closer the data comes to the figure, also known as the slope of the ascending curve, the better the individual's sensitivity. Consider the curve on the right of Figure 10E.3. Here, it takes a large change in the stimulus to alter the percentage of too wide judgments. Thus, sensitivity is related to slope.

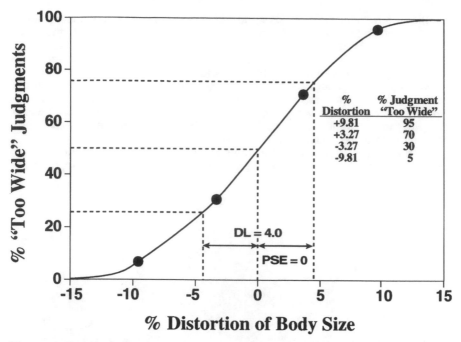

% Distortion	% Judgment "Too Wide"
+9.81	95
+3.27	70
-3.27	30
-9.81	5

% Distortion of Body Size (x-axis)

% "Too Wide" Judgments (y-axis)

DL = 4.0

PSE = 0

Figure 10E.2. Best fit cumulative normal sigmoid curve for "too wide" judgments presented at four levels of distortion. The PSE [point of subjective equality] corresponds to the percentage of body size distortion where the participant made 50% "too wide" judgments. The DL [difference threshold] reflects the amount of change in body size distortion necessary for the participant to detect a change in body size 50% of the time. Note that this study used adaptive probit estimation for determining sensitivity and bias. From "Methodological Issues in Assessment of the Perceptual Component of Body Image Disturbance," by R. M. Gardner, 1996, *British Journal of Psychology, 87*, p. 334. Copyright 1996 by the British Psychological Society. Reprinted with permission.

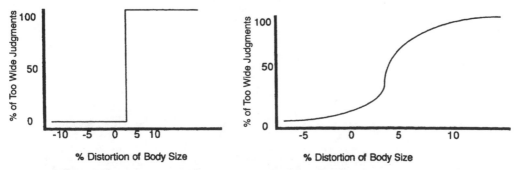

Figure 10E.3. Alternative relationships between the percentage of distortion in the stimulus and the proportion of "too wide" judgments: theoretical absolute threshold (left) and data from hypothetical participant with less sensitivity than those in Gardner's (1996) study (right).

Bias corresponds most closely to the 50% judgment point: the stimulus strength at which the participant reports a change in body size 50% of the time. That point could be the same, regardless of sensitivity. Given the same sensitivity, one person may have a higher criterion on the curve to report the presence of distortion. The two variables, sensitivity and bias, are mostly independent.

Gardner and colleagues (e.g., Gardner, Jones, & Bokenkamp, 1995) have adapted a variant of the signal detection method, called the *adaptive probit estimation.* This method allows for separation of sensory and nonsensory factors with fewer trials. In addition, one can derive the point of subjective equality (PSE) as an estimate of the individual's perceived actual size.

Perception is a result of the interplay of sensation and cognition. The cognitive–bias component is essential to perceiving a signal in a noisy world.

11

FUTURE DIRECTIONS: INTEGRATIVE THEORIES, MULTIDIMENSIONAL ASSESSMENTS, AND MULTICOMPONENT INTERVENTIONS

In the previous chapters, we examined a number of influences that have received varying levels of empirical support as explanatory factors for body image disturbance. The advantage of constructing individual chapters for each hypothesis or theory is that each approach can receive singular attention and examination. In addition, this tactic allowed us to blend the research overview with more clinically related assessment and treatment information specific to each model. Of course, two disadvantages are that no unitary approach captures the complexity of body image and all one-factor models are limited. For this reason, some researchers have begun to test multiple factors and suggest integrative models. In addition, researchers are beginning to offer comprehensive assessment batteries, with subscales designed to assess many of the risk and maintaining factors reviewed in our previous eight chapters. Finally, new and innovative treatment approaches promise to challenge, and possibly revolutionize, the content of interventions for body image disturbance. In this brief final chapter, we offer some of the most recent multifactorial approaches for theory, assessment, and treatment and note avenues for future research.

INTEGRATIVE THEORETICAL APPROACHES

The model developed by Cash (1996), illustrated in Figure 11.1, is perhaps the most unified current model. This model is based on Cash's extensive research and available data. Its central feature is a separation of historical and proximal influences, which might also be conceptualized as early developmental–causal and maintaining factors. In our review of factors in this book, we extensively covered two of his historical factors: physical attributes and cultural and interpersonal socialization. Chapters on sociocultural factors, social feedback, interpersonal issues, and feminist views, among others, detailed the vast influence of American society and the interpersonal spheres. Physical attributes, such as being overweight, were also examined, and the particular bodily experiences of being female were explored in chapters 1, 7, and 8.

It is interesting to note that we found little in the way of an organized database for Cash's personality attributes box, yet if we take a broad view of "personality" as certain individual difference variables, our examination of the moderating influence of factors such as internalization of societal values and sex-role orientation (chapter 3), degree of social comparison (chapter 4), a history of negative appearance-related feedback (chapter 5), and sexual orientation (chapter 1) is indicative of the role of dispositional

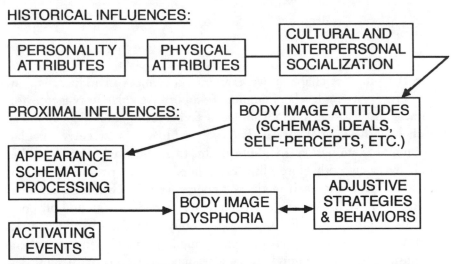

Figure 11.1. A model of historical and proximal influences. These influences jointly affect body image, producing dysphoria that leads to the use of behaviors and strategies to reduce the accompanying distress. From "The Treatment of Body Image Disturbance" (p. 85), by T. F. Cash, in J. K. Thompson (Ed.), *Body Image, Eating Disorders, and Obesity: An Integrative Guide for Assessment and Treatment*, 1996, Washington, DC: American Psychological Association. Copyright 1996 by the American Psychological Association. Reprinted with permission.

moderators of level of disturbance. Proximal influences in the model, such as schemas and schematic processing, clearly reflect the recent emergence of cognitive models as deserving a central location in any theory of body image—an area we covered in chapter 10. Activating events, consisting of any type of internal or external cue or perhaps a life stressor, were mentioned in the context of conditioning and avoidance in our chapter on behavioral influences.

Although Cash's model has not yet received empirical testing, various researchers, who are using primarily covariance structure modeling procedures, have evaluated certain components of the model. Veron-Guidry, Williamson, and Netemeyer (1997) evaluated social pressure for thinness, self-esteem, and depression as factors in the prediction of body dysphoria for female adolescents (ages 8–13). Both personality variables were significantly related to the social pressure factor; however, neither was a significant predictor of body image. Nonetheless, the social pressure measure did significantly predict body image, which was also a significant predictor of eating disturbance (see Figure 11.2).

Williamson et al. (1995) also tested the effects of social influence (perceived pressure regarding weight), performance anxiety, and self-appraisal on body image in a group of 98 female college athletes. All three factors predicted concern with appearance, which, as with the previous study, also significantly predicted level of eating disturbance (see Figure 11.3).

Stice, Shaw, and Nemeroff (1998), in a multifactorial model of bulimic symptoms, dietary restraint, and negative affect, tested the contributions of body mass, perceived social pressure, and internalization of ideal body standards in the prediction of body satisfaction (see Figure 11.4). All factors were significant, with the perceived pressure having a direct effect on body image and internalization having an indirect effect.

J. K. Thompson, Coovert, et al. (1995) evaluated the effects of teasing, maturational status, and actual degree of obesity on body image. It is interesting to note that the level of obesity did not directly affect body satisfaction but was mediated by teasing level: Only those individuals who were also teased had high levels of dissatisfaction (see Figure 11.5).

J. K. Thompson, Coovert, and Stormer (in press) directly addressed the social comparison factor as a mediator of body image. In a sample of female college students, they found that the effect of teasing on body image was mediated through social comparison, suggesting that "negative verbal feedback may engender deleterious social comparison processes that augment the possibility of appearance concerns" (also see Figure 11.6).

Finally, in Figure 11.7, we present an integrative heuristic for future research on the diverse factors that affect body image and the consequent effects of body image disturbance on closely associated conditions, such as eating disturbance and global psychological functioning (i.e., self-esteem,

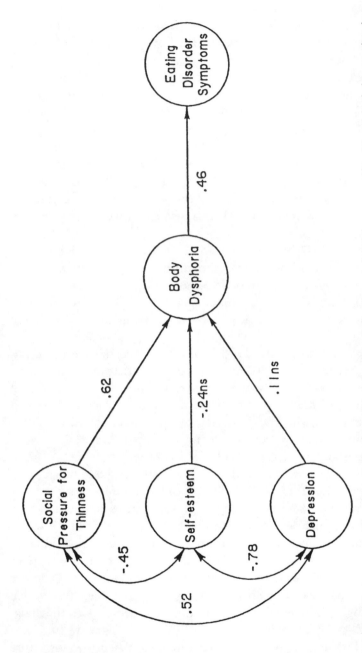

Figure 11.2. A covariance structural model testing the role of social pressure for thinness, self-esteem, and depression in producing body dysphoria. The findings indicate that only social pressures are significantly related to body dysphoria, which in turn significantly predicts eating disorder symptoms. From "Structural Equation Modeling of Risk Factors for the Development of Eating Disorder Symptoms in Female Athletes," by D. A. Williamson, R. G. Netemeyer, L. P. Jackman, D. A. Anderson, C. L. Funsch, and J. Y. Rabalais, 1995, *International Journal of Eating Disorders, 17*, p. 389. Copyright 1995 by John Wiley & Sons, Inc. Reprinted by permission of John Wiley & Sons, Inc.

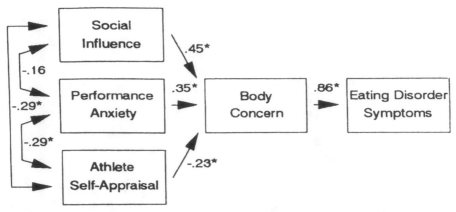

Figure 11.3. A covariance structural model testing the role of social influence, performance anxiety, and self-appraisal in producing body concern. The results indicate that all three factors are significant in the prediction of body concern, which is also a significant predictor of eating disorder symptoms. From "Structural Modeling Analysis of Body Dysphoria and Eating Disorder Symptoms in Preadolescent Girls," by S. Veron-Guidry, D. A. Williamson, and R. G. Netemeyer, 1997, *Eating Disorders: The Journal of Treatment and Assessment, 5*, p. 23. Copyright 1997 by Brunner/Mazel Inc. Reprinted with permission.

depression). These two models focus on our tripartite model of core influences: peers, parents, and media. Figure 11.7A indicates that these three sources of influence lead to social comparisons regarding appearance and internalization of societal values (internalization is also affected indirectly by social comparison). Both social comparison and internalization lead to body dissatisfaction, which influences restrictive and bulimic eating disturbances. Bulimia has a reciprocal relationship with global psychological functioning (e.g., J. K. Thompson, Coovert, et al., 1995).

Figure 11.7B is a competing model that moves the psychological functioning variable to the middle of the sequence. Specifically, in this model, self-esteem and depression become mediators between the three core influences (peers, parents, media) and increased frequency of comparison and internalization. For instance, this model, as opposed to the prior one, suggests that individuals low in self-esteem and high in depression are more vulnerable to factors that produce an awareness of appearance pressures and thus are more likely to engage in social comparison and internalization, leading to body dissatisfaction.

MULTIDIMENSIONAL ASSESSMENT

Throughout this book, we focused on the examination and presentation of scales (many of which have been reproduced in appendixes) that would allow the clinician and researcher to measure a specific component

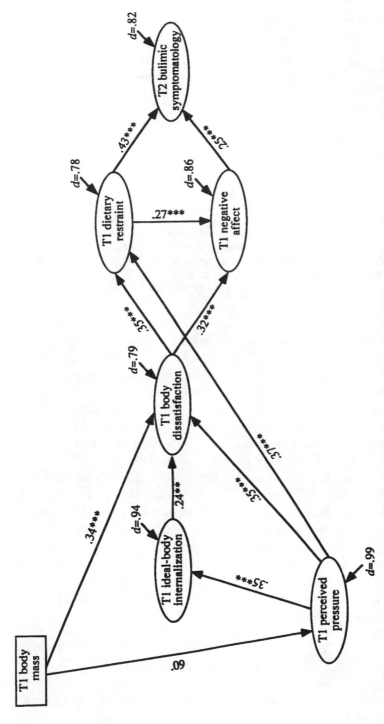

Figure 11.4. A covariance structural model evaluating the direct and indirect influences of body mass, perceived pressures to be thin, and internalization of societal body ideals on body dissatisfaction. As the asterisk indicates, all paths—with the exception of the path from body mass to perceived pressures—were significant. T1 = Time 1; T2 = Time 2. ** *p* < .05. *** *p* < .01. From "Dual Pathway Model of Bulimia Nervosa: Longitudinal Support for Dietary Restraint and Affect-Regulation Mechanisms," by E. Stice, H. Shaw, and C. Nemeroff, 1998, *Journal of Social and Clinical Psychology, 17,* p. 139. Copyright 1998 by Guilford Press. Reprinted with permission of the Guilford Press.

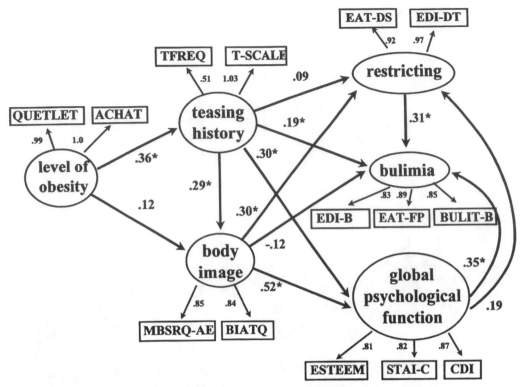

Figure 11.5. A covariance structural model evaluating the direct effects of level of obesity on teasing and both direct and indirect effects of level of obesity on body image disturbance. The findings suggest that the effect of weight status on body image is indirectly mediated through teasing. Teasing also has a significant impact on bulimia but not on restriction level. Body image disturbance is a significant predictor of restriction level and psychological function but not bulimia. ACHAT = age-based weight percentile; BIATQ = Body-Image Automatic Thoughts Questionnaire; CDI = Children's Depression Inventory; EAT-D = Eating Attitudes Test–Diet; EAT-FP = Eating Attitudes Test–Food Preoccupation; EDI-B = Eating Disorder Inventory–Bulimia; EDI-DT = Eating Disorder Inventory–Drive for Thinness; ESTEEM = self-esteem; MBSRQ-AE = Multidimensional Body Self-Relations Questionnaire–Appearance Evaluation scale; QUETLET = (weight ÷ height)^2; STAI-C = State–Trait Anxiety Inventory–Children; TFREQ = teasing frequency; T-SCALE = Teasing Scale. * = significant pathways. From "Development of Body Image, Eating Disturbance, and General Psychological Functioning in Female Adolescents: Covariance Structural Modeling and Longitudinal Investigations," by J. K. Thompson, M. Coovert, K. Richards, S. Johnson, and J. Cattarin, 1995, *International Journal of Eating Disorders, 18*, p. 231. Copyright 1995 by John Wiley & Sons, Inc. Reprinted by permission of John Wiley & Sons, Inc.

of body image or a hypothesized associated variable (e.g., peer teasing, media pressures). In fact, almost all of the available measures were developed by authors with the goal of measuring one, or at most two, specific variables. Certainly, there is a logic to the strategy of selecting mea-

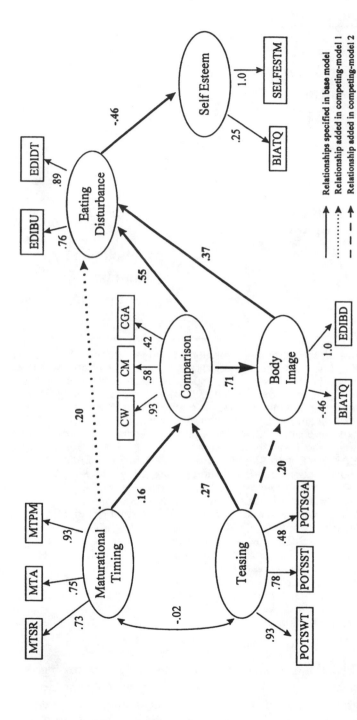

Figure 11.6. A covariance structural model evaluating the direct effects of maturational timing and teasing on appearance comparison, the direct and indirect effects of teasing on body image disturbance, and the direct effects of appearance comparison and body image disturbance on eating disturbance. The findings suggest the competing Model 2, which includes the dashed line from teasing to body image, is the best fit of the data. Thus, teasing is directly related to comparison and body image; teasing also indirectly produces body image through its effect on comparison. Body image and comparison have direct effects on eating disturbance. BIATQ = Body-Image Automatic Thoughts Questionnaire; CGA = comparison–general appearance; CM = comparison–muscularity; CW = comparison–weight; EDIBD = Eating Disorder Inventory–Body Dissatisfaction subscale; EDIBU = Eating Disorder Inventory–Bulimia; EDIDT = Eating Disorder Inventory–Drive for Thinness; MTA = maturational timing–age; MTPM = maturational timing–peer menarche; MTSR = maturational timing–subjective ratios; POTSGA = Perception of Teasing Scale–General Appearance; POTSST = Perception of Teasing Scale–Site Specific Teasing; POTSWT = Perception of Teasing Scale–Weight Teasing; SELFESTM = self-esteem. From J. K. Thompson, Coovert, and Stormer (in press).

sures based on their documented psychometric properties and relevance for the presenting symptomatology of a particular client—in effect, creating your own multidimensional assessment battery. In fact, this idiographic, hypothesis-testing model of clinical practice is one that others have advocated (e.g., J. K. Thompson & Williams, 1987).

However, there is also an advantage to the presence in one's assessment armamentarium of a multifactorial scale, designed for the measurement of multiple factors. Perhaps the most comprehensive instrument currently available for the assessment of the multiple components of body image is that developed by Cash and colleagues (T. A. Brown, Cash, & Mikulka, 1990; Cash, 1996, 1997). His Multidimensional Body Self-Relations Questionnaire has subscales that assess (a) appearance evaluation, (b) appearance orientation (e.g., cognitive–behavioral investment in appearance), and (c) body satisfaction (the Body Areas Satisfaction scale). Several of Cash's other scales, including the Body Image Ideals Scale and the Situational Inventory of Body-Image Dysphoria, when added to his Multidimensional Body Self-Relations Questionnaire create perhaps the most impressive multicomponent approach for the assessment of body image disturbance (see Cash, 1996, 1997, for guidelines). (Note that many of these scales are contained in this book's appendixes to specific chapters, and information is presented in tables within chapters.)

The development of a multidimensional assessment of risk factors instrument has only recently intrigued researchers, perhaps because the field of basic research in this area is still quite new. However, one recent measure, the McKnight Risk Factor Survey (see Appendix 11A), has been developed to fill this gap (Shisslak et al., in press). This scale has been extensively piloted, and the current version is the third iteration of the original scale. It was administered to 651 fourth- through twelfth-grade girls, and psychometric properties were described (Shisslak et al., in press). The McKnight scale consists of 17 domains that assess risk and protective factors for disordered eating behaviors. Many of these domains are consistent with factors noted throughout this book as influences for the development and maintenance of body image disturbance—a facet of the scale that makes it appropriate for consideration as a tool for body image assessment. For example, such factors as weight-related teasing, the role of one's social group in modeling weight concern, media modeling, and sports pressure to be thin are some of the domains assessed. In addition, personality and psychological functioning factors, such as perfectionism, confidence, and depression, are also included. Certainly, this newly emerged multidimensional scale should receive serious consideration as an adjunct to the other scales noted throughout our book for the measurement of risk and associated features.

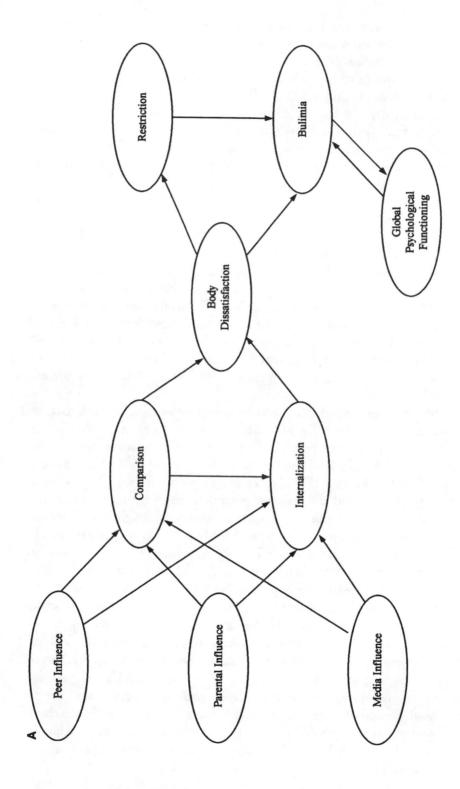

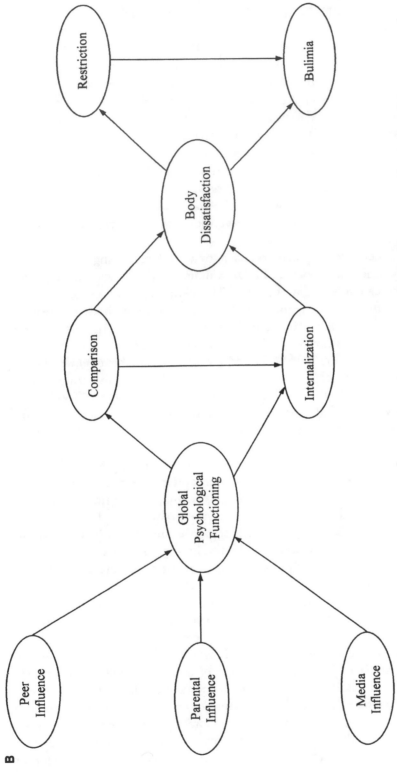

Figure 11.7. Two hypothetical integrative models for the development of body image disturbance. A indicates that three sources of influence (peers, parents, media) lead to social comparison and internalization; these two factors, in turn, lead to body dissatisfaction, which influences both types of eating disturbances. Bulimia has a reciprocal relationship with global psychological functioning. B moves the psychological functioning factor to an earlier stage, suggesting that it mediates between the three formative influences (peers, parents, media) and the development of social comparison tendencies and internalization of societal values.

MULTIFACTORIAL TREATMENT

At the outset of chapter 2, we noted that several strategies had been developed for treating body image disturbance. We also noted that the multicomponent cognitive–behavioral procedures developed by Cash (1995b, 1996, 1997) and J. C. Rosen (1996a, 1996b, 1997) had received extensive empirical validation as efficacious for the modification of many different components of body image disturbance. These approaches contain several strategies that target the cognitive and behavioral aspects of disturbance (e.g., chapters 9 and 10) and have procedures that address a sociocultural influence and social comparison processes (chapter 3 and 4). Therefore, in a sense, we are well on the way in terms of research progress in the area of multicomponent intervention methods and the empirical evaluation of treatment packages.

One recent development offers a new and refreshing approach to treatment—one made possible by the unique technological advances afforded to researchers leading into the 21st century. Riva (1998, in press) is at the forefront of the application of virtual reality methods for treating body image disturbance. His procedure, labeled virtual environment for body image modification (VEBIM) is a Pentium-based immersive virtual reality system (Pentium II 266 MHz, 64 megaRAM, graphic engine, Matrox Millennium II with 8Mb WRAM). His VEBIM uses a five-zone virtual environment, which was developed using the Sense 8 World ToolKit for Windows (V. 2.02). A description of the five zones and the tactics relevant to the assessment and treatment of body image disturbance is contained in Exhibit 11.1.

One of the outstanding aspects of this treatment approach is its multicomponent angle: Cognitive, behavioral, and perceptual aspects of disturbance are targeted. Cognitive strategies include countering, alternative interpretation, label shifting, and deactivating the illness belief. From a behavioral perspective, exposure with response prevention is used; visual-motor (perceptual) techniques include developing an awareness of any perceptual problems along with modification consisting of imagery exercises. Table 11.1 contains a complete detailing of these strategies.

In the one empirical study to date with the VEBIM method, it was found to reduce dissatisfaction in a group of women "attending a virtual reality conference" (Riva, 1998, p. 166) in comparison to a control group. Thus, this technique needs much more empirical testing before we can understand its efficacy for a broad range of individuals with diverse body image issues. In addition, to date, we do not have follow-up data on this method. Therefore, it would be premature to offer it as a procedure equivalent to the often-tested cognitive–behavioral strategies of Cash and J. C. Rosen. However, this virtual reality procedure, and the many similar ones that are sure to be developed in the near future, deserves to receive rigorous

EXHIBIT 11.1
Characteristics of the Virtual Environment

The first two zones are designed both to give the participant a minimum level of skill in perceiving, moving through, and manipulating objects in virtual reality and to focus attention on eating and food choice. The two environments can also be used by the therapist for a comprehensive assessment of stimuli that could elicit abnormal eating behavior. This assessment is normally part of the temptation exposure with response prevention protocol. The next three zones are designed to modify the body experience of the participant.

Zone 1: In this zone, the participant becomes acquainted with the appropriate control device, the head mounted display, and the recognition of collisions. To move into the next zone, participants have to weigh themselves on a virtual balance. The balance is used for two functions:

- as an inevitable obstacle for the user, who must focus his or her attention on this object, representing the importance of the "weight" dimension in the experiences to come thereafter.
- if needed by the therapist, as a display of the initial weight of the participant, as acquired in the dialogue box at the beginning of body image virtual reality system.

Zone 2a and 2b: These zones show a kitchen (2a) and office (2b). Each of these rooms is furnished with typical items and contains different foods and drinks. When the user decides to "eat" or "drink" something, all he or she has to do is "touch" a specific item. In this way, the food is "eaten" and the corresponding caloric intake is automatically recorded in a text file, which is later used to calculate the total intake of calories. At the end of the second zone is located a second virtual balance. According to the "eaten" food and to the caloric intake inserted at the beginning of body image virtual reality system, the balance shows the new weight of the participant (in kilograms).

Zone 3: In this zone, the participant is exposed to a series of panels that are textured with pictures of models, in the typical way of the advertising world. The images are used as stimuli to support a cognitive approach: The elicited feelings are subject to an analysis by the therapist according to the label shifting and objective counters methods. The feelings and their associated beliefs are identified, broken down into their logical components, replaced with two or more descriptive words, and then analyzed.

Zone 4: In this zone, the user finds a large mirror. Standing by it, the participant can look at his or her real body, previously digitized using an Epson Photo PC camera. The vision of his or her body usually elicits in the user strong feelings that can be matched using the counterattacking and countering cognitive methods. The mirror is also used, as indicated by S. C. Wooley and Wooley (1985), to instruct the user to imagine himself or herself as different on several dimensions, including size, race, and being larger or smaller in particular areas. The user is also asked to imagine himself or herself as younger, older, before and after eating (how one feels and looks) as well as before and after academic–vocational and social successes and failures.

Zone 5: This zone consists of a long corridor, ending with a room containing four doors of different dimensions. The participant can move into the last zone only by choosing the door corresponding exactly to his or her width. This procedure is the same procedure indicated by S. C. Wooley and Wooley (1985) to improve the awareness of body distortion.

From "Virtual Environment for Body Image Modification: Virtual Reality System in the Treatment of Body Image Disturbances," by G. Riva, in press, *Computers in Human Behavior.* Copyright by Elsevier Science. Reprinted with permission from Elsevier Science.

TABLE 11.1
Therapeutic Methods Integrated Into the Virtual Environment
for Body Image Modification

Method	Procedure	Description
Cognitive	Countering	Once a list of distorted perceptions and cognitions is developed, the process of countering these thoughts and beliefs begins. In countering, the patient is taught to recognize the error in thinking, and substitute more appropriate perceptions and interpretations.
	Alternative interpretation	The patient learns to stop and consider other interpretations of a situation before proceeding to the decision-making stage. The patient develops a list of problem situations, evoked emotions, and interpretative beliefs. The therapist and patient discuss each interpretation and if possible identify the kind of objective data that would confirm one of them as correct.
	Label shifting	The patient first tries to identify the kinds of negative words she uses to interpret situations in her life, such as bad, terrible, obese, inferior, and hateful. The situations in which these labels are used are then listed. The patient and therapist replace each emotional label with two or more descriptive words.
	Deactivating the illness belief	The therapist first helps the client list her beliefs concerning eating disorders. The extent to which the illness model influences each belief is identified. The therapist then teaches the client a cognitive/behavioral approach to interpreting maladaptive behavior and shows how bingeing, purging, and dieting can be understood from this framework.

testing as a potential approach for the modification of body image disturbance. Perhaps a first step might be the comparison of Riva's (1998, in press) VEBIM with Cash and J. C. Rosen's cognitive–behavioral approach.

There are also many other tasks left to be done in the treatment arena. For instance, there has actually been very little work in the examination of procedures for challenging an acceptance of societal ideals (chapter 3; see also M. P. Levine & Smolak, in press; and Stormer & Thompson, 1995, 1998). Basic research in the area of social comparison is just beginning, and there is minimal work on assessment and treatment in this area. The focus on appearance-related commentary and interpersonal issues related to body image, although yielding a wealth of anecdotal and descriptive evidence and a few appropriate measures, has yet to produce empirically grounded intervention strategies. Finally, although there is general agreement that feminist approaches offer a multitude of techniques

TABLE 11.1 (*Continued*)

Method	Procedure	Description
Behavioral	Temptation exposure with response prevention	The rationale of temptation exposure with response prevention is to expose the individual to the environmental, cognitive, physiological, and affective stimuli that elicit abnormal behaviors and to prevent them from occurring. The TERP protocol is usually divided into three distinct phases: (1) comprehensive assessment of eliciting stimuli, (2) temptation exposure extinction sessions, and (3) temptation exposure sessions with training in alternative response.
Visual-motorial	Awareness of the distortion	The patients are instructed to develop an awareness of the distortion. This is approached by a number of techniques including the presentation of feedback regarding one's self-image. Videotape feedback is also usually used. Patients are videotaped engaging in a range of activities.
	Modification of the body image	The patients are instructed to imagine themselves as different on several dimensions, including size, race, and being larger or smaller in particular areas. They also are asked to imagine themselves as younger, older, what they look and feel like before and after eating, as well as before and after academic–vocational and social successes and failures.

Note. TERP = temptation exposure with response prevention. From "Virtual Environment for Body Image Modification: Virtual Reality System in the Treatment of Body Image Disturbance," by G. Riva, in press, *Computers in Human Behavior*. Copyright by Elsevier Science. Reprinted with permission from Elsevier Science.

that may serve as primary or ancillary treatments for many individuals with body image problems, particularly those with abusive sexual experiences, these approaches have yet to receive substantial empirical testing (Kearney-Cooke & Striegel-Moore, 1997).

Prevention of body image disturbance is an area of inquiry related to the treatment that should receive great attention in the coming years (M. P. Levine, in press; M. P. Levine & Smolak, in press). Researchers are not only conducting controlled studies to elucidate effective strategies for preventing body image problems in adolescence but have also advocated the targeting of wider audiences through social marketing approaches (M. P. Levine, in press; J. K. Thompson & Heinberg, in press). Social marketing has been defined as the "adaptation of commercial marketing techniques to programs designed to influence the voluntary behavior of target audiences to improve their personal welfare and that of the society of which they are a part" (Andreasen, 1994, p. 110). With regard to body image, it is suggested that the media may glamorize eating and shape-related disorders through pairings with celebrities, the lack of negative consequences of extreme behaviors (e.g., starvation, excessive exercise), or both to achieve an unrealistic weight (J. K. Thompson & Heinberg, in press). A most difficult but necessary task will be to cooperate with all forms of media in the goal of producing messages that reduce, rather than promote, an obsession with appearance. For instance, the development of television shows for children (or adults, for that matter) that address the negative psychological effects of teasing others about appearance, is one such strategy based on social marketing.

CONCLUSIONS

We are just beginning to understand the complex interrelationships among variables thought to produce and maintain negative feelings regarding one's appearance. From a research perspective, future investigations should further detail the importance and uniqueness of the factors explored throughout this book. However, we encourage more detective work that is designed to uncover novel influences that have not yet been described. In addition, testing multiple factors through covariance structure prospective research designs should be a primary goal of future research (Vandenburg & Thompson, 1998).

A strong database exists for the clinical assessment and management of body image problems. Cognitive–behavioral treatment strategies and a wealth of assessment methods have received empirical validation and should be integrated into any clinician's battery of clinical approaches. Feminist strategies are essential in the treatment of certain cases, particularly those with a component of sexual abuse–harassment and interpersonal–societal issues that pertain to the unique situations encountered by women in American society. Many other approaches, ranging from exercise to virtual reality to "fat acceptance" programs, have been suggested as interventions for body image problems. As we enter the 21st century— at a time when life expectancy is increasing and baby beauty pageants are all the rage—it is likely that new theoretical, assessment, and treatment paradigms will emerge to help psychologists comprehend and cope with these and multiple other influences that are sure to affect body image in the next millennium.

Domain	Scale	Question content
Maturity	Reaction to Body Changes scale	Two questions combined: ■ How bothered are you about your body changing? ■ How bothered are you about others noticing your body changes?
	Period scale	Have you gotten your first period yet?
	Period Started scale	If yes, what grade were you in when you got your first period?
Psychological	Weight Control Behaviors scale	Six questions combined: In the past year, how often have you tried to lose weight? In the past year, how often have you tried to lose weight by ■ starving (not eating) for a day or more? ■ cutting back on what you ate? ■ skipping meals? ■ exercising? ■ eating less sweets or fatty foods?
	Overconcern With Weight and Shape scale	Five questions combined: In the past year, how often have you ■ thought about having fat on your body? ■ felt fat? ■ thought about wanting to be thinner? ■ worried about gaining two pounds? In the past year, how much has your weight made a difference in how you feel about yourself?
Eating disorder	Binge scale	Two questions combined: In the past year, how often ■ have you kept eating and eating and felt like you could not stop? ■ did you eat a lot of food in a short amount of time when it was not a meal or a holiday?
	Purge scale	Three questions combined: In the past year, how often have you tried to lose weight by ■ taking diet pills? ■ taking laxatives or "water" pills? ■ making yourself throw up after you ate?
Weight teasing	Incidence scale	Four questions combined: In the past year, how often ■ have you been teased about your weight? ■ has your brother or sister made fun of you because of your weight? ■ have girls made fun of your weight? ■ have boys made fun of you because of your weight?

Appendix continues

Domain	Scale	Question content
	Effect scale	Four questions combined: ■ If you have been teased about your weight in the past year, how much has it changed the way you feel about yourself? ■ If boys have teased you about your weight in the past year, how much has it changed the way you feel about yourself? ■ If girls have teased you about your weight in the past year, how much has it changed the way you feel about yourself? ■ Have you changed your weight so as not to be teased?
	Adult Teasing scale	Three questions combined: In the past year, how often has ■ your father made a comment to you about your weight or your eating that made you feel bad? ■ a teacher or coach made a comment to you about your weight that made you feel bad? ■ your mother made a comment to you about your weight or your eating that made you feel bad?
Body appearance/ appraisal		Three questions combined: In the past year, how often have you ■ felt ugly? ■ felt pretty? ■ been happy with the way your body looks?
Parents	Family Eating Disorder scale	Has anyone in your family ever had an eating disorder?
	Concern With Thinness scale	Two questions combined: In the past year, how important has it been ■ to your mother that you be thin? ■ to your father that you be thin?
Mother diets		In the past year, how often has your mother tried to lose weight?
Social group	Weight Rejection scale	Two questions combined: In the past year, how much do you think ■ your weight made boys not like you? ■ your weight made girls not like you?
	Concern With Peer Thinness scale	Three questions combined: ■ In the past year, how often have your friends talked about wanting to lose weight? ■ In the past year, how important has it been to your friends that you be thin? ■ In the past year, how important has it been to your friends that they be thin?

Appendix continues

Domain	Scale	Question content
	Eating scale	Two questions combined: In the past year, how often have you changed ■ your eating when you were around girls or young women? ■ your eating when you were around boys?
Dating	Started Dating scale	Have you started to date?
	Grade When Starting Dating scale	If yes, what grade were you in when you started to date?
	Pressure to Date scale	In the past year, have you felt pressured by friends to date?
Life events	Life Events in Past Year scale	Six questions combined: Do you go to a different school now than you did last year? Has anyone important to you died? In the past year, ■ have you broken up with a boyfriend? ■ have you lost a friend (e.g., because of a fight or a move)? ■ have any of your pets died? ■ have your parents separated or divorced?
	Bothered by Life Events scale	Six questions combined: ■ Different school? ■ Broken up with boyfriend? ■ Lost a friend? ■ Pet died? ■ Parents separated? ■ Someone died?
Coping (middle and high school only)		Three questions combined: When you experience something that is stressful, how often do you ■ say to yourself "this isn't real"? ■ use alcohol or drugs to get through it? ■ give up trying to deal with it?
Demographics	SES–Mom Education	How much school has your mother had?
	SES–Dad Education	How much school has your father had?
	Ethnicity scale	Which one of the groups below best describes what you consider yourself to be?
	Acculturation scale	What is the main language you speak at home?
	Family status	Are your parents separated or divorced?
Media modelling		In the past year, how much have you tried to look like the girls or women you see on television or in magazines?
Confidence		Three questions combined: In the past year, how often did you feel sure of yourself? Have you liked things about yourself? Have you been happy just the way you are?

Appendix continues

Domain	Scale	Question content
Support	Number of People Talk To scale	Nine questions combined: Please circle any of the people you talk to when you have a problem: ■ Mother/stepmother ■ Father/stepfather ■ Brother/stepbrother ■ Sister/stepsister ■ Friend ■ Coach ■ Teacher ■ No one ■ Other
	Having Someone There for You scale	Three questions combined: In the past year, have you had someone ■ you can count on to listen to you when you need to talk? ■ to love you and make you feel wanted? ■ to have a good time with?
	Sharing scale	Three questions combined: In the past year, how often have you had someone ■ to give you good advice about a problem? ■ to share your most private worries and fears with? ■ to help you understand a problem when you needed it?
Substance use		Three questions combined: In the past year, how often did you ■ drink alcohol? ■ smoke cigarettes? ■ use drugs (not medicine)?
Bothered by substance pressure		Three questions combined: If yes, how much has this pressure ■ to drink alcohol bothered you? ■ to smoke cigarettes bothered you? ■ to use drugs bothered you?
Gain weight		In the past year, how often have you tried to gain weight?
School performance		In the past year, how have you been doing in school?
Safety		Two questions combined: In the past year, have you felt ■ unsafe or threatened at school? ■ unsafe or threatened outside of school?
Depression symptoms		Six questions combined: In the past year, how often did you ■ feel worthless? ■ notice you didn't have as much energy as you usually do? ■ feel "down in the dumps" or "depressed"?

Appendix continues

Domain	Scale	Question content
Activities		■ feel hopeful about the future? ■ have trouble concentrating? ■ have trouble enjoying the activities you usually enjoy? Specify the number of days of the week that you usually had activities outside of school (e.g., music, sports, girl scouts) in the past year. Are you ever in more than one activity a day?
Perfectionism (middle and high school only)	Based on EDI model	Five questions combined: ■ Only outstanding performance is good enough in my family. ■ As a child I tried very hard to avoid disappointing my parents and teachers. ■ I hate being less than the best at things. ■ I feel that I must do things perfectly or not do them at all. ■ I have extremely high goals.
Perfectionism (elementary only)		Four questions combined: ■ My family expects me to do well in everything. ■ I try to never disappoint my parents and teachers. ■ I hate when I am not the best at what I do. ■ If I can't be really good at something, I don't want to do it at all.
Emotional eating	Eat Less scale	Three questions combined: In the past year, how often did you eat less than usual ■ when you were bored? ■ to try to make yourself feel better? ■ when you were upset?
	Eat More scale	Three questions combined: In the past year, how often did you eat more than usual ■ when you were bored? ■ to try to make yourself feel better? ■ when you were upset?
Look good		Two questions combined: ■ In the past year, how often have people said you look good? ■ In the past year, how important has it been that you look good for boys?
Sports pressure to be thin		Six questions combined: In the past year, have you been a cheerleader or songleader? Are you training to become a professional dancer or ballerina?

Appendix continues

Domain	Scale	Question content
		In the past year, have you trained for competition in ■ ice skating? ■ swimming? ■ gymnastics? ■ track and field?
Physical health symptoms		Two questions combined: In the past year, how often have you had ■ headaches? ■ stomachaches?
Healthy behaviors		Two questions combined: In the past year, how often ■ have you tried to be more healthy by exercising? ■ did you watch what you were eating to keep your weight the same?
Parents involved in school		In the past year, how involved have your parents been with your school?
Watchful eating because of medical problem		In the past year, have you watched what you were eating because of a medical problem (e.g., diabetes, food allergies, or ulcers)?
Bothered by bad touches— sexual pressure	(elementary only)	In the past year, have you worried about "bad touches" from other kids?
	(middle and high school only)	In the past year, have you felt pressured to have sex?
Parent Stunkard scores	(mother)	Provide the number of the figure below that best looks like the most you have ever seen your real (biological) mother weigh.
	(father)	Provide the number of the figure below that best looks like the most you have ever seen your real (biological) father weigh.
Watchful eating		Three questions combined: In the past year, how often did you watch what you were eating ■ to lose weight? ■ to be healthy? ■ to keep your weight the same?

Note. SES = socioeconomic status; EDI = Eating Disorder Inventory. Adapted from the McKnight Risk Factor Survey by C. Shisslak et al. (in press). Reprinted with permission by the authors. Note that this scale is currently under revision.

REFERENCES

Adler, J., & Rosenberg, D. (1992, October 19). Must boys always be boys? *Newsweek*, p. 77.

Agell, G., & Rothblum, E. D. (1991). Effects of clients' obesity and gender on the therapy judgements of psychologists. *Professional Psychology: Research and Practice, 22*, 223–229.

Ahmad, S., Waller, G., & Verduyn, C. (1994). Eating attitudes among Asian schoolgirls: The role of perceived parental control. *International Journal of Eating Disorders, 15*, 91–97.

Alfonso, V. C., & Allison, D. B. (1993, August). *Further development of the Extended Satisfaction With Life Scale*. Paper presented at the 101st Annual Convention of the American Psychological Association, Toronto, Ontario, Canada.

Alfonso, V. C., Allison, D. B., Rader, D. E., & Gorman, B. S. (1996). The Extended Satisfaction With Life Scale: Development and psychometric properties. *Social Indicators Research, 38*, 275–301.

Allison, D. B., Hoy, K., Fournier, A., & Heymsfield, S. B. (1993). Can ethnic differences in men's preferences for women's body shapes contribute to ethnic differences in female obesity? *Obesity Research, 1*, 425–432.

Altabe, M. N. (1996). Issues in the assessment and treatment of body image disturbance in culturally diverse populations. In J. K. Thompson (Ed.), *Body image, eating disorders, and obesity: An integrative guide to assessment and treatment* (pp. 129–147). Washington, DC: American Psychological Association.

Altabe, M. N. (1998). Ethnicity and body image: Quantitative and qualitative analysis. *International Journal of Eating Disorders, 23*, 153–159.

Altabe, M. N., & Sanocki, T. (1996, November). *Body image and visual search*. Paper presented at the 30th annual convention of the Association for the Advancement of Behavior Therapy, New York, NY.

Altabe, M. N., & Thompson, J. K. (1990). Menstrual cycle, body image, and eating disturbance. *International Journal of Eating Disorders, 9*, 395–402.

Altabe, M. N., & Thompson, J. K. (1992). Size estimation vs. figural ratings of body image disturbance: Relation to body dissatisfaction and eating dysfunction. *International Journal of Eating Disorders, 11*, 397–402.

Altabe, M. N., & Thompson, J. K. (1994). Body image. In V. S. Ramachandran (Ed.), *Encyclopedia of human behavior* (Vol. 1, pp. 407–414). New York: Academic Press.

Altabe, M. N., & Thompson, J. K. (1995). Body image disturbance: Advances in assessment and treatment. In L. Vandecreek, S. Knapp, & T. L. Jackson (Eds.), *Innovations in clinical practice: A source book* (pp. 89–110). Sarasota, FL: Professional Resource Press.

Altabe, M. N., & Thompson, J. K. (1996). Body image: A cognitive self-schema? *Cognitive Therapy and Research, 20*, 171–193.

American Psychiatric Association. (1980). *Diagnostic and statistical manual of mental disorders* (3rd ed.). Washington, DC: Author.

American Psychiatric Association. (1987). *Diagnostic and statistical manual of mental disorders* (3rd ed., rev.). Washington, DC: Author.

American Psychiatric Association. (1994). *Diagnostic and statistical manual of mental disorders* (4th ed.). Washington, DC: Author.

American Psychological Association. (1996). *Research agenda for psychosocial and behavioral factors in women's health.* Washington, DC: Author.

American Society of Plastic and Reconstructive Surgeons. (1996). *1996 plastic surgery statistics.* Arlington Heights, IL: Author.

Anders, S. L., & Tucker, J. S. (1997, August). *The social control of health behavior in marriage.* Paper presented at the 105th Annual Convention of the American Psychological Association, Chicago, IL.

Andersen, A. E., & DiDomenico, L. (1992). Diet vs. shape content of popular male and female magazines: A dose–response relationship to the incidence of eating disorders. *International Journal of Eating Disorders, 11,* 283–287.

Anderson, C. A., Miller, R. S., Riger, A. L., Dill, J. C., & Sedikides, C. (1994). Behavioral and characterological attributional styles as predictors of depression and loneliness: Review, refinement, and test. *Journal of Personality and Social Psychology, 66,* 549–558.

Andreasen, A. R. (1994). Social marketing: Its definition and domain. *Journal of Public Policy & Marketing, 13,* 108–114.

Andrews, B. (1995). Bodily shame as a mediator between abusive experiences and depression. *Journal of Abnormal Psychology, 104,* 277.

Askevold, R. (1975). Measuring body image: Preliminary report on a new method. *Psychotherapy and Psychosomatics, 26,* 71–76.

Attie, I., & Brooks-Gunn, J. (1987). Weight concerns as chronic stressors in women. In R. C. Barnett, L. Biener, & G. K. Baruch (Eds.), *Gender and stress* (pp. 218–254). New York: Free Press.

Attie, I., & Brooks-Gunn, J. B. (1989). Development of eating problems in adolescent girls: A longitudinal study. *Developmental Psychology, 25,* 70–79.

Barber, N. (1995). The evolutionary psychology of physical attractiveness: Sexual selection and human morphology. *Ethology and Sociobiology, 16,* 395–424.

Barber, N. (1998). The slender ideal and eating disorders: An interdisciplinary "telescope" model. *International Journal of Eating Disorders, 23,* 295–307.

Barrios, B. A., Ruff, G. A., & York, C. I. (1989). Bulimia and body image: Assessment and explication of a promising construct. In W. G. Johnson (Ed.), *Advances in eating disorders* (Vol. 2, pp. 67–89). New York: JAI Press.

Beebe, D. W., Hombeck, G. N., Schober, A., Lane, M., & Rosa, K. (1996). Is body focus restricted to self-evaluation? Body focus in the evaluation of self and others. *International Journal of Eating Disorders, 20,* 415–422.

Bem, S. L. (1981). *The Bem Sex Role Inventory: Professional manual.* Palo Alto, CA: Consulting Psychologists Press.

Benedikt, R., Wertheim, E., & Love, A. (1998). Eating attitudes and weight-loss attempts in female adolescents and their mothers. *Journal of Youth and Adolescence, 27,* 43–57.

Ben-Tovim, D. I., & Crisp, A. H. (1984). The reliability of estimates of body width and their relationship to current measured body size among anorexic and normal subjects. *Psychological Medicine, 14,* 843–846.

Ben-Tovim, D. I., Walker, M. K., Murray, H., & Chin, G. (1990). Body size estimates: Body image or body attitude measures. *International Journal of Eating Disorders, 9,* 57–68.

Beren, S. E., Hayden, H. A., Wilfley, D. E., & Grilo, C. M. (1996). The influence of sexual orientation on body dissatisfaction in adult men and women. *International Journal of Eating Disorders, 20,* 135–141.

Beren, S. E., Hayden, H. A., Wilfley, D. E., & Striegel-Moore, R. H. (1997). Body dissatisfaction among lesbian college students. *Psychology of Women Quarterly, 21,* 431–445.

Bergner, M., Remer, P., & Whetsell, C. (1985). Transforming women's body image: A feminist counseling approach. *Women and Therapy, 4,* 25–38.

Bernstein, N. R. (1990). Objective bodily damage: Disfigurement and disability. In T. F. Cash & T. Pruzinsky (Eds.), *Body images: Development, deviance, and change* (pp. 131–148). New York: Guilford.

Biggs, S. J., Rosen, B., & Summerfield, A. B. (1980). Video-feedback and personal attribution in anorexic, depressed, and normal viewers. *British Journal of Medical Psychology, 53,* 249–254.

Biloukha, O. O., & Utermohlen, V. (1997, July). *The role of Western mass media in influencing ideal body image and some aspects of eating behavior in Ukrainian women.* Paper presented at the annual meeting of the Society for the Study of Ingestive Behavior, Baltimore, MD.

Birch, L. L. (1990). Development of food acceptance patterns. *Developmental Psychology, 26,* 515–519.

Blair, S. H., Kohl, H. W., Barlow, C. E., Paffenbarger, R. S., Gibbons, L. W., & Macera, C. A. (1995). Changes in physical fitness and all-cause mortality: A prospective study of healthy and unhealthy men. *Journal of the American Medical Association, 273,* 1093–1098.

Blichert-Toft, M. (1992). Breast-conserving therapy for mammary carcinoma: Psychosocial aspects, indications and limitations. *Annuals of Medicine, 24,* 445–461.

Blitzer, J. R., Rollins, N., & Blackwell, A. (1961). Children who starve themselves: Anorexia nervosa. *Psychosomatic Medicine, 23,* 369–383.

Blood, S. K. (1996). The dieting dilemma—Factors influencing women's decision to give up dieting. *Women and Therapy, 18,* 109–118.

Blouin, A. G., & Goldfield, G. S. (1995). Body image and steroid use in male bodybuilders. *International Journal of Eating Disorders, 18,* 159–165.

Bonnier, P. L. (1905). L'aschematie. *Revue Neurologie, 54,* 605–621.

Borchert, J., & Heinberg, L. J. (1996). Gender schema and gender-role discrepancy as correlates of body image. *Journal of Psychology: Interdisciplinary and Applied, 130,* 547–559.

Boskind-Lodahl, M. (1976). Cinderella's stepsisters: A feminist perspective on anorexia nervosa and bulimia. *Signs: Journal of Women in Culture and Society, 2,* 35–41.

Bowden, P. K., Touyz, S. W., Rodriguez, P. J., Hennsley, R., & Beumont, P. J. V. (1989). Distorting patient or distorting instrument? Body shape disturbance in patients with anorexia nervosa and bulimia. *British Journal of Psychiatry, 155,* 196–201.

Bradbury, E. (1994). The psychology of aesthetic plastic surgery. *Aesthetic and Plastic Surgery, 18,* 301–305.

Broadstock, M. R., & Gason, R. (1992). Effects of suntan on judgments of healthiness and attractiveness by adolescents. *Journal of Applied Social Psychology, 22,* 157–175.

Brodie, D. A., Slade, P. D., & Rose, H. (1989). Reliability measures in disturbing body image. *Perceptual and Motor Skills, 69,* 723–732.

Brody, J. E. (1997, August 6). Focus is on diagnosis as melanoma rates soar. *New York Times,* p. B9.

Brooks-Gunn, J., Attie, I., Burrow, C., Rosso, J. T., & Warren, M. P. (1989). The impact of puberty on body and eating concerns in athletic and nonathletic contexts. *Journal of Early Adolescence, 9,* 262–290.

Brooks-Gunn, J., & Warren, M. P. (1985). The effects of delayed menarche in different contexts: Dance and non-dance students. *Journal of Youth and Adolescence, 14,* 285–300.

Brown, L. S. (1989). Fat oppressive attitudes and the feminist therapist: Directions for change. *Women and Therapy, 8,* 19–30.

Brown, T. A., Cash, T. F., & Mikulka, P. J. (1990). Attitudinal body-image assessment: Factor analysis of the Body Self-Relations Questionnaire. *Journal of Personality Assessment, 55,* 135–144.

Browne, G., Byrne, C., Brown, B., Pennock, M., Streiner, D., Roberts, R., Eyles, P., Truscott, D., & Dabbs, R. (1985). Psychosocial adjustment of burn survivors. *Burns, 12,* 28–35.

Brownell, K. D. (1991). Dieting and the search for the perfect body: Where physiology and culture collide. *Behavior Therapy, 22,* 1–12.

Brownell, K. D., & Rodin, J. R. (1994). The dieting maelstrom: Is it possible and advisable to lose weight? *American Psychologist, 49,* 781–791.

Bruch, H. (1962). Perceptual and conceptual disturbances in anorexia nervosa. *Psychosomatic Medicine, 24,* 187–194.

Bruch, H. (1973). *Eating disorders: Obesity, anorexia, and the person within.* New York: Basic Books.

Bruch, H. (1978). *The golden cage: The enigma of anorexia nervosa.* Cambridge, MA: Harvard University Press.

Bryant-Waugh, R. J., Cooper, P. J., Taylor, C. L., & Lask, B. D. (1996). The use of the Eating Disorder Examination with children: A pilot study. *International Journal of Eating Disorders, 19,* 391–397.

Burgess, E. W., & Wallen, P. (1944). Personal appearance and neuroticism as related to age at marriage. *Human Biology, 16,* 15–22.

Burns, G. L., & Farina, A. (1992). The role of physical attractiveness in adjustment. *Genetic, Social, & General Psychology Monographs, 118,* 157–194.

Buss, D. M. (1989). Sex differences in human mate selection: Evolutionary hypotheses tested in 37 cultures. *Behavioral and Brain Sciences, 12,* 1–49.

Butow, P., Beumont, P., & Touyz, S. (1993). Cognitive processes in dieting disorders. *International Journal of Eating Disorders, 14,* 319–329.

Butters, J. W., & Cash, T. F. (1987). Cognitive-behavioral treatment of women's body-image dissatisfaction. *Journal of Consulting and Clinical Psychology, 55,* 889–897.

Button, E. J., Loan, P., Davies, J., & Sonuga-Barke, E. J. S. (1997). Self-esteem, eating problems, and psychological well-being in a cohort of schoolgirls aged 15–16: A questionnaire and interview study. *International Journal of Eating Disorders, 21,* 39–47.

Cachelin, F. M., Striegel-Moore, R. H., & Elder, K. A. (1998). Realistic weight perception and body size assessment in a racially diverse community sample of dieters. *Obesity Research, 6,* 62–68.

Caldwell, M. B., Brownell, K. D., & Wilfley, D. E. (1997). Relationship of weight, body dissatisfaction, and self-esteem in African-American and White female dieters. *International Journal of Eating Disorders, 22,* 127–130.

Carr-Nangle, R. E., Johnson, W. G., Bergeron, K. C., & Nangle, D. W. (1994). Body image changes over the menstrual cycle in normal women. *International Journal of Eating Disorders, 16,* 267–273.

Carter, J. C., Stewart, D. A., Dunn, V. J., & Fairburn, C. G. (1997). Primary prevention of eating disorders: Might it do more harm than good? *International Journal of Eating Disorders, 22,* 167–172.

Cash. T. F., Winstead, B. A., & Janda, L. H. (1986). Body Image Survey report: The great American shape-up. *Psychology Today, 24,* 30–37.

Cash, T. F. (1987). *The psychosocial effects of male pattern balding: A scientific study* (a technical report for the Upjohn Company). New York: Manning, Selvage, & Lee.

Cash, T. F. (1989). The psychosocial effects of male pattern balding. *Patient Care, 1,* 18–23.

Cash, T. F. (1990a). Losing hair, losing points? The effects of male pattern baldness on social impression formation. *Journal of Applied Social Psychology, 20,* 154–167.

Cash, T. F. (1990b). The psychology of physical appearance: Aesthetics, attributes, and images. In T. F. Cash & T. Pruzinsky (Eds.), *Body images: Development, deviance and change* (pp. 51–79). New York: Guilford Press.

Cash, T. F. (1991). *Body-image therapy: A program for self-directed change.* New York: Guilford.

Cash. T. F. (1992). The psychological effects of androgenetic alopecia in men. *Journal of the American Academy of Dermatology, 26,* 926–931.

Cash, T. F. (1994a). Body-image attitudes: Evaluation, investment, and affect. *Perceptual and Motor Skills, 78,* 1168–1170.

Cash, T. F. (1994b). The Situational Inventory of Body-Image Dysphoria: Contextual assessment of a negative body image. *The Behavior Therapist, 17,* 133–134.

Cash, T. F. (1995a). Developmental teasing about physical appearance: Retrospective descriptions and relationships with body image. *Social Behavior and Personality, 23,* 123–130.

Cash, T. F. (1995b). *What do you see when you look in the mirror? Helping yourself to a positive body image.* New York: Bantam Books.

Cash, T. F. (1996). The treatment of body image disturbances. In J. K. Thompson (Ed.), *Body image, eating disorders, and obesity: An integrative guide for assessment and treatment* (pp. 83–107). Washington, DC: American Psychological Association.

Cash, T. F. (1997). *The body image workbook: An 8-step program for learning to like your looks.* Oakland, CA: New Harbinger.

Cash, T. F., Ancis, J. R., & Strachan, M. D. (1997). Gender attitudes, feminist identity, and body images among college women. *Sex Roles, 36,* 433–447.

Cash, T. F., Counts, B., & Huffine, C. E. (1990). Current and vestigial effects of overweight among women: Fear of fat, attitudinal body image, and eating behaviors. *Journal of Psychopathology and Behavioral Assessment, 12,* 157–167.

Cash, T. F., & Henry, P. E. (1995). Women's body images: The results of a national survey in the U.S.A. *Sex Roles, 33,* 19–28.

Cash, T. F., & Hicks, K. L. (1990). Being fat versus thinking fat: Relationships with body image, eating behaviors, and well-being. *Cognitive Therapy and Research, 14,* 327–341.

Cash, T. F., & Horton, C. E. (1990). *A longitudinal study of satisfaction with plastic surgery.* Unpublished manuscript, Old Dominion University.

Cash, T. F., & Labarge, A. S. (1996). Development of the Appearance Schemas Inventory: A new cognitive body-image assessment. *Cognitive Therapy and Research, 20,* 37–50.

Cash, T. F., Lewis, R. J., & Keeton, P. (1987, March). *Development and validation of the Body-Image Automatic Thoughts Questionnaire: A measure of body-related cognitions.* Paper presented at the meeting of the Southeastern Psychological Association, Atlanta, GA.

Cash, T. F., Novy, P. L., & Grant, J. R. (1994). Why do women exercise? Factor analysis and further validation of the Reasons for Exercise Inventory. *Perceptual and Motor Skills, 78,* 539–544.

Cash, T. F., Price, V. H., & Savin, R. C. (1993). Psychological effects of androgenetic alopecia on women: Comparisons with balding men and with female control subjects. *Journal of the American Academy of Dermatology, 29,* 568–575.

Cash, T. F., & Pruzinsky, T. (1990). *Body images: Development, deviance, and change*. New York: Guilford.

Cash, T. F., & Roy, R. E. (in press). Pounds of flesh: Weight, gender, and body images. In J. Sobal & D. Maurer (Eds.), *Interpreting weight: The social management of fatness and thinness*. Hawthorne, NY: Aldine de Gruyter.

Cash, T. F., & Szymanski, M. L. (1995). The development and validation of the Body-Image Ideals Questionnaire. *Journal of Personality Assessment, 64*, 466–477.

Cattarin, J., & Thompson, J. K. (1994). A three-year longitudinal study of body image and eating disturbance in adolescent females. *Eating Disorders: The Journal of Prevention and Treatment, 2*, 114–125.

Cattarin, J., Williams, R., Thomas, C. M., & Thompson, J. K. (in press). The impact of televised images of thinness and attractiveness on body image: The role of social comparison. *Journal of Social and Clinical Psychology*.

Centers for Disease Control and Prevention. (1996). *1996 Surgeon General's report on physical activity and health*. Atlanta, GA: Author.

Changing Faces. (1996). *The psychology of facial disfigurement*. London: Author.

Chernin, K. (1981). *The obsession: Reflections on the tyranny of slenderness*. New York: Harper & Row.

Clark, D. A., Feldman, J., & Channon, S. (1989). Dysfunctional thinking in anorexia and bulimia nervosa. *Cognitive Therapy and Research, 13*, 377–387.

Cogan, J. C., Bhalla, S. K., Sefa-Dedeh, A., & Rothblum, E. D. (1996). A comparison study of United States and African students on perceptions of obesity and thinness. *Journal of Cross-Cultural Psychology, 27*, 98–113.

Cole, B., & Gealth, A. (1989). *Art of the Western world*. New York: Summit Books.

Cole, C. L. (1985). A group design for adult female survivors of childhood incest. *Women and Therapy, 4*, 71–82.

Collins, M. E. (1991). Body figure perceptions and preferences among preadolescent children. *International Journal of Eating Disorders, 10*, 199–208.

Connors, M. E. (1996). Developmental vulnerabilities for eating disorders. In L. Smolak, M. Levine, & R. Streigel-Moore (Eds.), *The developmental psychopathology of eating disorders* (pp. 285–310). Hillsdale, NJ: Erlbaum.

Connors, M. E., & Morse, W. (1993). Sexual abuse and eating disorders: A review. *International Journal of Eating Disorders, 13*, 1–11.

Cooley, C. H. (1922). *Human nature and the social order* (rev. ed.). New York: Scribner.

Cooper, M. (1997). Do interpretive biases maintain eating disorders? *Behaviour Research and Therapy, 35*, 619–626.

Cooper, M. J., & Fairburn, C. G. (1992). Selective processing of eating, weight and shape related words in patients with eating disorders and dieters. *British Journal of Clinical Psychology, 31*, 363–365.

Cooper, P. J., Taylor, M. J., Cooper, Z., & Fairburn, C. G. (1987). The development and validation of the Body Shape Questionnaire. *International Journal of Eating Disorders, 6,* 485–494.

Crago, M., Shisslak, C. M., & Estes, L. S. (1996). Eating disturbances among American minority groups: A review. *International Journal of Eating Disorders, 19,* 239–248.

Crandall, C. S. (1988). The social contagion of binge eating. *Journal of Personality and Social Psychology, 55,* 588–598.

Cusumano, D. L., & Thompson, J. K. (1997). Body image and body shape ideals in magazines: Exposure, awareness and internalization. *Sex Roles, 37,* 701–721.

Davies, K., & Wardle, J. (1994). Body image and dieting in pregnancy. *Journal of Psychosomatic Research, 38,* 787–799.

Davis, C., Dionne, M., & Lazarus, L. (1996). Gender-role orientation and body image in women and men: The moderating influence of neuroticism. *Sex Roles, 34,* 493–505.

Davis, C., & Katzman, M. (1997). Charting new territory: Body esteem, weight satisfaction, depression, and self-esteem among Chinese males and females in Hong Kong. *Sex Roles, 36,* 449–459.

Davis, P. (1997, November 23). Is Barbie for real? *St. Petersburg Times,* p. F1.

Davis, S. (1990). Men as success objects and women and sex objects: A study of personal advertisements. *Sex Roles, 23,* 43–50.

Deaux, K., & Wrightsman, L. S. (1984). *Social psychology in the 80s.* Monterey, CA: Brooks/Cole.

dePalma, M. T., Koszewski, W. M., Case, J. G., Barile, R. J., dePalma, B. F., & Oliaro, S. M. (1993). Weight control practices of lightweight football players. *Medicine and Science in Sports and Exercise, 25,* 694–701.

Dibiase, W. J., & Hjelle, L. A. (1968). Body-image stereotypes and body-type preferences among male college students. *Perceptual and Motor Skills, 27,* 1143–1146.

Dionne, M. (1992). *Feminist ideology as a predictor of body dissatisfaction in women.* Unpublished master's thesis, York University, North York, Ontario, Canada.

Dionne, M., Davis, C., Fox, J., & Gurevich, M. (1995). Feminist ideology as a predictor of body dissatisfaction in women. *Sex Roles, 33,* 277–287.

Dowd, M. (1997, March 22). The latest wrinkle. *New York Times,* p. 19.

Downs, A. C., & Harrison, S. K. (1985). Embarrassing age spots or just plain ugly? Physical attractiveness stereotyping as an instrument of sexism on American television commercials. *Sex Roles, 13,* 9–19.

Dreger, A. (1998, July 28). When medicine goes too far in the pursuit of normality. *New York Times,* p. B10.

Drewnowski, A., Kurth, C. L., & Krahn, D. D. (1995). Effects of body image on dieting, exercise, and anabolic steroid use in adolescent males. *International Journal of Eating Disorders, 17,* 381–386.

Dunning, J. (1997, July 16). Pursuing perfection, dancing with death. *New York Times*, pp. B1, B8.

Dworkin, S. H. (1988). Not in man's image: Lesbians and the cultural oppression of body image. *Women and Therapy, 8*, 27–39.

Dworkin, S. H., & Kerr, B. A. (1987). Comparison of interventions for women experiencing body image problems. *Journal of Counseling Psychology, 34*, 136–140.

Eldredge, K. L., & Agras, W. S. (1996). Weight and shape overconcern and emotional eating in binge eating disorder. *International Journal of Eating Disorder, 19*, 73–82.

Ellis, M. L. (1989). Women: The mirage of the perfect image. *Arts in Psychotherapy, 16*, 263–276.

Evans, E. D., Rutberg, J., Sather, C., & Turner, C. (1991). Content analyses of contemporary teen magazines for adolescent females. *Youth & Society, 23*, 99–120.

Fabian, L. J., & Thompson, J. K. (1989). Body image and eating disturbance in young females. *International Journal of Eating Disorders, 8*, 63–74.

A facelift? It's just what I wanted. (1997, June 11). *St. Petersburg Times*, p. D4.

Fahy, T. A., & O'Donoghue, G. (1991). Eating disorders in pregnancy. *Psychological Medicine, 21*, 577–580.

Fairburn, C. G., & Beglin, S. J. (1990). Studies of the epidemiology of bulimia nervosa. *American Journal of Psychiatry, 147*, 401–408.

Fairburn, C. G., & Cooper, Z. (1993). The Eating Disorder Examination (12th ed.). In C. G. Fairburn & G. T. Wilson (Eds.), *Binge eating: Nature, assessment, and treatment* (pp. 3–14). New York: Guilford.

Fairburn, C. G., Cooper, R. J., Cooper, M., McKenna, F. P., & Anastasiades, P. (1991). Selective information processing in bulimia nervosa. *International Journal of Eating Dirorders, 10*, 415–442.

Faith, M. S., & Allison, D. B. (1996). Assessment of psychological status among obese persons. In J. K. Thompson (Ed.), *Body image, eating disorders, and obesity: An integrative guide for assessment and treatment* (pp. 365–387). Washington, DC: American Psychological Association.

Faith, M. S., Leone, M., & Allison, D. B. (1997). The effects of self-generated comparison targets, BMI, and social comparison tendencies on body image appraisal. *Eating Disorders: Journal of Treatment and Prevention, 5*, 34–46.

Fallon, A. E. (1990). Culture in the mirror: Sociocultural determinants of body image. In T. F. Cash & T. Pruzinsky (Eds.), *Body images: Development, deviance and change* (pp. 80–109). New York: Guilford Press.

Fallon, A. E., & Rozin, P. (1985). Sex differences in perceptions of desirable body shape. *Journal of Abnormal Psychology, 94*, 102–105.

Fallon, P., & Wonderlich, S. A. (1997). Sexual abuse and other forms of trauma. In D. M. Garner & P. E. Garfinkel (Eds.), *Handbook of treatment for eating disorders* (2nd ed., pp. 394–414). New York: Guilford.

Faludi, S. (1991). *Backlash: The undeclared war against American women*. New York: Crown.

Fatal gunfight may have been the result of taunting over weight. (1997, January 19). *Orlando Sentinel*, p. A5.

Fawzy, F. I., & Fawzy, N. W. (1994). A structured psychoeducational intervention for cancer patients. *General Hospital Psychiatry, 16*, 149–192.

Feinberg, L. S. (1996). *Teasing: Innocent fun or sadistic malice?* Far Hills, NJ: New Horizon.

Feingold, A. (1990). Gender differences in effects of physical attractiveness on romantic partner attraction: A comparison across five research paradigms. *Journal of Personality and Social Psychology, 59*, 981–993.

Feingold, A. (1992). Good-looking people are not what we think. *Psychological Bulletin, 111*, 304–341.

Feingold, A., & Mazzella, R. (1996). Gender differences in body image are increasing. *The General Psychologist, 32*, 90–98.

Felson, R. B. (1985). Reflected appraisal and the development of the self. *Social Psychology Quarterly, 48*, 71–78.

Fernandez, R., & Vandereycken, W. (1994). Influence of video-confrontation on the self-evaluation of anorexia nervosa patients. *Eating Disorders: The Journal of Treatment and Prevention, 2*, 135–140.

Festinger, L. (1954). A theory of social comparison processes. *Human Relations, 7*, 117–140.

Finkelhor, D. (1984). *Child sexual abuse*. New York: Free Press.

Fisher, E., & Thompson, J. K. (1994). A comparative evaluation of cognitive–behavioral therapy (CBT) versus exercise therapy (ET) for the treatment of body image disturbance: Preliminary findings. *Behavior Modification, 18*, 171–185.

Fisher, E., & Thompson, J. K. (1998). *Social comparison and body image: An investigation of body comparison processes using multidimensional scaling*. Unpublished manuscript, University of South Florida.

Fisher, M. (1992). Parents' views of adolescent health issues. *Pediatrics, 90*, 335–341.

Fisher, S. (1986). *Development and structure of the body image*. Hillsdale, NJ: Erlbaum.

Fisher, S. (1990). The evolution of psychological concepts about the body. In T. F. Cash & T. Pruzinsky (Eds.), *Body images: Development, deviance, and change* (pp. 3–20). New York: Guilford.

Fisher, S., & Cleveland, S. E. (1968). *Body image and personality*. New York: Dover Press.

Foa, E. B., Stekette, G., & Rothbaum, B. O. (1989). Behavioral/cognitive conceptualizations of post-traumatic stress disorder. *Behavior Therapy, 20*, 155–176.

Forston, M. T., & Stanton, A. L. (1992). Self-discrepancy theory as a framework for understanding bulimic symptomatology and associated distress. *Journal of Social and Clinical Psychology, 11*, 103–118.

Franko, D. L., & Orosan-Weine, P. (in press). The prevention of eating disorders: Empirical, methodological and conceptual considerations. *Clinical Psychology: Science and Practice.*

Franko, D. L., & Walton, B. E. (1993). Pregnancy and eating disorders: A review and clinical implications. *International Journal of Eating Disorders, 13*, 41–48.

Franks, V. (1986). Sex stereotyping and diagnosis of psychopathology. *Women and Therapy, 5*, 219–232.

Franzoi, S. L., & Herzog, M. E. (1987). Judging physical attractiveness: What body aspects do we use? *Personality and Social Psychology Bulletin, 13*, 19–33.

Freedman, R. (1986). *Beauty bound.* Lexington, MA: Heath.

Freeman, R. F., Thomas, C. D., Solyom, L., & Hunter, M. A. (1984). A modified video camera for measuring body image distortion: Technical description and reliability. *Psychological Medicine, 14*, 411–416.

Freeman, R., Touyz, S., Sara, G., Rennie, C., Gordon, E., & Beumont, P. (1991). In the eye of the beholder: Processing body shape information in anorexic and bulimic patients. *International Journal of Eating Disorders, 10*, 709–714.

French, S. A., Story, M., Remafedi, G., Resnick, M. D., & Blum, R. W. (1996). Sexual orientation and prevalence of body dissatisfaction and eating disordered behaviors: A population-based study of adolescents. *International Journal of Eating Disorders, 19*, 119–126.

Friedman, M. A., & Brownell, K. D. (1995). Psychological correlates of obesity: Moving to the next research generation. *Psychological Bulletin, 117*, 3–20.

Friedman, M. A., Dixon, A. E., Brownell, K. D., Whisman, M. A., & Wilfley, D. E. (in press). Marital status, marital satisfaction, and body image dissatisfaction. *International Journal of Eating Disorders.*

Friedman, S. S. (1996). Girls in the 90's. *Eating Disorders: The Journal of Treatment and Prevention, 4*, 238–244.

Furman, K., & Thompson, J. K. (1998). *Body image and teasing: The effects of exposure via vignettes.* Unpublished manuscript, University of South Florida.

Furnham, A., & Baguma, P. (1994). Cross-cultural differences in the evaluation of male and female body shapes. *International Journal of Eating Disorders, 15*, 81–89.

Furnham, A., Dias, M., & McClelland, A. (1998). *The role of body weight, waist-to-hip ratio and breast size in judgments of female attractiveness.* Unpublished manuscript, University College of London.

Furnham, A., Tan, T., & McManus, C. (1997). Waist-to-hip ratio and preferences for body shape: A replication and extension. *Personality and Individual Differences, 22*, 539–549.

Furnham, A., Titman, P., & Sleeman, E. (1994). Perception of female body shapes as a function of exercise. *Journal of Social Behavior and Personality, 9*, 335–352.

Gaesser, G. A. (1996). *Big fat lies: The truth about your weight and your health.* New York: Fawcett Columbine.

Gardner, R. M. (1996). Methodological issues in assessment of the perceptual component of body image disturbance. *British Journal of Psychology, 87,* 327–337.

Gardner, R. M., & Bokenkamp, E. D. (1996). The role of sensory and nonsensory factors in body size estimations of eating disorder subjects. *Journal of Clinical Psychology, 52,* 3–15.

Gardner, R. M., Friedman, B. N., & Jackson, N. A. (1998). Methodological concerns when using silhouettes to measure body image. *Perceptual and Motor Skills, 86,* 387–395.

Gardner, R. M., Gallegos, V., Martinez, R., & Espinoza, T. (1989). Mirror feedback and judgments of body size. *Journal of Psychosomatic Research, 33,* 603–607.

Gardner, R. M., Gardner, E. A., & Morrell, J. A. (1990). Body image of sexually and physically abused children. *Journal of Psychiatric Research, 24,* 313–324.

Gardner, R. M., Jones, L. C., & Bokenkamp, E. D. (1995). Comparison of three psychophysical techniques for estimating body-size perception. *Perceptual and Motor Skills, 80,* 1379–1390.

Gardner, R. M., Martinez, R., & Sandoval, Y. (1987). Obesity and body image: An evaluation of sensory and non-sensory components. *Psychological Medicine, 17,* 927–932.

Gardner, R. M., & Moncrieff, C. (1988). Body image distortion in anorexics as a non-sensory phenomenon: A signal detection approach. *Journal of Clinical Psychology, 44,* 101–107.

Gardner, R. M., Sorter, R. G., & Friedman, B. N. (1997). Developmental changes in children's body images. *Journal of Social Behavior and Personality, 12,* 1019–1036.

Garfinkel, P. E., & Garner, D. M. (1982). *Anorexia nervosa: A multidimensional approach.* New York: Brunner/Mazel.

Garfinkel, P. E., Moldofsky, H., & Garner, D. M. (1979). The stability of perceptual disturbances in anorexia nervosa. *Psychological Medicine, 9,* 703–708.

Garfinkel, P. E., Moldofsky, H., Garner, D. M., Stancer, H. C., & Coscina, D. U. (1978). Body awareness in anorexia nervosa: Disturbances in "body image" and "satiety." *Psychosomatic Medicine, 40,* 487–498.

Garner, D. M. (1991). *Eating Disorder Inventory—2: Professional manual.* Odessa, FL: Psychological Assessment Resources.

Garner, D. M. (1997, January/February). The Body Image Survey. *Psychology Today,* 32–84.

Garner, D. M., & Garfinkel, P. E. (1981). Body image in anorexia nervosa: Measurement, theory, and clinical implications. *International Journal of Psychiatry in Medicine, 11,* 263–284.

Garner, D. M., Garfinkel, P. E., Rockert, W., & Olmsted, M. P. (1987). A prospective study of eating disturbances in the ballet. *Psychosomatics, 48,* 170–175.

Garner, D. M., Garfinkel, P. E., Schwartz, D., & Thompson, M. (1980). Cultural expectations of thinness in women. *Psychological Reports, 47*, 483–491.

Garner, D. M., Garner, M. V., & Van Egeren, L. F. (1992). Body dissatisfaction adjusted for weight: The body illusion index. *International Journal of Eating Disorders, 12*, 263–272.

Garner, D. M., Olmsted, M. P., & Polivy, J. (1983). Development and validation of a multi-dimensional eating disorder inventory for anorexia nervosa and bulimia. *International Journal of Eating Disorders, 2*, 15–34.

Gerrard, J. (1991). The teasing syndrome in facially deformed children. A.N.Z. *Journal of Family Therapy, 12*, 147–154.

Gettelman, T. E., & Thompson, J. K. (1993). Actual differences and stereotypical perceptions in body image and eating disturbance: A comparison of male and female heterosexual and homosexual samples. *Sex Roles, 29*, 545–562.

Ghizzani, A., Pirtoli, L., Bellezza, A., & Velicogna, F. (1995). The evaluation of some factors influencing the sexual life of women affected by breast cancer. *Journal of Sex and Marital Therapy, 21*, 57–63.

Gilbert, S., & Thompson, J. K. (1996). Feminist explanations of the development of eating disorders: Common themes, research findings, and methodological issues. *Clinical Psychology: Science and Practice, 3*, 183–202.

Gilbert, S., & Thompson, J. K. (1998). *Body image and mood changes in competitive interactions: Winning or losing against an opposite-sexed peer on a gender-based task.* Unpublished manuscript, University of South Florida.

Giles, T. R. (1988). Distortion of body image as an effect of conditioned fear. *Journal of Behavior Therapy and Experimental Psychiatry, 19*, 143–146.

Gillespie, B. L., & Eisler, R. M. (1992). Development of the Feminine Gender Role Stress Scale: A cognitive/behavioral measure of stress, appraisal, and coping for women. *Behavior Modification, 16*, 426–438.

Glanz, K., & Lerman, C. (1992). Psychosocial impact of breast cancer: A critical review. *Annals of Behavioral Medicine, 14*, 204–212.

Gleason, N. A. (1995). A new approach to disordered eating—Using an electronic bulletin board to confront social pressure on body image. *Journal of American College Health, 44*, 78–80.

Gleghorn, A. A., Penner, L. A., Powers, P. S., & Schulman, R. (1987). The psychometric properties of several measures of body image. *Journal of Psychopathology and Behavior Assessment, 9*, 230–218.

Glidden, C. E., & Tracey, T. J. (1989). Women's perceptions of personal versus sociocultural counseling interventions. *Journal of Counseling Psychology, 36*, 54–62.

Glucksman, M., & Hirsch, J. (1969). The response of obese patients to weight reduction: III. The perception of body size. *Psychosomatic Medicine, 31*, 1–17.

Goldfield, A., & Chrisler, J. C. (1995). Body stereotyping and stigmatization of obese persons by first graders. *Perceptual and Motor Skills, 81*, 909–910.

Goldsmith, D., & Thompson, J. K. (1989). The effect of mirror confrontation and size estimation accuracy feedback on perceptual inaccuracy in normal females who overestimate body size. *International Journal of Eating Disorders, 8,* 437–444.

Gonzalez-Lavin, A., & Smolak, L. (1995, March). *Relationships between television and eating problems in middle school girls.* Paper presented at the meeting of the Society for Research in Child Development, Indianapolis, IN.

Goodman, N., Dornbusch, S. M., Richardson, S. A., & Hasdorf, A. H. (1963). Variant reactions to physical disabilities. *American Sociological Review, 28,* 429–435.

Goodman, W. C. (1995). *The invisible woman: Confronting weight prejudice in America.* Carlsbad, CA: Gürze Books.

Gortmaker, S. L., Must, A., Perrin, J. M., Sobol, A. M., & Dietz, W. H. (1993). Social and economic consequences of overweight in adolescence and young adulthood. *New England Journal of Medicine, 329,* 1008–1012.

Gottheil, E., Backup, C. E., & Cornelison, F. S. (1969). Denial and self-image confrontation in a case of anorexia nervosa. *Journal of Nervous and Mental Disease, 148,* 238–250.

Graber, J. A., Brooks-Gunn, J., Paikoff, R. L., & Warren, M. P. (1994). Prediction of eating problems: An 8-year study of adolescent girls. *Development Psychology, 30,* 823–834.

Grady, D. (1998, July 21). Cosmetic breast enlargements are making a comeback. *New York Times,* p. B13.

Grant, J., & Cash, T. F. (1995). Cognitive-behavioral body-image therapy: Comparative efficacy of group and modest-contact treatments. *Behavior Therapy, 26,* 69–84.

Grant, P. (1996, May). If you could change your breasts . . . . *Self,* 186–189, 210–211.

Grilo, C. M., Wilfley, D. E., Brownell, K. D., & Rodin, J. (1994). Teasing, body image, and self-esteem in a clinical sample of obese women. *Addictive Behaviors, 19,* 443–450.

Gupta, M. A., & Schork, N. J. (1993). Aging-related concerns and body image: Possible future implications for eating disorders. *International Journal of Eating Disorders, 14,* 481–486.

Haiken, E. (1997). *Venus envy: A history of cosmetic surgery.* Baltimore: Johns Hopkins University Press.

Haimovitz, D., Lansky, L. M., & O'Reilly, P. (1993). Fluctuations in body satisfaction across situations. *International Journal of Eating Disorders, 13,* 77–84.

Hall, C. C. I. (1995). Asian eyes: Body image and eating disorders of Asian and Asian American women. *Eating Disorders: The Journal of Treatment and Prevention, 3,* 8–19.

Handy, B. (1997, June 9). Are we not men's magazines? *Newsweek,* p. 87.

Hangen, J. D., & Cash, T. F. (1991, November). *Body-image attitudes and sexual functioning in a college population.* Poster session presented at the annual meeting of the Association for Advancement of Behavior Therapy, New York, NY.

Harris, R. J. (1994). A *cognitive psychology of mass communication* (2nd ed.). Hillsdale, NJ: Erlbaum.

Harris, S. M. (1995). Family, self, and sociocultural contributions to body-image attitudes of African-American women. *Psychology of Women Quarterly, 19*, 129–145.

Hastings, T., & Kern, J. M. (1994). Relationships between bulimia, childhood sexual abuse and family environment. *International Journal of Eating Disorders, 15*, 103–111.

Hay, G. G. (1970). Dysmorphophobia. *British Journal of Psychiatry, 140*, 399–406.

Head, H. (1926). *Aphasia and kindred disorders of speech*. Cambridge, England: Cambridge University Press.

Heatherton, T. F., Mahamedi, F., Striepe, M., Field, A. E., & Keel, P. (1997). A 10-year longitudinal study of body weight, dieting, and eating disorder symptoms. *Journal of Abnormal Psychology, 106*, 117–125.

Heffernan, K. (1996). Eating disorders and weight concerns among lesbians. *International Journal of Eating Disorders, 19*, 127–138.

Heinberg, L. J. (1996). Theories of body image: Perceptual, developmental, and sociocultural factors. In J. K. Thompson (Ed.), *Body image, eating disorders, and obesity: An integrative guide to assessment and treatment* (pp. 27–48). Washington, DC: American Psychological Association.

Heinberg, L. J., Fauerbach, J. A., Spence, R. J., & Hackerman, F. (1997). Psychologic factors involved in the decision to undergo reconstructive surgery after burn injury. *Journal of Burn Care and Rehabilitation, 7*, 374–380.

Heinberg, L. J., Haythornthwaite, J. A., Rosofsky, W., McCarron, P., & Clarke, A. (1996, November). *Body image predicts weight loss compliance in elderly African-Americans*. Paper presented at the annual meeting of the Association for the Advancement of Behavior Therapy, New York, NY.

Heinberg, L. J., & Thompson, J. K. (1992a). The effects of figure size feedback (positive vs. negative) and target comparison group (particularistic vs. universalistic) on body image disturbance. *International Journal of Eating Disorders, 12*, 441–448.

Heinberg, L. J., & Thompson, J. K. (1992b). Social comparison: Gender, target importance ratings, and relation to body image disturbance. *Journal of Social Behavior and Personality, 7*, 335–344.

Heinberg, L. J., & Thompson, J. K. (1995). Body image and televised images of thinness and attractiveness: A controlled laboratory investigation. *Journal of Social and Clinical Psychology, 7*, 335–344.

Heinberg, L. J., Thompson, J. K., & Stormer, S. (1995). Development and validation of the Sociocultural Attitudes Toward Appearance Questionnaire (SATAQ). *International Journal of Eating Disorder, 17*, 81–89.

Heinberg, L. J., Wood, K. C., & Thompson, J. K. (1995). Body image. In V. I. Rickert (Ed.), *Adolescent nutrition: Assessment and management* (pp. 136–156). New York: Chapman & Hall.

Herman-Giddens, M. E., Slora, E. J., Wasserman, R. C., Bourdony, C. J., Bhapkar,

M. V., Koch, G. G., & Hasemeier, C. M. (1997). Secondary sexual characteristics and menses in young girls seen in office practice: A study from the
Pediatric Research in Office Settings Network. *Pediatrics, 99*, 505–512.

Hesse-Biber, S. J. (1996). *Am I thin enough yet? The cult of thinness and the commercialization of identity*. New York: Oxford University Press.

Higgins, E. T. (1987). Self-discrepancy: A theory relating self and affect. *Psychological Review, 94*, 319–340.

Higgins, E. T., & Brendl, C. M. (1995). Accessibility and applicability: Some
"activation rules" influencing judgment. *Journal of Experimental Social Psychology, 31*, 218–243.

Hill, A. J., Weaver, C., & Blundell, J. E. (1990). Dieting concerns of 10-year-old
girls and their mothers. *British Journal of Clinical Psychology, 29*, 346–348.

Hoelter, J. W. (1984). Relative effects of significant others on self-evaluation. *Social
Psychology Quarterly, 47*, 255–262.

Humphrey, L. L. (1986). Family relations in bulimic–anorexic and nondistressed
families. *International Journal of Eating Disorders, 5*, 223–232.

Humphrey, L. L. (1989). Observed family interactions among subtypes of eating
disorders using structural analysis of social behavior. *Journal of Clinical and
Consulting Psychology, 57*, 206–214.

Huon, G. F. (1995). The Stroop color-naming task in eating disorders: A review
of the research. *Eating Disorders: The Journal of Treatment and Prevention, 3*,
124–132.

Huon, G. F., & Brown, L. B. (1989). Assessing bulimics' dissatisfactions with their
body. *British Journal of Clinical Psychology, 28*, 283–284.

Iijima Hall, C. C. (1995). Asian eyes: Body image and eating disorders of Asian
and Asian American women. *Eating Disorders: The Journal of Treatment and
Prevention, 3*, 8–19.

Irving, L. M. (1990). Mirror images: Effects of the standard of beauty on the self-
and body-esteem of women exhibiting varying levels of bulimic symptoms.
Journal of Social and Clinical Psychology, 9, 230–242.

Jackman, L. P., Williamson, D. A., Netemeyer, R. G., & Anderson, D. A. (1995).
Do weight preoccupied women misinterpret ambiguous stimuli related to body
size? *Cognitive Therapy and Research, 19*, 341–355.

Jackson, L. A., Sullivan, L. A., & Rostker, R. (1988). Gender, gender role, and
body image. *Sex Roles, 19*, 429–443.

Jacobi, L., & Cash, T. (1994). In pursuit of the perfect appearance: Discrepancies
among self-ideal percepts of multiple physical attributes. *Journal of Applied
Social Psychology, 24*, 379–396.

Janet, P. (1903). *Les obsessions et la psychasthenie*. Paris, France: Felix Alcan.

Jasper, K. (1993). Monitoring and responding to media messages. *Eating Disorders:
The Journal of Treatment and Prevention, 1*, 109–114.

Johnson, C. E., & Petrie, T. A. (1995). The relationship of gender discrepancy to
eating disorder attitudes and behaviors. *Sex Roles, 33*, 405–416.

Johnson, M. A. (1989). Variables associated with friendship in an adult population. *Journal of Social Psychology, 129,* 379–390.

Johnson, W. G., & Torgrud, L. J. (1996). Assessment and treatment of binge eating disorder. In J. K. Thompson (Ed.), *Body image, eating disorders, and obesity: An integrative guide for assessment and treatment* (pp. 321–343). Washington, DC: American Psychological Association.

Joiner, G. W., & Kushubeck, S. (1996). Acculturation, body image, self-esteem, and eating-disorder symptomatology in adolescent Mexican-American women. *Psychology of Women Quarterly, 20,* 419–435.

Joiner, T. E., Schmidt, N. B., & Singh, D. (1994). Waist-to-hip ratio and body dissatisfaction among college women and men: Moderating role of depressed symptoms and gender. *International Journal of Eating Disorders, 16,* 199–203.

Jones, J. L., & Leary, M. R. (1994). Effects of appearance-based admonitions against sun exposure on tanning intentions in young adults. *Health Psychology, 13,* 86–90.

Jourard, S. M., & Secord, P. F. (1955). Body cathexis and the ideal female figure. *Journal of Abnormal and Social Psychology, 50,* 243–246.

Kahneman, D., & Tversky, A. (1973). On the psychology of prediction. *Psychological Review, 80,* 237–251.

Kalodner, C. R. (1997). Media influences on male and female non-eating disordered college students: A significant issue. *Eating Disorders: The Journal of Treatment and Prevention, 5,* 47–57.

Kaufman, L. (1980). Prime-time nutrition. *Journal of Communication, 30,* 37–46.

Kearney-Cooke, A., & Striegel-Moore, R. H. (1994). Treatment of childhood sexual abuse in anorexia nervosa and bulimia nervosa: A feminist psychodynamic approach. *International Journal of Eating Disorders, 15,* 305–319.

Kearney-Cooke, A., & Striegel-Moore, R. (1997). The etiology and treatment of body image disturbance. In D. M. Garner & P. E. Garfinkel (Eds.), *Handbook of treatment for eating disorders* (2nd ed., pp. 295–306). New York: Guilford.

Keeton, P., Cash, T. F., & Brown, T. A. (1990). Body image of body images? Comparative, multidimensional assessment among college students. *Journal of Personality Assessment, 54,* 213–240.

Kelly, G. A. (1955). *The psychology of personal contacts.* New York: Norton.

Kelson, T. R., Kearney-Cooke, A., & Lansky, L. M. (1990). Body-image and body-beautification among female college students. *Perceptual and Motor Skills, 71,* 281–289.

Kilbourne, J. (1994). Still killing us softly: Advertising and obsession with thinness. In P. Fallon, M. A. Katzman, & S. C. Wooley (Eds.), *Feminist perspectives on eating disorders* (pp. 395–418). New York: Guilford Press.

Killen, J. D., Taylor, C. B., Hayward, C., Haydel, K. F., Wilson, D. M., Hammer, L., Kraemer, H., Blair-Greiner, A., & Strachowski, D. (1996). Weight concerns influence the development of eating disorders: A 4-year prospective study. *Journal of Consulting and Clinical Psychology, 64,* 936–940.

Klesges, R. C., Coates, T. J., Brown, G., Sturgeon-Tillish, J., Moldenhauer-Klesges,

L. M., Holzer, B., Woolfrey, J., & Vollmer, J. (1983). Parental influences on children's eating behavior and relative weight. *Journal of Applied Behavior Analysis, 16,* 371–378.

Koff, E., & Bauman, C. L. (1997). Effects of wellness, fitness, and sport skills programs on body image and lifestyle behaviors. *Perceptual and Motor Skills, 84,* 555–562.

Koff, E., & Benavage, A. (1998). Breast size perception and satisfaction, body image, and psychological functioning in Caucasian and Asian-American college women. *Sex Roles, 38,* 655–673.

Kolata, G. (1997, July 13). The fearful price of getting thin. *New York Times,* p. E3.

Kowalski, R., Simons, A., Snyder, C., Houston, E., Davis, B., & Pritchett, R. (1997, August). *"I was only kidding!" Victims' and perpetrators' perceptions of teasing.* Paper presented at the 105th Annual Convention of the American Psychological Association, Chicago, IL.

Kruglanski, A. W., & Mayseless, O. (1990). Classic and current social comparison research: Expanding the perspective. *Psychological Bulletin, 108,* 195–208.

Kuczmarski, R. J., Flegal, K. M., Campbell, S. M., & Johnson, C. L. (1994). Increasing prevalence of overweight among US adults. The National Health and Nutrition Examination Surveys, 1960 to 1990. *Journal of the American Medical Association, 272,* 205–211.

Kumanyika, S. K. (1994). The cultural aspects of weight control. *Weight Control Digest, 4,* 345–352.

Lacey, J. H., & Smith, G. (1987). Bulimia nervosa: The impact of pregnancy on mother and baby. *British Journal of Psychiatry, 150,* 777–781.

Lakoff, R. T., & Scherr, R. L. (1984). *Face value: The politics of beauty.* Boston: Routledge & Kegan Paul.

Larkin, J., Rice, C., & Russell, V. (1996). Slipping through the cracks: Sexual harassment, eating problems, and the problem of embodiment. *Eating Disorders: The Journal of Treatment and Prevention, 4,* 5–26.

Larrubia, E. (1996, August 27). Obese boy, fearing ridicule, hangs self. *Tampa Tribune,* p. B1.

Lasegue, E. C. (1873). De l'anoréxie hystérique. *Archives Générales de Médecine, 21,* 385–403.

Lawrence, M. (1979). Anorexia nervosa—The control paradox. *Women's Studies International Quarterly, 2,* 93–101.

Lawrence, M. (1984). Education and identity: Thoughts on the social origins of anorexia. *Women's Studies International Forum, 7,* 201–209.

LeBow, M. D. (1995). *Overweight teenagers: Don't bear the burden alone.* New York: Plenum Press.

Lerner, R. M., & Jovanovic, J. (1990). The role of body image in psychosocial development across the life span: A developmental contextual perspective. In T. F. Cash & T. Pruzinsky (Eds.), *Body images: Development, deviance, and change* (pp. 110–127). New York: Guilford.

Levine, M. P. (1994). Beauty myth and the beast: What men can do and be to help prevent eating disorders. *Eating Disorders: The Journal of Treatment and Prevention, 2,* 101–113.

Levine, M. P. (in press). Prevention of eating disorders and eating problems. In R. Lemberg (Ed.), *Controlling eating disorders with facts, advice, and resources* (2nd ed.). Phoenix, AZ: Oryx Press.

Levine, M. P., & Smolak, L. (1992). Toward a model of the developmental psychopathology of eating disorders: The example of early adolescence. In J. H. Crowther, S. E. Hobfoll, D. L. Tennenbaum, & M. A. P. Stephens (Eds.), *The etiology of bulimia nervosa: The individual and family context* (pp. 59–80). Washington, DC: Hemisphere.

Levine, M. P., & Smolak, L. (1996). Media as a context for the development of disordered eating. In L. Smolak & M. P. Levine (Eds.), *The developmental psychopathology of eating disorders: Implications for research, prevention, and treatment* (pp. 235–257). Mahwah, NJ: Erlbaum.

Levine, M. P., & Smolak, L. (in press). The mass media and disordered eating: Implications for primary prevention. In G. Van Noordenbos & W. Vandereyecken (Eds.), *Primary prevention of eating disorders.* London: Athlone.

Levine, M. P., Smolak, L., & Hayden, H. (1994). The relation of sociocultural factors to eating attitudes and behaviors among middle school girls. *Journal of Early Adolescence, 14,* 471–490.

Levine, M. P., Smolak, L., Moodey, A. F., Shuman, M. D., & Hessen, L. D. (1994). Normative developmental challenges and dieting and eating disturbances in middle school girls. *International Journal of Eating Disorders, 15,* 11–20.

Levine, P. (1988). "Bulimic" couples: Dynamics and treatment. *Family Therapy Collections, 25,* 89–104.

Lewis, R. J., Cash, T. F., Jacobi, L., & Bubb-Lewis, C. (1997). Prejudice toward fat people: The development and validation of the Antifat Attitudes Test. *Obesity Research, 5,* 297–307.

Lohr, S. (1998, March 5). It takes a child to raze a village. *New York Times,* p. D1.

Lopez, E., Blix, G. G., & Blix, A. G. (1995). Body image of Latinas compared to body image of non-Latina White women. *Health Values, 19,* 3–10.

Lull, J., Mulac, A., & Rosen, L. S. (1983). Feminism as a predictor of mass media use. *Sex Roles, 9,* 165–177.

Lunner, K., Wertheim, E., Halvarsson, K. S., Thompson, J. K., Paxton, S., & MacDonald, F. (1998). *A cross-cultural examination of body image and eating disturbance in Swedish, Australian, and United States samples.* Unpublished manuscript, University of South Florida.

Macgregor, F. (1990). Facial disfigurement: Problems and management of social interaction and implications for mental health. *Aesthetic Plastic Surgery, 14,* 249–257.

Madan-Swain, A., Brown, R. T., Sexson, S. B., Baldwin, K., Pais, R., & Ragab, A.

(1994). Adolescent cancer survivors: Psychosocial and familial adaptation. *Psychosomatics, 35,* 453–459.

Major, B., Testa, M., & Bylsma, W. H. (1991). Responses to upward and downward social comparisons: The impact of esteem-relevance and perceived control. In J. Suls & T. A. Wills (Eds.), *Social comparison: Contemporary theory and research* (pp. 237–260). Hillsdale, NJ: Erlbaum.

Mann, T., Nolen-Hoeksema, S., Huang, K., Burgard, D., Wright, A., & Hanson, K. (1997). Are two interventions worse than none? Joint primary and secondary prevention of eating disorders in college females. *Health Psychology, 16,* 215–225.

Mark, S. K., & Crowther, J. H. (1997, August). *Body dissatisfaction and relationship satisfaction in dating couples.* Paper presented at the 105th Annual Convention of the American Psychological Association, Chicago, IL.

Marks, I., & Mishan, J. (1988). Dysmorphophobic avoidance with disturbed bodily perception: A pilot study of exposure therapy. British Journal of Psychiatry, 152, 674–678.

Markus, H. (1977). Self-schemata and processing information about the self. *Journal of Personality and Social Psychology, 17,* 60–71.

Markus, H., Hamill, R., & Sentis, K. P. (1987). Thinking fat: Self-schemas for body weight and the processing of weight relevant information. *Journal of Applied Social Psychology, 17*(1), 60–71.

Marsh, H. W., & Parker, J. W. (1984). Determinants of student self-concept: Is it better to be a relatively large fish in a small pond even if you don't learn to swim as well? *Journal of Personality and Social Psychology, 47,* 213–231.

Martin, J. E. (1989). The role of body image in the development of bulimia. *British Journal of Occupational Therapy, 52,* 262–265.

Martin, M. C., & Kennedy, P. F. (1993). Advertising and social comparison: Consequences for female preadolescents and adolescents. *Psychology & Marketing, 10,* 513–530.

Martinez, E. T., & Spinetta, M. (1997). Behavior therapy in Argentina. *The Behavior Therapist, 20,* 171–174.

Martz, D. M., Handley, K. B., & Eisler, R. M. (1996). The relationship between feminine gender role stress, body image, and eating disorders. *Psychology of Women Quarterly, 19,* 493–508.

Maude, D., Wertheim, E. H., Paxton, S., Gibbons, K., & Szmukler, G. (1993). Body dissatisfaction, weight loss behaviours, and bulimic tendencies in Australian adolescents with an estimate of female data representativeness. *Australian Psychologist, 28,* 128–132.

Mazur, A. (1986). U.S. trends in feminine beauty and overadaptation. *Journal of Sex Research, 22,* 281–303.

McAllister, W. R., & McAllister, D. E. (1995). Two-factor fear theory: Implications for understanding anxiety-based clinical phenomena. In W. O'Donohue & L. Krasner (Eds.), *Theories of behavior therapy: Exploring behavior change* (pp. 145–171). Washington, DC: American Psychological Association.

McCarthy, M. (1990). The thin ideal, depression and eating disorders in women. *Behaviour Research and Therapy, 28*, 205–215.

McDonald, D., & Thompson, J. K. (1992). Eating disturbance, body image dissatisfaction, and reasons for exercising: Gender differences and correlational findings. *International Journal of Eating Disorders, 11*, 289–292.

McGill, J., Lawlis, F., Selby, D., Mooney, V., & McCoy, C. E. (1983). The relationship of Minnesota Multiphasic Personality Inventory (MMPI) profile clusters to pain behaviors. *Journal of Behavioral Medicine, 6*, 677–692.

McGrath, E., Keita, G. P., Strickland, B. R., & Russo, N. F. (1990). *Women and depression: Risk factors and treatment issues.* Washington, DC: American Psychological Association.

McHugh, P. (1997, February 2). Shrinking psychology into science. *Baltimore Sun,* p. K4.

McKenzie, S. J., Williamson, D. A., & Cubic, B. A. (1993). Stable and reactive body image disturbances in bulimia nervosa. *Behavior Therapy, 24*, 195–207.

McKinley, N. M. (1995). Women and objectified body consciousness: A feminist psychological analysis. *Dissertation Abstracts International, 56*, 05B. (University Microfilms No. 9527111)

McKinley, N. M. (1997). *Women and objectified body consciousness: Mothers' and daughters' body experience in cultural, developmental, and familial context.* Unpublished manuscript, Alleghany College.

McKinley, N. M. (1998). Gender differences in undergraduates' body esteem: The mediating effect of objectified body consciousness and actual–ideal weight discrepancy. *Sex Roles, 39*, 113–123.

McKinley, N. M., & Hyde, J. S. (1996). The Objectified Body Consciousness Scale: Development and validation. *Psychology of Women Quarterly, 20*, 181–215.

McLorg, P. A., & Taub, D. E. (1987). Anorexia nervosa and bulimia: The development of deviant identities. *Deviant Behavior, 8*, 177–189.

Mead, G. H. (1934). *Mind, self, and society.* Chicago, IL: University of Chicago.

Mendelson, B. K., & White, D. R. (1985). Development of self-body-esteem in overweight youngsters. *Developmental Psychology, 21*, 90–96.

Mendelson, B. K., White, D. R., & Mendelson, M. J. (1998). *Manual for the Body-Esteem Scale for Adolescents and Adults.* Unpublished manuscript, Center for Research in Human Development, Montreal, Quebec, Canada.

Meyers, A. W., Klesges, R. C., Winders, S. E., Ward, K. D., Peterson, B. A., & Eck, L. H. (1997). Are weight concerns predictive of smoking cessation? A prospective analysis. *Journal of Consulting and Clinical Psychology, 65*, 448–452.

Miller, D. T., Turnbull, W., & McFarland, C. (1988). Particularistic and universalistic evaluation in the social comparison process. *Journal of Personality and Social Psychology, 55*, 908–917.

Mock, V. (1993). Body image in women treated for breast cancer. *Nursing Research, 42*, 153–157.

Moreno, A., & Thelen, M. H. (1993). Parental factors related to bulimia nervosa. *Addictive Behaviors, 18*, 681–689.

Morselli, E. (1886). Sulla dismorfofobia e sulla tafefobia. *Nolletinno della Accademia di Genova, 6*, 110–119.

Mowrer, O. W. (1960). *Learning theory and behavior.* New York: Wiley.

Moyer, A. (1997). Psychosocial outcomes of breast-conserving surgery versus mastectomy: A meta-analytic review. *Health Psychology, 16*, 284–298.

Moyer, D. M., DiPietro, L., Berkowitz, R. I., & Stunkard, A. J. (1997). Childhood sexual abuse and precursors of binge eating in an adolescent female population. *International Journal of Eating Disorders, 21*, 23–30.

Murnen, S. K., & Smolak, L. (1997). Femininity, masculinity, and disordered eating: A meta-analytic review. *International Journal of Eating Disorders, 22*, 231–242.

Murray, S. H., Touyz, S. W., & Beumont, P. J. V. (1995). The influence of personal relationships on women's eating behavior and body satisfaction. *Eating Disorders: Journal of Treatment and Prevention, 3*, 243–252.

Murray, S. H., Touyz, S. W., & Beumont, P. J. V. (1996). Awareness and perceived influence of body ideals in the media: A comparison of eating disorder patients and the general community. *Eating Disorders: The Journal of Treatment and Prevention, 4*, 33–46.

Myers, A., & Rosen, J. C. (1998). *Obesity stigmatization and coping: Relation to mental health symptoms, body image, and self-esteem.* Unpublished manuscript, University of Vermont.

NAAFA denounces *The Nutty Professor.* (1996, July/August). *NAAFA Newsletter, 24,* p. 10.

Nagel, K. L., & Jones, K. H. (1992). Sociological factors in the development of eating disorders. *Adolescence, 27*, 107–111.

Nassar, M. (1988). Culture and weight consciousness. *Journal of Psychosomatic Research, 32*, 573–577.

Nathanson, D. L. (1989). Understanding what is hidden: Shame in sexual abuse. *Psychiatric Clinics of North America, 12*, 381.

Nemeroff, C. J., Stein, R. I., Diehl, N. S., & Smilack, K. M. (1994). From the Cleavers to the Clintons: Role choices and body orientation as reflected in magazine article content. *International Journal of Eating Disorders, 16*, 167–176.

Nevid, J. S. (1984). Sex differences in factors of romantic attraction. *Sex Roles, 11*, 401–411.

Newman, J. P., Wallace, J. F., Strauman, T. J., Skolaski, R. L., Oreland, K. M., Mattek, P. W., Elder, K. A., & McNeely, J. (1993). Effects of motivational significant stimuli on the regulation of dominant responses. *Journal of Personality and Social Psychology, 65*, 165–175.

Newman, L. (1986). *Good enough to eat.* Ithaca, NY: Firebrand Books.

Neziroglu, F., McKay, D., Todaro, J., & Yaryura-Tobias, J. A. (1996). Effect of cognitive behavior therapy on persons with body dysmorphic disorder and comorbid Axis II diagnoses. *Behavior Therapy, 27,* 67–77.

Nichter, M., & Nichter, M. (1991). Hype and weight. *Medical Anthropology, 13,* 249–284.

Norris, D. L. (1984). The effects of mirror confrontation on self-estimation of body dimension in anorexia nervosa, bulimia, and two control groups. *Psychological Medicine, 14,* 835–842.

Norton, K. I., Olds, T. S., Olive, S., & Dank, S. (1996). Ken and Barbie at life size. *Sex Roles, 34,* 287–294.

O'Connor, P. J., Lewis, R. D., & Boyd, A. (1996). Health concerns of artistic women gymnasts. *Sports Medicine, 21,* 321–325.

O'Connor, P. J., Lewis, R. D., & Kirchner, E. M. (1995). Eating disorder symptoms in female college gymnasts. *Medicine and Science in Sports and Exercise, 27,* 550–555.

O'Connor, P. J., Lewis, R. D., Kirchner, E. M., & Cook, D. B. (1996). Eating disorder symptoms in former female college gymnasts: Relations with body composition. *American Journal of Clinical Nutrition, 64,* 840–843.

Ogletree, S. M., Williams, S. W., Raffeld, P., Mason, B., & Fricke, K. (1990). Female attractiveness and eating disorders: Do children's television commercials play a role? *Sex Roles, 22,* 791–797.

O'Hanlon, A. (1997, January 5). A sense of scale. *The Washington Post Magazine,* 11–34.

Olweus, D. (1991). Bully/victim problems among schoolchildren: Basic facts and effects of a school based intervention program. In D. J. Pepler & K. H. Rubin (Eds.), *The development and treatment of childhood aggression* (pp. 411–448). Hillsdale, NJ: Erlbaum.

Olweus, D. (1993). Bully/victim problems among schoolchildren: Long-term consequences and an effective intervention program. In S. Hodgins (Eds.), *Mental disorder and crime* (pp. 317–349). Newbury Park, CA: Sage.

Oliver, K. K., & Thelen, M. H. (1996). Children's perceptions of peer influence on eating concerns. *Behavior Therapy, 27,* 25–39.

Orbach, S. (1978a). *Fat is a feminist issue.* New York: Paddington Press.

Orbach, S. (1978b). *Fat is a feminist issue: A self-help guide for compulsive overeaters.* New York: Berkley Books.

Palmer, R. L., Oppenheimer, R., Dignon, A., Chaloner, D. A., & Howells, K. (1990). Childhood sexual experiences with adults reported by women and eating disorders: An extended series. *British Journal of Psychiatry, 156,* 699–703.

Parker, S., Nichter, M., Vuckovic, N., Sims, C., & Ritenbaugh, C. (1995). Body image and weight concerns among African American and White adolescent females: Differences that make a difference. *Human Organization, 54,* 103–114.

Partridge, J. (1990). *Changing faces: The challenge of facial disfigurement.* London: Penguin.

Partridge, J. (1996). *When burns affect the way you look: Helping yourself towards successful rehabilitation*. Bristol, UK: Taylor Brothers.

Pasman, L., & Thompson, J. K. (1988). Body image and eating disturbance in obligatory runners, obligatory weightlifters, and sedentary individuals. *International Journal of Eating Disorders, 7*, 759–769.

"A pathology of thinness" is plaguing Argentine girls. (1997, July 4). *St. Petersburg Times*, p. A14.

Pedersen, E. L., & Markee, N. L. (1991). Fashion dolls: Representations of ideals of beauty. *Perceptual and Motor Skills, 73*, 93–94.

Penner, L., Thompson, J. K., & Coovert, D. L. (1991). Size overestimation among anorexics: Much ado about very little? *Journal of Abnormal Psychology, 100*, 90–93.

Peplau, L. A., & Conrad, E. (1989). Beyond nonsexist research: The perils of feminist methods in psychology. *Psychology of Women Quarterly, 13*, 379–400.

Perlick, D., & Silverstein, B. (1994). Faces of female discontent: Depression, disordered eating, and changing gender roles. In P. Fallon, M. A. Katzman, & S. C. Wooley (Eds.), *Feminist perspectives on eating disorders* (pp. 77–93). New York: Guilford Press.

Perpina, C., Hemsley, D., Treasure, J., & de Silva, P. (1993). Is the selective information processing of food and body words specific to patients with eating disorders? *International Journal of Eating Disorders, 14*, 359–366.

Persall, S. (1997, June 3). Nicholas Cage would cast Superman in his own image. *St. Petersburg Times*, p. D1.

Perspectives. (1997a, May 12). *Newsweek*, p. 29.

Perspectives. (1997b, June 9). *Newsweek*, p. 27.

Pertschuk, M. J., Sarwer, D. B., Wadden, T. A., & Whitaker, L. A. (1998). Body image dissatisfaction in male cosmetic surgery patients. *Aesthetic Plastic Surgery, 22*, 20–24.

Petersen, A. C., Schulenberg, J. E., Abramowitz, R. H., Offer, D., & Jarcho, H. D. (1984). The Self-Image Questionnaire for Young Adolescents (SIQYA): Reliability and validity studies. *Journal of Youth and Adolescence, 13*, 93–11.

Petersons, M., Phillips, E, & Steinhaus, N. (1996). Prevalence of eating-disordered behaviors among fashion merchandising majors. *Eating Disorders: The Journal of Treatment and Prevention, 4*, 256–263.

Petrie, T. A., Austin, L. J., Crowley, B. J., Helmcaup, A., Johnson, C. E., Lester R., Rogers, R., Turner, J., & Walbrick, K. (1996). Sociocultural expectations of attractiveness for males. *Sex Roles, 35*, 581–601.

Phares, V. (1992). Where's poppa? The relative lack of attention to the role of fathers in child and adolescent psychopathology. *American Psychologist, 47*, 656–664.

Phillips, K. A. (1996). *The broken mirror: Understanding and treating body dysmorphic disorder*. New York: Oxford University Press.

Phillips, K. A., McElroy, S. L., Keck, P. E., Pope, H. G., & Hudson, J. I. (1993).

Body dysmorphic disorder: 30 cases of imagined ugliness. *American Journal of Psychiatry, 150,* 302–308.

Pick, A. (1922). Storung der orientierung am eigenen korper. *Psychologische Forschung, 1,* 303–315.

Pierce, J. W., & Wardle, J. (1996). Body size, parental appraisal, and self-esteem in blind children. *Journal of Child Psychology and Psychiatry, 37,* 205–212.

Pierce, K. (1990). A feminist theoretical perspective on the socialization of teenage girls through *Seventeen* magazine. *Sex Roles, 23,* 491–500.

Pike, K. (1995). Bulimic symptomatology in high school girls: Toward a model of cumulative risk. *Psychology of Women Quarterly, 19,* 373–396.

Pike, K., & Rodin, J. (1991). Mothers, daughters, and disordered eating. *Journal of Abnormal Psychology, 100,* 198–204.

Pipher, M. (1994). *Reviving Ophelia: Saving the lives of adolescent girls.* New York: Grosset/Putnam.

Pitts, C., & Waller, G. (1993). Self-denigratory beliefs following sexual abuse. Association with the symptomatology of bulimic disorders. *International Journal of Eating Disorders, 11,* 407–410.

Polivy, J., Herman, C. P., Olmsted, M. P., & Jazwinsky, C. (1984). Restraint and bingeing: From laboratory models to clinical practice. In R. C. Hawkins II, W. J. Fremouw, & P. F. Clement (Eds.), *Binge eating: Theory, research, and treatment.* New York: Wiley.

Pope, H. G., Gruber, A. J., Choi, P., Olivardia, R., & Phillips, K. A. (1997). "Muscle dysmorphia": An underrecognized form of body dysmorphic disorder? *Psychosomatics, 38,* 548–557.

Pope, H. G., & Hudson, J. I. (1992). Is childhood sexual abuse a risk factor for bulimia nervosa? *American Journal of Psychiatry, 149,* 455–463.

Pope, H. G., & Hudson, J. I. (1995). Does childhood sexual abuse cause adult psychiatric disorders? Essentials of methodology. *Journal of Psychiatry & Law,* 363–381.

Powers, P. S. (1980). *Obesity: The regulation of weight.* Baltimore: Williams & Wilkins.

Probst, M., Vandereycken, W., Van Coppenolle, H., & Pieters, G. (1995). Body size estimation in eating disorder patients: Testing the video distortion method on a life-size screen. *Behaviour Research and Therapy, 33,* 985–990.

Probst, M., Vandereycken, W., Vanderlinden, J., & Van Coppenolle, H. (1998). The significance of body size estimation in eating disorders: Its relationship with clinical and psychological variables. *International Journal of Eating Disorders, 24,* 167–174.

Pruzinsky, T. (1992). Social and psychological effects of major craniofacial deformity. *Cleft Palate–Craniofacial Journal, 29,* 578–584.

Pruzinsky, T. (1996). Cosmetic plastic surgery and body image: Critical factors in patient assessment. In J. K. Thompson (Ed.), *Body image, eating disorders, and obesity: An integrative guide for assessment and treatment* (pp. 83–107). Washington, DC: American Psychological Association.

Pruzinsky, T., & Cash, T. F. (1990). Integrative themes in body image development, deviance and change. In T. F. Cash & T. Pruzinsky (Eds.), *Body images: Development, deviance, and change* (pp. 337–349). New York: Guilford Press.

Pyszczynski, T., Greenberb, J., & LaPrelle, J. (1985). Social comparison after success and failure: Biased search for information consistent with a self-serving conclusion. *Journal of Experimental Social Psychology, 21*, 195–211.

Radke-Sharpe, N., Whitney-Saltiel, D., & Rodin, J. (1990). Fat distribution as a risk factor for weight and eating concerns. *International Journal of Eating Disorders, 9*, 27–36.

Rand, C. S. W., & Kuldau, J. M. (1990). The epidemiology of obesity and self-defined weight problem in the general population: Gender, race, age, and social class. *International Journal of Eating Disorders, 9*, 329–343.

Raphael, F. J., & Lacey, J. H. (1992). Sociocultural aspects of eating disorders. *Annals of Medicine, 24*, 293–296.

Reed, D. L., Thompson, J. K., Brannick, M. T., & Sacco, W. P. (1991). Development and validation of the Physical Appearance State and Trait Anxiety Scale (PASTAS). *Journal of Anxiety Disorders, 5*, 323–332.

Rice, C. (1996). Trauma and eating problems: Expanding the debate. *Eating Disorders: The Journal of Treatment and Prevention, 4*, 197–237.

Richardson, S. A., Goodman, N., Hasdorf, A. H., & Dornbusch, S. M. (1961). Cultural uniformity in relation to physical disabilities. *American Sociological Review, 26*, 241–247.

Rieger, E., Schotte, D. E., Touyz, S. W., Beumont, P. J. V., Griffiths, R., & Russell, J. (1998). Attentional biases in eating disorders: A visual probe detection procedure. *International Journal of Eating Disorders, 23*, 199–205.

Rieves, L., & Cash, T. F. (1996). Social developmental factors and women's body-image attitudes. *Journal of Social Behavior and Personality, 11*, 63–78.

Riva, G. (1998). Modifications of body-image induced by virtual reality. *Perceptual and Motor Skills, 86*, 163–170.

Riva, G. (in press). Virtual environment for body image modification: Virtual reality system in the treatment of body image disturbances. *Computers in Human Behavior.*

Riva, G., & Molinari, E. (1995). Body image and social attitude in growth-hormone-deficient adults. *Perceptual and Motor Skills, 80*, 1083–1088.

Robinson, B. E., & Bacon, J. G. (1996). The "If Only I Were Thin . . . " treatment program: Decreasing the stigmatizing effects of fatness. *Professional Psychology: Research and Practice, 27*, 175–183.

Robinson, E., Clarke, A., & Cooper, C. (1996). *The psychology of facial disfigurement: A guide for health professionals.* Bristol, UK: Taylor.

Robinson, E., Rumsey, N., & Partridge, J. (1996). An evaluation of the impact of social interaction skills training for facially disfigured people. *British Journal of Plastic Surgery, 49*, 281–289.

Rodin, J., & Ickovics, J. R. (1990). Women's health: Review and research agenda as we approach the 21st century. *American Psychologist, 45*, 1018–1034.

Rodin, J., Silberstein, L. R., & Striegel-Moore, R. H. (1985). Women and weight: A normative discontent. In T. B. Sonderegger (Ed.), *Psychology and Gender: Nebraska Symposium on Motivation, 1984* (pp. 267–307). Lincoln: University of Nebraska Press.

Rolland, K., Farnill, D., & Griffiths, R. A. (1997). Body figure perceptions and eating attitudes among Australian schoolchildren aged 8 to 12 years. *International Journal of Eating Disorders, 21*, 273–278.

Root, M. P. (1990). Disordered eating in women of color. *Sex Roles, 22*, 525–536.

Root, M. P. (1991). Persistent disordered eating as a gender specific post-traumatic response to sexual assault. *Psychotherapy: Theory, Research and Practice, 28*, 96–102.

Root, M. P., & Fallon, P. (1988). The incidence of victimization experience in a bulimic sample. *Journal of Interpersonal Violence, 3*, 161–173.

Root, M. P., Fallon, P., & Friedrich, W. N. (1986). *Bulimia: A systems approach to treatment.* New York: Norton.

Rorty, M., & Yager, J. (1996). Histories of childhood trauma and complex post-traumatic sequelae in women with eating disorders. *Psychiatric Clinics of North America, 19*, 773–791.

Rorty, M., Yager, J., & Rossotto, E. (1994). Childhood sexual, physical, and psychological abuse and their relationship to comorbid psychopathology in bulimia nervosa. *International Journal of Eating Disorders, 16*, 317–334.

Rosen, J. C. (1992). Body image disorder: Definition, development, and contribution to eating disorders. In J. H. Crowther, D. L. Tennenbaum, S. E. Hobfoll, & M. A. P. Stephens (Eds.), *The etiology of bulimia: The individual and family context* (pp. 157–177). Washington, DC: Hemisphere.

Rosen, J. C. (1996a). Body dysmorphic disorder: Assessment and treatment. In J. K. Thompson (Ed.), *Body image, eating disorders, and obesity: An integrative guide for assessment and treatment* (pp. 149–170). Washington, DC: American Psychological Association.

Rosen, J. C. (1996b). Improving body image in obesity. In J. K. Thompson (Ed.), *Body image, eating disorders, and obesity: An integrative guide for assessment and treatment* (pp. 425–440). Washington, DC: American Psychological Association.

Rosen, J. C. (1997). Cognitive–behavioral body image therapy. In D. M. Garner & P. E. Garfinkel (Eds.), *Handbook of treatment for eating disorders* (pp. 188–201). New York: Guilford.

Rosen, J. C., & Cash, T. F. (1995). Learning to have a better body image. *Weight Control Digest, 5*, 411–416.

Rosen, J. C., & Gross, J. (1987). Prevalence of weight reducing and weight gaining in adolescent girls and boys. *Health Psychology, 6*, 131–147.

Rosen, J. C., Orosan-Weine, P., & Tang, T. (1997). Critical experiences in the development of body image. *Eating Disorders: The Journal of Treatment and Prevention, 5*, 191–204.

Rosen, J. C., & Ramirez, E. (in press). A comparison of eating disorders and body dysmorphic disorder on body image and psychological adjustment. *Journal of Psychosomatic Research*.

Rosen, J. C., & Reiter, J. (1996). Development of the Body Dysmorphic Disorder Examination. *Behaviour Research and Therapy, 34*, 755–766.

Rosen, J. C., Reiter, J., & Orosan, P. (1995a). Assessment of body image in eating disorders with the Body Dysmorphic Disorder Examination. *Behaviour Research and Therapy, 33*, 77–84.

Rosen, J. C., Reiter, J., & Orosan, P. (1995b). Cognitive behavioral body image therapy for body dysmorphic disorder. *Journal of Consulting and Clinical Psychology, 63*, 263–269.

Rosen, J. C., Saltzberg, E., & Srebnik, D. (1989). Cognitive behavior therapy for negative body image. *Behavior Therapy, 20*, 293–404.

Rosen, J. C., Srebnik, D., Saltzberg, E., & Wendt, S. (1991). Development of a body image avoidance questionnaire. *Psychological Assessment, 3*, 32–37.

Rosen, M. D. (1997, Spring). Can this marriage be saved? *Ladies' Home Journal*, p. 2.

Rosenthal, E. (1991, September 24). Cosmetic surgeons seek new frontiers. *New York Times*, p. C1.

Roth, D., & Armstrong, J. (1993) Feelings of Fatness Questionnaire: A measure of the cross-situational variability of body experience. *International Journal of Eating Disorders, 14*, 349–358.

Roth, G. (1982). *Feeding the hungry heart*. New York: Penguin Books.

Rothblum, E. D. (1992). The stigma of women's weight: Social and economic realities. *Feminism & Psychology, 2*, 61–73.

Rothblum, E. D. (1994). "I'll die for the revolution but don't ask me not to diet": Feminism and the continuing stigmatization of obesity. In P. Fallon, M. A. Katzman, & S. C. Wooley (Eds.), *Feminist perspectives on eating disorders* (pp. 53–76). New York: Guilford Press.

Rothblum, E. D., Brand, P. A., Miller, C. T., & Oetjen, H. A. (1990). The relationship between obesity, employment discrimination and employment-related victimization. *Journal of Vocational Behavior, 37*, 251–266.

Rothblum, E. D., Miller, C. T., & Garbutt, B. (1988). Stereotypes of obese female job applicants. *International Journal of Eating Disorders, 7*, 277–283.

Rozin, P., & Fallon, A. (1988). Body image, attitudes to weight, and misperceptions of figure preferences of the opposite sex: A comparison of men and women in two generations. *Journal of Abnormal Psychology, 97*, 342–345.

Ruble, D. N. (1983). The development of social comparison processes and their role in achievement-related self-socialization. In E. T. Higgins, D. N. Ruble, & W. W. Hartup (Eds.), *Social cognition and social development: A sociocultural perspective* (pp. 134–157). Cambridge, England: Cambridge University Press.

Rucker, C. E., III, & Cash, T. F. (1992). Body images, body-size perceptions, and eating behaviors among African-American and White college women. *International Journal of Eating Disorders, 12*, 291–299.

Ruff, G. A., & Barrios, B. A. (1986). Realistic assessment of body image. *Behavioral Assessment, 8,* 237–252.

Russell, G. F. M. (1970). Anorexia nervosa: Its identity as in illness and its treatment. In J. H. Price (Ed.), *Modern trends in psychological medicine* (Vol. 2, pp. 131–164). London: Butterworths.

Ryan, J. (1996). *Little girls in pretty boxes: The making and breaking of elite gymnasts and figure skaters.* New York: Doubleday.

Rybarczyk, B., Nyenhuis, D. L., Nicholas, J. J., Cash, S. M., & Kaiser, J. (1995). Body image, perceived social stigma, and the prediction of psychosocial adjustment to leg amputation. *Rehabilitation Psychology, 40,* 95–110.

Rydall, A. C., Rodin, G. M., Olmsted, M. P., Devenyi, T. G., & Daneman, D. (1997). Disordered eating behavior and microvascular complications in young women with insulin-dependent diabetes mellitus. *New England Journal of Medicine, 336,* 1849–1854.

Sanftner, J. L., Crowther, J. H., Crawford, P. A., & Watts, D. D. (1996). Maternal influences (or lack thereof) on daughters' eating attitudes and behaviors. *Eating Disorders: The Journal of Treatment and Prevention, 4,* 147–159.

Santonastaso, P., Favaro, A., Ferrara, S., Sala, A., & Zanetti, T. (1995). Prevalence of body image disturbance in a female adolescent sample: A longitudinal study. *Eating Disorders: The Journal of Treatment and Prevention, 3,* 342–350.

Sarwer, D. B. (1997). The "obsessive" cosmetic surgery patient: A consideration of body image dissatisfaction and body dysmorphic disorder. *Plastic Surgical Nursing, 17,* 193–197.

Sarwer, D. B., Bartlett, S. P., Bucky, L. P., LaRossa, D., Low, D. W., Pertschuk, M. J., Wadden, T. A., & Whitaker, L. A. (1998). Bigger is not always better: Body image dissatisfaction in breast reduction and breast augmentation patients. *Plastic and Reconstructive Surgery, 101,* 1956–1961.

Sarwer, D. B., Pertschuk, M. J., Wadden, T. A., & Whitaker, L. A. (in press). Psychological investigations in cosmetic surgery: A look back and a look ahead. *Plastic and Reconstructive Surgery.*

Sarwer, D. B., Wadden, T. A., & Foster, G. D. (in press). Assessment of body image dissatisfaction in obese women: Specificity, severity, and clinical significance. *Journal of Consulting and Clinical Psychology.*

Sarwer, D. B., Wadden, T. A., Pertschuk, M. J., & Whitaker, L. A. (1998). The psychology of cosmetic surgery: A review and reconceptualization. *Clinical Psychology Review, 18,* 1–22.

Sarwer, D. B., Wadden, T. A., Pertschuk, M. J., & Whitaker, L. A. (in press). Body image dissatisfaction and body dysmorphic disorder in 100 cosmetic surgery patients. *Plastic and Reconstructive Surgery.*

Sarwer, D. B., Whitaker, L. A., Wadden, T. A., & Pertschuk, M J. (1997). Body image dissatisfaction in women seeking rhytidectomy or blepharoplasty. *Aesthetic Surgery Journal, 17,* 230–234.

Scalf-McIver, L., & Thompson, J. K. (1989). Family correlates of bulimic characteristics in college females. *Journal of Clinical Psychology, 45,* 467–472.

Scharlott, B. W., & Christ, W. G. (1995). Overcoming relationship-initiation barriers: The impact of a computer-dating system on sex role, shyness, and appearance inhibitions. *Computers in Human Behavior, 11,* 191–204.

Schefer, D. (1997). *What is beauty?* New York: Universe.

Schilder, P. (1914). *Selbstewusstsein und personlichkeithewusstsein.* Berlin, Germany: Springer.

Schilder, P. (1923). *Das koerperschema.* Berlin, Germany: Springer.

Schilder, P. (1950). *The image and appearance of the human body.* New York: International Universities Press.

Schlundt, D. G., & Bell, C. (1993). Body image testing system: A microcomputer program for assessing body image. *Journal of Psychopathology and Behavioral Assessment, 15,* 267–285.

Schlundt, D. G., Jarrell, M. P., & Johnson, W. G. (1983). A naturalistic functional analysis of eating behavior in bulimia and obesity. *Advances in Behavior Research and Therapy, 7,* 149–162.

Schneider, K. S. (1996, June 3). Mission impossible. *People, 45,* pp. 65–74.

Schreiber, G. B., Robins, M., Striegel-Moore, R., Obarzanek, E., Morrison, J. A., & Wright, D. J. (1996). Weight modification efforts reported by Black and White preadolescent girls: National Heart, Lung, and Blood Institute Growth and Health Study. *Pediatrics, 98,* 63–70.

Schulman, R. G., Kinder, B. N., Powers, P. S., Prange, M., & Gleghorn, A. A. (1986). The development of a scale to measure cognitive distortions in bulimia. *Journal of Personality Assessment, 50,* 630–639.

Schwartz, D., Phares, V., Tantleff-Dunn, S., & Thompson, J. K. (in press). Body image, psychological function, and parental feedback regarding physical appearance. *International Journal of Eating Disorders.*

Schwartz, D. M., Thompson, M. G., & Johnson, C. L. (1981). Anorexia nervosa and bulimia: The socio-cultural context. *International Journal of Eating Disorders, 1,* 20–36.

Schwerin, M. J., Corcoran, K. J., Fisher, L., Patterson, D., Askew, W., Olrich, T., & Shanks, S. (1996). Social physique anxiety, body esteem, and social anxiety in bodybuilders and self-reported anabolic steroid users. *Addictive Behaviors, 21,* 1–8.

Scott, D. W. (1987). The involvement of psychosexual factors in the causation of eating disorders: Time for a reappraisal. *International Journal of Eating Disorders, 36,* 199–213.

Secord, P. F., & Jourard, P. F. (1953). The appraisal of body-cathexis: Body-cathexis and the self. *Journal of Consulting Psychology, 17,* 343–347.

Segal, Z. V. (1988). Appraisal of the self-schemata construct in cognitive models of depression. *Psychological Bulletin, 103,* 147–162.

Seid, R. P. (1994). Too "close to the bone": The historical context for women's obsession with slenderness. In P. Fallon, M. A. Katzman, & S. C. Wooley (Eds.), *Feminist perspectives on eating disorders* (pp. 3–16). New York: Guilford Press.

Selvini-Palazzoli, M. (1974). *Self-starvation—From the intrapsychic to the transpersonal approach to anorexia nervosa* (A. Perans, Trans.). London: Human Context Books.

Serdula, M. K., Collins, M. E., Williamson, D. F., Anda, R. F., Pamuk, E., & Byers, T. E. (1993). Weight control practices of U.S. adolescents and adults. *Annals of Internal Medicine, 119,* 667–671.

Shapiro, J. P., Baumeister, R. F., & Kessler, J. W. (1991). A three-component model of children's teasing: Aggression, humor, and ambiguity. *Journal of Social and Clinical Psychology, 10,* 459–472.

Shaw, J., & Waller, G. (1995). The media's impact on body image: Implications for prevention and treatment. *Eating Disorders: The Journal of Treatment and Prevention, 3,* 115–123.

Shisslak, C. M., Renger, R., Sharpe, T., Crago, M., McKnight, K. M., Gray, N., Bryson, S., Estes, L. S., Parnaby, O. G., Killen, J., & Taylor, C. B. (in press). Development and evaluation of the McKnight Risk Factor Survey (MRFS-III) for assessing potential risk and protective factors for disordered eating in preadolescent and adolescent girls. *International Journal of Eating Disorders.*

Shontz, F. C. (1974). Body image and its disorders. *International Journal of Psychiatry in Medicine, 5,* 461–471.

Shore, R. A., & Porter, J. E. (1990). Normative and reliability data for 11 to 18 year olds on the Eating Disorder Inventory. *International Journal of Eating Disorders, 9,* 201–208.

Siever, M. D. (1994). Sexual orientation and gender as factors in socioculturally acquired vulnerability to body dissatisfaction and eating disorders. *Journal of Consulting and Clinical Psychology, 62,* 252–260.

Silberstein, L. R., Striegel-Moore, R. H., & Rodin, J. (1987). Feeling fat: A woman's shame. In H. B. Lewis (Ed.), *The role of shame in symptom formation* (pp. 98–108). Hillsdale, NJ: Erlbaum.

Silverstein, B., Carpman, S., Perlick, D., & Perdue, L. (1990). Nontraditional sex role aspirations, gender identity conflict and disordered eating among college women. *Sex Roles, 23,* 687–695.

Silverstein, B., & Perdue, L. (1988). The relationship between role concerns, preferences for slimness and symptoms of eating problems among college women. *Sex Roles, 18,* 101–106.

Silverstein, B., Perdue, L., Peterson, B., & Kelly, E. (1986). The role of the mass media in promoting a thin standard of bodily attractiveness for women. *Sex Roles, 14,* 519–532.

Silverstein, B., Perdue, L., Peterson, B., Vogel, L., & Fantini, D. A. (1986). Possible causes of the thin standard of bodily attractiveness for women. *International Journal of Eating Disorders, 5,* 907–916.

Silverstein, B., Perdue, L., Wolf, C., & Pizzolo, C. (1988). Bingeing, purging and estimates of parental attitudes regarding female achievement. *Sex Roles, 19,* 723–733.

Silverstein, B., Peterson, B., & Perdue, L. (1986). Some correlates of the thin standard of bodily attractiveness for women. *International Journal of Eating Disorders, 5,* 895–905.

Simpson, W. S., & Ramberg, J. A. (1992). Sexual dysfunction in married female patients in anorexia and bulimia nervosa. *Journal of Sex and Marital Therapy, 18,* 44–54.

Sjostrom, L., & Stein, N. (1996). *Bullyproof: A teacher's guide on teasing and bullying for use with fourth and fifth grade students.* Wellesley, MA: National Education Association Professional Library.

Slade, P. D. (1977). Awareness of body dimensions during pregnancy: An analogue study. *Psychological Medicine, 7,* 245–252.

Slade, P. D. (1982). Towards a functional analysis of anorexia nervosa and bulimia nervosa. *British Journal of Clinical Psychology, 21,* 67–79.

Slade, P. D. (1985). A review of body-image studies in anorexia nervosa and bulimia nervosa. *Journal of Psychiatric Research, 19,* 255–265.

Slade, P. D., Dewey, M. E., Newton, T., Brodie, D., & Kiemle, G. (1990). Development and preliminary validation of the Body Satisfaction Scale (BSS). *Psychology and Health, 4,* 213–220.

Slade, P. D., & Russell, G. F. M. (1973). Awareness of body dimensions in anorexia nervosa: Cross-sectional and longitudinal studies. *Psychological Medicine, 3,* 188–199.

Slap, G. B., Khalid, N., Paikoff, R. L., Brooks-Gunn, J., & Warren, M. P. (1994). Evolving self-image, pubertal manifestations, and pubertal hormones: Preliminary findings in young adolescent girls. *Journal of Adolescent Health, 15,* 327–335.

Smeets, M. A. M. (1997). The rise and fall of body size estimation research in anorexia nervosa: A review and reconceptualization. *European Eating Disorders Review, 5,* 75–95.

Smeets, M. A. M., Smit, F., Panhuysen, G. E. M., & Ingleby, J. D. (in press). Body Perception Index: Benefits, pitfalls, ideas. *Journal of Psychometric Research.*

Smith, D. E., Thompson, J. K., Raczynski, J. M., & Hilner, J. (in press). Body image among men and women in a biracial cohort: The CARDIA Study. *International Journal of Eating Disorders.*

Smith, P. K., & Sharp, S. (1994). *School bullying: Insights and perspectives.* London: Routledge.

Smolak, L., & Levine, M. P. (1994). Toward an empirical basis for primary prevention of eating problems with elementary school children. *Eating Disorders: The Journal of Treatment and Prevention, 2,* 293–307.

Smolak, L., & Levine, M. P. (1996). Adolescent transitions and the development of eating problems. In L. Smolak, M. P. Levine, & R. Striegel-Moore (Eds.), *The developmental psychopathology of eating disorders: Implications for research, prevention, and treatment* (pp. 207–233). Mahwah, NJ: Erlbaum.

Smolak, L., Levine, M. P., & Gralen, S. (1993). The impact of puberty and dating on eating problems among middle school girls. *Journal of Youth and Adolescence, 22,* 355–368.

Smolak, L., Levine, M. P., & Schermer, F. (1998). A controlled evaluation of an elementary school primary prevention program for eating problems. *Journal of Psychosomatic Research, 44*, 339–354.

Smolak, L., Levine, M. P., & Schermer, F. (in press). Lessons from lessons: An evaluation of an elementary school prevention program. In G. Noordenbos & W. Vandereycken (Eds.), *The prevention of eating disorders*. London: Athlone.

Smolak, L., Levine, M. P., & Striegel-Moore, R. (Eds.). (1996). *The developmental psychopathology of eating disorders: Implications for research, prevention, and treatment*. Mahwah, NJ: Erlbaum.

Smuts, R. W. (1992). Fat, sex, class, adaptation and cultural change. *Ethology and Sociobiology, 13*, 523–542.

Snyder, M., Tanke, E. D., & Berscheid, E. (1977). Social perception and interpersonal behavior: On the self-fulfilling nature of social stereotypes. *Journal of Personality and Social Psychology, 35*, 656–666.

Sobal, J., & Stunkard, A. J. (1989). Socioeconomic status and obesity: A review of the literature. *Psychological Bulletin, 105*, 260–275.

Spence, J. T., & Helmreich, R. L. (1978). Gender, sex roles, and the psychological dimension of masculinity and femininity. In J. T. Spence & R. L. Helmreich (Eds.), *Masculinity and femininity: Their psychological dimensions, correlates, and antecedents* (pp. 3–18). Austin: University of Texas Press.

Spillman, D. M., & Everington, C. (1989). Somatotypes revisited: Have the media changed our perception of the female body image? *Psychological Reports, 64*, 887–890.

Sprecher, S., & McKinney, K. (1987). Barriers in the initiation of intimate heterosexual relationships. *Journal of Social Work and Human Sexuality, 5*, 97–110.

Stanley, A. (1996, August 14). New face of Russian capitalism. *New York Times*, p. C16.

Steiger, H., Liquornik, K., Chapman, J., & Hussain, N. (1991). Personality and family disturbances in eating-disorder patients: Comparison of "restrictor" and "binger" to normal controls. *International Journal of Eating Disorders, 10*, 510–512.

Stein, A., & Fairburn, C. G. (1989). Children of mothers with bulimia nervosa. *British Medical Journal, 299*, 777–778.

Stein, A., & Fairburn, C. G. (1996). Eating habits and attitudes in the postpartum period. *Psychosomatic Medicine, 58*, 321–325.

Stein, A., & Wooley, H. (1996). The influence of parental eating disorders on young children: Implications of recent research for some clinical interventions. *Eating Disorders: The Journal of Treatment and Prevention, 4*, 139–146.

Stein, A., Wooley, H., Cooper, S. D., & Fairburn, C. G. (1994). An observational study of mothers with eating disorders and their infants. *Journal of Child Psychology and Psychiatry, 35*, 733–748.

Stein, K. F., & Hedger, K. M. (1997). Body weight and shape self-cognitions, emotional distress, and disordered eating in middle adolescent girls. *Archives of Psychiatric Nursing, 11*, 264–275.

Stern, S. (1991). Managing opposing currents: An interpersonal psychoanalytic technique for the treatment of eating disorders. In C. L. Johnson (Ed.), *Psychodynamic treatment of anorexia nervosa and bulimia* (pp. 3–33). New York: Guilford Press.

Stern, S., Dixon, K., Jones, D., Lake, M., Nemzer, E., & Sansone, R. (1989). Family environment in anorexia nervosa and bulimia. *International Journal of Eating Disorders, 8*, 25–31.

Sternberg, L., & Blinn, L. (1993). Feelings about self and body image during adolescent pregnancy. *Families in Society, 74*, 282–290.

Stice, E. (1994). Review of the evidence for a sociocultural model of bulimia nervosa and an exploration of the mechanisms of action. *Clinical Psychology Review, 14*, 1–29.

Stice, E., & Agras, W. S. (1998). Predicting the onset and remission of bulimic behaviors during adolescence: A longitudinal grouping analysis. *Behavior Therapy, 29*, 257–276.

Stice, E., Killen, J. D., Hayward, C., & Taylor, C. B. (in press). Age of onset for binge eating and purging during adolescence: A four-year survival analysis. *Journal of Abnormal Psychology*.

Stice, E., Nemeroff, C., & Shaw, H. (1996). A test of the dual pathway model of bulimia nervosa: Evidence for restrained-eating and affect-regulation mechanisms. *Journal of Social and Clinical Psychology, 15*, 340–363.

Stice, E., Schupak-Neuberg, E., Shaw, H. E., & Stein, R. I. (1994). Relation of media exposure to eating disorder symptomatology: An examination of mediating mechanisms. *Journal of Abnormal Psychology, 103*, 836–840.

Stice, E., & Shaw, H. E. (1994). Adverse effects of the media portrayed thin-ideal on women and linkages to bulimic symptomatology. *Journal of Social and Clinical Psychology, 13*, 288–308.

Stice, E., Shaw, H., & Nemeroff, C. (1998). Dual pathway model of bulimia nervosa: Longitudinal support for dietary restraint and affect-regulation mechanisms. *Journal of Social and Clinical Psychology, 17*, 129–149.

Stice, E., Ziemba, C., Margolis, J., & Flick, P. (1996). The dual pathway model differentiates bulimics, subclinical bulimics, and controls: Testing the continuity hypothesis. *Behavior Therapy, 27*, 531–549.

Stone, S. D. (1995). The myth of bodily perfection. *Disability and Society, 10*, 413–424.

Stormer, S. M., & Thompson, J. K. (1995, November). *The effect of media images and sociocultural beauty ideals on college-age women: A proposed psychoeducation program*. Poster session presented at the meetings of the Association for the Advancement of Behavior Therapy, New York, NY.

Stormer, S. M., & Thompson, J. K. (1996). Explanations of body image disturbance: A test of maturational status, negative verbal commentary, social comparison, and sociocultural hypotheses. *International Journal of Eating Disorders*, *19*, 193–202.

Stormer, S., & Thompson, J. K. (1998, November). *An evaluation of a media-focused psychoeducational program for body image distrubance.* Paper presented at the annual meeting of the Association for the Advancement of Behavior Therapy, Washington, DC.

Story, M., French, S. A., Resnick, M. D., & Blum, R. W. (1995). Ethnic/racial and socioeconomic differences in dieting behaviors and body image perceptions in adolescents. *International Journal of Eating Disorders*, *18*, 173–179.

Strauman, T. J., & Higgins, E. T. (1987). Automatic activation of self-discrepancies and emotional syndromes: When cognitive structures influence affect. *Journal of Personality and Social Psychology*, *53*, 1004–1014.

Strauman, T. J., Vookles, J., Berenstein, V., Chaiken, S., & Higgins, E. T. (1991). Self-discrepancies and vulnerability to body dissatisfaction and disordered eating. *Journal of Personality and Social Psychology*, *61*, 946–956.

Striegel-Moore, R. H. (1993). Etiology of binge eating: A developmental perspective. In C. G. Fairburn & G. T. Wilson (Eds.), *Binge eating—Nature, assessment, and treatment* (pp. 144–172). New York: Guilford.

Striegel-Moore, R. H. (1994). A feminist agenda for psychological research on eating disorders. In P. Fallon, M. A. Katzman, & S. C. Wooley (Eds.), *Feminist perspectives on eating disorders* (pp. 438–454). New York: Guilford Press.

Striegel-Moore, R. H. (1995). A feminist perspective on the etiology of eating disorders. In K. D. Brownell & C. G. Fairburn (Eds.), *Eating disorders and obesity: A comprehensive handbook* (pp. 224–229). New York: Guilford Press.

Striegel-Moore, R., & Kearney-Cooke, A. (1994). Exploring parents' attitudes and behaviors about their children's physical appearance. *International Journal of Eating Disorders*, *15*, 377–385.

Striegel-Moore, R., & Marcus, M. (1995). Eating disorders in women: Current issues and debates. In A. Stanton & S. Gallant (Eds.), *Psychology of women's health: Progress and challenges in research and application* (pp. 445–487). Washington, DC: American Psychological Association.

Striegel-Moore, R., McAvay, G., & Rodin, J. (1986). Psychological and behavioral correlates of feeling fat in women. *International Journal of Eating Disorders*, *5*, 935–947.

Striegel-Moore, R., Schreiber, G. B., Pike, K. M., Wilfley, D. E., & Rodin, J. (1995). Drive for thinness in Black and White preadolescent girls. *International Journal of Eating Disorders*, *18*, 59–69.

Striegel-Moore, R., Silberstein, L. R., & Rodin, J. (1986). Toward an understanding of risk factors for bulimia. *American Psychologist*, *41*, 246–263.

Striegel-Moore, R., & Smolak, L. (1996). The role of race in the development of eating disorders. In L. Smolak, M. P. Levine, & R. Striegel-Moore (Eds.), *The developmental psychopathology of eating disorders: Implications for research, prevention, and treatment* (pp. 259–284). Mahwah, NJ: Erlbaum.

Striegel-Moore, R. H., Tucker, N., & Hsu, J. (1990). Body image dissatisfaction and disordered eating in lesbian college students. *International Journal of Eating Disorders, 9*, 493–500.

Striegel-Moore, R. H., Wilfley, D. E., Caldwell, M. B., Needham, M. L., & Brownell, K. D. (1996). Weight-related attitudes and behaviors of women who diet to lose weight: A comparison of Black dieters and White dieters. *Obesity Research, 4*, 109–116.

Stroop, J. R. (1935). Studies of interference in serial verbal reactions. *Journal of Experimental Psychology, 18*, 643–662.

Strowman, S. R. (1996). *The relation between media exposure and body satisfaction: An examination of moderating variables derived from social comparison theory.* Unpublished doctoral dissertation, University of New Hampshire, Durham.

Stunkard, A. J., & Burt, V. (1967). Obesity and the body image: II. Age at onset of disturbances in the body image. *American Journal of Psychiatry, 123*, 1443–1447.

Stunkard, A. J., & Mendelson, M. (1967). Obesity and body image: I. Characteristics of disturbances in the body image of some obese persons. *American Journal of Psychiatry, 123*, 1296–1300.

Stunkard, A. J., & Sobal, J. (1995). Psychosocial consequences of obesity. In K. D. Brownell (Ed.), *Eating disorders and obesity: A comprehensive handbook* (pp. 417–421). New York: Guilford.

Stunkard, A. J., Sorenson, T. I., & Schulsinger, F. (1983). Use of the Danish Adoption Register for the study of obesity and thinness. In S. Kety, L. P. Rowland, R. L. Sidman, & S. W. Matthysse (Eds.), *The genetics of neurological and psychiatric disorders* (pp. 115–120). New York: Raven Press.

Sugarman, A. (1991). Bulimia: A displacement from psychological self to body self. In C. L. Johnson (Ed.), *Psychodynamic treatment of anorexia nervosa and bulimia* (pp. 3–33). New York: Guilford Press.

Swallow, S. R. (1995). Social comparison behavior and low self-regard: Empirical developments and therapeutic implications. *The Behavior Therapist, 18*, 72–73.

Swallow, S. R., & Kuiper, N. A. (1988). Social comparison and negative self-evaluations: An application to depression. *Clinical Psychology Review, 8*, 55–76.

Swallow, S. R., & Kuiper, N. A. (1992). Mild depression and frequency of social comparison behavior. *Journal of Social and Clinical Psychology, 11*, 167–180.

Szekely, E. A. (1989). From eating disorders to women's situations: Extending the boundaries of psychological inquiry. *Counseling Psychology Quarterly, 2*, 167–184.

Szymanski, L. A., & Seime, R. J. (1997). A re-examination of body image distortion: Evidence against a sensory explanation. *International Journal of Eating Disorders, 21*, 175–180.

Szymanski, M. L., & Cash, T. F. (1995). Body-image disturbances and self-discrepancy theory: Expansion of the Body-Image Ideals Questionnaire. *Journal of Social and Clinical Psychology, 14*, 134–146.

Tantleff-Dunn, S., & Thompson, J. K. (1995). Romantic partners and body image disturbance: Further evidence for the role of perceived–actual disparities. *Sex Roles, 33*, 589–605.

Tantleff-Dunn, S., & Thompson, J. K. (1997, November). *Breast and chest size satisfaction: Relation to overall level of body dissatisfaction.* Paper presented at the Association for the Advancement of Behavior Therapy, Miami, FL.

Tantleff-Dunn, S., & Thompson, J. K. (1998). Body image and appearance-related feedback: Recall, judgment, and affective response. *Journal of Social and Clinical Psychology, 17*, 319–340.

Tantleff-Dunn, S., Thompson, J. K., & Dunn, M. E. (1995). The Feedback on Physical Appearance Scale (FOPAS): Questionnaire development and psychometric evaluation. *Eating Disorders: The Journal of Treatment and Prevention, 3*, 332–341.

Tantleff-Dunn, S., Thompson, J. K., Sellin-Wolters, S., & Ashby, A. (1997, August). *Breast and chest size: Ideals and stereotypes over six years.* Paper presented at the 105th Annual Convention of the American Psychological Association, Chicago, IL.

Tassinary, L. G., & Hansen, K. A. (1998). A critical test of the waist-to-hip-ratio hypothesis of female physical attractiveness. *Psychological Science, 9*, 150–155.

Tennis fan sues Letterman. (1996, February 6). *St. Petersburg Times*, p. B2.

Thelen, M. H., & Cormier, J. F. (1995). Desire to be thinner and weight control among children and their parents. *Behavior Therapy, 26*, 85–99.

Then, D. (1992, August). *Women's magazines: Messages they convey about looks, men, and careers.* Paper presented at the 100th Annual Convention of the American Psychological Association, Washington, DC.

Thomas, C. M., Keery, H., Williams, R., & Thompson, J. K. (1998, November). *The Fear of Appearance Evaluation Scale: Development and preliminary validation.* Paper presented at the Association for the Advancement of Behavior Therapy, Washington, DC.

Thomas, C. M., & Thompson, J. K. (1998). *Social comparison: Effects of live versus videotaped conditions on mood and body image.* Unpublished manuscript, University of South Florida.

Thomas, J. O. (1998). *An investigation of the individual differences in mental representations of supermodels.* Unpublished manuscript, Hope University College, University of Liverpool, Liverpool, England.

Thompson, B. (1996). Multiracial feminist theorizing about eating problems: Refusing to rank oppressions. *Eating Disorder, 4*, 104–114.

Thompson, J. K. (1990). *Body image disturbance: Assessment and treatment.* Elmsford, NY: Pergamon Press.

Thompson, J. K. (1991). Body shape preferences: Effects of instructional protocol and level of eating disturbance. *International Journal of Eating Disorders, 10*, 193–198.

Thompson, J. K. (1992). Body image: Extent of disturbance, associated features, theoretical models, assessment methodologies, intervention strategies, and a proposal for a new *DSM-IV* diagnostic category—Body image disorder. In M. Hersen, R. M. Eisler, & P. M. Miller (Eds.), *Progress in behavior modification* (Vol. 28, pp. 3–54). Sycamore, IL: Sycamore.

Thompson, J. K. (1995). Assessment of body image. In D. Allison (Ed.), *Handbook of assessment methods for eating behaviors and weight-related problems* (pp. 119–148). Thousand Oaks, CA: Sage.

Thompson, J. K. (1996a). Assessing body image disturbance: Measures, methodology, and implementation. In J. K. Thompson (Ed.), *Body image, eating disorders, and obesity: An integrative guide for assessment and treatment* (pp. 49–81). Washington, DC: American Psychological Association.

Thompson, J. K. (1996b). Body image, eating disorders, and obesity: An emerging synthesis. In J. K. Thompson (Ed.), *Body image, eating disorders, and obesity: An integrative guide for assessment and treatment* (pp. 1–20). Washington, DC: American Psychological Association.

Thompson, J. K. (1998). Discussion of Sarwer et al. (Bigger is not always better: Body image dissatisfaction in breast reduction and breast augmentation patients). *Plastic and Reconstructive Surgery, 101,* 1962–1963.

Thompson, J. K., & Altabe, M. N. (1991). Psychometric qualities of the Figure Rating Scale. *International Journal of Eating Disorders, 10,* 615–619.

Thompson, J. K., Altabe, M. N., Johnson, S., & Stormer, S. (1994). A factor analysis of multiple measures of body image disturbance: Are we all measuring the same construct? *International Journal of Eating Disorders, 16,* 311–315.

Thompson, J. K., Berland, N. W., Linton, P. H., & Weinsier, R. (1986). Assessment of body distortion via a self-adjusting light beam in seven eating disorder groups. *International Journal of Eating Disorders, 7,* 113–120.

Thompson, J. K., Cattarin, J., Fowler, B., & Fisher, E. (1995). The Perception of Teasing Scale (POTS): A revision and extension of the Physical Appearance Related Teasing Scale (PARTS). *Journal of Personality Assessment, 65,* 146–157.

Thompson, J. K., Coovert, D. L., Pasman, L., & Robb, J. (1993). Body image and food consumption: Three laboratory studies of perceived caloric content. *International Journal of Eating Disorders, 14,* 445–457.

Thompson, J. K., Coovert, M. D., Richards, K. J., Johnson, S., & Cattarin, J. (1995). Development of body image, eating disturbance, and general psychological functioning in female adolescents: Covariance structure modeling and longitudinal investigations. *International Journal of Eating Disorders, 18,* 221–236.

Thompson, J. K., Coovert, M. D., & Stormer, S. (in press). Body image, social comparison, and eating disturbance: A covariance structure modeling investigation. *International Journal of Eating Disorders.*

Thompson, J. K., & Dolce, J. J. (1989). The discrepancy between emotional vs. rational estimates of body size, actual size, and ideal body ratings. *Journal of Clinical Psychology, 45,* 473–478.

Thompson, J. K., Fabian, L. J., Moulton, D., Dunn, M., & Altabe, M. N. (1991).

Development and validation of the Physical Appearance Related Teasing Scale. *Journal of Personality Assessment, 56*, 513–521.

Thompson, J. K., & Heinberg, L. J. (1993). A preliminary test of two hypotheses of body image disturbance. *International Journal of Eating Disorders, 14*, 59–64.

Thompson, J. K., & Heinberg, L. J. (in press). The media's influence on body image disturbance and eating disorders: We can blame them but can we rehabilitate them? *Social Issues.*

Thompson, J. K., Heinberg, L. J., & Clarke, A. (1996). Treatment of body image disturbance in eating disorders. In J. K. Thompson (Ed.), *Body image, eating disorders, and obesity: An integrative guide for assessment and treatment* (pp. 303–319). Washington, DC: American Psychological Association.

Thompson, J. K., Heinberg, L., & Marshall, K. (1994). The Physical Appearance Behavior Avoidance Test (PABAT): Preliminary findings. *The Behavior Therapist, 17*, 9–10.

Thompson, J. K., Heinberg, L. J., & Tantleff, S. (1991). The Physical Appearance Comparison Scale (PACS). *The Behavior Therapist, 14*, 174.

Thompson, J. K., & Pasman, L. (1991). The Obligatory Exercise Questionnaire. *The Behavior Therapist, 14*, 137.

Thompson, J. K., Penner, L., & Altabe, M. (1990). Procedures, problems and progress in the assessment of body images. In T. F. Cash & T. Pruzinsky (Eds.), *Body images: Development, deviance, and change* (pp. 21–48). New York: Guilford Press.

Thompson, J. K., & Psaltis, K. (1988). Multiple aspects and correlates of body figure ratings: A replication and extension of Fallon and Rozin (1985). *International Journal of Eating Disorders, 7*, 813–818.

Thompson, J. K., & Spana, R. E. (1988). The adjustable light beam method for the assessment of size estimation accuracy description, psychometrics, and normative data. *International Journal of Eating Disorders, 7*, 521–526.

Thompson, J. K., & Tantleff, S. T. (1992). Female and male ratings of upper torso: Actual, ideal, and stereotypical conceptions. *Journal of Social Behavior and Personalty, 7*, 345–354.

Thompson, J. K., & Tantleff-Dunn, S. T. (1998). Assessment of body image disturbance in obesity. *Obesity Research, 6*, 375–377.

Thompson, J. K., & Thompson, C. M. (1986). Body size distortion and self-esteem in asymptomatic normal weight males and females. *International Journal of Eating Disorders, 5*, 1061–1068.

Thompson, J. K., & Williams, D. E. (1987). An interpersonally-based cognitive–behavioral psychotherapy. In M. Hersen, R. M. Eisler, & P. M. Miller (Eds.), *Progress in behavior modification* (Vol. 21, pp. 230–258). New York: Sage.

Thompson, M. A., & Gray, J. J. (1995). Development and validation of a new body-image assessment tool. *Journal of Personality Assessment, 64*, 258–269.

Thompson, S. H., & Corwin, S. J., & Sargent, R. G. (1997). Ideal body size beliefs and weight concerns of fourth-grade children. *International Journal of Eating Disorders, 21*, 279–284.

Thornton, B., & Maurice, J. (1997). Physique contrast effect: Adverse impact of idealized body images for women. *Sex Roles, 37*, 433–439.

Tiggemann, M., & Pennington, B. (1990). The development of gender differences in body-size dissatisfaction. *Australian Psychologist, 25*, 306–311.

Tiggemann, M., & Pickering, A. S. (1996). Role of television in adolescent women's body dissatisfaction and drive for thinness. *International Journal of Eating Disorders, 20*, 199–203.

Tiggemann, M., & Rothblum, E. D. (1988). Gender differences in social consequences of perceived overweight in the United States and Australia. *Sex Roles, 18*, 75–86.

Tobin, D. L., & Griffing, A. S. (1996). Coping, sexual abuse, and compensatory behavior. *International Journal of Eating Disorders, 20*, 143–148.

Touyz, S. W., Beumont, P. J. V., Collins, J. K., & Cowie, L. (1985). Body shape perception in bulimia and anorexia nervosa. *International Journal of Eating Disorders, 4*, 261–265.

A toxic beauty. (1997, June 2). *Newsweek*, p. 82.

Tudahl, L. A., Blades, B. C., & Munster, A. M. (1987). Sexual satisfaction in burn patients. *Journal of Burn Care and Rehabilitation, 8*, 292–293.

van Buren, D. J., & Williamson, D. A. (1988). Marital relationships and conflict resolution skills of bulimics. *International Journal of Eating Disorders, 7*, 735–741.

Vandenburg, P., & Thompson, J. K. (1998, November). *A covariance structure modeling investigation of body image disturbance: The role of internalization of media pressures as a mediator between body dissatisfaction and eating disturbance.* Paper presented at the Association for the Advancement of Behavior Therapy, Washington, DC.

van Strien, T. (1989). Dieting, dissatisfaction with figure, and sex role orientation in women. *International Journal of Eating Disorders, 8*, 455–462.

Vernberg, E. M., Ewell, K. K., Beery, S. H., Freeman, C. M., & Abwender, D. A. (1995). Aversive exchanges with peers and adjustment during early adolescence: Is disclosure helpful? *Child Psychiatry and Human Development, 26*, 43–59.

Veron-Guidry, S., & Williamson, D. A. (1996). Development of a body image assessment procedure for children and preadolescents. *International Journal of Eating Disorders, 20*, 287–293.

Veron-Guidry, S., Williamson, D. A., & Netemeyer, R. G. (1997). Structural modeling analysis of body dysphoria and eating disorder symptoms in preadolescent girls. *Eating Disorders: The Journal of Treatment and Prevention, 5*, 15–27.

Vitousek, K. B., & Hollon, S. D. (1990). The investigation of schematic content and processing in eating disorders. *Cognitive Therapy and Research, 14*, 191–214.

von Hippel, W., Hawkins, C., & Narayan S. (1994). Personality and perceptual expertise: Individual differences in perceptual identification. *Psychological Science, 5*, 401–406.

Wagner, S., Halmi, K. A., & Maguire, T. V. (1987). The sense of personal ineffectiveness in patients with eating disorders: One construct or several? *International Journal of Eating Disorders, 6*, 495–505.

Waller, G. (1993). Association of sexual abuse and borderline personality disorder in eating disordered women. *International Journal of Eating Disorders, 13*, 259–263.

Waller, G., Hamilton, K., Rose, N., & Sumra, J. (1993). Sexual abuse and body-image distortion in the eating disorders. *British Journal of Clinical Psychology, 32*, 350–352.

Waller, G., Hamilton, K., & Shaw, J. (1992). Media influences on body size estimation in eating disordered and comparison subjects. *British Review of Bulimia and Anorexia Nervosa, 6*, 81–87.

Wardle, J., & Collins, E. (1998). *Body dissatisfaction—Social and emotional influences in adolescent girls.* Unpublished manuscript, University College, London, England.

Weiner, K. E., & Thompson, J. K. (1997). Overt and covert sexual abuse: Relationship to body image and eating disturbance. *International Journal of Eating Disorders, 22*, 273–284.

Weinraub, B. (1996, November 14). Barbara Streisand, still not pretty enough. *New York Times*, pp. B1, B4.

Wertheim, E. H., Paxton, S. J., Schutz, H. K., & Muir, S. L. (1997). Why do adolescent girls watch their weight? An interview study examining sociocultural pressures to be thin. *Journal of Psychosomatic Research, 42*, 345–355.

Wichstrom, L. (1994). Predictors of Norwegian adolescents' sunbathing and use of sunscreen. *Health Psychology, 13*, 412–420.

Wichstrom, L. (1995). Social, psychological and physical correlates of eating problems. A study of the general adolescent population in Norway. *Psychological Medicine, 25*, 567–579.

Wilfley, D. E., Schreiber, G. B., Pike, K. M., Striegel-Moore, R. H., Wright, D. J., & Rodin, J. (1996). Eating disturbance and body image: A comparison of a community sample of adult Black and White women. *International Journal of Eating Disorders, 20*, 377–387.

Williamson, D. A. (1996). Body image disturbances in eating disorders: A form of cognitive bias? *Eating Disorders: The Journal of Treatment and Prevention, 4*, 47–58.

Williamson, D. A., Anderson, D. A., & Gleaves, D. H. (1996). Anorexia nervosa and bulimia nervosa: Structured interview methodologies and psychological assessment. In J. K. Thompson (Ed.), *Body image, eating disorders, and obesity: An integrative guide for assessment and treatment* (pp. 225–252). Washington, DC: American Psychological Association.

Williamson, D. A., Cubic, B. A., & Gleaves, D. H. (1993). Equivalence of body image disturbances in anorexia and bulimia nervosa. *Journal of Abnormal Psychology, 102,* 177–180.

Williamson, D. A., Davis, C. J., Bennett, S. M., Goreczny, A. J., & Gleaves, D. H. (1989). Development of a simple procedure for assessing body image disturbances. *Behavioral Assessment, 11,* 433–446.

Williamson, D. A., Netemeyer, R. G., Jackman, L. P., Anderson, D. A., Funsch, C. L., & Rabalais, J. Y. (1995). Structural equation modeling of risk factors for the development of eating disorder symptoms in female athletes. *International Journal of Eating Disorders, 17,* 387–393.

Wilson, G. T. (1996). Acceptance and change in the treatment of eating disorders and obesity. *Behavior Therapy, 27,* 417–439.

Winfield, C., & Thompson, J. K. (1997). *Recent developments in the search for a behavioral measure of body image disturbance.* Unpublished manuscript, University of South Florida.

Winklepleck, J., Restum, E. J., & Strange, B. (Eds.). (1993). *Gale directory of publications and broadcast media* (125th ed., Vols. 1 & 2). Detroit, MI: Gale Research.

Wiseman, C. V., Gray, J. J., Mosimann, J. E., & Ahrens, A. H. (1992). Cultural expectations of thinness in women: An update. *International Journal of Eating Disorders, 11,* 85–89.

Wiseman, C. V., Gunning, F. M., & Gray, J. J. (1993). Increasing pressure to be thin: 19 years of diet products in television commercials. *Eating Disorders: The Journal of Treatment and Prevention, 1,* 52–61.

Witchel, A. (1997, March 12). At size 14, a model figure. *New York Times,* p. B1.

Wolf, N. (1990). *The beauty myth.* London, UK: Vintage.

Wonderlich, S. (1992). Relationship of family and personality factors in bulimia. In J. H. Crowther, D. L. Tennenbaum, S. E. Hobfoll, & M. A. P. Sephens (Eds.), *The etiology of bulimia nervosa* (pp. 103–126). Washington, DC: Hemisphere.

Wood, J. V. (1989). Theory and research concerning social comparisons of personal attributes. *Psychological Bulletin, 106,* 231–248.

Wood, K. C., Altabe, M., & Thompson, J. K. (1998). *The Commentary Interpretation Scale: A measure of judgment of neutral appearance commentary.* Unpublished manuscript, University of South Florida.

Wood, K. C., Becker, J. A., & Thompson, J. K. (1996). Body image dissatisfaction in preadolescent children. *Journal of Applied Developmental Psychology, 17,* 85–100.

Wooley, O. W., & Roll, S. (1991). The Color-a-Person Body Dissatisfaction Test: Stability, internal consistency, validity, and factor structure. *Journal of Personality Assessment, 56,* 395–413.

Wooley, S. C. (1991). Uses of countertransference in the treatment of eating disorders: A gender perspective. In C. L. Johnson (Ed.), *Psychodynamic treatment of anorexia nervosa and bulimia* (pp. 3–33). New York: Guilford Press.

Wooley, S. C. (1995). Feminist influences on the treatment of eating disorders. In

K. D. Brownell & C. G. Fairburn (Eds.), *Eating disorders and obesity: A comprehensive handbook* (pp. 294–298). New York: Guilford.

Wooley, S. C., & Wooley, O. W. (1983). Should obesity be treated at all? *Psychiatric Annals, 13,* 884–888.

Wooley, S. C., & Wooley, O. W. (1985). Intensive outpatient and residential treatment for bulimia. In D. M. Garner & P. E. Garfinkel (Eds.), *Handbook of psychotherapy for bulimia and anorexia* (pp. 391–403). New York: Guilford Press.

Yesalis, C. E., Barsukiewicz, C. K., Kopstein, A. N., & Bahrke, M. S. (1997). Trends in anabolic–androgenic steroid use among adolescents. *Archives of Pediatric and Adolescent Medicine, 151,* 1197–1206.

Yoshimura, K. (1995). Acculturative and sociocultural influences on the development of eating disorders in Asian-American females. *Eating Disorders: The Journal of Treatment and Prevention, 3,* 216–228.

Zakin, D. F. (1983). Physical attractiveness, sociability, athletic ability, and children's preferences for their peers. *Journal of Psychology, 115,* 117–122.

Zlotnick, C., Hohlstein, L. A., Shea, M. T., Pearlstein, T., Recupero, P., & Bidadi, K. (1996). The relationship between sexual abuse and eating pathology. *International Journal of Eating Disorders, 20,* 129–134.

AUTHOR INDEX

Brodie, D., 60
Brodie, D. A., 295
Brody, J. E., 47
Brooks-Gunn, J., 30, 31, 36, 88, 105,
    111, 177
Brown, L. B., 55
Brown, L. S., 214
Brown, R. T., 47
Brown, T. A., 11, 26, 59, 60, 319
Browne, G., 109
Brownell, K. D., 25, 33, 42, 43, 72, 87,
    153, 154, 187
Bruch, H., 6, 35, 219, 221, 290
Bryant-Waugh, R. J., 61
Bubb-Lewis, C., 72
Burgess, E. W., 5
Burns, G. L., 183, 190–192
Burrow, C., 31
Burt, V., 6, 42
Buss, D. M., 89
Butow, P., 282, 287, 288, 302
Butters, J. W., 64, 258, 259
Button, E. J., 33
Byers, T. E., 22, 23
Bylsma, W. H., 127

Cachelin, F. M., 59
Caldwell, M. B., 25, 33, 153
Campbell, S. M., 50
Carpman, S., 222
Carr-Nangle, R. E., 31
Carter, J. C., 67
Cash, T., 6–9, 11, 12, 20, 26, 27, 29, 42–
    43, 46, 52, 56, 57, 59, 60, 63–
    65, 68, 72, 74, 79, 87, 107–110,
    116, 129, 130, 134, 137–139,
    147, 152, 154, 163, 165, 170,
    189, 190, 193–195, 198–199,
    205, 207, 227, 253, 257–264,
    267, 284, 286, 288, 290, 312,
    319, 322, 324
Cattarin, J., 36, 43, 103, 132, 155, 157,
    162, 164, 172, 317
Centers for Disease Control and Preven-
    tion, 43
Chaiken, S., 276
Chaloner, D. A., 238
Changing Faces, 44
Channon, S., 284
Chapman, J., 182
Chernin, K., 215, 218, 221

Choi, P., 41
Chrisler, J. C., 111
Christ, W. G., 186
Clark, D. A., 284, 287
Clarke, A., 8, 39, 43, 63, 110
Cleveland, S. E., 5
Cogan, J. C., 34
Cole, B., 90
Cole, C. L., 219
Collins, E., 154, 160
Collins, M. E., 22, 23, 53, 57, 87
Connors, M. E., 182, 183, 220
Conrad, E., 213
Cook, D. B., 46
Cooley, C. H., 190
Cooper, C., 110
Cooper, M., 278, 279
Cooper, P. J., 56, 61, 279
Cooper, S. D., 179
Cooper, Z., 61, 279
Coovert, D. L., 291
Coovert, J. K., 254
Coovert, M. D., 36, 43, 134, 135, 155,
    313, 315, 317, 318
Cormier, J. F., 180, 181, 197
Cornelison, F. S., 297
Corwin, S. J., 33
Counts, B., 43
Crago, M., 33
Crandall, C. S., 184
Crawford, P. A., 177
Crisp, A. H., 294
Crowther, J. H., 177, 187
Cubic, B. A., 254, 291
Cusumano, D. L., 96–98, 112–115, 122

Daneman, D., 32
Dank, S., 105
Davies, K., 31
Davies, J., 33
Davis, C., 34, 65, 224, 226, 227
Davis, C. J., 57
Davis, P., 106
Davis, S., 187
Deaux, K., 190
dePalma, M. T., 46
de Silva, P., 279
Dewey, M. E., 60
Devenyi, T. G., 32
Dias, M., 61

Dibiase, W. J., 93
DiDomenico, L., 96, 106
Diehl, N. S., 96
Dietz, W. H., 50
Dignon, A., 238
Dill, J. C., 160
Dionne, M., 65, 224, 227, 229, 230
DiPietro, L., 237
Dixon, A. E., 187
Dolce, J. J., 254, 291
Dornbusch, S. M., 111
Dowd, M., 70
Downs, A. C., 101
Dreger, A., 189
Drewnowski, A., 107
Dunn, M., 161, 162, 164, 173
Dunn, V. J., 67
Dunning, J., 45
Dworkin, S. H., 64, 218, 221, 228

Eisler, R. M., 229
Elder, K. A., 59
Eldredge, K. L., 37
Ellis, M. L., 230
Espinoza, T., 297
Estes, L. S., 33
Evangelista, L., 85
Evans, E. D., 97
Everington, C., 93
Ewell, K. K., 160

Fabian, L. J., 154, 161, 162
Fahy, T. A., 31
Fairburn, C. G., 31–32, 61, 67, 176, 179, 211, 279
Faith, M. S., 42, 61, 132, 135, 137
Fallon, A., 46, 85, 87, 88, 91, 134, 180, 187, 190
Fallon, P., 188, 237, 240, 242–244
Faludi, S., 216
Fantini, D. A., 222
Farina, A., 183, 191, 192
Farnill, D., 33
Fauerbach, J. A., 109
Favaro, A., 34
Fawzy, F. I., 47
Fawzy, N. W., 47
Feinberg, L. S., 239
Feingold, A., 3, 5, 32, 60, 187

Feldman, J., 284
Felson, R. B., 190
Fernandez, R., 66, 297
Ferrara, S., 34
Fesnick, M. D., 33
Festinger, L., 126
Field, A. E., 37–38
Finkelhor, D., 240
Fisher, E., 74, 135, 136, 143, 157, 172, 260
Fisher, S., 4–7, 19, 135
Flegal, K. M., 50
Flick, P., 112
Foa, E. B., 161
Forston, M. T., 276
Foster, G. D., 70
Fournier, A., 59
Fowler, B., 157, 172
Fox, J., 65, 227
Franko, D. L., 31, 67
Franks, V., 221
Franzoi, S. L., 86
Freedman, R., 87, 93
Freeman, C. M., 160
Freeman, R., 280, 281, 295
French, S. A., 33, 108, 228
Freud, S., 5
Fricke, K., 101
Friedman, B. N., 57, 293
Friedman, M. A., 42, 187
Friedman, S. S., 113
Friedrich, W. N., 188
Funsch, C. L., 314
Furman, K., 155
Furnham, A., 29, 59, 61, 78, 88

Gaesser, G. A., 74
Gallegos, V., 297
Garbutt, B., 111
Gardner, E. A., 293
Gardner, R. M., 57, 292–293, 295, 297, 298, 307, 309, 310
Garfinkel, P. E., 6, 46, 87, 94, 216, 217, 295
Garner, D. M., 6, 46, 54, 59, 87, 92, 94, 98, 99, 106, 152, 176, 216, 217, 221
Garner, M. V., 59
Gason, R., 48
Gealth, A., 90
Gerrard, J., 74

Gettelman, T. E., 190, 227
Ghizzani, A., 47
Gibbons, K., 34
Gilbert, S., 22, 48, 211–216, 218–221,
    226, 232, 236
Giles, T. R., 252, 253
Gillespie, B. L., 229
Glanz, K., 47
Gleason, N. A., 113
Gleaves, D. H., 57, 61, 291
Gleghorn, A. A., 295
Glidden, C. E., 226
Glucksman, M., 295
Goldfield, A., 111
Goldfield, G. S., 30, 41, 107
Goldsmith, D., 66, 298
Gonzalez-Lavin, A., 100–103, 105
Goodman, N., 111
Goodman, W. C., 85, 111
Goreczny, A. J., 57
Gorman, B. S., 59
Gortmaker, S. L., 50
Gottheil, E., 297
Graber, J. A., 36
Grady, D., 27
Gralen, S., 30, 104, 128
Grant, J., 8, 47, 64
Grant, P., 27
Gray, J. J., 53, 57, 76, 86, 101, 216
Greenberb, J., 127
Griffing, A. S., 237, 238, 241
Griffiths, R. A., 33
Grilo, C. M., 32, 43, 154, 228
Gross, J., 108
Gruber, A. J., 41
Gunning, F. M., 101, 216
Gupta, M. A., 113
Gurevich, M., 65, 227

Hackerman, F., 109
Haiken, E., 71
Haimovitz, D., 256
Hall, C. C. I., 28
Halmi, K. A., 220
Hamill, R., 275
Hamilton, K., 99, 217, 237
Handley, K. B., 229
Handy, B., 106
Hangen, J. D., 198, 207
Hansen, K. A., 61
Harris, R. J., 93, 100

Harris, S. M., 108
Harrison, S. K., 101
Hasdorf, A. H., 111
Hastings, T., 220, 238
Hawkins, C., 280
Hay, G. G., 7
Hayden, H., 12, 32–33, 96, 98, 99, 112,
    115, 165, 183, 185, 196, 202–
    204, 228, 232
Haythornthwaite, J. A., 8, 43
Hayward, C., 36
Head, H., 5
Heatherton, T. F., 37–38
Hedger, K. M., 285, 287, 306
Heffernan, K., 228, 232
Heinberg, L. J., 8, 30, 39, 43, 63, 85, 87,
    94, 98, 102, 103, 105, 109, 112,
    114, 119, 125, 128, 129, 131–
    133, 135, 136, 138, 140, 141,
    171, 212, 216–218, 224, 226,
    256, 258, 259, 325, 326
Helmreich, R. L., 229
Hemsley, D., 279
Henry, P. E., 26, 87
Herman, C. P., 186
Herman-Giddens, M. E., 31
Herzog, M. E., 86
Hesse-Biber, S. J., 118, 125, 214
Hessen, L. D., 30, 184
Heymsfield, S. B., 59
Hicks, K. L., 42
Higgins, E. T., 274, 275, 276, 285
Hill, A. J., 177
Hilner, J., 25
Hirsch, J., 295
Hjelle, L. A., 93
Hoelter, J. W., 190
Hollon, S. D., 283
Hombeck, 130
Horton, C. E., 68
Howells, K., 238
Hoy, K., 59
Hsu, J., 228
Hudson, J. I., 41, 220, 236–238
Huffine, C. E., 43
Humphrey, L. L., 182
Huon, G. F., 55, 279, 281
Hussain, N., 182
Hyde, J. S., 228, 229

Ickovics, J. R., 213

Iijima Hall, C. C., 108
Ingleby, J. D., 293
Irving, L. M., 99, 131, 217

Jackman, L. P., 277, 314
Jackson, L. A., 224
Jackson, N. A., 57
Jacobi, L., 27, 29, 72, 134, 189, 190
Janda, L. H., 6
Janet, P., 7
Jarcho, H. D., 60
Jarrell, M. P., 186
Jasper, K., 94, 116, 119
Jazwinski, C., 186
Johnson, C. E., 224, 226
Johnson, C. L., 50, 184
Johnson, M. A., 184
Johnson, S., 11, 36, 43, 52, 155, 317
Johnson, W. G., 31, 37, 186
Joiner, G. W., 109
Joiner, T. E., 60
Jones, J. L., 48
Jones, K. H., 90, 214
Jones, L. C., 310
Jourard, S. M., 5
Jovanovic, J., 111, 189
Jung, C., 5

Kahneman, D., 276
Kaiser, J., 110
Kalodner, C. R., 99
Katzman, M., 34
Kaufman, L., 100
Kearney-Cooke, A., 66, 87, 163, 180,
    181, 195, 197, 214, 219, 227,
    231, 241, 244, 245, 325
Keery, H., 160
Keck, P. E., 41
Keel, P., 37–38
Keeton, P., 284, 258
Keita, G. P., 30
Kelly, E., 99, 100, 216, 217
Kelly, G. A., 280
Kelson, T. R., 87, 227
Kennedy, P. F., 101
Kern, J. M., 220, 238
Kerr, B. A., 64
Kessler, J. W., 158, 159
Khalid, N., 31

Kiemle, G., 60
Kilbourne, J., 215
Killen, J. D., 35, 36
Kirchner, E. M., 46
Klesges, R. C., 176
Koff, E., 28, 59, 74
Kolata, G., 43
Kopstein, A. N., 32
Kowalski, R., 155
Krahn, D. D., 107
Kruglanski, A. W., 126
Kuczmarski, R. J., 50
Kuiper, N. A., 139
Kuldau, J. M., 86, 108
Kumanyika, S. K., 108
Kurth, C. L., 107
Kushubeck, S., 109

Labarge, A. S., 284, 286
Lacey, J. H., 87, 90, 94, 179, 217
Lakoff, R. T., 93, 94
Lane, A., 130
Lansky, L. M., 87, 227, 256
LaPrelle, J., 127
Larkin, J., 221, 223, 235, 244
Larrubia, E., 151
Lasegue, E. C., 186
Lask, B. D., 61
Lawlis, F., 116
Lawrence, M., 215, 221
Lazarus, L., 224
Leary, M. R., 48
LeBow, M. D., 13
Leone, M., 132
Lerman, C., 47
Lerner, R. M., 111, 189
Levine, M. P., 12, 30–31, 67, 94–100,
    104, 112, 115, 118, 120, 128,
    165, 183, 184, 185, 193, 196,
    200–204, 324
Levine, P., 188
Lewis, R. D., 46
Lewis, R. J., 72, 73, 284
Linton, P. H., 6
Liquornik, K., 182
Loan, P., 33
Lohr, S., 85
Lopez, E., 109
Love, A., 176
Lull, J., 218
Lunner, K., 34, 154

MacDonald, D., 8, 47
Macgregor, F., 44, 74
Madan-Swain, A., 47
Maguire, T. V., 220
Mahamedi, F., 37–38
Major, B., 127
Mann, T., 67, 68
Marcus, M., 220
Margolis, J., 112
Mark, S. K., 187
Markee, N. L., 105
Marks, I., 261
Markus, H., 275, 282–285
Marsh, H. W., 126
Marshall, K., 258, 259
Martin, J. E., 216
Martin, M. C., 101
Martinez, E. T., 34
Martinez, R., 291, 297
Martz, D. M., 229
Mason, B., 101
Maude, D., 34
Maurice, J., 99
Mayseless, O., 126
Mazur, A., 88, 91, 93, 215
Mazzella, R., 5, 32, 60
McAllister, D. E., 252
McAllister, W. R., 252
McAvay, G., 86, 128
McCarron, P., 8, 43
McCarthy, M., 88
McClelland, A., 61
McCoy, C. E., 116
McElroy, S. L., 41
McFarland, C., 126
McGill, J., 116
McGrath, E., 30
McHugh, P., 95
McKay, D., 65
McKenna, F. P., 279
McKenzie, S. J., 254
McKinley, N. M., 228, 229, 234
McKinney, K., 186
McLorg, P. A., 219, 220
McManus, C., 61
Mead, G. H., 190
Mendelson, B. K., 55, 60, 80
Mendelson, M., 6, 42, 60
Meyers, A. W., 48
Mikulka, P. J., 11, 26, 59, 319
Miller, R. S., 160
Miller, C. T., 111

Miller, D. T., 126, 127
Mishan, J., 261
Mock, V., 47
Molinari, E., 109
Molnar, A., 85
Moncrieff, C., 192–202
Moodey, A. F., 30, 184
Mooney, F., 116
Moreno, A., 163, 177, 180, 195
Morrell, J. A., 293
Morrison, J. A., 24
Morse, W., 220
Morselli, E., 7, 39
Mosimann, J. E., 86, 216
Moulton, D., 161, 162
Mowrer, O. W., 252
Moyer, D. M., 47, 237, 238
Muir, S. L., 96
Mulac, A., 218
Munster, A. M., 109
Murnen, S. K., 224
Murray, S. H., 112, 115, 176, 192
Must, A., 50
Myers, A., 72

NAAFA, 73, 171
Nagel, K. L., 90, 214
Nangle, D. W., 31
Narayan, S., 280
Nassar, M., 88
Nathanson, D. L., 241
Needham, M. L., 25, 153
Nemeroff, C., 96, 104, 112, 114, 313, 316
Netemeyer, R. G., 36, 277, 313–315
Nevid, J. S., 187
Newman, J. P., 280–281, 284
Newman, L., 240
Newton, T., 60
Neziroglu, F., 65
Nicholas, J. J., 110
Nichter, M., 46, 95, 108
Norris, D. L., 297, 298
Norton, K. I., 105, 106
Novy, P. L., 8, 46
Nyenhuis, D. L., 110

Obarzanek, E., 24
O'Connor, P. J., 46

O'Donoghue, G., 31
Oetjen, H. A., 111
Offer, D., 60
Ogletree, S. M., 101, 105
O'Hanlon, A., 211
Olds, T. S., 105
Olivardia, R., 41
Olive, S., 105
Oliver, K. K., 105, 162, 184, 193, 195
Olmsted, M. P., 32, 46, 186
Olweus, D., 168
Oppenheimer, R., 238
Orbach, S., 218
O'Reilly, P., 256
Orosan, P., 41, 62
Orosan-Weine, P., 67, 254, 256

Paikoff, R. L., 31, 36
Palmer, R. L., 238
Pamuk, E., 22, 23
Panhuysen, G. E. M., 293
Parker, J. W., 126
Parker, S., 108
Partridge, J., 74, 109, 110
Pasman, L., 47, 254
Paxton, S., 34, 96
Pedersen, E. L., 105
Penner, L., 254, 291
Pennington, B., 57
Peplau, L. A., 213
Perdue, L., 92, 94, 95, 99, 100, 216, 217, 222
Perrin, J. M., 50
Perlick, D., 222
Perpina, C., 279
Persall, S., 151
Pertschuk, M. J., 68, 70
Peterson, A. C., 56, 60
Peterson, B., 92, 94, 95, 99, 100, 216, 217, 222
Petersons, M., 46
Petrie, T. A., 106, 107, 224, 226
Phares, V., 164, 180
Phillips, E., 46
Phillips, K. A., 7, 8, 28, 29, 39, 41, 48, 185, 252
Pick, A., 5
Pickering, A. S., 85, 101, 102
Pierce, J. W., 45, 97
Pike, K., 108, 177, 194, 197, 232
Pipher, M., 13

Pirtoli, L., 47
Pitts, C., 241
Pizzolo, C., 222
Polivy, J., 186
Pope, H. G., 41, 46, 220, 236–238
Porter, J. E., 54
Powers, P. S., 88
Price, V. H., 29
Probst, M., 297
Probst, V., 296
Pruzinsky, T., 7, 9, 12, 70, 109
Psaltis, K., 134, 154
Pyszczynski, T., 127

Rabalais, J. Y., 314
Raczynski, J. M., 25
Rader, D. E., 59
Radke-Sharpe, N., 60
Raffeld, P., 101
Ramberg, J. A., 238
Ramirez, E., 41
Rand, C. S., 86, 108
Raphael, F. J., 87, 90, 94, 217
Reed, D. L., 56, 60, 256, 259
Reiter, J., 41, 62, 82
Remafedi, G., 33, 228
Remer, P., 65, 212
Resnick, M. D., 108, 228
Restum, E. J., 95
Rice, C., 220, 221, 235, 236
Richards, K. J., 36, 43, 155, 317
Richardson, S. A., 111
Rieger, E., 280, 281
Rieves, L., 129, 130, 152, 154, 165, 193–195, 205
Riger, A. L., 160
Ritenbaugh, C., 108
Riva, G., 109, 322–325
Robb, J., 254
Robins, M., 24
Robinson, B. E., 72, 116
Robinson, E., 74, 110
Rockert, W., 46
Rodin, G. M., 32
Rodin, J., 6, 35, 42, 43, 60, 72, 86, 87, 108, 119, 128, 135, 154, 177, 181, 213, 224, 232
Roll, S., 54
Rolland, K., 33
Rollins, N., 178
Root, M. P., 108, 188, 219, 240

Rorty, M., 235, 238, 241
Rosa, M., 130
Rose, N., 237
Rosen, B., 297
Rosen, J. C., 7, 8, 12, 35, 36, 39–43,
          62–65, 72, 82, 86, 108, 116,
          138, 140, 170, 197, 199, 253,
          254, 256–260, 263, 264, 269,
          322, 324
Rosen, L. S., 218
Rosen, M. D., 192
Rosenberg, D., 235
Rosenthal, E., 175
Rosofsky, W., 8, 43
Rosso, J. T., 31
Rossotto, E., 238
Rostker, R., 224
Roth, D., 258
Roth, G., 185
Rothbaum, B. O., 161
Rothblum, E. D., 4, 34, 111, 215
Roy, R. E., 43, 72
Rozin, P., 87, 134, 180, 187, 190
Ruble, D. N., 126
Rucker, C. E., III, 26, 108
Ruff, G. A., 294
Rumsey, N., 74
Russell, G. F. M., 6, 290, 294
Russell, V., 221, 235
Russo, N. F., 30
Rutberg, J., 97
Ryan, J., 46
Rybarczyk, B., 110, 113, 115
Rydall, A. C., 32

Sacco, W. P., 60, 256
Sala, A., 34
Saltzberg, E., 64, 259, 269
Sandoval, Y., 291
Sanftner, J. L., 177, 178, 180
Sanocki, T., 280, 281
Santonastaso, P., 34
Sargent, R. G., 33
Sarwer, D. B., 68, 70
Sather, C., 97
Savin, R. D., 29
Scalf-McIver, L., 182
Scharlot, B. W., 186
Schefer, D., 86, 93, 95, 126, 235
Schermer, F., 67
Scherr, R. L., 93, 94

Schilder, P., 5
Schlundt, D. G., 59, 186
Schmidt, N. B., 60
Schneider, K. S., 35, 183
Schober, G. N., 130
Schork, N. J., 113
Schreiber, G. B., 21, 24, 108, 232
Schulenberg, J. E., 60
Schulman, R. G., 286
Schulsinger, F., 57
Schupak-Neuberg, E., 102
Schutz, H. K., 96
Schwartz, D., 87, 164, 184, 216, 217
Schwerin, M. J., 107
Scott, D. W., 186
Secord, P. F., 5
Sedikides, C., 160
Sefa-Dedeh, A., 34
Segal, Z. V., 276
Seid, R. P., 215
Seime, R. J., 292
Selby, D., 116
Sellin-Walters, S., 27
Selvini-Palazzoli, M., 219
Sentis, K. P., 275
Serdula, M. K., 20–23
Sexson, S. B., 47
Shapiro, J. P., 158, 159
Sharp, S., 168
Shaw, H., 99, 102, 103, 104, 112, 114,
          313, 316
Shaw, J., 99, 116, 217
Shisslak, C., 33, 319, 332
Shontz, F. C., 5
Shore, R. A., 54
Shuman, M. D., 30, 184
Siever, M. D., 227, 228
Silberstein, L. R., 6, 35, 86, 87, 92, 94,
          134, 181, 224
Silverstein, B., 92, 94, 95, 99, 100, 216,
          217, 222, 230
Simpson, W. S., 238
Sims, C., 108
Singh, D., 60
Sjostrom, L., 168
Slade, P. D., 6, 31, 35, 55, 60, 290, 294
Slap, G. B., 31
Sleeman, E., 29, 59, 78
Smeets, M. A. M., 293
Smilack, K. M., 96
Smit, F., 293
Smith, D. E., 25

Smith, G., 179
Smith, P. K., 168
Smolak, L., 12, 30–31, 33, 67, 94–105, 112, 115, 118, 120, 128, 165, 183–185, 193, 196, 202–204, 224, 324
Smuts, R. W., 91
Snyder, M., 191
Sobal, J., 49–50, 88
Sobol, A. M., 50
Sonuga-Barke, E. J. S., 33
Sorenson, T. I., 57
Sorter, R. G., 293
Spana, R. E., 294
Spence, J. T., 229
Spence, R. J., 109
Spillman, D. M., 93
Spinetta, M., 34
Sprecher, S., 186
Srebnik, D., 64, 269
Srebnik, E., 259
Stanley, A., 85
Stanton, A. L., 276
Steiger, H., 182
Stein, A., 31–32, 176, 179, 200
Stein, K. F., 285, 287, 306
Stein, N., 168
Stein, R. I., 96, 102
Steinhaus, N., 46
Stekette, G., 161
Stern, S., 183, 219
Sternberg, L., 31
Stewart, D. A., 67
Stice, E., 1–4, 36, 97, 99, 102, 103, 112–114, 115, 123, 124, 313, 316
Stone, S. D., 111, 213
Stormer, S., 11, 52, 94, 98, 114, 116, 118, 133, 134, 135, 140, 313, 318, 324
Story, M., 33, 108, 228
Strachan, M. D., 227
Strange, B., 95
Strauman, T. J., 276, 285
Strickland, B. R., 30
Striegel-Moore, R., 6, 12, 24, 25, 33, 35, 59, 66, 86, 87, 92, 94, 108, 128, 134, 153, 163, 165, 180, 181, 195, 197, 212, 214, 217, 219, 220, 223, 224, 228, 231, 232, 241, 244, 245, 325
Striepe, M., 37–38
Stroop, J. R., 279

Strowman, S. R., 113, 114, 136, 138, 144
Stunkard, A. J., 6, 42, 49–50, 53, 57, 88, 237
Sugarman, A., 219
Sullivan, L. A., 224
Summerfield, A. B., 297
Sumra, J., 237
Swallow, S. R., 139
Szekely, E. A., 218
Szmukler, G., 34
Szymanski, L. A., 292
Szymanski, M. L., 134, 137, 138, 147, 284, 286

Tan, T., 61
Tang, T., 254, 256
Tanke, E. D., 191
Tantleff, S., 27, 28, 53, 57, 77, 87, 128, 136, 141, 156, 190
Tantleff-Dunn, S., 27, 30, 42, 61, 72, 155–157, 162, 164, 167, 173, 187, 188, 278
Tassinary, L. G., 61
Taub, D. E., 219, 220
Taylor, C. B., 36
Taylor, C. L., 61
Testa, M., 127
Texas, 27
Thelen, M. H., 105, 162, 163, 177, 180, 181, 184, 193, 195, 197
Then, D., 98
Thomas, C. M., 103, 132, 160, 174
Thomas, J. O., 297
Thompson, B., 213, 220, 228, 232
Thompson, J. K., 4–8, 11, 12, 25, 27–28, 29–31, 35–36, 39, 42, 43, 46–48, 52, 53, 57–61, 63, 65–68, 74, 77, 80, 85, 86, 94, 96–98, 102, 103, 112–116, 118, 119, 122, 128, 129, 131–136, 138, 140, 141, 143, 154–157, 160–162, 164, 171–174, 182, 187, 188, 190, 211–223, 226, 227, 236, 239, 240, 242, 247, 254, 256, 258–260, 265, 268, 276, 278, 285, 287, 291–294, 298, 301, 305, 313, 315, 317–319, 324, 326
Thompson, M., 87, 216, 217

SUBJECT INDEX

Balanchine, George, 45
Baldness, 29, 107–108
Barbie dolls, 105–106
BDDE. *See* Body Dysmorphic Disorder Examination
BED. *See* Binge eating disorder
Behavioral aspects of body image disturbance, 89, 251–269
 assessment of, 257–260, 264–269
 research background, 253–257
 treatment strategies, 260–263
Bem Sex Role Inventory, 229
Beverly Hills 90210, 101
Biases, 274, 276–278
Binge eating disorder (BED), 38, 228
Blacks. *See* African Americans
Blepharoplasty, 28
Blindness, 45
BMI. *See* Body mass index
Body boundary, 5
Bodybuilders, 41, 46
Body Comparison Scale, 135, 142–143
Body concern, 10
Body dissatisfaction, 89
 and eating disorders, 35–36
 and social comparison, 131–132
Body distortion, 10
Body dysmorphia, 10
Body dysmorphic disorder, 7, 8, 11, 39–41
Body Dysmorphic Disorder Examination (BDDE), 41, 62, 82, 254
Body dysphoria, 10
Body esteem, 10
Body-Esteem Scale, 55, 60, 80
Body-Esteem Scale Revised, 55
Body Exposure in Sexual Activities Questionnaire, 194, 198, 206–207
Body image
 See also Body image disturbance
 appearance-based aspects of, 4
 and appearance-related feedback, 154–155
 critical experiences in development of, 255–256
 definitions of, 4, 9–12
 and power–control, 218–221
 and social comparison, 128–134
Body Image Assessment, 54
Body-Image Automatic Thoughts Questionnaire, 284, 286

Body Image Avoidance Questionnaire, 258, 259, 269
Body Image Comparison Scale, 135, 137
Body Image Diary, 257, 264
Body image disorder, 11
Body image disturbance, 89
 See also Behavioral aspects of body image disturbance; Treatment
 continuum model of, 7–8
 costs of, 48–50
 definition of, 10
 history of research on, 5–7
Body-Image Ideals Questionnaire, 137, 138, 145–147, 284–286
Body Mapping Questionnaire, 55
Body mass index (BMI), 21, 25
Body percept, 11
Body satisfaction, 10
Body Satisfaction Scale, 55
Body schema, 5, 10, 11, 272–274
Body–Self Relations Questionnaire, 79
Body Shape Questionnaire, 56
Body Weight and Shape Self-Schema Scale, 287, 306
Bogosian, Eric, 235
Brain damage, modifications in self-image produced by, 5
Brambilla, Francesco, the Younger, 89
Brawdy, Tawnya, 235, 238–239
Breast/Chest Rating Scale, 27, 53, 77
Breast–chest size, 27–28
Breast implants, 27
Bronstein, Jane, 151
Brow lifts, 28
Bulimia Cognitive Distortions Scale, 286
Bulimia nervosa, 6, 35, 188, 241
 and achievement anxieties, 222
 DSM definition of, 11–12
 and influence of mass media, 94
 prevalence of, 48, 211
Bulimic Symptomatology Within the Friendship Network Scale, 197
Bullying, 167–169
Bust-to-waist ratio, 92

Cage, Nicholas, 151
Canada, 227
Cancer, 47–48
Cash, T. F., 52, 63, 116, 259–260, 312–313

Ethnicity, 21, 24–27, 33–34
Evaluation/affect, 52
Exercise
  motivations for, 88
  as treatment for body image distur-
    bance, 73–74
Extended Satisfaction With Life Scale,
    54, 59
Eyelid surgery, 28

Face lifts, 28
Facial features, 28
Facilitation, 274, 279
Family dynamics, 180–183
Family History of Eating Survey, 163,
    195, 197
Fat prejudice, 43
Fear of Negative Appearance Evaluation
    Scale, 174
Feedback, appearance related, 151–174.
  See also Interpersonal factors
  assessment of, 161–166, 172–174
  and body image, 154–155
  children, interventions for, 166–169
  experimental manipulation of, 155–
    156
  methodological issues, 156–157, 165–
    166
  prevalence of, 152–156
  theoretical explanations of, 158–161
  and treatment for body image distur-
    bance, 166–171
Feedback on Physical Appearance Scale
    (FOPAS), 155, 162, 164, 165,
    173
Feelings of Fatness Questionnaire, 258
Female puberty, 30–31
Feminine Gender Role Stress Scale
    (FGRS), 229
Feminism, 13
Feminist approaches to body image dis-
    turbance, 211–234
  and anxieties about achievement, 221–
    223
  assessment, 228–229, 233–234
  gay–lesbian body image issues, 227–
    228
  and heterogeneity of discontent, 224–
    228
  research methods, 212–213
  and sex-role orientation, 224, 226–227

and sociocultural theories, 214–218
treatment, 65–66, 230–231
and weight as power–control, 218–
    221
FGRS. See Feminine Gender Role Stress
    Scale
Figure Rating Scale, 53
Findsen, Canute, 151
Fisher, S., 6–7
Fitzjames, Louise, 45
Food and Drug Administration, 27
FOPAS. See Feedback on Physical Ap-
    pearance Scale
Forehead lifts, 28

Gay men, 32, 33, 190
Gender differences, 30–32, 38
  See also Men; Women
Gender roles, 224, 226–227
Ghana, 34
"Gibson Girl," 91
Glamour, 95, 96
Good Housekeeping, 92, 96
Goodman, W. C., 111–112
GQ, 106
Grable, Betty, 91
Graham, Samuel John, 151

Hair loss, male pattern, 29, 107–108
Harassment. See Sexual abuse–harassment
Harpers Bazaar, 92
Heart, Lung, and Blood Institute, 21, 24
Hershey's, 118
High school students, 20–21
Homosexuality, 32–33, 190, 227–228
Hurricane effect, 283–284

Ideal Body Internalization Scale–Revised,
    114, 123
If Only I Were Thin treatment program,
    113
Information processing, 274, 276–278
Integrative theoretical approaches, 312–
    318, 320–321
Interference, 274, 279
Interpersonal factors, 175–207
  See also Feedback, appearance-related
  assessment of, 193–198, 202–207
  family dynamics, 180–183

Upward comparisons, 127

VEBIM. *See* Virtual environment for
     body image modification
Vestigial body image, 43
Video confrontation procedures, 66
Virtual environment for body image
     modification (VEBIM), 322–325
Visual Analogue Scale, 259, 268
Visual impairment, 44–45
Vocational status, 45–46
Vogue, 92, 99

Waist-to-hips ratio (WHR), 60–61,
     89–90
Weight modification efforts
   and ethnicity, 21, 24–25
   gender differences in, 38
   and sense of control, 218–221
Weight
   prejudice, 111–112
   satisfaction, 10

Weight–size discrepancy, assessment of,
     52, 57–59
Western societies, sociocultural influences
     in, 85–87, 125, 212
WHR. *See* Waist-to-hips ratio
Woman's Day, 92
Women
   See also Feminist approaches to body
     image disturbance
   breast–chest ratings by, 27–28
   cosmetic surgery for, 27
   hair loss in, 29
   lesbian, 32, 227–228
   surveys of, 20–23
   weight modification efforts among
     young Black, 21, 24–25
   weight–size and body image of Black,
     26
Women's magazines, 92, 95, 216
Women's Movement, 211–212, 215, 229
Wood, J. V., 127

Young Miss, 95
Youth Risk Behavior Survey, 20–22

ABOUT THE AUTHORS

J. Kevin Thompson, PhD, is a professor of psychology in the Department of Psychology at the University of South Florida in Tampa. He received his PhD in clinical psychology at the University of Georgia in 1982 and has been at the University of South Florida since 1985. He previously authored *Body Image Disturbance: Assessment and Treatment* (Pergamon Press, 1990) and edited *Body Image, Eating Disorders, and Obesity: An Integrative Guide for Assessment and Treatment* (American Psychological Association, 1996). He has been on the editorial board of the *International Journal of Eating Disorders* since 1990. His research interests in the field of body image include developmental factors, sociocultural variables, and assessment issues.

Leslie J. Heinberg, PhD, is an assistant professor in the Department of Psychiatry and Behavioral Sciences at the Johns Hopkins University School of Medicine. She received her PhD in clinical psychology from the University of South Florida in 1993. She completed a predoctoral internship at the Medical University of South Carolina and followed with a 2-year fellowship specializing in behavioral medicine at the Johns Hopkins University School of Medicine. She has been a member of the Johns Hopkins faculty since 1995. She has written three book chapters and published extensively in the area of body image, eating disorders, chronic pain, and women's health. Her research interests in the field of body image include sociocultural influences, diverse populations, and the effects of disfiguring illnesses and injuries on body image.

Madeline Altabe, PhD, is an adjunct assistant professor in the Department of Psychology at the University of South Florida in Tampa, where she also has a private practice. She received her BA from New College in Sarasota, Florida, in 1987 and her PhD from the University of South Florida in

1991. She has written extensively in the area of body image, including chapters in *Innovations in Clinical Psychology, An Encyclopedia of Clinical Psychology,* and *Body Image, Eating Disorders, and Obesity: An Integrative Guide for Assessment and Treatment.* Her research interests in the field of body image include cognition, cultural diversity, and examining eating disorders from a cognitive perspective.

Stacey Tantleff-Dunn, PhD, is an assistant professor in the Department of Psychology at the University of Central Florida in Orlando, where she is the director of the Laboratory for the Study of Eating, Appearance, and Health (LEAH). She received her BA from Georgetown University in 1989 and her PhD from the University of South Florida in 1995. She has published extensively in the area of body image, including articles on breast–chest size preferences, social comparison processes, and cognitive-processing models. Her research interests in the field of body image include interpersonal factors, appearance-related feedback, cosmetic surgery, and developing a school-based antiteasing program. She also has a part-time private practice.

BAY PATH COLLEGE   HATCH LIBRARY

3 0376 00113 2065